*Recollections of
an Argyllshire Drover*

ERIC R. CREGEEN
1921 – 1983

'Recollections of an Argyllshire Drover' and other West Highland Chronicles

ERIC R. CREGEEN

EDITED BY MARGARET BENNETT

GRACE NOTE PUBLICATIONS
OCHTERTYRE

Hardcover first published in 2004
by John Donald Publishers,
an imprint of Birlinn Ltd

Paperback first published in 2013
by Grace Note Publications C.I.C.
Grange of Locherlour,
Ochtertyre, PH7 4JS,
Scotland
www.gracenotepublications.co.uk
books@gracenotereading.co.uk

ISBN 978-1-907676-46-8

Copyright © Estate of Eric R. Cregeen 2004, 2013
Editorial Introduction copyright © Margaret Bennett 2004, 2013

All rights reserved. No part of this publication may be
reproduced, stored, or transmitted in any form, or by
any means, electronic, mechanical or photocopying,
recording or otherwise, without the express written
permission of the publisher

British Library Cataloguing-in-Publication Data
A catalogue record for this book is available from the British Library

Scottish Natural Heritage
Dualchas Nàdair na h-Alba
All of nature for all of Scotland
Nàdar air fad airson Alba air fad

CONTENTS

1. Editorial Introduction — 1
2. Extra-mural Classes in the West Highlands — 13
3. In Partnership: Adult Education in the County of Argyll — 21
4. Recollections of an Argyllshire Drover — 31
5. Flailing in Argyll — 49
6. The Tacksmen and their Successors: a Study of Tenurial Reorganisation in Mull, Morvern and Tiree in the Early Eighteenth Century — 51
7. Oral Sources for The Social History of the Scottish Highlands and Islands — 109
8. Oral Tradition and Agrarian History in the West Highlands — 123
9. Donald Sinclair: Oral Tradition of Tiree — 141
10. Donald Morrison: Oral Tradition of Mull — 164
11. Tiree Bards and their Bardachd — 194
12. Oral Tradition and History in a Hebridean Island — 221
13. Tradition and Change in the West Highlands of Scotland: A Case Study — 251
14. Bibliography of Eric R. Cregeen's Published Works — 265

1
EDITORIAL INTRODUCTION

> Eric Cregeen was a social scientist of the highest order. We talk a lot about being interdisciplinary these days – there are research grants and institutes to encourage it – but he was instinctively at once a very fine historian and a very fine anthropologist. All these years later, one re-reads his work with a delight in its freshness, accessibility and insight, and realises what a blow to scholarship his early death was. He was not only far in advance of his time, but no-one since has put the two disciplines together so effectively to illuminate the life of the Highlands.
>
> – Professor T.C. Smout, St Andrews, November 2003

Scotland's first writer to rely upon oral tradition to record social and cultural history was, arguably, Martin Martin at the close of the seventeenth century. His research was largely based upon what we now call 'fieldwork', using techniques that have become standard to generations of researchers, both scholarly and amateur. Quite simply (or so it seems), he interviewed ordinary folk in their own language, closely observed their surroundings, wrote about what he heard and saw, then disseminated the information in his published works. Martin Martin's two books, *A Voyage to St Kilda* (1698) and *A Description of the Western Isles of Scotland circa 1695* (1703), soon became a source of inspiration to generations of travellers and writers, even to those who later criticised his efforts. Martin himself, however, made no claim to definitive expertise: '. . . if I have been so happy as to oblige the republic of learning with anything that is useful I have my design. I hold it enough for me to furnish my observations . . .'.[1]

Until the twentieth century, historians concentrating on manuscript and other written records seemed to have had an abiding suspicion of evidence based on oral tradition, despite the fact that their sources must have begun with the spoken word in the first place. Writers who did not profess to be historians, however, such as Hugh Miller, Anne Grant of Laggan, Elizabeth Grant of Rothiemurchus, Walter Scott, and many others, nevertheless gave invaluable accounts of the social history of their time.

In 1878, the foundation of the Folklore Society encouraged enthusiasts all over the British Isles to interview people from every walk of life, to write down traditional lore, along with descriptions and explanations of the social context, and all available information on the function of the material. Judging by the impressive range of books that were published under the imprint of the Society, the call to collect seems to have been answered largely by clergymen, dominies and a few ladies with time on their hands. Despite the fact that the Folklore Society lent a strong element of respectability to such books, the list of writers was by no means dominated by university lecturers.

The formation of the American Folklore Society in 1888 and the establishment of the *Journal of American Folklore* were important to collectors on both sides of the Atlantic, as the new publication welcomed contributions from every nation that peopled America. By so doing, it raised the profile of the discipline world-wide, facilitating discussions that were to influence scholars and hobbyists alike. In 1893, the first International Folklore Congress was held in Chicago, attracting anthropologists, literature scholars, historians, theologians, biographers, and scientists from many fields, affirming once and for all that traditional knowledge and oral history – folklore – had much to offer in all areas of the arts, humanities and social sciences. Such was the international platform upon which major contributors would stand from that time forth.

The growing awareness of the importance of oral history gave rise to the movement in Britain, and eventually, in 1973, a group of eminent scholars founded the Oral History Society under the leadership of Paul Thompson (University of Essex).[2] One of the key players in the early days of the Society was Eric Cregeen (1921–1983), both as speaker and participant in their earliest conferences, and as contributor to the newly established journal, *Oral History*. The calibre of participants is evident from the discussion that followed Cregeen's 1974 conference paper, 'Oral Sources for The Social History of the Scottish Highlands and Islands'. Names such as Charles Parker (the BBC's pioneering oral-history programme maker), Seán Ó Súilleabháin of the Irish Folklore Commission, renowned Scottish historian Christopher Smout, George Ewart Evans (the famous Suffolk folklorist), Robin Page Arnot, University of Wales (social and political activist, and founder of Labour Research Department) and eminent scholars from the University of Edinburgh's School of Scottish Studies, Alan Bruford and John MacQueen were among them. The collective aim, summed up by Cregeen, was that the oral historian should primarily be concerned 'with those sections of society which are unlikely to leave behind them any quantity of memoirs, diaries, or correspondence from which history can subsequently be written'.[3]

In 1977, the annual conference of the Oral History Society was held in Edinburgh, and the following year, the Scottish Oral History Group was formed[4]. Eric Cregeen was appointed Chairman, and, as his Introduction to their first publication shows, the organisation could not have begun on surer footing:

> [O]ral history is not something for the social and economic historian only. David Edge of Edinburgh University's Science Research Unit has already brilliantly demonstrated how it may be applied to particular fields by his study of the development of research in astrophysics (see *Oral History*, vol. 4, no. 2). Science, medicine, law, education, politics, music, literature, journalism and the arts are proper fields for oral history research. We must as a group have a multidisciplinary approach and encourage and assist projects of the most diverse kinds, providing a forum free from religious, political and social bias, for the discussion of whatever may be of human interest. . ..
>
> Oral History presents us with a rich and diverse store of source-material, ranging from the ponderous utterances of politicians to the unpremeditated reflections of the elderly and it mirrors the thoughts, attitudes and experiences of people from all walks of life. It is as near as you can get to the history of everyman and to everyman's history. But this does not make it an easy option exempt from the control of disciplined thinking. Its source materials are not to be treated as sacred texts capable of solving all our historical problems. On the contrary they demand from those who use them not only enthusiastic and wide sympathy for the human condition but an alert and critical judgement and sufficient detachment to weigh the recorded testimony. It is our aim to make the approach and methods of oral history better known and more widely used in the investigation of Scottish life. The recordings we make now will be a powerful aid to future generations living in a much-changed society.[5]

One of the most striking examples demonstrating not only the importance, but also the power, of memory and oral history is conveyed in a recording, made by Cregeen in the late fifties, of Dugald MacDougall, an Argyllshire drover. He was born in 1866, and at the age of 91, his personal memories spanned not only his own lifetime, but also that of his parents and grandparents. And, most remarkable of all, he could report details they had told to him, thus taking us back several generations to the early 1700s.[6] Although this phenomenon was, in Dugald's day, common throughout Gaelic Scotland, where the oral tradition of the *taigh cèilidh* was the norm, it had hardly been recognised by historians as evidence of social or cultural history. And, to reiterate the words of the far-sighted collector, the recordings are undoubtedly 'a powerful aid to future generations living in a much-changed society'.

Cregeen's devotion to language, culture and tradition no doubt had its roots in earliest childhood. His mother's people were from Peel and his father's people, the Cregeens, came from the south-west of the Island. Eric's maternal grandfather farmed and also had a smithy on Peel quay. In those days Manx could be heard in daily conversation and school holidays left lasting impressions on Eric as well as his brother Allan and sister Sheila. The children willingly worked on the farm to help their grandfather and liked to accompany him on walks around Peel Hill and along the southern coast.

Eric's nephew, David Cregeen, recalled the family also had significant Scottish connections:

> Their paternal grandmother was from Scotland, south of Edinburgh. His father was James Pentland Cregeen and he was born and brought up in Liverpool. His mother was a Radcliffe – she was Manx though originally the Radcliffes were an English-Scottish family from the north of England and related to the Stewarts. They had come as Jacobite exiles, Roman Catholics, and joined distant relations already living on the Isle of Man. They were landowners and famers on the west side of the island, around Peel. His grandfather owned much of Peel Hill and surrounding countryside, which is where he kept goats. As a child, I was taken to look for them, but they had become wild after my great-grandfather's death. Oddly enough, Manx was not spoken in the Radcliffe home because they considered themselves English-Scottish. Nevertheless, Eric, his sister Sheila and their cousin Jack Irving became leading people in the revival of the Manx language and in recording the oral history of the island.[7] Latterly the Radcliffes were a strong Methodist family and Eric's uncle and aunt were very well known missionaries in China – his cousin, Mary Sheaff, wrote a book about their lives there before the Maoist revolution, *From Tortoise Hill: A Story of China* (published in 2007). Her father, Eric's uncle Norman Warren, had the dubious distinction of teaching Mao to swim – Mao refers to it in his autobiography.[8]

In his early teens, Eric began to keep a notebook of Manx words and phrases, in an effort to study the language of his forebears, which, by then, was on the verge of extinction.[9] By the time he enrolled as a student of history at Cambridge University Eric Cregeen was clearly devoted to and passionate about his interests and benefited from the excellent academic rigour that was to stand him in good stead for the rest of his career. Also an avid reader of anthropology, his strength lay in the fact that he was able to combine the many facets of several disciplines and, at the same time, draw upon his own experience to develop, perfect and practise the skills of the oral historian.

In 1948, with several years of experience behind him, he was appointed Assistant Director of the Manx Museum with a remit to collect the oral traditions of the Isle of Man. The position (which lasted till 1950) was supported financially by the Irish Folklore Commission (founded in 1935), which also provided training in folklore fieldwork. To this day, the voices of Manx tradition bearers, systematically recorded by Cregeen and his colleagues, preserve a living account of island life. They are a testimony to the dedication of those who continued recording till 1974 when the last native speaker passed away.

Cregeen's research into the history and oral traditions of the West Highlands of Scotland, which forms the core of this book, began in 1954 when the University of Glasgow, in partnership with Argyll County Council Education Committee, appointed him as extra-mural tutor in Argyll. Although several Scottish universities have since developed extra-mural curricula, the concept was yet in its infancy. Challenged by the fact that 'Legislation has laid it down that the subjects taught . . . must be cultural not vocational' ['Extra-Mural Venture', *MacTalla*, 1954, 8], the new appointee wasted no time in planning a curriculum, which, to this day, stands as one of the most exciting ever offered. At the same time, he not only set out his aims and objectives in running such a course, but also wrote an evaluation of *why* such classes are important. Half a century on, his words retain freshness and enthusiasm combined with a profound wisdom, which is almost eerily prophetic. Extra-mural classes in the twenty-first century might well begin by reading aloud the words of Eric Cregeen to all who teach or come to learn:

> Extra-mural classes stand or fall purely by their cultural values . . . It is learning for its own sake, for the pleasure it brings, for the sanity and balance it can give to life. These are healthy things and help to safeguard civilised values. Ours is an age of technology. The demanding governments and industry have resulted in the expansion of those universities that produce technical experts. We have all met some of these experts and trembled to think of the power they exert over our destinies. If we are not to become ridded by philistinism more people inside and outside the universities must be trained to think honestly and to read widely . . .
>
> To the radio and the cinema, television has been added as one more of our amenities. These things have undoubted value both in entertainment and education, but they make it very easy to become passive instead of creative in our approach to life and leisure. Whenever an extra-mural class exists it stands for the triumph of curiosity over passivity, of constructiveness over mental sloth.

There was, and is, no question of whether the 'venture' would be successful or not. In the intervening years, extra-mural classes have become established all over Scotland, having gone from strength to strength. Few who have benefited from them, however, may know of the pioneers in the field. Oral historian to the core, Eric Cregeen recorded a colourful account of his own experience:

> I came to Argyll as Resident Tutor knowing little about it except what I had read in an elderly ordnance gazetteer. It had informed me that the population was scattered ... It spoke at some length of 'the excessive humidity' of the West Highlands, and the added drawback of 'occasional, fitful, severe tempestuousness ...'.
>
> My arrival in the dusk of a September evening was in a steady torrent of rain that blanketed the landscape. It rained like that for the whole winter.

Nevertheless, the precipitation neither dampened his enthusiasm nor his sense of humour – 'I was daily drenched with buckets of well-intentioned cold water.' Finding himself in an area where there seemed to be no shortage of 'whist drives, dances, films, drama clubs, Gaelic choirs, church meetings' but 'few or no art galleries and museums, literary or learned societies' Cregeen recognised enormous potential. Were it possible 'to create an informed awareness about the Highlands [this] could in turn lead to a keener appreciation of problems of world proportions ...'. Cregeen's ideals were not for the faint-hearted. He sought out the best speakers he could find and brought them to areas where higher education was hitherto inaccessible. One of those early classes included 'four teachers ... a Polish cobbler, two very live-minded civil engineers from the hydroelectric scheme, several retired people, some manual workers and two lairds'. He also met his future wife, Lily, art teacher in Campbeltown, whom he married in 1958. Even the celebration of their wedding seems to reflect the warmth and loyalty of Eric's association with those who became part of his Argyll years, as one of his former guest speakers, by that time a firm friend, was the best man – Hamish Henderson.

In the days before computer-generated images and electronic devices that churn out instant publicity, Lily thought little of producing posters. The timelessness of her artwork, such as the evocative poster (see plate section), fittingly reflects her appreciation of Eric's interests. In a note sent to me in November 2003, Lily recalled the lively scene:

> I remember Calum Maclean coming to lecture. Hamish, of course. Bill Nicolaisen. And Hugh MacDiarmid came to speak on Jacobitism! That is a story all on it own, getting H. MacD. to the venue on time! All sorts of people – judges, prison governors, opera singers, geologists, marine biologists, artists, priests, landowners, etc. [Eric] did some of the archaeology and history himself. It was a very busy house ... He was very happy in those extra-mural years ...

Professor W.F.H. (Bill) Nicolaisen, folklorist and renowned authority on Scottish place-names, warmly remembers the early sixties when he became part of that extra-mural circuit:

> I gave two lectures for him in Tiree and one in Inveraray. He had an excellent relationship with local people . . . One of his main contacts and helpers was Marion Campbell of Kilberry. My main memory of Eric is of a fine person, a good friend, and an excellent scholar and organiser.[10]

While working tirelessly to bring a wide range of subjects to his audiences, Cregeen also continued to expand his own research and broaden his understanding of the culture: 'I need to extend my knowledge of Gaelic and do more fieldwork in the islands on such matters as traditional building styles, industries and social habits in the past two centuries . . .' Former colleague, Dr John MacInnes, recalled that from time to time Eric resorted to Manx Gaelic, which was quite intelligible to his interviewee. He also became one of the foremost researchers in the archives housed in Inveraray Castle, particularly the estate papers and records of the Dukes of Argyll. By sifting through reams of documents, letters, ledgers, diaries that had hitherto gathered dust, and in combing library stacks, Cregeen's investigations unearthed vital information on the social and economic life of the area – practical details, such as precise numbers and prices of cattle, the exact income from rentals – and took account of the views held by landowners and factors of the time. During those years he edited two important books, *Inhabitants of the Argyll Estate 1779*, (Scottish Record Society, Edinburgh, 1963) and *Argyll Estate Instructions: Mull, Morven, Tiree, 1771–1805* (Scottish History Society, Edinburgh, 1964).

By the time he moved on to take up a new post at the University of Edinburgh's School of Scottish Studies in 1966, Eric Cregeen was more than equipped to further his investigation into the history and traditions of the West Highlands. Aside from the university requirements of preparing courses, lecturing to students and supervising postgraduate projects, a position at the School of Scottish Studies seemed the best place to continue recording oral testimonies and traditions, as it is also Scotland's major sound archive.

It was scarcely surprising therefore, that Cregeen's work caught the attention of scholars and general readers from far and wide. Ernest Gellner, Professor of Philosophy at Cambridge, for example, claimed that his research and writing exemplified 'all the best features of both social history and anthropology'. After listening to his presentation of a conference paper based on excerpts from the Argyll Estate papers, along with tape-recorded accounts from oral tradition, Gellner wrote to Cregeen encouraging him to publish, as he considered him to be 'uniquely qualified to write the book that is needed'. Though Eric continued his dedicated work of research and writing, sadly he was scarcely at the peak of his career before his untimely death in 1983.

Without a doubt, however, the influence of Cregeen's work extended to scholars and students on both sides of the Atlantic, as my own experience as a postgraduate student in the Folklore Department of Memorial University of Newfoundland can confirm. It was Professor Herbert Halpert, the distinguished North American folklorist, who first drew my attention to Cregeen's approach. Halpert had trained in anthropology (with notable 'legends' such as Franz Boaz and Ruth Benedict) before arriving at the 'folklore methodology' that was to characterise his work: 'To enable one to "get inside" a culture, as it were, it is important that the actual words of the informants [be] obtained.'[11] As a great exponent of 'the study of the community and the study of the folklore that the community produces',[12] Halpert was instantly excited by Cregeen's work, and advised all his students pay close attention to it, as much for the *contextual* setting as for the actual folklore *content*. The point becomes crystal clear, for example, in Cregeen's introductory note to the Tiree tradition-bearer Donald Sinclair:

> When he was telling of the great storm, you were there on the shore, watching the boats founder, and felt the terror and the pity of it. Then the melancholy would go from his voice, and his face would light up and his eyes shine as he recounted some wild escapade of one of his ancestors. The width of his sympathies and the rich complexity of his nature were part of his greatness as a *seanchaidh*.

Although I did not have the privilege of learning directly from him, I acknowledge that it was Eric Cregeen who originally suggested that I publish my own first book, when, reluctantly (and only at Halpert's insistence), I placed the manuscript of my Newfoundland thesis on Mr Cregeen's desk at the School of Scottish Studies.[13]

Years on, leading scholars who were students during Eric Cregeen's lectureship continue to acknowledge his characteristic generosity, encouragement and inspiration. Prof. Donald Meek, widely known for his important contribution to Gaelic scholarship, records his personal gratitude – 'My final debt is perhaps the greatest.'

> I was introduced to the living tradition of Gaelic song and its role within the community in the early 1970s, when I was invited to accompany the late Eric Cregeen, of the School of Scottish Studies, on his field-trips in my native island of Tiree. As my friend and later my colleague at the University of Edinburgh, Eric taught me to appreciate the historical value of song . . .[14]

Aside from Cregeen's two books mentioned above, the articles in this volume represent only half of his published work, to say nothing of his many unpublished papers. While this anthology aims to demonstrate the depth and the wide scope of his output, the majority of the items are selected from research that relied largely upon oral tradition and tape-recorded interviews. The fresh approach of combining historical records of books and manuscripts with transcriptions of tape-recorded folk memories demonstrates that, in his day, Eric Cregeen was one of Britain's leading exponents in the field. Admittedly, as editor of the collection, the choice has also been influenced by my own professional training in education and in folklore scholarship. All the same, I have included two of his historical essays, which not only complement his work on the oral traditions of the West Highlands but also show his prowess as a scholar in that field.

There can be little doubt, that, had he lived, Eric Cregeen's major work would have derived from what has come to be known as 'The Tiree Project', which he initiated and planned shortly after joining the School of Scottish Studies:

> The Tiree investigation developed from a series of field-trips commencing in 1968, made with the purpose of recording from the lips of the islanders such oral traditions as survived on topics already familiar to me from earlier documentary research.[15]

Nevertheless, the project did produce several important articles and features, and there is probably no area better represented than Tiree in the archives of the School of Scottish Studies. Copies of Cregeen's Tiree recordings have also been deposited in *An Iodhlann*, the museum-archive on the island, where they can be accessed by the public.

Meanwhile, it is only right and fitting that Scotland honour a bright intellectual who made such an excellent contribution to the understanding and appreciation of West Highland life and culture. Though the first edition of this anthology appeared twenty years after his death, and the revised second edition in 2013, it will hopefully begin to acknowledge the debt owed to the diligent scholarship and generosity of Eric Cregeen.

NOTES ON THE EDITING

The work adheres faithfully to Cregeen's original presentation and writing style, apart from a few minor clarifications [generally noted in square brackets within the text]. It would have been impractical (and presumptuous) to attempt an update of cross-references such as those that are the hallmark of modern academic articles. Besides, the essays are of their time, and well able to stand reprinting. Only in very few instances, where the reader might gain a false impression of the subject, have I added a note to sharpen the focus, make an essential connection to current circumstances, or explain obscurities, which would have been clear in their day. References to the century (e.g. 'this century') have been updated to avoid confusion.

Several of the articles contain anglicised plurals of Gaelic words which have gained currency with English speakers, such as *seanchaidhs, ceilidhs*. These have been retained throughout the anthology, though, strictly speaking, the Gaelic ending would be more correct – *ceilidhean*. Non-standard orthography reflecting local dialect or pronounciation has also been retained.

As the papers originally appeared in a wide range of publications, I have attempted to conform to one 'house-style', with as little disturbance as possible of Cregeen's own presentation. In the two articles originally published in *Oral History*, for the sake of clarity an occasional sentence has been restructured, as the original had obviously relied upon the intonation and expression of an oral delivery of the paper.

To the best of my ability I have generally indicated these small changes by using ellipses for words omitted and square brackets within the text for words added. For example:

> ... a few unusual Mull waulking songs were recorded [in the 1950s] by Calum Maclean from the late Capt. Dugald MacCormick, but it is remarkable to find someone in Mull [in the 1970s] who ... actually remembers seeing a waulking ...

Where these conventions proved to be too clumsy, an endnote has been added, indicating clearly [Ed.] that it is the editor's comment and not in the original text.

It will become evident that there are occasional 'repeats' in the collection, usually verbatim transcriptions of a tape-recording, or occasionally an opinion or persuasion that was crucial to Cregeen's philosophy. I have intentionally left them intact, for not only would removal disturb the flow of his prose, but also the fact that they are repeated only emphasises their importance to his work.

ACKNOWLEDGEMENTS

I would like to thank Lily Cregeen who asked me to take on this project – encouraged by friend and colleague Professor Ted Cowan, I agreed with some trepidation, aware that this adventure into print would be filled with interest and discovery, yet fearful I might linger too long on irresistible sidetracks. Consulting at each stage with her daughters Kirsty and Nicola, Lily herself has shown a depth of commitment and affection that is deeply moving. I have no doubt whatsoever that, while the anthology will be a lasting tribute to Eric, my association with it has also nurtured an enduring friendship with Lily. I am sincerely grateful for this dimension, which enriches my life.

I wish to acknowledge my indebtedness to The Carnegie Trust for the Universities of Scotland (who, in the early 1960s, supported the publication of Eric Cregeen's two books) for assisting my travel to the West Highlands. I also appreciated discussions with Professor Ted Cowan (University of Glasgow), Hugh Cheape (National Museums of Scotland and the University of the Highlands and Islands), Dr. John MacInnes (former colleague at the University of Edinburgh) and Eric's nephew David Cregeen. Andrew Simmons and Hugh Andrews at Birlinn supported the publication of the first edition, which was much appreciated by the Cregeen family.

As this edition was going to press to coincide with the 2013 Crieff and Strathearn Drovers' Tryst, Scottish Natural Heritage supported cultural events to celebrate the wisdom of the Gaelic-speaking drovers (*Eòlas nan Dròbhairean*). Since this enabled so many people to experience the landscape, ecology, culture and language that inspired Cregeen, the encouragement of Scottish Natural Heritage is gratefully acknowledged.

Finally, my eternal gratitude goes to Marie Salton, valued friend and proof-reader, whose good humour always added pleasure to a very worthwhile project – sadly she is no longer with us, and much missed for all her encouragement and scholarly support to me over many years as well as her warm friendship.

Margaret Bennett
Honorary Professor of Antiquities
Royal Scottish Academy
Edinburgh, 2013

NOTES

1. Martin Martin, *Description . . .*, 1884 edn. pp. xvi–xvii.
2. See also, Paul Thompson, *The Voice of the Past* (Oxford 1978).
3. Eric Cregeen, 'Oral History', *Phonographic Bulletin,* No. 29 (March 1981) p.11. I am grateful to The Society of Archivists, Film and Sound Group website (2003) for this reference, cited in the thesis of David Bishop, 'The Role of the Archivist in the Collecting of Oral History', University of Liverpool, 1998. The website of the International Institute of Social History, (Glasgow-based) also flags up Cregeen as a 'noted exponent of oral history' (2003).

4. See also, Margaret Bennett, 'The Growth of the Oral History Movement in Scotland: The Legacy of Eric Cregeen' *Oral History*, No. 37 (2009): 43-51.
5. *The Scottish History Group: Newsletter,* No. 1. pp. 1–2. After three 'Newsletters', the publication was re-named *By Word of Mouth.*
6. In 2007, the Year of Highland Culture, a group of young crofters proposed that, in the absence of a mart in Skye, the cattle could be walked from Lochalsh to Dingwall. West Highland Free Press reporter Iain MacKinnon, himself a crofter, referred to the 2004 edition of this book as he explained, 'The primary purpose will be to celebrate a tradition that was for hundreds of years an integral part of the way of life in the Highlands and Islands. Although direct memory of the droving days is now all but gone, there are, in south Skye, still tantalising reminders of it… further afield other accounts of the drovers have been preserved. One of the most important of them belongs to Dugald MacDougall, an Argyllshire drover, born in 1866. He was recorded in the 1950s by Eric Cregeen… His paper based on Dugald MacDougall's recollections is a unique account of the droving way of life and the warmth of his writing style, which continues throughout the piece, speaks volumes about Cregeen's feelings towards the subject of his research.'
7. Sheila later studied Archaeology and it is a testimony to her work in that area that the Centre for Manx Studies has set up a special collection of her projects, 'The Sheila Cregeen Archive'.
8. Email, David Cregeen, Sept. 20, 2013. (See also, Bennett, op cit. 2009.)
9. Interestingly, his namesake, Archibald Cregeen (1774–1841), began collecting vocabulary, carols and ballads, proverbs and idioms while he was an apprentice marble mason. The collection was published in 1838.
10. Personal correspondence, 2003.
11. H. Halpert, 'Suggestions for the Collector', *Hoosier Folklore,* 1.1. (1942): 37. See also 'Coming into Folklore More Than Fifty Years Ago', *Journal of American Folklore,* 105. 418 (1992): 442–457.
12. H. Halpert, in *Four Symposia on Folklore. Held at the Midcentury International Folklore Conference, 1950,* (Ed. Stith Thompson, Bloomington, Indiana, 1953) p. 320
13. 'Some Aspects of the Scottish Gaelic Traditions of the Codroy Valley, Newfoundland' was the thesis, later re-written and published as *The Last Stronghold: Scottish Gaelic Traditions in Newfoundland,* 1989.
14. Donald E. Meek (editor), *Tuath is Tighearna: Tenants and Landlords, An Anthology of Gaelic Poetry of Social and Political Protest from the Clearances to the Land Agitation (1800–1890),* p. 3, Preface (Scottish Gaelic Texts Society, Aberdeen, 1996). Prof. Meek dedicates the book jointly to Eric Cregeen and Hector Kennedy, the Tiree singer recorded on that visit.
15. Written in 1983, published posthumously in *Scottish Studies,* 1998.

2
EXTRA-MURAL CLASSES IN THE WEST HIGHLANDS
Scottish Adult Education, Vol. 20, 1957, pp. 6–10

In 1954 the University of Glasgow Extra-Mural Committee decided to extend its work into the more outlying parts of its province. Agreements were made with Ayrshire, the Stewartry of Kirkcudbright and Argyll. A member of the Extra-Mural Department staff was in each case to be assigned as Resident Tutor in the county. Argyll Education Committee agreed to bear a proportion of the expenses of the experiment and from the first gave it every encouragement. Both the Director and the Assistant Director of Education were sympathetic to the aims we had in view and were familiar with Extra-Mural classes at Dunoon. But Dunoon is not Argyll and their success in a watering-place on the Clyde, geographically and spiritually linked to Glasgow, could be no guarantee that such classes would take root in a county vast in extent, thinly populated, rural, almost archaic in character. Much of it consists of islands with an ancient language and traditional ways that seemed to offer no point of contact with orthodox adult education. The rest of the county bravely masquerades as mainland but is, in fact, a mass of islands deeply divided by lochs and mountains and tenuously connected by awkwardly placed land-bridges. The winding roads and the steamers bring visitors and newspapers, groceries and incomers, but deep down there is an insularity and attachment to old faiths that are poles apart from the outlook and habits of the city folk.

I came to Argyll as Resident Tutor knowing little about it except what I had read in an elderly Ordnance Gazetteer. It had informed me that the population was scattered, living mostly in small towns and villages numbering some hundreds at the outside, and that there were, besides Dunoon, only two towns with a population of six thousand. It spoke at some length of 'the excessive humidity' of the West Highlands, and the added drawback of 'occasional, fitful, severe tempestuousness'. My arrival in the dusk of a September evening was in a steady torrent of rain that blanketed the landscape. It rained like that for the whole winter. The leading inhabitants whom I interviewed in the first weeks were curious about my mission, friendly and ready with advice. In nearly every case this advice was that I should try the neighbouring town, where interest was sure to be stronger than it was in the immediate vicinity. I was daily drenched with buckets of well-intentioned cold water. Sometimes, it is true, I found individuals who were keenly interested. There was a minister's wife who was whole-heartedly for an Extra-Mural class until she learned that it had nothing to do with interior decorating.

But the prophets proved wrong and the first meeting was an astounding success. Well over a hundred people came to hear a lecture on geology in the Highlands by Professor George. It was no flash in the pan. Since that time classes have been established in many parts of Argyll and there is still room for expansion. A profound need exists in the Highlands for the kind of intellectual stimulus that Extra-Mural classes can give. Other activities there are in abundance in every Highland village – whist drives, dances, films, drama clubs, Gaelic choirs, church meetings. But there are few or no art galleries and museums, literary or learned societies or opportunities of education beyond the technical stage. My impression after three years of working in Argyll is that, with the right tutors, the possibilities of adult education in the Highlands are enormous. The difficulties lie not in creating a demand – it is there already – but in meeting this demand imaginatively and at the highest level possible.

My first class was at Inveraray, mainly because the headmaster of the Grammar School was encouraging. For three successive winters a class has been held there, dealing with different aspects of the history and archæology of Celtic Britain in a linked series of lectures. Last winter seventeen students enrolled. They included four teachers (always a valuable asset in a class), a Polish cobbler, two very live-minded civil engineers from the hydro-electric scheme, several retired people, some manual workers and two lairds. The lairds recruit and bring several students with them from ten miles away and are full of ideas for future courses. The average age of the class is probably nearer fifty than forty, but the level of interest and discussion would be hard to beat, and for the tutor the class is a sheer pleasure. Admittedly, there are certain limits to discussion in a class of this composition, but it has seemed to me that the first duty of a tutor is to try to understand and respect his students' attitudes and values, not to dynamite them. A distinguished visiting lecturer who laid about him with some vehemence produced from this class some of the best public speaking I have heard; but he would have wrecked the class if he had taken a full course.

Ten classes were held last winter in Argyll, excluding Dunoon. There are seven centres – Tobermory, Oban, Inveraray, Lochgilphead, Tarbert, Carradale and Campbeltown. Two hundred and ninety students enrolled and maintained an average attendance of 75 per cent. It has been possible to offer a fairly varied programme of studies. Twelve students studied art appreciation at Campbeltown and thirty studied the development of song at Oban. A course on the geology and natural history of the Highlands ran for sixteen weeks at Oban and Lochgilphead, with 46 and 35 students respectively, whilst at Tarbert a much smaller group was concerned with modern Scottish writing and had the inspiration of a young tutor whose appointment to the inspectorate of schools shortly after is a sore loss to Extra-Mural work in Argyll. We have flourishing history and archaeology classes where no television mast has raised its horns, and at Lochgilphead a psychology class which has continued for three years and has taken a new aspect of the subject each session. The tutor is a psychiatrist at the County Mental Hospital, whose staff have from the beginning shown a lively and practical interest in Extra-Mural work. The other part-time tutors, too, are outstandingly good, and one's only complaint is that they cannot undertake more lecturing. Glasgow is too far away to provide more than an occasional lecturer. Quite ordinary requests for subjects like geology and literature have to be answered by an apology.

My own classes account for about half of the syllabus and usually form the spearhead of penetration when a new centre is opened up. Because of the tutor shortage, my courses are limited to between twelve and eighteen lectures, so that I can visit a larger number of centres. Individuals who attend all the lectures benefit from a linked series of forty or more lectures carried on over a period of three years, which is tantamount to a cohesive course at a college or university.[1] At Campbeltown I gave a class on prehistoric archaeology in the first year and followed it by a class on Early Scotland the second year. In both of these courses the background of European and wider influences was constantly referred to, but most of the illustrations were Scottish, and more particularly Highland. In the third year I ventured into medieval and modern history in a study of the social and cultural development of the Highlands, and sometime in the future I hope to complete the series of possibly fifty lectures by studies of traditional life and folk-culture in the Highlands and Islands. But before I reach the final series I need to extend my knowledge of Gaelic and do more fieldwork in the islands on such matters as traditional building styles, industries and social habits in the past two centuries. My work in organising a similar survey in the Isle of Man some years ago will help in this.

At Lochgilphead, which is the chief centre in mid-Argyll, the interest aroused by Extra-mural classes coincided with a growing local pride in the amazing concentration of ancient monuments in the district, and the result was the formation of a new society, the Natural History and Antiquarian Society of mid-Argyll. It is doing excellent work in promoting excavation and encouraging its members to report new archaeological finds. The value of Extra-Mural classes has been proved by the discovery of numerous sites of real importance by members of classes. Foresters have been particularly valuable allies. It was owing to a forester at Tobermory that recently a prehistoric house-site in Mull, in which trees had already been planted, was brought to notice and rescued from certain oblivion.

There was immense satisfaction in seeing Extra-mural classes take root in Mull, for this was the first of the islands to be tackled. All the problems of a sparse population, poverty of communications and an ill-balanced distribution of age-groups were found in Mull in an extreme form. Fraser Darling's *Highland Survey* (1955) has only the most dismal predictions for the island. Yet the Extra-mural class, which meets about eight times a year at monthly intervals, is wonderfully alive. It consists of over fifty people, who come from Tobermory, Salen, Dervaig, and even places thirty miles away. They are a mixture of shopkeepers, doctors, farmers, foresters, customs officers, ministers, schoolteachers, retired people and craftsmen. One feels that they represent the island fairly, and that their support of the class is an expression of their pride in Mull, their curiosity to learn more about their history and archaeology, and their amazing Gaelic zest for a ceilidh. In the discussions after the lecture I have heard foresters make contributions that would be a credit to any class. The local blacksmith and the ironmonger are true tradition-bearers.[2] They will also dispute about the precise meaning of a Gaelic place-name. Such men are the salt of Extra-Mural education in the Highlands. They have a limited formal education, but good minds and skilful hands and an independence of outlook that one envies. There is an Edwardian feeling about society in Mull, and a distinction between gentry and the ordinary families, which is alien to the modern world.[3] I have no desire to upset the social order, merely to educate, and I have found some of our stoutest allies among the old leading families as well as amongst the manual workers. In a year or two I hope that the class, with its leader, Ursula Betts, will have gathered material for a complete archaeological survey of the island, and perhaps will form an archaeological club with an independent existence.

Carradale is a small fishing village in Kintyre with a developing forestry industry. It has six boats and a wrecked pier, but at last the Secretary of State has approved the building of a new pier. Almost yearly the herring fleet has diminished, and the fishermen have known hard times. Carradale has several able leaders and a lively sense of community. The first year of lectures was well supported, but there were not enough young people. This year I waited until the boats and the crews were home in spring, then held a short course on Marine Studies designed for the fishermen. Millport Marine Station sent one of their young scientists to lecture on the habits of fish, the research work done at Millport and similar stations, the effects of advances in fishing vessels and methods.

Half of the class of forty-odd people were fishermen and their wives, and there were as many young men as middle-aged. This is the sort of class that should be held at all the fishing villages and towns in Argyll.

Another type of class arose as a response to the perennial tutor-shortage. As there was no permanent single tutor available to conduct a science class, a course was arranged that could be given by a team of twelve. It was entitled 'The Geology and Natural History of the Highlands' and was given at Oban and Lochgilphead on successive evenings (the expense was reduced in this way). It began with a geological survey of the Highlands, followed by a geographical survey, and then a series of studies on the flora and fauna of the land and sea. It was not purely academic, for throughout there was a human bias and an appreciation of the problems and potentialities of the Highlands. A lecture on forestry could not ignore the social changes that are being produced by the Forestry Commission's programme, nor could the lecturer evade the challenge of farmers and agricultural advisers in the class. A lecture on seaweed was fascinating to the botanical, but alginate industries have a modern economic relevance and kelp-burning a century or so ago made fortunes for landlords and, at the cost of wearisome labour, staved off emigration for a few years for thousands of crofters. There was a class of 46 at Oban and of 35 at Lochgilphead, and the practical experience and specialised knowledge of the forestry men and the agriculturalists gave a keener edge to the discussions. One saw the same thing at Carradale where the dominant element in the class was the fishermen.

The lecturers were drawn from four university departments, the Nature Conservancy, the Forestry Commission, and two marine research stations, but the change of personnel hardly seemed to matter. The inner unity of the course and the personality of the class asserted themselves and removed all doubts as to the healthiness of this type of course. It is to be expanded from sixteen to twenty lectures by exploiting the marine side more fully, and will be given at new centres next session. Last session we had a permanent chairman in each class to ensure continuity and a reception for the lecturer. This time we shall experiment with a different student as chairman at each meeting.

After three years, Extra-Mural work in the West Highlands has become established over a wide area, and it is still at the pioneer stage. In the coming winter, if all goes well, Tiree will, be included in the programme. Out there, five or six hours' sail from Oban, you are in a different world. Thatched houses, more archaic in appearance than anything in the British Isles, crouch like something prehistoric beside the spick-and-span new co-operative store. Gaelic is used by old and young. Cattle and sheep graze the machair land, but the crofters are taking to the idea of growing tulip bulbs and may steal some of the Dutchman's trade.[4] North of Oban, too, there are villages like Ballachulish where a class could be organised. But time and energy are limited, and a resident tutor dare not become an organiser and nothing more, or his classes will suffer. Besides planning and organising, travelling and mixing with the community (a knowledge of Gaelic is almost an essential), he must read in every spare minute and be as active at the frontiers of his subject as in the familiar hinterland. Further expansion will depend greatly on what part-time tutors can do. I look forward to seeing a team of part-time tutors, most of them locally resident and fully mobile, conducting classes at a standard as high as those which exist at present. But mobility in the West Highlands will only come when helicopters cross the mountains and lochs in a tenth of the time that a car takes to go round them. There are so many unpredictable factors that one cannot forecast the shape of Extra-Mural work in the future, but one can express one's hopes and preferences and general aims.

Classes on specific orthodox subjects such as geology and botany will come when a tutor is available, but in the meantime general courses of the kind already attempted are valuable in themselves, for they bring isolated facts and ideas into new and significant relationships. At the end of the course, no-one has been trained to be a botanist, a zoologist or a geologist, but the members of the class have become aware how a botanist or a geologist thinks and works, and why a knowledge of geology and of soil-structure is important to botany.

Art and music, religion and philosophy, economics and politics, all have a part to play in Extra-Mural developments in the Highlands. Already some or all of these subjects have been studied in the larger centres, where there are more teachers, doctors and others with wider horizons of thought, but I fancy that a class on European music in a small rural centre would at present gather together a mere handful of people. The Highlands have, however, a strong tradition of native song and of pipe music, unsurpassed by any folk-music in the world. Starting from this point there are infinite possibilities in developing the study of music in the Highlands, and particularly in the islands. The most successful Extra-Mural lecture I ever heard in Argyll was given by a collector of folk-song, but he would be the first to admit that he could gain more from the class in the collection of traditional music than they could learn from him.

The history of the Highlands and archaeology in most of the Highlands have been grossly neglected, yet both offer great opportunities in education. There is no lack of dusty volumes on local traditions, but the bulk of them are quite unscientific and appeal to the woolly-minded romantic. Many clan histories and traditions fall into this category, but this is no reason to avoid the immensely interesting topic of clanship, to trace its origins in early Gaelic society and in feudalism and to assess its effects in moulding the development of the Highlands. No study will sooner correct the false and romantic notions that have gained currency. I tried to be as impartial as possible in my treatment of the clan struggles of the sixteenth century, perhaps too much, as I realised when an elderly man of crofting stock expressed his interest but added, 'But you weren't half hard enough on those damned Campbells.' There is all the satisfaction of teaching a subject in which the students feel themselves to have a stake and in which the tutor can advance his own knowledge and wisdom by contact with his students. The line between student and tutor disappears in the discussion period and the class becomes an active research group. A whole world of anthropological studies lies waiting to be explored in the Highlands and Islands, and Extra-Mural classes can play an important role in this work.

The Highlands and Islands are poor in comparison with the rest of the country. They are suffering from centuries of misuse and neglect. Once-flourishing communities are shrinking away through lack of opportunities of gainful employment, through depopulation and the handicaps of remoteness and heavy freight charges. The young and enterprising are expected, indeed encouraged, to leave. Various bodies exist, such as the Highland Panel and the Crofters' Commission, whose task it is to try to restore the social and economic health of this region. One of the aims of Extra-Mural work should be the forming of groups in Highland counties to study these questions and propose remedies, and in general to create an informed awareness about the Highlands. This could in turn lead to a keener appreciation of problems of world proportions.

Being a resident tutor in Argyll does not spell intellectual isolation. The classes are stimulating enough, and, besides these, there are the informal discussions that go on in the Highlands until one and two o'clock in the morning, gathered round the fire with a few cronies and a visiting folklorist or poet. Some of the visiting lecturers have become legendary figures already and their amiable eccentricities are recalled again and again. They drank enough whisky to sink a dozen ships or slept without pyjamas, but they awakened interest and planted ideas that will go on growing. Sometimes we talk about the Highlander and his foibles. I confess I have a weakness for him and his country, and the long road home from a class at the other end of the county is often cheered by a parting shot from a friend and the moon lighting up the Sound of Jura.

EDITORIAL NOTES

1. The original text had: 'None of them is termed a tutorial, but a linked series of forty or more lectures carried on over a period of three years is tantamount to a tutorial.' The current university usage of 'tutorial' does not, in this context, convey the meaning. [Ed.]
2. Cregeen made invaluable tape-recordings of Mull blacksmith, Angus (Angie) Henderson who had an extensive of knowledge of local history and Gaelic tradition. [Ed.]
3. After the Second World War, Mull began to develop its current reputation as 'the Officers' Mess' – a place where moneyed folk from the south, often ex-military, could buy up larger properties and set themselves up as self-styled 'gentry'. The majority, who seemed to consider themselves a cut above the general population of crofters and fishermen, did not fit the old Highland pattern where the landowners and tenants had mutual respect for each other and a common understanding of Gaelic culture. [Ed.]
4. Despite efforts and aspirations, bulb-growing did not become established. [Ed.]

3

IN PARTNERSHIP: ADULT EDUCATION IN THE COUNTY OF ARGYLL

Scottish Adult Education, Vol. 30, 1960, pp. 14–21

In his Introduction at the Scottish Adult Education conference held in Dunblane in 1960 (published in the December issue of the journal, 1960, pp. 14–16), Mr T. G. Henderson, Director of Education for Argyll, set the scene for this Illustrated Lecture delivered by Eric Cregeen. He summarised the background to the Adult Education project originally proposed by the partnership of Glasgow University and Argyll County Council Education Committee, and admitted he doubted the practicality of delivering such an ambitious idea: 'It is one thing to be a convert to a creed and quite another to take the faith out and make it flower . . . I must confess that I myself had some misgivings as to how the experiment would work out.' Visualising not only several potential pitfalls but, even more importantly, the pressing need for 'patience, ingenuity, and infinite goodwill' along with 'the co-operation from powerful agencies like the Press and the BBC' along with 'the best possible organisation at local and regional levels,' he continued: 'Above all, we need leaders, men and women with special gifts for the job and dedicated to it, with a warm humanity as well as a true scholarship, and with a zeal for the work that is often hard and sometimes very frustrating. I believe that in Mr Cregeen we in Argyll have such a leader . . .' The Director of Education then took pleasure in handing over the session to the Resident Tutor Eric Cregeen, who delivered the following lecture. [Ed.]

ILLUSTRATED LECTURE

It was an act of faith when the University of Glasgow and West of Scotland Extra-Mural Committee and the Argyll County Council Education Committee decided in 1954 to bring this West Highland county within the orbit of extra-mural education. Not that rural areas have been neglected by adult education agencies in the past. In Scotland the largely rural county of Dumfries had already proved that extra-mural classes and the small town were not incompatible. But Argyll belongs geographically and culturally to the Highland zone, and the Highland zone is a law unto itself. Problems of remoteness, lack of communications, depopulation, age structure, outlook and sheer distance exist in so extreme a form as to present a new problem altogether. And in 1954 no regular extra-mural organisation existed in any Highland area to provide guidance or encouragement. That some of these problems have been overcome and a regular system of adult classes established over most of the county is an achievement that could only have been carried out by a partnership between university and local education authority blessed by mutual trust and the happiest of relations. The university could provide trained tutors, with access to the resources of the Extra-Mural Committee and to the experience of colleagues. The authority, on its side, gave generous financial support, the framework of its educational services, the co-operation of its experienced staff, and the sympathetic backing of an education committee who are fortunate in having a director of education with vision and understanding among his many virtues. As resident tutor I have had problems, but never problems in which I had not the greatest possible help from both university and authority.

Successful extra-mural classes had already been held at Dunoon, but this was no real guide to us in approaching the educational needs of this vast, sprawling, thinly populated region. Even the idea of extra-mural classes was unknown and when one early meeting was attended by a minister's wife who expected from an extra-mural tutor something new on interior decorating, it made one wonder what the uninformed laity might take him for. In Oban and Campbeltown, towns which had a population of around 6,000 and 7,000 respectively, we might hope for support from shopkeepers, professional men, women and housewives. Beyond this there was a large question mark. What about the fishing villages, the forestry workers, the farmers and crofters who are the backbone of the county? What about the small villages and towns of between two or three hundred and twelve or thirteen hundred, which are the characteristic population centres? And what about the people of the islands of Argyll? In spite of emigration a significant proportion still live in large islands like Mull and Islay (each the size of a normal county) or small ones like Lismore, Coll and Tiree. We were assured by knowledgeable men that we might just as well forget about these. Wrapped in their Celtic twilight the Gaelic-speaking communities would regard us as another alien, disintegrating influence. Certainly if we were to succeed we had to appeal to the representatives of the ancient, submerged culture of the West and North. This challenge was not so daunting as some others.

How, in the first place, organise a regular system of adult classes in a county so lacking in normal transport that country dwellers could not reach the nearest town or village in the evening, and so remote from Glasgow that the normal service of university teachers was out of the question? The roads are usually good, but tortuous, following the windings of the lochs for many a mile when a bridge or a ferry would save one thirty or forty miles. My road to Dunoon leads round the head of Loch Fyne and the shores of Loch Eck, over seventy miles of varied and impressive scenery, when as the crow flies the distance is but 25 miles. In Argyll, though, even the crows take a zigzag course. I found myself acquiring a trans-Atlantic attitude towards distances as my car sped hundreds of miles a week between class centres as remote from one another as Tiree and Campbeltown. Island piers lashed by high winds in the dark of a winter's morning became familiar, though not less horrid through custom. I counted myself lucky if I could on occasion go by plane instead.

This physical problem of scattered, inaccessible places, had a social counterpart which was just as challenging. For a couple of centuries the Highlands have been drained by constant emigration, indeed for longer. Not only are great areas so thinly populated now that normal services of any kind are vastly expensive and yet inadequate, but the population that remains is aged and deprived of many of its best sons and daughters. To a remarkable degree in Highland counties lairds and ministers shoulder responsibilities that should be carried by the rank and file of the community. I had grave doubts whether in such an environment an adult education class, which flourishes on individual initiative and self-expression, could survive. This social problem is not wholly solved, but I was to find the strongest ally that we had, in our hopes and plans, lay in the people of Argyll. In every part of the county I found there existed an appetite for adult education, a discriminating appetite if you like, that might reject the dished-up cold baked meats of the university diet, but that one might call the human hunger and thirst after understanding that somehow survives in most people the pressure-cooking of our youthful education. This, the true inspiration of education anywhere and at any time, whether of young or of old, ensured a measure of success for this venture in Argyll.

How do things stand now after six years of extra-mural work? There are eleven centres where classes are held, nine of which are regular centres where one, two or three classes are held every year. In the mainland centres these courses are held weekly over a term or a session, with the sixteen-week course as the most characteristic. The islands of Mull, Tiree and Islay have a regular monthly meeting through nine or ten months of the year, supplemented by fieldwork of a kind that I shall discuss shortly. Within a year we expect to have at least one centre in every district of

Argyll capable of sustaining a class: – in Cowal, Dunoon; in Mid-Argyll, Lochgilphead and Inveraray; in Kintyre, Campbeltown, Carradale and Tarbert; in Lorne, Oban, Ballachulish and perhaps Dalmally; in Mull, Tobermory; in Islay, Bowmore; and in Tiree, Cornaigmore. Open lectures are held in outlying areas, but the keynote of our policy is the regular class, with lecture, discussion, a reading programme and the fullest sense of belonging to an adult education movement. This is as true for the islands as for the mainland. We have regarded the founding of classes in Mull (in 1955), in Tiree (in 1957) and in Islay (in 1959) as important for social as well as educational reasons. About half of the total of 300 enrolled students are in the islands. After the first two years, which saw the founding of the mainland classes and one island class, expansion has been forced on us by local demand, frequently expressed through the Community Panels, and so urgent and genuine that our over-taxed and groaning organisation has had to extend its range still further. It is difficult to be hard-hearted when one knows that students are keen enough to drive up to 30 or 40 miles to a class and home again afterwards. I can think of nine or ten such cases without reflection.

We have been hampered by a shortage of local tutors and by the complete absence of internal University teachers except for single lectures. Yet the programme of studies is wide and varied, including most of the normal adult studies. Out of ten classes being held this year, five run for between fifteen and twenty meetings, and one is a tutorial. In history and archaeology, which are my own particular province, each of four or five centres has had – and survived – between forty and fifty lectures on a developing theme, with an emphasis on the Highlands. We have managed to weld together teams of lecturers from university departments and research organisations to conduct courses in science and social studies. In this way we have succeeded in dealing with human biology, psychology, medical progress, environmental studies, and this year a study of crime. The latter course combines the contributions of a moral philosopher, a psychologist, a lawyer, a prison governor, a forensic scientist, a deputy chief constable, a probation officer, a remand home superintendent, an after-care inspector, and an American exchange teacher. For this class over thirty students have enrolled. Forced upon us as a necessity, the team course has shown that it has its own set of virtues. We hope to continue to provide courses of first-rate quality in the sciences in Argyll. But with more than sixty tutors to plan for in last year's programme you can understand how delighted the resident tutor is when he finds a tutor able to conduct a course on his own.

Enrolments vary widely, but they average about thirty per class, with a 70 per cent to 80 per cent attendance. Where there have been disappointing results the fault has usually lain with the resident tutor in failing to plan with a good enough knowledge of local interests.

However well conceived a course may be, it must be planned with a particular centre in mind. It must be aimed at the right level, and also at the right angle, of interest, and it must be flexible, so that it develops in the direction suited best to the students' particular needs. It is better that students should be made to strain slightly rather than stoop.

'A man's reach should exceed his grasp, or what's heaven for?'

Meeting places are village halls, which are usually cold and too big, schools and sometimes hotels. Particularly in the country people look on the school as a usual centre for activities, and one has the advantage of using the school equipment. But surely it is high time that every community of a reasonable size had at least one properly furnished and equipped room, with adult-sized chairs and no inkpots to use as ashtrays, for adult classes. And a large town or city should be able to afford an adult education centre with a refectory and a library as well as rooms suitable for classes. One cannot achieve the status of a major educational activity for adult classes when they are not regarded as deserving of suitable and special accommodation.

Have we in Argyll made an impression on all sections of the community? In the towns, not as much as we should like. Our membership there approximates to the white-collared worker and housewife type of class one is familiar with. It is rarely that we attract the manual worker or the well-to-do upper middle class, whose values are very often thoroughly materialistic. But in country districts we have a more general appeal to all sections of the community, and our influence is important. It is a matter I think of social cohesion, and has nothing to do with the character of the work in the two types of community. Rural society is possibly more stratified in Argyll than in urban society, but there is greater social cohesion and unity, and it is normal for all sections of the community to take part in common activities – church, drama clubs, agricultural meetings, ceilidhs of one kind and another – whereas in towns you 'stick to your own kind' much more, to quote *West End Story*. Hence it is that an extra-mural class in a country town or village or island is simply the community in one of its aspects. This has its problems too, in that the class reflects the moods of the community and takes longer to assert its own character and produce its own leaders. I have analysed the occupations of a typical extra-mural class in one of the small islands with a population of about a thousand. The thirty-seven members of the class in 1959–60 include: the district clerk, the policeman, the postmaster, the pier-master, a motor mechanic; three shopkeepers, two retired people, nine teachers, five crofters, eight housewives, and one lord. Most are Gaelic-speaking. The subject of the year's studies was the social and economic history of the Scottish islands since the eighteenth century, with special studies of the industries, population movements, social organisation and the stories and songs of the Hebrides. Discussions were long and fascinating, for they often threw up unrecorded information and traditions about this island, and I remember my irritation at losing my sleep when, between six and eight o'clock next morning on the boat, the captain and policeman insisted on continuing the discussion. If you arouse local and regional interest and pride, the interest can be led outwards in widening circles of knowledge, and this year's more widely-based course in the same island has gathered an equally representative class.

I need to say something here about my own approach to history. I was trained in the economic-minded school of Cambridge history, with its faint but not unpleasing cynicism. I was as much interested in archaeology and anthropology as in history when I came to Argyll, having worked professionally in antiquities and folklore in the Isle of Man, and I was as anxious to learn as to teach. Earlier experiences in collecting oral traditions proved unexpectedly valuable for one could get one's own students to make their own history.

Some of these were new thoughts to Highland classes but they had many of the answers in their own recollections and traditions and daily experience. From the pooled information of any of the country classes one can reconstruct much of the vanished social scene, recover the half-forgotten place-names, locate ruined settlements and piece together the life and occupations of their denizens. With the backing and co-operation of the archaeology branch of the Ordnance Survey we are aiming to record the pattern of settlement before the clearances, perhaps over the whole of Argyll. Through the classes a number of valuable sound recordings have been made, containing material of great interest to students in many fields, and we aim to build up as large a body of such material as possible, both in English and Gaelic.

Mr Cregeen then played an excerpt from a Gaelic recording made by a prominent member of the class in Mull [Angie Henderson], the blacksmith at Tobermory, whose mind was a storehouse of traditional knowledge. Here he was describing the precise techniques used in making spades, forks, ploughs, salmon poaching spears, etc., in the smithy, in reply to Mr Cregeen's questions in Manx Gaelic.

Others have contributed on traditional farming methods, the making of lazy-beds, the different types of implement, and the management of stock, or on the construction of archaic types of house, providing the particular term used for each part and process. In this respect we have turned to advantage the high age-structure of Highland classes. In some ways, the older, the better, and every ninety-year-old is sure of a free drink.

At every stage the work has been done by co-operation. Had it not been for the initiative of one class member and the technical skill of another, Dugald, a frail old man of ninety, the last of the Highland drovers, would not have made just six months before he died the finest and fullest account of the life and work of a drover that has ever been made. It is stored in the archives of Edinburgh University, since unfortunately we have not developed this side of historical studies at Glasgow and have not the facilities for forming a library of recordings.

Mr Cregeen then played a number of excerpts from the 40 minutes' account.

Haldane's book, *The Drove Roads of Scotland*, is excellent history, but I recommend Dugald's reminiscences if you want to know the story from the drover's angle, told by a great natural storyteller. Many of the topographical and other notes in the published version were supplied by elderly members of the class at Inveraray after they had heard the recording for which they were themselves so much responsible and had discussed the historical development of the Highland cattle industry. But classes from one end of Argyll to the other have contributed to the study of the subject.

This approach to historical and related studies serves a threefold purpose. (1) It unites a class in a type of project for which they require no long and special training and which is ideally suited to a mature and adult mind. (2) It bases education on what is already familiar to them and awakens an interest and pride in what they often take for granted by showing them how it is related to wider issues. (3) And it achieves its results in fields of research where there is an urgent need for a great deal of work. It is important in such a region as the Highlands, where a whole way of life is fast vanishing, but it is just as important in recording, for example, the whole lore of the East Coast fishing communities, and that of the equally close-knit mining communities, and a whole host of industries and crafts and facets of social life in towns and cities all over Scotland (to go no further than that), not to speak of the recording of dialects and all the rich diversity of speech found within this country.

It is perhaps in archaeology that extra-mural work in Argyll has made its greatest impression so far. As we all know, archaeology has enjoyed a wave of popularity in recent years, which has not yet been broken. The television experts, and the supremely entertaining Sir Mortimer Wheeler, have played their part in extending its popularity, but the BBC, like ourselves, came in when a great public interest in this, as in other deeply cultural subjects, was evinced after the War. Certainly it existed in the West Highlands in 1954, where few television masts were to be seen. The classes in archaeology, which we established, have the advantage of seeing all around them the monuments and fragments of a succession of cultures. In four districts archaeological surveys are now in progress, two of which, in Mull and Cowal, we initiated, and two in Mid-Argyll and Islay, our students are assisting with. The striking growth of local interest and co-operation in the recording of unknown or previously unpublished sites is reflected in the consecutive issues of *Discovery and Excavation: Scotland*, an annual archaeological reporter. The 1955 issue contains four pages of Argyll notes. There are nine pages devoted to Argyll in 1956, eight in 1957, fourteen (a third of the book) in 1958, and eighteen in 1959. Much of this information is from extra-mural students, the most active and important single group being forestry workers.

It need not be stressed how valuable an educated public can be in such matters. Scores of finds and sites, which would otherwise have been lost to archaeology, are now rescued, investigated and published. Museums have gained. Public bodies concerned with antiquities have gained. In Islay, Mull and Cowal an extra-mural student has become the official Ordnance Survey Archaeological correspondent. And the Royal Commission on Ancient and Historical Monuments has, in the light of the recent progress in Argyll, decided to give Argyll precedence in its survey of the Scottish counties. It has been our policy to devolve responsibility and encourage initiative as much as possible and to promote the funding of new, autonomous societies for furthering local studies in archaeology, natural history, etc. Through our work and encouragement, three new Natural History and Antiquarian Societies have come into being: Part of Mid-Argyll in 1955, that of Mull in 1959, and that of Islay in the same year. They have a total membership of around 300. Each has this year sponsored an excavation. The Mull society has financed and organised one entirely on their own, the others have sought our assistance. In Mid-Argyll prompt action saved a unique Iron Age settlement from being destroyed by the contractors' bulldozer. My services as director of the excavation were provided by the Extra-Mural Committee with some financial help. The rest of the finance and most of the labour were furnished by the Society. It was mostly the under-thirties who helped during the two or three months of excavation to recover the post-holes of the houses of the settlement, the workshops, tools, and the great surrounding ditch, which had been twice renewed and contained a quite intact oven of earth and stones. We found the signs of a conflagration which must have destroyed the settlement at one stage – reddened stones, calcined bones and charcoal, fire-burnt posts in the post-holes, burnt wattle-and-daub walls, and quantities of charred and perfectly preserved barley. After another season (if the contractors can be held off so long), several students will be sufficiently trained to carry out at least rescue operations.

I have stressed the archaeological and folkloristic aspects of the work done with these groups. They have indeed come to play a very useful part in the study of Scottish antiquities. They have direct relations with official and semi-official bodies, and with research workers in universities, museums, etc. But their potential in natural history is equally great and simply requires developing. Already the Millport Marine Station, the Nature Conservancy, botanists and others are finding the groups valuable allies and reporters, but there is need for a naturalist to assist with the development of other aspects of local studies. Here I should say that I do not favour the term Local Studies as applied to extra-mural work. It is for one thing nonsense to apply the term local to a county of 2,000 square miles. But more fundamentally we are concerned with the particular only as illustrative of the general, and use the appeal and familiarity of the local to introduce a wider perspective. To have a department of local studies at a university is ludicrous. There, subject matter either is the local history and culture of a particular area, in which case it has no claim to academic status, or it is a branch of human history and anthropology, based on the study of the characteristics of a submerged peasant life.

I conclude this survey of the work in Argyll of this partnership of university and [education] authority by alluding to the fishing communities at Campbeltown, Tarbert and Carradale. We chose the small fishing village of Carradale as a suitable centre for a short course of Spring lectures on marine biology and economics in 1956. We got excellent support from the fishermen and their families, with whom I had established friendly contacts, and the friendly interest of Mrs [Naomi] Mitchison. We have held successful extra-mural courses there since then and have developed marine studies in the other fishing centres. But we were hampered in our treatment of the history of the industry by the paucity of good historical studies of this industry which made the fortunes of so many Lowland burghs and in the eighteenth and nineteenth centuries was the principal hope of the evicted and the landless. I began a long and fascinating enquiry into the fishing industry in Scotland – those sturdy little villages on the east that since the seventeenth century have represented the vigour and courage and spartan simplicity of Scottish life, the Shetland haaf fishing in their prefabricated Norwegian boats, the Ayrshire ports, and not least the developments in the Clyde lochs and the Highlands. But details of the construction of boats and nets, the methods of fishing in use, and the folklore of fishing and the internal economy of the boats were difficult to come by. I resorted to the fishermen in the classes and the older men to whom they could introduce me. Though much of the information I was after had gone forever, the search was rewarding. The following recordings will demonstrate this best.

There followed a number of recordings to illustrate the varying patterns of boat building over the years and the variety of fishing practice.

Through a large number of recordings of this kind supplemented by material I had collected in Man, it was possible to let the story of the industry be built up by the men engaged in it, creating a more complete and human picture than one can possibly get in any other way. The class itself was, with the help of the tutor, teaching itself, and seeing things in a new perspective. It should be done on the east coast and in Shetland, and then we can let loose some real controversies among the fishermen of different parts.

In conclusion I want to emphasise the importance of the relationship between tutor and student. The tutor has the advantages that derive from study, training and wide contacts. The student, however ill-educated in the strict sense, has been schooled by life itself. His adulthood and experience merit respect and consideration and offer a basis for his studies. The positions of tutor and student must often be reversed. Those who are concerned in this partnership in Argyll have no doubts that adult education is as important as the education of the child, that indeed, the education of the child loses point if, at adulthood – at the very time when he is free from the earlier pressure to pass examinations and 'get on' – he is deprived of the opportunity to grow mentally and spiritually and reach his full maturity. In this belief we have endeavoured not only to bring education into the field and the fishing boat, the distillery and the croft, the schoolroom and the manse, but also to derive inspiration from the occupations and concerns of men and women in their homes and at their work. In education as in every other worthy pursuit, nothing of human interest is alien to us.

4
RECOLLECTIONS OF AN ARGYLLSHIRE DROVER WITH HISTORICAL NOTES ON THE WEST HIGHLAND CATTLE TRADE

Scottish Studies, Vol. 3, Part 2, 1959, pp. 143–163

The last of the true Argyllshire drovers died at the age of 91 in Minard, on the shores of Loch Fyne, in April 1957. Other men are still alive in the district who went with cattle to the Falkirk Trysts, but they were not drovers in the sense that Dugald MacDougall was; they simply acted as cattle-men, taking the beasts by road and track to a distant market. Dugald was much more. In his young days – he was born in 1866 – he worked with four uncles who were farmers and cattle-dealers in the parish of Kilmichael Glassary. The spring and summer found him out in the islands buying young cattle. Autumn brought the big trysts at Falkirk, and from about 1886 until the late 1890s Dugald MacDougall took part in most of the droves that went to the October tryst. He came, moreover, of a family of drovers. His uncles, his grandfather, his great-great-uncles followed this business in successive generations. He was the repository of a droving tradition that dated from the eighteenth century and that was localised in Mid-Argyll. His forebears lived in North Knapdale, a secluded parish on the west coast, which has the closest links with the islands of Islay and Jura, the breeding grounds of some of the finest Highland cattle. They bought cattle in these islands and in the neighbouring parishes, and sold them after grazing them to English and Lowland buyers at the Falkirk Tryst. This same pattern of business was followed by successive generations of the family for over a hundred years, coming to an end with the subject of this article, Dugald, at the end of the nineteenth century.

In the six months before he died the old drover was thinking and talking a great deal about his droving years. He was ninety years old at this time. His memory was good and his powers of expression unimpaired. In November 1956 he made a remarkable sound recording.[1] He had never previously used, or even seen, a recording machine, yet he answered a series of questions on his life and experiences with a fullness of detail and a spontaneity of expression that give his account a unique value. It lasts for forty minutes and is in English, but he could equally well have spoken in his native Gaelic. Indeed the language he uses is Gaelic in its essential thought-forms and colour as well as more obviously in its cadences and pronunciations.[2] The facts of a drover's life are there, probably more fully than in any extant oral source; but the account is more than a piece of informative social history; it acquires from the old man's telling and the artless changes of his mood a compelling and moving quality.

The facts of Dugald MacDougall's life are soon set down. He was born in 1866 on a small farm called Craig Murail in the low hills north of Lochgilphead. An aunt at Bellanoch brought him up, and when she married the miller at Kilmartin he lived with them at the mill-house near the ruins of Carnasserie Castle. He had a job for five years in the estate office of the Malcolms of Poltalloch, and then at nineteen years of age he joined his four uncles, who were called MacLellan and had two farms in the district. These were his droving years. In 1899, or thereabouts, he moved to the farm of Craiganterve, near Ford at the southern end of Loch Awe. Craiganterve is still remembered as having been the best farm in the district and a model for the whole neighbourhood during his tenancy. He was here for forty-four years, saw his family grow up, became an elder in the Church and served as Clerk to the Kilmartin Parish Council. After he retired to live with his daughter at Minard, he was often to be seen taking a walk along the road, a spare figure, slightly bowed, with a handsome kindly face, a curly grey beard, and a surprisingly full head of white, wavy hair.

Dugald's reminiscences were of the native West Highland cattle. For centuries these small, hardy, black cattle had been bred for export on the mainland, but especially in the islands, of Argyll. The trysts at Crieff, Falkirk and Glasgow already feature in the rentals of the Lochfyneside estate of Campbell of Knockbuy in the 1730s,[3] a period when Crieff was pre-eminent and when droving and cattle-stealing were still liable to be confused, not least in the minds of the drovers. From his home, not a mile distant from where Dugald lived in his later years, Archibald Campbell, seceond laird of Knockbuy, carried on a successful cattle-dealing business in partnership with his kinsman, Campbell of Inverawe, with a turnover of 2,000 cattle in the year 1739–40. These beasts, purchased in the islands of Islay, Jura and Mull, and from the West Highland mainland as far north as Moidart, were grazed on the parks about Knockbuy (the present-day Minard) until they were ready to be driven to the Lowland trysts and ultimately into England.

Knockbuy Papers, accounts dated May 1739 to 20 March 1740, state that the outlay on buying 3,323 cattle was £5,482 17s. 2$^{5}/_{8}$d. Of those, 1,342 were kept for wintering and the rest sold. Knockbuy's accounts for the sale of 1,981 cattle are of interest. The number lost by accident or sickness during the long journeys is remarkably small – only ten proved totally unsaleable.

	Numbers	£. s. d.
Sold to my L. Ross at 30 Sh each	9	13.10.0.
Sold at the July Tryst 1739	147	294.0.0.
To my L. Elphinston	10	17.10.0.
Sold by Inverawe in England of Conjunct Cattle	666	1,607.13.11.
Sold at Creif by Knockbuy of Do.	1,127	2,254.0.0.
Sold by Castle Stewart of these that were left lame on the English road at Ninive [?Moniaive]	7	9.0.0.
To 4 Stotes of the Conjunct Catle put in Knokbuy's own drove to make up his numbers	4	9.0.0.
To 2 Stotes that dyed, one at Falkirk, Sold by James Campbell, the other in Larigdochart, Sold by Do. McKeck, both for	2	1.5.0.
Dy'd at Portaskaig 2, of the Mull Stotes 2, in Lincoln Shyre 1 left rot'n, in all	5	
Dy'd at Ninive	2	
Lost of the Numr gon to Creif marcat	1	
	1,980	4,205.19.5.
Sold lame for 10 lib Scots inde	1	16.8.
	1,981	4,206.16.1.

Knockbuy reckons the total outlay on buying and transporting 1,981 cattle at £3,809 4s. 10^{1}/$_{3}$d. The net profit is stated as £387 11s. 2^{2}/$_{3}$d.

By the mid-1700s, the 'spirit of improvement' had already, it seems, communicated its quickening influence to the shores of Loch Fyne and the lairds of Mid-Argyll, and Knockbuy appears as one of the earliest of the pioneers of stock-breeding in the Highlands. The enclosures at Minard were an indispensable part of his plan for raising the standard of his Highland cattle by breeding only from the finest beasts. His success was marked. '... [T]he Galloway gentlemen,' he writes in February 1744, 'acknowledge these several years past my cattle were inferior to no highlanders grazed with them; which demonstrates Argyllshire is as capable as Galloway for that purpose, though the latter has run away with the profit for many years back, which proper attention and application might alwise preserve to the Shire of Argyll.' In a letter to Campbell of Stonefield he urged the Duke should follow suit. Whether indeed the ambitious programme of agricultural and industrial reforms launched by the dukes of Argyll in the next decades was inspired, at least in part, by the advice and practice of Knockbuy, or not, there is no doubt that having a neighbour as active and enterprising as Archibald Campbell must have served to keep the ducal improvers on their toes.[4]

Smaller farmers had little interest in improvements, and the bulk of Highland cattle continued undersized and puny. But the movement which Knockbuy had so early pioneered in Mid-Argyll gained impetus. By the end of the eighteenth century many lairds in the West Highlands subscribed to, and practised, the new principles of selective breeding; none to more effect than Campbell of Shawfield, whose estate in Islay bred animals that took pride of place among the Highland cattle (MacDonald 1811, pp. 422 ff., 623 ff.)[5] It is no wonder that Dugald MacDougall's droving ancestors dealt largely in the product of the Islay grazings, nor that Bakewell himself declared, too late, 'that he wished he had laid the foundations of his improved breed with the kyloe or West Highland cow, for it wanted only size to be perfect' (Sinclair 1831: pt. 1, 264; Smith 1805: 243).

Already by the 1760s professional drovers appear in the Knockbuy rentals as substantial tenants. They were prosperous enough by the late seventies to rent two or three farms at seventy or eighty pounds sterling.[6] Possibly here in Argyll, as in Galloway (Haldane 1952: 51, 65), this professional class superseded Knockbuy and the other drover-lairds in their cattle-dealing functions, and by their increased specialisation enabled the Scottish supply of cattle to keep pace with the mounting demand in the South. Too often, however, the insufficiency of their capital hampered them. When allied to a lack of moral scruples, it caused an alarming frequency of bankruptcies among drovers and brought the whole class of drovers into disrepute (Haldane 1952: 49–52). But there appears to be something more solid and reliable about the late eighteenth century Mid-Argyll drovers than there was about their contemporaries in Galloway. If the *Statistical Account* does not applaud their virtues, it is equally silent about their failings. The regular appearance over a fairly long period of the same names in Knockbuy's rental against farms wide in extent and highly rented, inspires confidence in such men as Charles Young, John McKellar and John Macfarlane. In a shire where lairds as active and experienced in cattle-dealing as Knockbuy had blazed the trail, and where their power was considerable, it may be that drovers as a class acquired habits of regularity and honesty in advance of the rest of the country.

Dugald MacDougall begins his account with a story which he heard as a little boy from his grandfather MacLellan who had Gallcoille farm in North Knapdale and carried on business as a drover and cattle-dealer. It was a story which, he confessed, he heard many times before he could understand it, and it concerned two uncles of his grandfather, who were drovers in Knapdale, 'bought the cattle at the farms where they were reared, you know, and . . . took them away to the markets of the South and to the markets where they could get them sold. It was to the markets of the South they had this lot.' They bought on credit ' . . . they didn't pay them. The bargain was that they would give so much for them, and pay them when they came back after selling them in the markets of the South. But they found that the price that they could get for them there wouldn't meet the price that they had to pay the people at home. They were going to drop money themselves, and they were going to be the occasion of the people at home dropping money too, because they would be disappointed not to get the price at which they sold them.' Many drovers at this period – the late eighteenth or early nineteenth century – would not have scrupled to fail their creditors:

> Well, they considered. The one spoke to the other, what [was] the best thing they could do. And the other brother advised him and he said, 'The only thing that I can do, that I can think we ought to do, and keep our own credit, and do the best we can for the people at home, is take them back, every one of these animals, to the owner that had them when he sold them, and deliver them to the owner at his own farm, where we bought them, and tell them that that's the best thing we can do. We can't pay the money that we ought to pay, but there's your animals as we found them.' So they had so much confidence in them after that that they would give them any cattle they wanted without paying for them; they could take them away to sell and pay them when they came back.

The rustic innocence of these droving brothers evidently found a ready response in a community more fearful of defaulting drovers than insistent on the uttermost farthing.[7] This engaging story forms a fitting preface to Dugald's account.

These may have been the first drovers in the family, the men who founded the long tradition followed by Dugald's grandfather, then by his four sons, Dugald's uncles, and finally by Dugald himself. As cattle-dealers, they required grazing lands. The uncles had two farms, Barmolloch and Ardnackaig. Barmolloch is an upland farm three miles south of Ford, with hilly land on either side, but a prospect northward of a broad glen opening out into the wooded parkland of Ederline. Ardnackaig is situated on the west coast of North Knapdale, upon the Sound of Jura. On the good Barmolloch pastures the brothers summered their cattle. Hugh MacLellan was the business head and had charge of the buying and selling. The Islay trysts in May and June offered the finest cattle in the West, a consequence of Shawfield's careful breeding.

Dugald went with Hugh in the spring of the year to buy young cattle in Islay and Jura. One story which told about his uncle Hugh MacLellan, (unfortunately not recorded in sound), described Hugh coming with cattle over the Colintraive ferry. The cattle were frightened by the noise of their hooves on the wooden pier and scattered. They were lost for some time. Hugh sent a telegram home to Barmolloch: 'Cattle retreated. Hugh defeated. Send reinforcements'. Hugh MacLellan, I am told by Mrs Ann MacDougall, was not a man to be easily beaten.

The black cattle of the West Highlands could fetch the highest prices at Falkirk. But changes were afoot that did not always please the older farmers. 'There was more black ones in these days, black ones. But they got, when they got like everything else, into fancy things, they did away with the black ones. There's hardly any left of the black cattle.' This departure from a sober black for coats of many colours – brindled, dun, brown, yellow and red – Dugald viewed as a regrettable piece of frivolity, but cross-breeding was something far more serious: 'They wouldn't go in for crosses, not by any [means]. One of the uncles especially had a great horror o' crosses. Nothing but the pure Highland native cattle, you know, bullocks and heifers.' In this objection they were in good company, for the learned Dr Smith had laid it down as axiomatic that 'crossing the true Highland breed with any other ought to be avoided . . . The native cattle are always the hardiest cattle and the best feeders.' The improving lairds had reached the same conviction after experimenting with crosses between the native cattle and Galloways and other breeds. In the end they found the English buyer much preferred the West Highland beast (Smith 1805: 250).

The Barmolloch drovers brought the Islay cattle over the ferry at Port Askaig to Jura, and drove them by the eastside road to the ferry at Lagg.[8] The road to Lagg was building and still incomplete in 1805. The chief proprietor, Campbell of Jura, challenged the right of Campbell of Islay to use the new road for the passage of his cattle to the ferry at Lagg, alleging that his droves were entitled to use the old hill-track only. Campbell of Islay, when he sold his estate in Jura to this proprietor, had made it a condition that the ferry charges from Islay to Jura and from Jura to the mainland should not be altered without his assent. He had not, however, foreseen what the consequences of his own improvements might be. MacDonald, in a footnote in the Appendix to his *General View*, pp. 618–9, brings these out significantly:

> In former times, the cattle exported from Islay for the mainland markets, were never strong enough for the journey until the middle of June, the driest and best season of the year. They were then driven by herdsmen thro' Jura by a hill-road (the shortest possible way) which went between the back of the farms, which are all on the eastern shore, and the mountainous ridge which occupies the middle and western parts of the island. They had freedom of pasturage gratis . . . during this journey. [This was one

of the rights he reserved at the time of the sale.] In consequence, however, of the late improvements carried on in Islay, the cattle of the proprietors and tenants are much earlier ready for the market than June, and indeed, are exported all the year round; and they are also much heavier and more unwieldy than they were in former times, and consequently cannot travel along the hill road.

At Lagg they were loaded into the ferry-boat. Dugald recollected that the bottom of the boat was thickly heaped with a protective layer of birch branches. The ferryman was called Lindsay, and he had a blind assistant. The cattle were carried to Keills and unloaded on to the jetty. There was no need for them to swim ashore, as the jetty sloped down to the water, and boats could be discharged in any state of the tide. Its corrugated surface, made of thin slabs of stone set vertically, would offer a ready foothold to the cattle as they scrambled ashore.

The herd made its way by Tayvallich and Bellanoch to Crinan Moss and Kilmichael and up the glen to Barmolloch. Here they remained to graze until they were ready to be sold at the Falkirk Tryst.

The Barmolloch men had other cattle grazing, bought at the local trysts at Lochgilphead and Kilmichael. The Kilmichael tryst was the more important, held on the last Wednesday of May in a field still called the Stance Field, situated within a curve of the River Add below the late eighteenth-century bridge at Kilmichael.[9] To refresh his memory, Dugald turned to a faded copy of Orr's *Scottish Almanac* for 1916, a thin paper-backed pamphlet containing miscellaneous information: 'The Rising and Setting of the Sun, the Phases of the Moon, with its Age, the Times of High Water at Glasgow, and a General Tide Table; also a Table of the Probable Weather that will occur during the Year, and a List of Fairs, Holidays and Fast Days kept in some of the Principal Towns in Scotland'. Information yet more exotic is to be found in its pages; a list of the Imperial Parliaments, the names, birthdays and marriages of all nine of Queen Victoria's children, and a splendid catalogue of the Sovereigns of Europe, no less than twelve in number if one includes Tsar Nicholas II and Sultan Mohamed V who succeeded his brother Abdul (deposed). Seven closely printed pages at the end of the almanac give details of the trysts of Scotland, classified according to their month. None, as Dugald explained, bears a specific date. 'There was no date; it was the day of the week, yes .... And you can see from this old almanac, you can see it there, the days of the week.' Here he reads aloud from it: 'Tuesday before last Wednesday ... Wednesday fortnight after Kilmichael in May, yes. And the Falkirk Tryst was the second Tuesday of October, and the day following he says in this almanac too.'[10]

For a century and a half the Falkirk Tryst occupied a unique place in the economic development and social life of Scotland. It was the annual meeting-place of English buyers and Scottish drovers, a gathering geographically almost as widely representative as the General Assembly. Here was congregated the cattle-surplus of all the Highland counties, beside beasts raised on Lowland farms. The export trade was worth about a quarter of a million pounds in the closing decade of the eighteenth century, and it was still expanding (Haldane 1952: 205 ff.). By Dugald MacDougall's time, the traffic had shrunk to a slender current compared with the full spate of the mid-nineteenth century. It was still, however, the principal cattle-market in Scotland, and its three trysts, in August, September and October, saw many Highland cattle sold to English and Lowland buyers.

The Barmolloch men attended the biggest of the trysts, held in October. There were other trysts where they sometimes did business, Doune in Perthshire and Carman Fair at Dumbarton, with its stance on the top of the hill above Renton: 'I was at that fair once, and there was only one house, a shepherd's house, up there. And the market-day the shepherd got a licence; he could sell spirits to the dealers or them that came with the cattle. That was the only house that was in it at Carman, up at the top of the hill, yes.' Kilmichael was the regular local market, and usually, 'when they were taken away from this district, as most of the older cattle were, it was to the Falkirk Trysts'.

By early October the cattle were in superb condition. 'After the summering and that they were splendid big animals ... oh grand big bullocks, just full of flesh and hair when they were sold at three and a half years old in October.' The heifers were sold off a year younger, but the bullocks were kept as long as there was grazing for them. The Barmolloch droves numbered fifty or sixty cattle. They could be handled by two men and their dogs. The seven-day journey of nearly a hundred miles of road and track began early enough to allow the cattle a rest for three days at the end of it before the Tryst commenced. The route which they followed was one which had been long used by drovers from Mid-Argyll. First the drove made for the old hill track leading from Loch Awe over the high moorland north of Loch Fyne to the farm of Auchindrain near Inveraray. Many of the drovers coming from Mull and Nether Lorne ferried their beasts across Loch Awe at Portinnisherrich (Haldane 1952: 90) and joined this track on the Leckan Muir. (They were from remote, unvisited regions to Dugald, who spoke of the northern Argyll and Inverness-shire islands as 'Mull and these places'.) The Barmolloch droves would emerge on to it two or three miles from its starting point at the medieval church of Kilneuair. It was a narrow track, about six feet wide, but dry and clean and well-drained, with a firm bottom of stones.

The first day with its unaccustomed fatigues and steep gradients was the hardest on the cattle. The road rises almost from sea-level to a loch-strewn terrain a thousand feet higher, apparently desolate but for sheep and predatory birds. It clambers to its summit at Loch a' Chaoruinn; here the drovers could ease off and look back over the winding track to the waters of Loch Awe, and in the distance, beyond the String of Lorne, the great hills of Jura and Mull.

A good drover was careful not to press his cattle too hard, especially at the outset. 'They were in full bloom, and full of flesh and hair. If you sweated them, the hair drooped down and never got up again into the same [condition]. The great secret was to take them there as good-looking as they were when they left home. One would think there was nothing but drive and force them on with a stick, but that wasn't allowed at all. They'd go quite nicely when they were left alone. The man that was in front – they didn't all stay behind – he took maybe twelve or so of the first cattle on, and the rest followed; and if these went into a gap, or found an open gate, and went in, you had only to get twelve out, whereas if you were all behind, you would have the whole sixty or fifty, and that spent time to get them back out again. There was an art in doing it right, properly; even suppose one would think it was a simple thing, there was an art in doing it properly too, to give man and beast a chance, yes'.

The old track can still be travelled on foot, but the surface has become pitted, eroded, and in places, water-logged. To the neglect of half a century and the effects of harsh weather was added more active ill-usage. The *Argyllshire Advertiser* announced on 20 August 1924, under the heading 'Motor Cycle Feat', that a local motor-cyclist had recently driven 'a machine of the well-known B.S.A. manufacture' from Ford to Inveraray 'by the old hill-road'. This no doubt praiseworthy individual initiated the trials which damaged the road beyond repair. Yet so late as 1914 or thereabouts a small boy called Archie Campbell, now living at Arrochar, travelled this road with his father, who was taking a drove of thirty young cattle from Oban to Mr Macfarlane's farm of Stronafyne at the head of Loch Long.

The route which the drovers followed from Auchindrain coincides fairly well with the present road through Inveraray, round the head of Loch Fyne, over the Rest and Be Thankful Pass to Arrochar, and thence by Tarbet and Loch Lomondside to Balloch. But in recent years, the old road over the Rest has been superseded by a new road with easier gradients. Along the west shore of Loch Lomond, too, the older road can frequently be seen escaping from the macadam bondage of the new, to make a brief excursion. The divergence of the new road from the old is particularly noticeable a quarter of a mile south of Inverbeg Inn; the latter crosses a crumbling eighteenth century bridge and climbs the slope of the hill, whilst the new road follows a course nearer the loch.

After Alexandria the drovers crossed the river at Bonhill. 'It was a wooden bridge that crossed [the Leven] at Bonhill, a wooden bridge. It's a fine concrete bridge now.' Here they turned to the left as if making for Jamestown and then took the old hill-road over the Cameron Muir. 'There was an old toll over there. It was Finnich Toll they called it. It was getting into disuse when I went there at first.' And so on to Killearn. From there the drovers' road led through Fintry, past Spittal Hill farm, and across the Kirk o' Muir. 'There's a big reservoir they tell me, converted now on the right hand side up there, a great big water works that wasn't there when we were going at all.' Carronbridge came next, and Denny, Dunipace and Dennyloanhead, and finally, Larbert, the end of the long journey.

Halting-places for a night's grazing existed all along the drovers' route. There were stances where custom gave the drover free unhindered access for his beasts, though a charge was made for the use of them. When there was no stance, accommodation could be obtained on farms for a payment of about ten shillings a score in Dugald's time. The Barmolloch drove must have reached the neighbourhood of the main Inveraray road on the first day, with a full dozen rough miles behind. Accommodation could be got on the stance at Auchnagoul or on farm land in the vicinity.[11] The old rights of free grazing at Inveraray, which are mentioned in the kirk-session records, had apparently escaped in the eighteenth-century improving movement.[12] 'The old town muir to be inclosed' reads a note of November 1758 written in the instructions to the Chamberlain of Argyll by the 3rd Duke (Fergusson n.d.). The loss of customary stances and the multiplication of turnpike pike tolls during the early nineteenth century added to the problems of the drovers and contributed to the decline of the Falkirk Tryst (Haldane 1952: 212 with note 4; 242-4).[13]

On the second night the drove might be in Glen Shira (as Duncan MacColl, Crarae, remembers) but more usually it reached the stance at Cairndow, an extensive area extending up the hillside on the east side of the head of the loch. 'There's a place – I can see the opening yet – where we went ... The stance came down to the road, but halfway up the hill it was fenced off. They couldn't get out of it altogether, but they had plenty of room, yes, they had plenty of room. But it will likely be getting into disrepair now like every other thing ... It's never used as a stance now.' Sadness and nostalgia for the past sometimes gently intrude into Dugald's recollections, but never for long. He quickly remembers his theme, and in imagination gathers his drove from the night's pasture and sets out briskly on the road.

On the third day the drove made its progress through Glen Finglas and over the Rest down to Loch Long and the stance on Stronafyne at Arrochar. The stance lies on the slope of the hill east of the head of

After Alexandria the drovers crossed the river at Bonhill. 'It was a wooden bridge that crossed [the Leven] at Bonhill, a wooden bridge. It's a fine concrete bridge now.' Here they turned to the left as if making for Jamestown and then took the old hill-road over the Cameron Muir. 'There was an old toll over there. It was Finnich Toll they called it. It was getting into disuse when I went there at first.' And so on to Killearn. From there the drovers' road led through Fintry, past Spittal Hill farm, and across the Kirk o' Muir. 'There's a big reservoir they tell me, converted now on the right hand side up there, a great big water works that wasn't there when we were going at all.' Carronbridge came next, and Denny, Dunipace and Dennyloanhead, and finally, Larbert, the end of the long journey.

Halting-places for a night's grazing existed all along the drovers' route. There were stances where custom gave the drover free unhindered access for his beasts, though a charge was made for the use of them. When there was no stance, accommodation could be obtained on farms for a payment of about ten shillings a score in Dugald's time. The Barmolloch drove must have reached the neighbourhood of the main Inveraray road on the first day, with a full dozen rough miles behind. Accommodation could be got on the stance at Auchnagoul or on farm land in the vicinity.[11] The old rights of free grazing at Inveraray, which are mentioned in the kirk-session records, had apparently escaped in the eighteenth-century improving movement.[12] 'The old town muir to be inclosed' reads a note of November 1758 written in the instructions to the Chamberlain of Argyll by the 3rd Duke (Fergusson n.d.). The loss of customary stances and the multiplication of turnpike pike tolls during the early nineteenth century added to the problems of the drovers and contributed to the decline of the Falkirk Tryst (Haldane 1952: 212 with note 4; 242–4).[13]

On the second night the drove might be in Glen Shira (as Duncan MacColl, Crarae, remembers) but more usually it reached the stance at Cairndow, an extensive area extending up the hillside on the east side of the head of the loch. 'There's a place – I can see the opening yet – where we went . . . The stance came down to the road, but halfway up the hill it was fenced off. They couldn't get out of it altogether, but they had plenty of room, yes, they had plenty of room. But it will likely be getting into disrepair now like every other thing . . . It's never used as a stance now.' Sadness and nostalgia for the past sometimes gently intrude into Dugald's recollections, but never for long. He quickly remembers his theme, and in imagination gathers his drove from the night's pasture and sets out briskly on the road.

On the third day the drove made its progress through Glen Finglas and over the Rest down to Loch Long and the stance on Stronafyne at Arrochar. The stance lies on the slope of the hill east of the head of strewn terrain a thousand feet higher, apparently desolate but for sheep and predatory birds. It clambers to its summit at Loch a' Chaoruinn; here the drovers could ease off and look back over the winding track to the waters of Loch Awe, and in the distance, beyond the String of Lorne, the great hills of Jura and Mull.

A good drover was careful not to press his cattle too hard, especially at the outset. 'They were in full bloom, and full of flesh and hair. If you sweated them, the hair drooped down and never got up again into the same [condition]. The great secret was to take them there as good-looking as they were when they left home. One would think there was nothing but drive and force them on with a stick, but that wasn't allowed at all. They'd go quite nicely when they were left alone. The man that was in front – they didn't all stay behind – he took maybe twelve or so of the first cattle on, and the rest followed; and if these went into a gap, or found an open gate, and went in, you had only to get twelve out, whereas if you were all behind, you would have the whole sixty or fifty, and that spent time to get them back out again. There was an art in doing it right, properly; even suppose one would think it was a simple thing, there was an art in doing it properly too, to give man and beast a chance, yes'.

The old track can still be travelled on foot, but the surface has become pitted, eroded, and in places, water-logged. To the neglect of half a century and the effects of harsh weather was added more active ill-usage. The *Argyllshire Advertiser* announced on 20 August 1924, under the heading 'Motor Cycle Feat', that a local motor-cyclist had recently driven 'a machine of the well-known B.S.A. manufacture' from Ford to Inveraray 'by the old hill-road'. This no doubt praiseworthy individual initiated the trials which damaged the road beyond repair. Yet so late as 1914 or thereabouts a small boy called Archie Campbell, now living at Arrochar, travelled this road with his father, who was taking a drove of thirty young cattle from Oban to Mr Macfarlane's farm of Stronafyne at the head of Loch Long.

The route which the drovers followed from Auchindrain coincides fairly well with the present road through Inveraray, round the head of Loch Fyne, over the Rest and Be Thankful Pass to Arrochar, and thence by Tarbet and Loch Lomondside to Balloch. But in recent years, the old road over the Rest has been superseded by a new road with easier gradients. Along the west shore of Loch Lomond, too, the older road can frequently be seen escaping from the macadam bondage of the new, to make a brief excursion. The divergence of the new road from the old is particularly noticeable a quarter of a mile south of Inverbeg Inn; the latter crosses a crumbling eighteenth century bridge and climbs the slope of the hill, whilst the new road follows a course nearer the loch.

the loch, behind the village. On the lower side it was limited by a wall, but above only by steep rocks. The drove road is still to be seen leaving the main road near the Roman Catholic church and re-emerging on the road to Tarbet a mile farther on. Mr MacFarlane was the farmer at Stronafyne, and he was himself accustomed to buying young cattle from the islands at Oban for selling eighteen months later at the Falkirk Tryst. The route taken by the Stronafyne drove lay along the shores of Loch Long to Faslane, where Mr MacFarlane's brother farmed, and then through Glen Fruin to Balloch and Larbert. After the decline of the Falkirk Tryst his droves went by the same route to the market at Stirling and continued to do so until 1916.[14] Dugald MacDougall was himself familiar with this route, as an old friend of his, Dugald MacIntyre, recalls. The latter was taking the Poltalloch drove to the Falkirk Tryst in one of the last years of the Tryst, probably in 1900. He met Dugald MacDougall with the Barmolloch drove at the stance at Cairndow. Both were making for the Tryst, but Dugald MacDougall had cattle to pick up on the way and left a day before Dugald MacIntyre. But the latter reached Larbert first, for his friend had travelled by the Loch Long–Glen Fruin route, picking up cattle from farms in Glen Douglas and probably, too, from Faslane. Farming connections of this kind continued frequently over many years and played no small part in deciding both the route and the halting-places of the droves, and from year to year it might be varied in detail.

After a night on the Stronafyne stance, Dugald would usually take the road down the shores of Loch Lomond as did the Poltalloch drover. The road was rougher and slightly more undulating than it is at present, but easier on the feet of cattle than the modern road-metal. Passing Firkin, three miles south of Tarbet, where droves might be seen leaving their night's grazing, he carried on to where the road, in its winding course, turns away from the loch by the inn at Inverbeg and climbs steeply into 'a fine glen they call Glen Douglas . . . There's farms up there, and it's there we put the cattle that night.' These were farms with which Barmolloch had business connections and where the drove would be reinforced with more beasts for the Tryst. Doune of Douglas farm is two miles along the glen and its spacious, well-walled enclosure by the river may often have provided the drove with a night's shelter and grazing. Higher up still is Invergroin, situated in the valley bottom, where a droving track from Arrochar drops down into Glen Douglas from between the great masses of Ben Reoch and Tullich Hill, to pass by Doune of Douglas, climb the slope to the south and descend to Luss by Glen Mallochan.

An experienced drover planned his journey carefully, and often put in a short day to rest his drove after a strenuous one and to refresh his beasts before a long trek.[15] On the fifth day, after the relative ease of the previous one, Dugald brought his cattle down to the lochside road at the Inverbeg Inn. Here was a stance opposite the inn which had formerly been used when the ferry plied across the loch to Rowardennan, taking the Argyllshire cattle on the shortest route to the Tryst. Sometimes they were swum across, with two experienced cattle, which were kept by the inn to lead them. But the ferry has gone beyond the memory of man, and survives only as a tradition in the locality. An old woman who died at Luss about 1952 at the age of 103 recollected her parents speaking of its existence.[16]

For Dugald and his uncles and their contemporaries the road to Falkirk Tryst stretched ahead through Luss and across the River Leven. With his drove refreshed and eager for the road, Dugald made for Killearn, more than twenty miles distant. He preferred the Bonhill crossing and the old hilltrack across the Cameron Muir rather than the bridge at Balloch and the Gartocharn road which was taken by the Poltalloch drove. Less than four miles beyond Bonhill and situated on the hill-road was the Merkins farm, where Mr Anderson allowed the drove to stay on many occasions. Eighteen miles was sometimes enough for a day, but if the drove was going well Dugald carried on farther before halting. His younger, lighter beasts were more than a match for the Poltalloch four-year-olds, which took nine days on the journey. By the sixth night the Barmolloch drove was at Carron Bridge with 'Laird Thomson as we called him'. The old man, whom the drovers accorded a courtesy-title in virtue of his owning his land, never refused grazing to any of the family of his friend, Dugald's grandfather. It was but a short journey after this. By the evening of the seventh day the cattle from the Barmolloch farm had joined some thousands of others on the stance at Stenhouse Muir on the outskirts of Larbert, where the Falkirk Trysts were held. Dugald and his companions could leave them to rest after the arduous trek whilst they sought the hospitable house of Mr Wilson, the blacksmith.

When the tryst opened on the Tuesday, buyers moved around the field to view the cattle, and the drovers showed off their stock to the best advantage. They kept the cattle 'in a close bunch, and got them to move round like that. And the buyer was standing outside, and he was seeing them all as they were coming round. And if possible, if there was one that wasn't so good, it was try to keep that one in the middle, let the rest keep him out of sight. The buyer saw them all, but they were all on the outside.' In the long run it was the quality of the cattle that counted, and the Barmolloch droves could compare with any cattle at the Tryst. Buyers learned to know the reliable drover with good beasts and formed a business connection that might last for years. Dugald remembered well 'a Mr Carr from Yorkshire', who regularly bought their heifers to rear calves; 'he took one calf off them. Likely it would be a cross – it might be a shorthorn bull – and let them rear the calf and then fatten them off to kill them . . . That was his rotation; buy more heifers when you sell off the ones you bought.'

The bullocks were fetching around sixteen pounds, but this was not clear profit; the expenses of the week's drove were to be deducted, and the buyer's *luck-money*, which amounted to a few pounds on the transaction (a custom still maintained and one which appears to have flourished in Knockbuy's day too).[17] The buyer, when he finally accepted the drover's price, clapped the latter's outstretched hand. And 'that', commented Dugald, as he smote his hands together with a resounding smack, 'that was the bargain sealed; and it was as good as suppose it was in a lawyer's book when they struck hands'.

When the cattle were sold, the Barmolloch men left for home, with money in their pockets for the next year's stock. But as the train carried them, at a speed considerably faster than they could walk, to Glasgow for the Ardrishaig steamer, the MacLellan brothers must have wondered how much longer the Falkirk Tryst could go on. In 1873 the railway line fingered its way up from Callander as far as Killin; two years later it had reached Tyndrum, Dalmally in 1877, and on 30 June 1880, Oban and the coast.[18] The progress of the railway meant the decline of the drover's craft. Cattle were conveyed from the most distant points to Larbert in a day. In the last years of the century, droves of a hundred and fifty or two hundred cattle were being driven from Kilchamaig farm on the west coast of Kintyre by Loch Aweside to Dalmally. Here they were loaded into ten trucks, specially ordered by Turner, 'the Kintyre cattle-king', for transporting to Larbert.[19] But the older-fashioned drovers continued to walk the cattle all the way, and Dugald and his uncles were at the Falkirk Tryst in the last years of the 1890s.

With the coming of railway communications, a new phenomenon made its appearance in Scotland's country towns – the auctioneer and the auction sale. Oban was a mere two days' trek from Barmolloch. Even the MacLellans took to selling at the new Oban market in their latter years. The end of the Falkirk Tryst came in 1901, and since then the race of drovers has virtually disappeared in Argyll. At Barmolloch, Dugald's cousins discontinued the old uncles' cattle-dealing business. The Tryst ground at Larbert has been turned into a golf-course. The drove-roads are a thing of the past.

Yet it is still common to meet men of middle age who took part in droving cattle to local auction sales before cattle-trucks became widely used. The Poltalloch cattle took two days on the road to Oban, spending a night at Cuilfail, and beasts from Eilean Righ in Loch Craignish were swum across to join the drove, whilst until the late war droves from Kilberry were making the three-day trek to Oban.[20]

Dugald MacDougall came of a long-lived family. He himself, at the age of ninety, could well have been taken for a man twenty years younger, and that in spite of the rheumatic pains in his legs. These he would refer to, with a wry smile, as 'the disabilities of age and the end of the journey'. His four bachelor-uncles, the MacLellans, all lived beyond fourscore years. His grandfather 'was ninety-four or ninety-five when he died, and he wouldn't have died then but he fell'. On a wild, stormy day in August 1956, in his ninety-first year, Dugald went to Oban to be presented to the Queen. It was a proud moment for him. He told her about his droving days and the many trysts that he attended. Three months later he made the recording. By the spring he was dead. Dugald MacDougall was as full of wisdom and kindliness as he was of years. The week he died he set his affairs in order with his usual serenity, like a drover coming to a tryst.

ACKNOWLEDGEMENTS

My thanks are due to Mrs Ann MacDougall for making it possible to record her father and for permission to publish the material; to Dr Iain MacCammond for help in recording; and to Sir George Campbell of Succoth, Bt., whose original suggestion led me to the drover's house. For access to the Kilberry and Knockbuy papers, and for permission to use them in the preparation of this article as well as for her kindness in drawing my attention to much relevant material in them, I am indebted to Miss Campbell of Kilberry. I am grateful to my wife for the initial maps (based on Haldane) and to Miss Isabel Catto for assistance with the transcription.

REFERENCES

Colville, Duncan (1958) Unpublished notes on Kintyre in the eighteenth century, incorporated in a lecture given at Campbeltown in December 1958.

Fergusson, Sir James (n.d.) Report on the archives at Inveraray Castle. File at Register House.

Haldane, A.R.B. (1952) *The Drove Roads of Scotland*. Edinburgh This is an invaluable guide. The author met Dugald MacDougall and refers to him briefly in his chapter on the drove roads of Argyll. My own study of a particular drover in a particular droving tradition and locality should be viewed against the great landscape of droving that Haldane has so admirably depicted in this work.

Kilberry Rentals. Unpublished eighteenth-century rentals at Kilberry Castle.

Knockbuy Papers. These unpublished papers at Kilberry Castle include eighteenth-century rentals, accounts and notes kept by Archibald Campbell, 2nd of Knockbuy, who lived 1693-1790.

MacDonald, James (1811) *General View of the Agriculture of the Hebrides*. Edinburgh.

MacDougall, Dugald. Recollections of droving, recorded in sound by the late Mr Dugald MacDougall, former drover, in November 1956, in his 91st year. A copy of the recording and a transcription have been deposited at the School of Scottish Studies.

Report, Crofter's Commision. (1884) *Report of the Commissioners of Inquiry into the Condition of the Crofters and Cottars in the Highlands and Islands of Scotland*, Appendix A: Report of Duncan Forbes to the Duke of Argyll.

Sinclair, Sir John (ed.) (1791–98) *The Statistical Account of Scotland*. Edinburgh.

Sinclair, Sir John (1831) *Analysis of the Statistical Account of Scotland*, 2 parts. Edinburgh.

Smith, Dr John (1805) *General View of the Agriculture of the County of Argyll*. London.

NOTES

1. School of Scottish Studies Archive, SA1958/194.
2. Inverted commas, when used here, indicate excerpts from Dugald MacDougall's account, unless referred to another source. Few modifications have been necessary, and those, slight ones to make plain the drover's meaning. Words I have inserted are in square brackets.
3. Typical entries are: 'two cowes to the Crieff drove, £33.6.8.' (1728) 'allowd this day 24 Decr. 1735 of the price of Cowes given in to the Drove, £12.7.4.'; 'by a cowe given to McKinley with the Drove went to Glasgow, £16.0.0.' (1728); 'allowd her son [Widow McIllevin's] a crown I owed him when out at the Falkirk Tryst and payd today 2 lib 14 sh. 4d.' (1732).
4. Sinclair 1791–98, Argyll parishes; Sir James Fergusson; Knockbuy rentals and papers; Kilberry rentals; Report 1884 (for Duncan Forbes's account, 1737); Colville 1958.

   Throughout the eighteenth century the Dukes of Argyll are found playing an important and often a leading role in the economic development of the county. Duncan Forbes's visit to Tiree and Mull in 1737 on behalf of the 2nd Duke marks an extension to these islands of a policy of agricultural reform that bore hard on the higher tenants, the tacksmen, but laid the foundations of improvement by granting longer leases to working farmers. The enterprises of the 3rd Duke (1743–61) and the 5th Duke (1770–1806) created at Inveraray a new castle and town, a noble park, and roads, bridges and plantations. From 1770, new leases for farms on the estate incorporated certain improvements as a condition of tenancy, and officials known as 'improvers' were employed to advise the Duke and the tenants. But in some directions Archibald Campbell, whose long life (1693–1790) spanned the greater part of the eighteenth century, was ahead of his noble neighbours, and especially in cattle-breeding. His experience in enclosing land at Minard, in breeding selectively for better types of horses and cattle, and in making use (from 1740) of such techniques as 'speaving' poorer beasts (an idea that he picked up from Galloway landowners) is discussed by him in a letter that he addressed to Archibald Campbell of Stonefield, Sheriff

Depute and Justice Depute of Argyll, on February 1744. The original of this highly interesting letter is among the Stonefield papers at Register House, and a copy exists at Kilberry Castle. It was written with the intention that it should be brought to the notice of the new (i.e. 3rd) Duke. Knockbuy stresses the importance of enclosing ground as 'absolutely necessary' to any improvements in stock, and advises that the enclosures at Inveraray should be employed as a kind of nursery, supplying 'the Gentlemen of the Shire' with carefully bred animals, which 'would soon spread a breed of fine black cattle over the whole shire'. A similar plan might be applied to horses. Knockbuy's recommendations range widely over the economic field. It would be interesting to learn precisely what direct influence they had on the Duke. It is surprising that he makes no allusion to potatoes. As early as 1735 this new crop, which was to play so great a part in the future development of the Highlands, appears in Knockbuy's rentals as an item in the payment of rents, and in 1736 the entry against the name of one tenant on the Kilberry estate (Knockbuy was one of the guardians and executors for the heir Colin, 7th of Kilberry) – 'to John McVretnie for Seed Butatos £4' – makes it clear and beyond doubt that potatoes were being cultivated. Archibald Campbell married Grizel, daughter of the 5th Kilberry, and their grandson eventually succeeded to Kilberry in 1798 on the death of Colin, the last of the old line of Kilberry.

5. MacDonald notes: 'So lately as 30 years ago the general average of the cattle of Skye and Mull brought as high prices as those of Islay ; but for the last ten years these two islands have sold their cattle at an average of £6, while that of Islay has been £8.10.0.: and the highest prices obtained for whole parcels or droves have been frequently in the proportion of two to one.' (1811: 423–4).

6. Tenants with the specific title of drovers first appear in the rentals in 1764, when Tunns is 'sett to Patrick McKellar, Drover, a seven years tack ... £25.0.0'. In 1781 Charles Young, drover, rented Achaghoile at Minard, for £58 13. 6d. and Upper Carron for £15 2. In the same year John McKellar, drover, rented Achabhialich and Kilmichaelbeg for £73 5s. 6d. In 1760 these two farms had been in the hands of nine tenants at rents totalling £35 15s. 10d. Much of the increase in rent would be due to the introduction of sheep. They first make their appearance in large numbers in 1762, when the laird commenced sheep-farming. I have no direct evidence that the drovers took up sheep-farming, but it is not unlikely that they used their higher ground for sheep. Lowland sheep-masters made several attempts to rent farms from Knockbuy in the seventies, but he resisted their offers, as he was not sure of their financial standing (Knockbuy Papers). He proved wise in the event, as most of them appear to have gone bankrupt in the period of the American War of Independence. (Sinclair 1794 [XIII]: 655). On one occasion a drover prevented a sheepmaster gaining entry to a farm: – 'North Moninirnich set to Lanarkmen but possessed violently by Patrick McKellar, Drover, who suspended my charge of removal which I have not discussed. The rent Patrick paid before was £28 2s. od. but the new rent is £41 besides fox-money.' (Knockbuy Rentals 1770).

Knockbuy, on the evidence of his letter of 2 February 1744, was already looking ahead to the day when sheep stocks in Argyll might be made more profitable. But there was one great obstacle: 'Till the fox is destroyed on the continent of Argyllshire, as in the Isles thairof, their can be very little improvement to be made of our sheep'. Nevertheless he advises breeding from good rams and commends the proprietors 'to be att pains to understand the methods us'd by the most considerable sheep stockers in the Low Country' [sic].

7. The only good cattle raised in North Knapdale, at the period when the drover brothers were operating, were those of the tacksmen. The cattle of the small tenants were 'scraggy and impoverished beasts' (Sinclair 1793 [VI]: 263). They must have been poor indeed if a three- or four-year-old weighing 360 to 400 lb was esteemed good (Smith 1805: 251). But the brothers would be dealing in the island cattle also. It should be noted, in further explanation of the story told by Dugald, that agreements made at this period between drovers and farmers were often of a fairly elastic type. Farmers might sell to drovers at a certain price but stipulate that the drovers should pay them more if prices at the tryst were higher than those agreed upon (Haldane 1952: 28).

8. The following items, from the Knockbuy cattle-dealing accounts in 1739–40 refer to Islay:

		£. s. d.
Bought from Shawfield 343 Stotes at 30 Sh. pr. peice and one at IIay at 16 Sh. 8 p.	344	515.6.8.
Bought from Sundries in Ilay in May, 1739	369	532.8.5 $^{1}/_{3}$
Their fferrieing from Ilay to Jura		5.2.4
Their proportion of £13.15.11 of Charges		3.15.11.

9. Information from Col. George Malcolm of Poltalloch and Mr John MacLachlan, Poltalloch. The latter recalls that a right to free grazing existed also on the greens at Kilmartin and Ford.

10. Some of the trysts appear in this almanac of 1916 as still regulated by the Julian Calendar. Strontian, for example, falls on the Friday following the third Thursday in June, Old Style. For drovers and farmers accustomed to the New Style the day would be a Tuesday instead of a Friday. Gaelic-speaking Argyllshire people know Falkirk as *An Eaglais Bhreac,* 'the speckled church', and one man over ninety applied this term to the Falkirk Tryst itself.

11. I omitted to question Dugald MacDougall about the first night's halt, but his daughter believes that it was at Brenachoille farm which lies beside the old hill-road a mile from its junction with the main road. Another informant, Dugald MacIntyre, made use of this stance for a Poltalloch drove about 1900, and thinks it probable that Dugald stayed there on occasions. However, drovers often varied their halts, and Duncan MacColl, now of Crarae, for many years farmer at Claonairi, near Inveraray, believes that he sometimes used the stance on the farm of Auchnagoul, which lies on the slope above the Bridge of Douglas. The last drove he recollects there was from Turner's farm at Kilchamaig near Whitehouse, Kintyre. Archie Campbell, Arrochar, mentioned in the text, also tells of staying a night at Auchnagoul with the drove from Oban. He recollects, too, that Auchindrain, which lies at the junction of the hill road and the Inveraray main road, was used by drovers and that the drovers' payments helped the crofters there to pay their rent.

12. Information regarding the right of grazing cattle at Inveraray from Mr Donald McKechnie, Bridge of Douglas, who further informs me that this right applied to the Cross Green and survived well into the nineteenth century.
13. The drovers won their action against the Earl of Breadalbane for interrupting the stance rights on the Moor of Rannoch in the Court of Session in 1848, but the decision of this court was reversed on appeal to the House of Lords.
14. Information from Mr Archie Campbell, Arrochar, aged 56.
15. Dugald MacIntyre, Lochgilphead, aged 81 or 82, who took Poltalloch cattle to Falkirk, describes this as common practice.
16. Informant, Robert Kerr, aged 69, inn-keeper at Inverbeg. He was brought up in Glen Fruin and was formerly the policeman at Luss.
17. In 1739 Knockbuy purchased 'from Duchra, including ½ Crown Lucks penny, 41 cattle £63.10.10'.
18. Information from Mr Alan Cameron, editor of the *Oban Times*.
19. Information from Duncan Currie, Tibertich, retired shepherd, aged 78. Mr Currie went with Kilchamaig cattle to the Falkirk Tryst, and was present at the last market in 1901. He saw railway trains and Glasgow for the first time and with immense enjoyment, on this occasion. His father, at one time a Mull shepherd, had accompanied droves of cattle from Falkirk Tryst into England.
20. Informants Miss Campbell of Kilberry and Mr John MacLachlan, Poltalloch.

5
FLAILING IN ARGYLL
Journal of the Society for Folk Life Studies,
Volume 3, 1965, p. 90

The flail appears to have been generally abandoned in many mainland parts of south and central Argyll as long as fifty years ago. Elderly people speak of having threshed with the flail regularly in their youth. An account given some years ago to me by Duncan McKeith, a man in his seventies living near Carradale in Kintyre, is typical of many. As boys, Duncan and his brother were given the job of threshing oats after school. They laid the sheaf on wooden planks in the barn, and struck alternately, working down the sheaf from the ears towards the butt twice, then turning the sheaf over and repeating the process. There were perforations in the planks to allow the grain to run out, and the draught created by the opposed doors of the barn being open blew the chaff away. Sometimes, instead of a second door, there was an aperture facing the door, known as a *sorn*, with a removable shutter.

Although the flail is a museum specimen in these mainland districts, it is none the less still employed in some crofting areas in Argyll when oats are required for the cattle during the winter. Older crofters and small farmers in the island of Tiree continue to use the flail. In the winter of both 1959 and 1960 I watched John MacKinnon threshing oats with the flail in his barn at Balephetrish. He is a small farmer and aged about seventy. He placed the sheaf on the hard earth floor, then keeping his arms fairly close to the body dealt rapid, forceful blows with the flail, wielding it over his right shoulder. Sometimes he would change direction without changing his grip and swing the flail with a deft backhand twist to the left across his body. The fast short blows of the flail in Tiree contrast strongly with the long unhurried strokes of Tuscan peasants which fall vertically down from high above the head.

Mr MacKinnon's flail was a rough affair, made of two stout sticks joined by a thick string. The handle was forty-six inches long, the striker thirty-three inches, and both were about one and a quarter inches in diameter. The striker, I was told, is often made of hazel root or oak. Whatever the timber, it would have to be imported into this completely tree-less island. The binding of string did duty for the usual sheepskin thong, which was either bound round the knobbed ends of the sticks (a groove was cut near the end of the sticks at Balephetrish) or fastened through holes in the ends.

Terms for the flail and its parts appear to vary from one district of Argyll to another. Informants in Kintyre and in the islands of Tiree and Islay call the flail *suist*, as they do also in the Isle of Man. In the Inveraray district of mid-Argyll and in the Crinan area on the coast of central Argyll, the term *suist* seems to be unknown, and instead Gaelic-speakers use *buailtean*, a word which elsewhere is restricted to the striker (the shorter stick). In Tiree the handle of the flail is called *lamh-chrann* and the leather thong *iall-shuiste*. In Kintyre the thong is *iallach*, on Lochfyneside *whang* and in Man, where the hide of the cow's knee was considered the best leather for this purpose, *cab-hoost*. '*Cho righinn ri iall-shuiste*', 'as tough as the flail thong', is a familiar Gaelic proverb.

6

THE TACKSMEN AND THEIR SUCCESSORS: A STUDY OF TENURIAL REORGANISATION IN MULL, MORVERN AND TIREE IN THE EARLY EIGHTEENTH CENTURY

Scottish Studies Vol. 13, Part 2, 1969, pp. 92–144

This article considers problems of social and economic change in the former MacLean of Duart lands appropriated by the earls of Argyll, and particularly the effects of the abolition of the system of great tacksmen in 1737. Based on a large body of unpublished documentary evidence, much of it only recently made available at Inveraray Castle, it reassesses the respective parts played by the family of Argyll and their tacksmen in the management of these insular districts and questions the accepted view that the tenurial reorganisation vastly improved conditions for the tenants in general.

'We have now entered finally on the times of peaceful industry' (Argyll 1887:263). In these words George, 8th Duke of Argyll, an outstanding champion of Victorian property and progress, summed up the tenurial reorganisation which his forebear had introduced into Morvern and the neighbouring islands of Mull, Tiree and Coll [See map, p. 53 and plate VI]. Its architects, John, 2nd Duke of Argyll, and his friend and Commissioner, Duncan Forbes of Culloden, Lord President of the Court of Session, would have been gratified by such a verdict. Forbes especially would have rejoiced to know that, as a consequence of his strenuous weeks of diplomacy and discomfort in the Inner Hebrides in the late summer of 1737, that clannish region had become a land of opportunity, progress and industry.

The Lord President had been principal manager of the Duke's business affairs since 1716, but it required a matter of unusual importance to bring him so far from the capital. Routine administration was left to the Chamberlain of Argyll or to one of his junior colleagues. The object of this expedition, however, was no less than the total reorganisation of the tenurial system that had hitherto governed the Duke's insular estates.

Culloden recorded the success of his mission in a report to the Duke immediately after his return to Inveraray (CCR 1884: 387–94). It expressed the sober satisfaction of a man who had carried out a difficult assignment to the best of his ability. Great tacksmen, or tenants-in-chief, had hitherto enjoyed a monopoly of the Duke's northern estate and had supported their kinsmen and followers on their holdings as sub-tenants. This was the custom on all Highland estates where the proprietor was a clan chief. Tacksmen were sometimes functionaries in the chief's service, such as harpers, historians and poets; sometimes heads of allied but unrelated followers; but most were relatives of the chief and heads of lineages or groups of kinsmen tracing their descent from the founder of the clan. The tacksmen were thus the chief's mainstay, serving to unify the clan proper of blood relations, and by their wider authority over their locality binding together all the diverse groups dwelling in the clan's territory into a political entity (Cregeen 1968: 161–5). Culloden reported that he had removed these tacksmen and put in their place some hundred tenants, large and small, to hold their farms directly from the Duke under written leases and on modern conditions. No longer subject to traditional prestations and labour services to the great chieftains, they would, he claimed, transform the backward agriculture of these remote districts, and, under the beneficent guidance of their landlord, bring undreamed-of prosperity both to themselves and to the Duke of Argyll. Such were the sanguine predictions of Culloden's report.

The mission was a notable victory for the Lord President. A man no longer young, travelling in physical discomfort in wet and boisterous weather (with no medical protection other than his rhubarb and gum pills), handicapped moreover by ignorance of the language, he had confronted and overcome a formidable coalition of interests in Mull and Tiree. By a series of skilful moves, and with the aid of his travelling companions, he had induced the sub-tacksmen and sub-tenants to bid for leases in defiance of the tacksmen, and now returned to Inveraray with most of the lands let at higher rents. The 8th Duke summed up the financial achievement thus: 'In the final result, Culloden had the satisfaction of reporting that these large insular estates had been re-let, with some little immediate increase of rent, and such new conditions, as would lay the foundations of indefinite improvement for the future' (Argyll 1887: 259). And his general conclusion on the great tenurial changes is contained in his comment on the terms of the new leases:

> In these words we see the symbol and consummation of a change which amounted to a revolution. In the abolition of all services, except a few strictly limited and defined, which were for purposes directly connected with the benefit of a whole district or of a large community, we see the

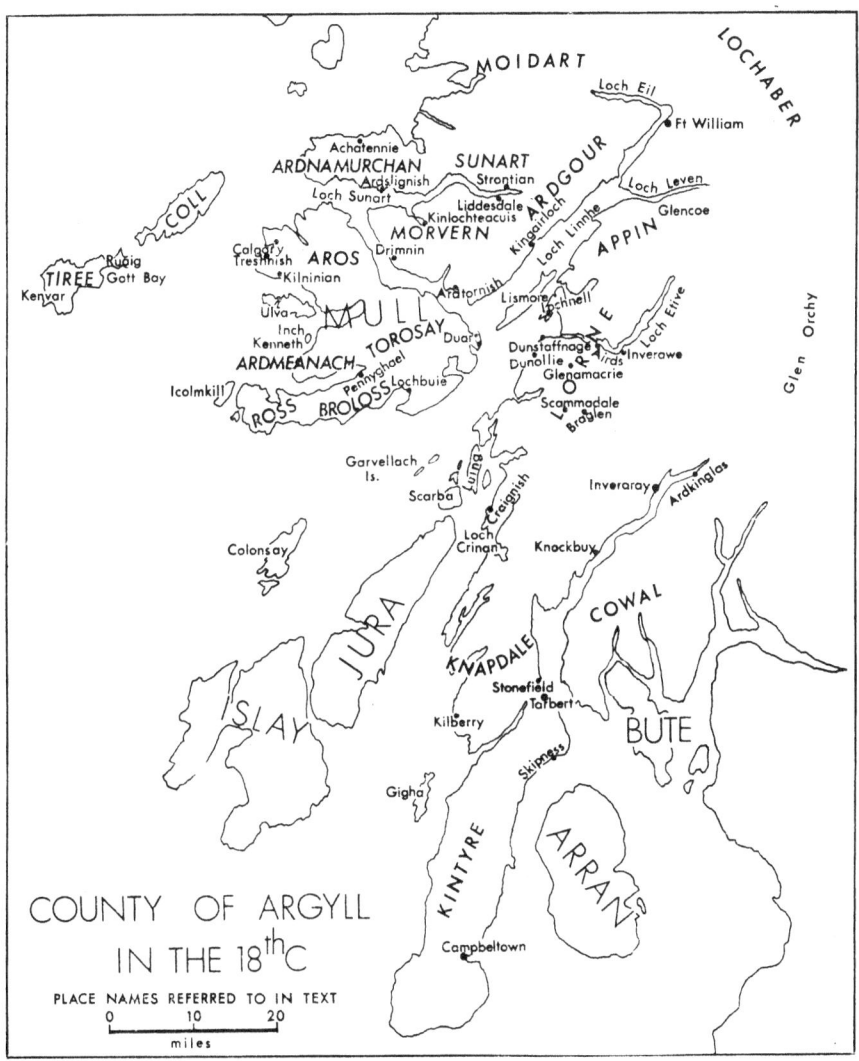

County of Argyll and neighbouring districts in the 18th century

last step, or almost the last, from the mediaeval to modern conditions of society. In the admission of a class to the benefits of leases who had hitherto been always tenants-at-will, and had in practice been often compelled to move from the necessity either of seeking protection or of rendering service, we see the elevation of a large portion of the people from a state of complete uncertainty and dependence to a state in which they could rely, and could make others rely, upon definite engagements' (Argyll 1887: 261–2).

In this view, an oppressive traditional system of land-tenure and social relations was swept away, and in its place there was established a beneficent modern system that opened the doors to technological advance, expanding production and higher revenues, giving the mass of the people, for the first time, a measure of freedom and security. There appear to have been no snags and no disappointments. Partly because of the persuasiveness with which both Culloden and the 8th Duke presented the case, partly perhaps because of a general predisposition in most people to identify change with progress, their eulogistic view of the tenurial reorganisation gained a ready acceptance, and with it Culloden's sweeping condemnation of the tacksmen. An authoritative modern textbook, for example, contains the statement (probably reflecting an attitude general among historians): 'In 1737 Forbes of Culloden reported on the tyranny and oppression of tacksmen in Mull, Morvern and Tiree, and his assessment was confirmed time and again in the course of the eighteenth century' (Hamilton 1963: 48).

The 8th Duke himself demurred against Culloden's extravagant attack on the tacksmen. They were, he said 'gentlemen in the best meaning of the term – men incapable of a dishonourable action, and disposed to deal as justly and humanely with their inferiors as was consistent with the standard of obligation universally recognised in their day and generation' (CCR 1884: 384). There is moreover a great deal of contemporary or near-contemporary literature to suggest that they were not the unfeeling monsters that Culloden represented, and this is supported in studies by modern historians like I.F. Grant and A. McKerral.[1] Perhaps the chief reason for treating Culloden's remarks with caution is the important role played by the tacksmen as the native leaders and natural cement of Highland society, a role which Dr Johnson observed and appreciated (Johnson 1825: 106–10, 172); and of all the commentators, travellers, reporters and observers in the Highlands in the eighteenth century, many of them notable, none brought to bear on the Highland scene so profound an insight into the nature of this society. If they were to be banished, he predicted that the chief, who depended on their company, would depart and the whole society decay: 'If the tacksmen be banished, who will be left to impart knowledge or impress civility?'

The time is ripe for a re-examination of the circumstances that led to the tenurial changes of 1737 and the part that the tacksmen had played in the earlier system. It is equally important to draw attention to the aftermath of these revolutionary changes and to reconsider the justice of the 8th Duke's conclusions. This article, in dealing with these problems, will be based largely on documentary material. Some of this material was known to the Duke, but probably the greater part was unknown to him and has not previously been studied.

The Argyll Conquest and Settlement of the Duart Lands

The system abolished in 1737 derived from the conquest and annexation of the estate of MacLean of Duart by the 9th Earl of Argyll. The estate, which comprised the bulk of Mull and of Morvern, part of Coll, almost the whole of Tiree, as well as a number of smaller islands, had been adjudged in 1659 to the 8th Earl (1st Marquess) of Argyll as the principal creditor of Sir Allan MacLean. The 9th Earl, restored to the estates of the forfeited Marquis in 1663, launched an invasion of Mull in 1674. The MacLeans resisted under Lachlan MacLean of Broloss – and more gallantly than the poet Iain Lom represented – but the opposition had virtually collapsed by 1678–80 and the Earl proceeded to settle large tacks of land on prominent Campbell chieftains who had played a part in the conquest. The Earl's own forfeiture for his refusal to subscribe to the Test Act of 1681 and his execution for rebellion in 1685 gave the MacLeans a brief respite, but with the fall of the Stuarts in 1688 and the final forfeiture of the MacLeans of Duart in 1691 the Campbell hegemony of the western seaboard and islands of Argyll became finally established.[2]

The dominance of the earls, later the dukes, of Argyll over this western region depended almost entirely on the Campbell tacksmen and on the loyal settlers whom they introduced. The danger of insurrection was always present, and the MacLean chieftains, to whom the Jacobite cause was attractive, among other reasons, as a means of regaining their ancient lands, could count on the attachment of the native population. The tacksmen were thus of great political and strategic importance, occupying a role similar to that of the Campbell colonists and Lowland planters settled in Kintyre in the Civil War period (McKerral 1948: 80–109), or the Scottish plantation in Northern Ireland in the early seventeenth century. They received from the Earls tacks (i.e. leases) of enormous extent, and therewith power to settle their lands, to hold courts, to collect revenue, in particular cases to garrison castles, and in general to administer and regulate their tack-lands.

The earliest tacks went mainly to Campbell families who had been prominent in the expeditions against the MacLeans, in particular those of Inverawe, Dunstaffnage, Craignish, Auchinbreck and Lochnell, with their cadets, as well as Islay cadets of the Calder branch. There cannot have been much colonisation before the last decade of the seventeenth century, for the conflict revived during the 9th Earl's forfeiture. Moreover, before they could settle, the tacksmen and their followers had to remove the earlier tenants and resistance must have been common. Campbell of Inverawe, who received a tack of the extensive districts of Aros and Morenish in Mull in 1696, was bound 'within the space of three years after the term of Whitsunday to remove such of the gentlemen of the name of McLean as are at present tennents and possessors of the island as hereafter he shall be directed to . . . and shall not set the samen lands or any part thereof in tack or tennandry either to them or to any other gentlemen of the said name of McLean during his tack without the consent and approbation of the said noble Earle . . . be obtained thereto first in wryte'. (ICP/M2 Tack to Inverawe).

Once the MacLeans and their friends were ejected – and a comparison of eighteenth-century rentals with those of the seventeenth century is proof of the extent of their dispossession – it required only a decade or two to establish families of land-hungry Campbells, predominantly from the mainland district of Lorne, in the more fertile areas. Campbell of Stonefield, whose half-brother was among the colonists, reported the existence of three principal settlements in Mull in 1732 – the Ross of Mull with Icolmkill [Iona], the south-eastern district of Torosay, and the northern district of Aros. These districts he described as 'sett in tack to gentlemen of the name of Campbell, who have gone a good length to plant their several districts with people of the same name or their friends, and, he continues, 'it must be acknowledged that the tenants are beginning to manage their lands better than the rest of the countrey' (Argyll 1887: 250; SL 3: 39–40). The Ross was dominated by cadets of the Dunstaffnage Campbells, Torosay by cadets of Lochnell, who were also widely distributed in Aros (ICP/M–JR 1715; ICP/M–Rentals 1742 and later; ICP/M–G). Morvern was too much a Cameron stronghold to be healthy for Campbell settlement, and Tiree and Coll too remote, but several Campbell families do appear to have settled early in Tiree and numerous farms were held there by Campbells who actually resided in Mull. At the beginning of the eighteenth century these remoter islands were in tack to Sir Archibald Campbell of Cluanes, who belonged to a cadet family of the Calder branch,[3] but in 1716 Sir James Campbell of Ardkinglas received a nineteen-year tack on condition that he planted Tiree and the two ends of Coll 'with tenants of the name of Campbell and such as have not taken part in the Rebellion, in place of the natives, who were for the most part guilty of the same' (Paton 1913: 151; 1915: 17).

The colonists were at first exposed to the raids and reprisals of the MacLeans, which reduced some to poverty, others probably to flight. Most of them, however, remained as a privileged, envied and sometimes hated, minority. (Cregeen 1968: 160) They may have shown occasional lapses and several settler families became suspect for their political or religious leanings, but normally the colonies were foci of loyalty to the Argyll ascendancy in the midst of a generally disaffected native population, and represented an element of considerable political and strategic importance in the West Highlands throughout much of the eighteenth century. Not only were they a source of military recruitment –

and the tacksmen were obliged by their leases to serve Argyll with the 'haill tenants and inhabitants' of their tack-lands 'in all hostages and other lawful expeditions as oft and whenever they shall be desyred or required therto . . .' (ICP/M2 Tack to Inverawe) – but they maintained a vigilant watch over disaffected neighbours, acted as an unpaid police force, provided intelligence of value to the Duke and Government concerning the whole western districts and actively discouraged any symptoms of Jacobite or Popish activity.[4]

The efficacy of the Campbell system was very much dependent, however, on successful colonisation. In Morvern the Campbell system failed signally to guarantee law and order and loyalty to the Government. The Duart lands in this district had been controlled by the Camerons and their chief, Locheil. In 1679, after their annexation they were set in tack to Cameron of Glendessary (Exhibits: 132). His tack expired in 1715 however and was not renewed. Instead Dugald Campbell of Craignish became tacksman (Paton 1913: 155), and settlers were introduced. The attempt to colonise was a complete failure. Like the peasants of Flanders and north-east France who, under their *droit de marché* defended their security of tenure against intruded tenants by acts of systematic violence (Bloch 1931: 183–5), the Camerons refused to be outed and operated a highly effective system of intimidation. Craignish and his uncle complained to the Duke two years after their tack commenced: 'Thus stands it with your tacksmen, and though the times are peaceable elsewhere, the government fixed and settled, they live as in a country yet to be conquered and still to be reduced to the peaceable possession of its proprietor and master.'[5] In 1717 the wretched tacksman had been robbed by the Camerons of the year's rents, and acts of terrorism – cattle-houghing, arson, threats – continued throughout the twenties and thirties, and proved so effective that would-be settlers were frightened away. Craignish had to sub-let his lands willy-nilly to the Camerons, as had also MacLean of Ardgour and MacLean of Kingairloch. Thus the Morvern lands, in spite of the Duke of Argyll's legal title, continued to be in the actual occupation of the Camerons and therefore controlled by Locheil. It is not surprising that it proved one of the main recruiting grounds of the Jacobites in 1745.

In Mull and Tiree, the Campbell system enjoyed greater success. True, clanship was declining in the 2nd Duke's time. The transfer of tacks to new tacksmen who were willing to pay a higher tack-duty inevitably weakened the strategic aspects of the system (ICP* 191 'State of the Duke of Argyle's Affaires', August 1716), and the increasing use of the shire levies must have affected the position of the tacksmen as military leaders of the clan. Nonetheless, in the islands the Campbell system did in fact serve to limit the areas of overt Jacobite activity. This was apparent in 1745, when there was no general rising here despite the widespread sympathy that the Jacobites enjoyed among the native population (Fergusson 1951: 99; ICP various papers).

The system of tacksmen in the insular districts was not simply a nexus of economic relations. It had been designed not only for the collection of revenue but for the reduction of hostile districts to order, for the settling of loyal colonists, for the administration of justice and policing of wide areas, and for political and strategic purposes that went a good deal beyond the simple collection of rent. Although it proved a failure in Morvern and in the islands – as will shortly be explained – was increasingly subordinated to the Duke's financial needs, the original functions of the great tacksmen continued to be in varying degrees highly necessary and actively exercised.

The Tacksmen and their Tenants

The tacksmen's holdings were not, in these recently annexed colonial territories, limited to the modest few farms characteristic of many Highland tacksmen.[6] Perhaps because of their colonial nature, they ranged over whole districts of many square miles, and each one was the equivalent of a considerable landed estate. In 1730 there were only seven tacksmen for the entire annexed lands. Icolmkill and the fertile Ross of Mull were in tack to Donald Campbell, brother to Campbell of Scammadale (a cadet family of Dunstaffnage). The enormous district of Aros in Mull was held by Archibald Campbell of Ballimore or Achatennie, brother to Sir Duncan Campbell of Lochnell, one of the most considerable of the Campbell chieftains. Torosay, the south-eastern district of Mull, was held by Colin Campbell of Braglen, another cadet of the Lochnell branch. To two members of the clan MacLean, distinguished for their firm Hanoverian principles, were assigned other tack-lands in the west of Mull: Morenish to Donald MacLean of Calgary, Treshnish to Mr John MacLean, minister of Kilninian, who had succeeded Mr John Beaton as minister of Kilninian in 1702 and was learned in Gaelic history and literature (J.L. Campbell and D. Thomson 1963: xiv, 22, 23–35). The entire Morvern lands were in tack to Dugald Campbell of Craignish, and the Duke's property in Coll and Tiree to Sir James Campbell of Ardkinglas, though he was represented by three important sub-tacksmen, Campbell of Clenamacrie, Campbell of Barnacarry and Alexander Maclachlan (CP 2970: 183–187). The tacksmen paid tack-duties ranging from £900 to £4,000 Scots, averaging a sum probably above the rental of most estates in Argyll (ICP/M–R 1730).

Whether the tacksman resided or not (and only in Mull was residence customary) he sub-let most of his tack-land. The greater part of it, or even the whole, was rented to a fairly small number of gentlemen who were his kinsmen or friends. They held their lands on privileged conditions and sometimes enjoyed written leases continuing for the period of the chief tacksman's lease. They paid rents which, though higher than they had been in the late seventeenth century, were still relatively lower than those of the other sub-tenants (ICP/M–JR 1715; CCR 1884: 388). Their holdings were commonly one, two, or more large farms, parts of which were in turn frequently sub-let.

The remainder of the tack-lands was sub-let to commoners who had a share in a jointly-held farm. Although their share in the land was small, these small tenants constituted the majority of a tacksman's sub-tenants. Duncan Forbes described these as 'tertenants' in his report of 1737 (CCR 1884: 388) and it was their interest that he claimed to be protecting against the oppressive tacksmen. They appear to have been held on a year-to-year basis without written leases. Their rents were relatively higher than those of the sub-tacksmen (ICP/M–JR 1715), and, although relaxations might be made in the event of general misfortune, their economic condition, being narrowly based, probably reflected fluctuations in trade and climate more quickly and sensitively than did that of the gentry. Their holdings, modest enough as they were, were further reduced by the widespread practice of sub-letting to kinsmen (Cregeen 1964: XXVII n).

A judicial rental of the Argyll lands of Morvern and Torosay taken in 1715 may be cited to illustrate how tacksmen allocated their lands. Torosay, in tack to Colin Campbell of Braglen,[7] consisted of twenty four pennylands.[8] Of these eight were let to thirty five joint tenants, whose average holding was rather more than a farthingland. The tacksman and his sons occupied four pennylands, and the remaining twelve pennylands were largely sub-let to six tenants – Archibald Campbell of Achindoun (3 pennylands), Donald Campbell of Achinard and his brother (2 pennylands), MacDougall of Ardmore (2 pennylands), John McKinvine (1 pennyland) and a family named MacPhail (1 pennyland). (This leaves out of account roughly two pennylands which were let in fairly modest shares but not to joint tenants.) Apart from a farthingland occupied by MacLean of Kingairloch and the holding of the McKinvines or MacKinnons (who appear to have been anciently there), little had been left of the old ascendancy.

At the same period, Cameron of Glendessary, as tackman of the Morvern lands, held 115 pennylands. Of these only a small fraction was let to joint-tenants, whose holdings averaged about 1½ pennylands (but the pennyland was not much more than a third of the pennyland in Mull); 84 pennylands, or three-quarters of the whole area, were occupied as large holdings. If one excludes Glendessary's own twenty pennylands, the rest ranged from three to ten pennylands and averaged six, which in Morvern was the equivalent of three merklands. Thus, both in Mull and Morvern, the tacksman's holding approximated in size to the 2½ merkland characteristic of the south-west Highlands.[9] Both large tenants and small sub-let part of their lands. For example, one of the four tenants of Kenlochteacus, Donald McAlister VcConil (alias Cameron) had a two pennyland, or one merkland, as his share, paying the tacksman £4 sterling and various payments in kind. He in turn sub-let two small portions, one a farthingland and one a half pennyland, to sub-tenants of the same surname as himself, at a rent that allowed him a slight profit (£16 Scots for the half pennyland). A large tenant, John McEan VcEan VcWilliam (alias Cameron), occupying the five pennyland of Aulistine, sub-let three pennylands to three sub-tenants named Cameron. Almost two-thirds of the Morvern lands were in the occupation of Camerons. MacLachlans, MacEacherns and s also appear as major tenants with holdings of 10, 11 and 5 pennylands respectively, but there is not a single Campbell named in the rental.

The tacksman reaped a profit as farmer of the rents of his district. In Tiree the tacksmen before 1737 received a money rent approximately 30 per cent above the tack-duty which they themselves paid to the Duke, viz. £423 as compared with £325 (CCR 1884: 390). In Mull the tackmen's surplus was comparable (see note 29). Sub-tacksmen and sub-tenants also derived some advantage from sub-letting, but in monetary terms it was not a great deal, representing in Morvern and Torosay a sum which was a fifth above their own rent for the land concerned, or even less (ICP/M–JR 1715). Possibly the principal advantage was that sub-tenants helped a tenant to pay his casualties and were a source of labour. Of Drumcragaig farm, the Sheriff recorded that 'the sub-tacksman has no benefit by them but that they free him of his pressand [present] sheep' (ICP/M–JR 1715).

Casualties paid to the tacksmen over and above the rent included a variety of farm produce – butter, cheese, poultry, eggs, sheep, veals and the like, and in Tiree a certain quantity of linen cloth.[10] Some were, or had been, due at stated seasons, like the 'Yuill and Pace presands' [presents] paid in Morvern in butter, cheese and veals. Others were irregular, like horse corn due from tenants in Tiree when the laird visited the island (MacPhail 1914: 291; and ICP, various papers). Such payments in kind were consumed in the household of the laird or the tacksman as there was no market for them, except briefly in Morvern and Sunart in the neighbourhood of the lead-mining settlements (CCR 1884: 390–1; ICP/L 'Minutes of Business 1744'). Casualties were valued at about a sixth of the total rent in Mull in the late seventeenth century; as the eighteenth century progressed they came to be no more than a twelfth or a fifteenth of rentals in the Highlands (Walker 1812 Vol. 2: 78). In addition to such casualties a supply might be required on extraordinary occasions, as for instance the cow claimed by Glendessary of each of his tenants when he purchased Lochbuy's lands in Morvern (ICP/M–JR 1715). At a tenant's death, the herezeld (heriot) was due to his master in the shape of his best beast or other property and in spite of having been abolished by Parliament in 1617, it continued to be levied well into the eighteenth century.

Beyond payments in money or kind, the tacksmen were accustomed to receive from their tenants a variety of personal services impossible to evaluate in money terms. The tacksman, as a chieftain of the clan, could require his tenants to follow him in the clan array or in creachs and other exploits. He could further require labour services in various kinds of agricultural work, in carriages, in thatching, cutting peats and the like. Exact data for the seventeenth and early eighteenth centuries are rarely available; by the second half of the eighteenth century a reliable observer estimated that subtenants generally worked regularly one day a week for the tacksman and extra days in seed-time and harvest, so that over the whole year a third of the sub-tenants' time was at the tacksman's disposal (Walker 1812 Vol. 2:54–5, 79–81). Buchanan quotes an instance of an even heavier burden of services in Scalpay, Harris, but it is significant that he observes that they had increased vastly, having been formerly eight or ten days in the year (Buchanan 1793: 52–3). Indeed the decay of local custom as the eighteenth century advanced may well have been accompanied in some cases by an increase in labour services, a situation which would find a parallel in the increasing burden of serfdom in Russia and Eastern Europe generally in the eighteenth century.[11]

Basically, the tenurial system which existed in the insular districts derived from traditional Highland clan relationships, in which claims to land and wealth depended on kinship to the chief or service to him. It neither aimed at nor achieved any sort of egalitarian social system. On the contrary, it was the duty of the commoners to maintain the gentry of the clan – the chief and the tacksmen, to follow them in war and serve them in peace.

Nevertheless in the clan system, aristocratic and hierarchic as it was, sentiment and ties of real or pretended kinship tended to soften the harsh lines of class distinction and to bind society together (Cregeen 1964: 161–5). Even on grounds of self-interest if on no other, chief and tacksmen were reluctant to lose tenants who were also fighting men, and assisted them in times of hardship by furnishing meal and other supplies, by waiving or reducing the rent or by allowing arrears to go unpaid for long periods.[12] Without entering here into a full examination of the social functions of the tacksmen, it is as well to recognise that they discharged important economic functions which their eighteenth-century critics usually overlooked. In a society which was conspicuously lacking in capital, it was the laird and tacksmen who sustained much of the agricultural production by loans of seed grain, cattle, implements and work-horses under the system of 'steel-bow' – an arrangement which frequently enabled young tenants to graduate eventually into farmers, with stock of their own.[13]

Fishing depended a good deal on their provision of boats and nets (Anderson 1785: 248; Gray 1957: 115–18). As merchants they supplied isolated communities with essential goods and raw materials which no professional class of merchants existed to provide (Anderson 1785 :165–7, 247–50), whilst by accepting rents in kind and organising the sale of these products in distant markets they performed the most important function of turning the Highlanders' products into cash.

One cannot assume, however, that even so early as 1720 or 1730, the norms of behaviour accepted in a more or less traditional society continued unaltered. Landed estates were beginning to come on to the market – a new phenomenon. In some parts of the Highlands it is evident that already a commercial outlook had begun to affect the relations of social classes. The wreck on the Irish coast of a vessel bound for the plantations brought to light in 1739 a sinister traffic in poor Highlanders carried on by certain Highland chiefs (Grant 1959: 404–9). It represents an extreme case but it is significant of the stirrings of a profound change in social relationships in the Highlands.

'The Tyranny of Tacksmen' – or a Grasping Duke?

Culloden may have been justified in speaking of 'the tyranny of tacksmen' in 1737. He was capable of observing the poverty of the mass of tenants and the inadequacy of the system of food production. A system which may have given the population certain advantages and safeguards against oppression in the seventeenth century may have ceased to work well in the eighteenth. Indeed there is every sign that the system, as it existed in the annexed districts in the early decades of the eighteenth century, was failing sadly to provide proper safeguards for the welfare of the generality of the population. 'They speak of above one hundred familys that have been reduced to beggary and driven out of the islands within these last seven years' (CCR 1884: 390). The Lord President perceived these symptoms of poverty and unrest and assumed that the whole fault lay with the monstrous tacksmen. 'Had the tacksmen been suffered to continue their extortions a few years longer', he wrote in 1737, 'the islands would have been dispeopled' (CCR 1884: 391).

On the other hand, he may have hit upon the wrong explanation, or a partial explanation, to explain the facts which he observed accurately enough. There is at least a strong case for arguing that the distress of tenants in the annexed lands was due not so much to the system of

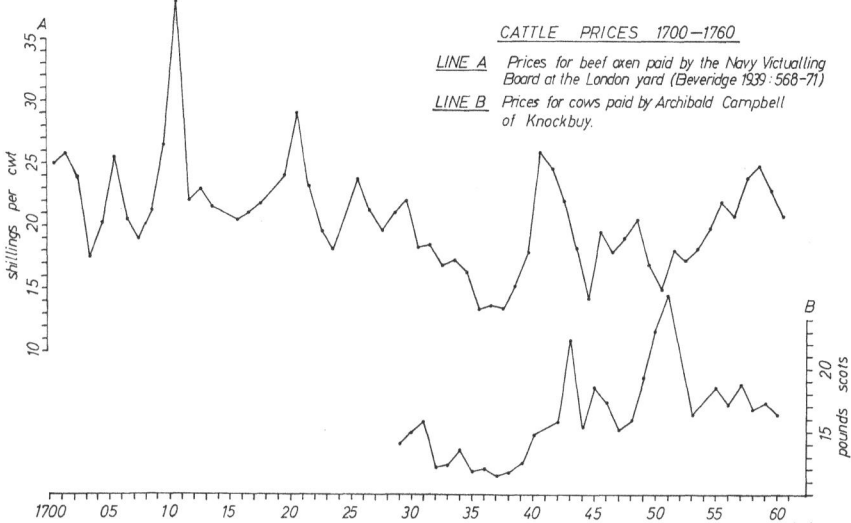

tacksmen as to the pressures which this system was being made to bear in a more commercial age. This case must be more closely examined.

John, 2nd Duke of Argyll, was a man of humane impulses. In theory, at least, he had a strong desire to assist the sub-tenants on his estates. He clearly cast himself in the role of their protector and champion against oppression. Among the sparse instructions that have survived, the following to his senior Chamberlain expresses this attitude:

> You are to enquire into the condition of the sub-tenants of Glenaray and Glenshyra, and particularly to examine what rent each of them pays for his possession to my tacksmen, and to report at Edinburgh in November what you find, and if they complain of any abuses you are to protect and redress them as far lawfully as you can' (ICP/M–L Instructions for Mr Archibald Campbell, 1729).

Stonefield wrote in October 1732 that the Duke 'desired that I go to Morvern to make some settlement between the tacksmen and tennents to prevent oppression or severity by the tacksmen by exorbitant exactions or otherwise. He likewise recommends the procuring of tacks to the sub-tennents' (SL 2: 64, 16 October 1732).

In practice, however, the Duke's management had a less beneficent aspect. He caused judicial rentals to be made when tacks expired and new ones were being negotiated – in Morvern and Torosay in 1715, in Tiree in 1727, in Morvern in 1732, to name only some of these occasions. They might have been expected, in this context of humane concern and intervention, occasionally to lead to some downward revision in the rentals. In fact, on each occasion, the immediate result was an increase in the rental, sometimes a large one, as in Tiree in 1727 and Morvern in 1732. Inevitably, and as a matter of course, the tacksmen passed the augmentations on to their sub-tenants. In 1732, for example, the intended tacksmen of Morvern successfully protested against an increased tack-duty levied from the previous Martinmas on the grounds that they had had insufficient warning to raise the rent of the sub-tenants for that year (SL 3:6–8, 6 March 1732).

At the judicial enquiry into the rentals of Torosay and Morvern in 1715, numerous tenants, speaking from long personal experience or as sons of former tenants, testified that money rents had never been so high. They were not exaggerating. The combined tack-duties of Mull, Morvern and Tiree climbed from £668 13s. 4d. Sterling in 1703 to about £1,300 in 1736. The rental of Tiree, which stood at £1,565 17s. 4d. Scots (about £130 Sterling) in 1674, had risen to £200 Sterling by 1706 and to £325 by 1727 (ICP/V65 'Memorial by Stonefield concerning Tyree' 1748). These were steep increases, even allowing for more settled conditions and good (though not rising) cattle prices (see graph), and they affected the tacksmen's tenants immediately and severely.

Rising tack-duties, then, were passed on to the sub-tenants and must have contributed to their plight, producing results which were a flagrant denial of the Duke's proclaimed concern for them. How did this contradiction come about? The 2nd Duke was by no means the first of his line to regard his estates as primarily a source of revenue rather than of manpower. Both his father, the 1st Duke, and his grandfather, the 9th Earl, of Argyll had a distinctly modern approach to land-owning. The rental of the Kintyre estate approximately doubled in the last fifty years of the seventeenth century (McKerral 1948: 86). One incident will illustrate with what business acumen affairs were handled. In 1690 the 10th Earl (later 1st Duke) was warned that offers for farms in Kintyre were likely to slump owing to the threatened migration of numbers of tacksmen and tenants across the narrow channel to Northern Ireland. Accompanied by a party of friends, he attended the auction of leases, and with their help succeeded in actually pushing rents up higher (ICP/M-L 'Particular State of the Lordship of Kintyre', n.d.) A Whig outlook combined with their familiarity with English land-owning attitudes and practices doubtless suggested to the earls this new kind of commercial estate management,[14] whilst a steady policy of aggrandisement and princely spending rendered it necessary.

Through the seventeenth century and into the eighteenth century the family of Argyll carried a load of inherited debt which was at once a symptom and a cause of their clamant financial needs. The 9th Earl, though restored to his family's estates in 1663, found revenue from his Scottish estates almost equalled by charges against it, the chief being debts of over a million merks (ICP/V62 'Private Accounts Estate'). The

2nd Duke succeeded to a family tradition grown already somewhat alien from their Highland background and to a family estate deeply in debt. His distant upbringing and education had given him the tastes of a great aristocrat, but little of the Highland chief's warm regard for his clan. With a large slice of the revenues of his Scottish estates assigned to creditors, including the whole of the tack-duties of Mull, Morvern and Tiree,[15] it could have been predicted that heavier demands would soon be made on his tacksmen. Growing power and fortune increased rather than diminished the Duke's expenses – houses and improvements, new estates in England and Scotland, and all the cost of maintaining the style required of a grandee in that opulent age.

The Duke's urgent demands for remittances from his Scottish lands are mirrored in the letters of his Chamberlains and in instructions to these officials. 'His Grace's occasion for money is so pressing', ran an instruction from the Duke's Commissioners to the Chamberlain of Argyll in 1705, 'that there is a necessity to use the outmost diligence against those lyable in payment without exception' (ICP*/87 'Instructions to the Chamberlane of Argyll', 1705). Fear of disappointing the Duke was enough to throw the Chamberlain into furious activity. James Campbell of Stonefield wrote, panic-stricken, to his deputy in Kintyre, 4 March 1728, that the Duke 'expects at least £4,000 Sterling, and if you doe not more than you mention there is no way for getting it in this place. I hope you will be so wise as to spare nobody upon any account whatsoever, otherwise your credit and mine is at stake, so for God's sake bestirr yourself to purpose as you wish well to your own interest and that of, Dear Sir, your ser^t., James Campbell. P.S. . . . for God's sake haste in the rent' (SL I: 43–4).

There is little in the correspondence of the Chamberlain or elsewhere to lead one to think that positive and far-sighted ideas of estate management engaged the attention of the 2nd Duke, much, on the other hand, to indicate that revenue was a constant preoccupation and that remoter goals were ordinarily subordinated to this. In so far as the Argyll estates remained solvent and reasonably well-managed, the credit is probably not a little due to the good sense of the trustees who administered the Scottish estates in his earlier years and to the experience and moderation of the two Campbell of Stonefield brothers, who acted successively as Chamberlain of Argyll under the 2nd Duke.

The steady pressure from above to maximise revenue undoubtedly altered the relationship of the tacksmen both to their kinsmen and to their sub-tenants. Their traditional role was more and more overshadowed by their role as financial agents of their chief. A significant piece of evidence from 1716 suggests that already the process was far advanced. On the agenda for the meeting of the 2nd Duke's Commissioners in August 1716 the following item occurs: 'That new rentalls be made of Mull,

Morvern and Tirrie conform to the report to be made by the Shereff [viz. James Campbell. See note 20] and Otter, who deponed the sub-tenants on the verity of their rents according to the Commissioners' order, and that the said lands be sett by way of roup [i.e. auction] or otherways as the Commissioners shall think just. It is to be observed that . . . the tacks of Aros and Morinish did expire a year agoe and the tacksmen renunced the same by way of instrument and they now design to compt as factors and not as tacksmen, which the Commissioners are to consider' (ICP* 191 'State of the Duke of Argyle's Affaires' August 1716).

Although in the event the proposal that the tacksmen of these districts of Mull should become simply officials of the Duke was not accepted, the fact that it should have been made is an indication that some tacksmen had come to conceive of themselves as more closely related to the Duke's administration than to the populations whom they controlled. The suggestion that tacks might be open to offers is also very significant. Clan chieftainries were not wont to be offered for sale in this fashion in the Highlands. The Duke's tacksmen in fact were rapidly being transformed into a quite new kind of creature. Tacksmen who had bid high for their tacks were unlikely to be capable of discharging the responsibilities formerly expected of local chieftains, but would have to recoup themselves at the natives' expense.

There seems little room for doubt, though, that the *fons et origo* of the new kind of tacksmen is to be sought in the highly commercial policies of the 2nd Duke, which had already resulted in Kintyre in the supersession of the existing tacksmen by the subtacksmen in 1710.[16] If the tacksmen were indeed the pincers, as Culloden alleged, then the Duke was undoubtedly the hammer, and his strokes had not been light.

As custom broke down as a regulator of the social body, sub-tenants might find themselves subject to unusual and unfair burdens. Thus, in 1706, the bailie of Tiree, in a memorial to the Duke's managers, recalled that

> when in Edinburgh in Summer last I gave in a representation for the inhabitants of Tirie anent a decreet obtained against them by Donald Campbell for their herezelds, which they would be pleased to consider, for the tenants cannot be obliged to pay herezelds to the Duke of Argyll but only to the tacksman, who has been in constant use to uplift the same, and the tacksman is only lyable for his own herezeld when it falls due, which is and has been the constant practise of the shyre past memory of man. So it's hoped the manadgers will not ordain the tenants to make double payment but may ordain the said Donald Campbell to discharge them for the forsaid decreet.' – ICP/V 65 'Memoriall for the Manadgers of the Duke of Argyle's Estate' (1706).

Thus the situation in the insular districts in the early decades of the eighteenth century was one of great confusion and contradiction. It was a situation that was to become familiar later in all the Highlands and in many other undeveloped areas of the world. The inhabitants, living neither wholly under their traditional clan system nor wholly under a free individualistic, commercial system, were exposed to conflicting demands. The increasing monetary demands of the modern landlord were superimposed on the customary demands of the tacksmen, whilst the tacksmen themselves were driven more and more into a situation where higher rents were all-important. The unfortunate tenants had the worst of both worlds, with neither the economic opportunities of the new nor the safeguards of the old. From the standpoint of a modern man like Duncan Forbes it must have appeared beyond doubt that the time had come to sweep away all the confusions and inconsistencies of the existing system and to introduce a purely commercial landlord-tenant relationship which would open wider opportunities of productivity and trade.

The Immediate Causes of the Tenurial Re-organisation

A silent revolution was thus in progress throughout the 2nd Duke's time, and was transforming land-tenure and the social system well before 1737, but until a comparatively short time before the Lord President denounced the tacksmen, there were few indications that the system as such was to be abolished. Characteristically, the Duke appears to have decided on a total change as a result of developments in the 1730s which convinced him that the tacksmen were of no further use to him and that the sub-tenants could offer higher rents.

It was Morvern, that most turbulent of the annexed territories, that acted as the catalyst.[17] In 1732, following the expiry of Campbell of Craignish's tack, Archibald Campbell of Stonefield was engaged in negotiating new tacks in Morvern. Because of the excessive control that the Camerons enjoyed there, Stonefield proposed to divide the land between the Camerons and the MacLachlans, so that the MacLachlans might be used as a counterpoise to the Camerons, on whom they had previously depended for land. Under this arrangement the Camerons would have to remove from a part of the area which they controlled. Before the tacks were ratified, however, the situation was abruptly changed by the death of Ewan Cameron, one of the intended tacksmen, and by the arrival of a petition, signed by some forty Morvern inhabitants who objected to the granting of the tacks and who offered, in return for leases, a rent equal to that expected of the tacksmen, with a sum sufficient to pay a factor's salary in addition.

These unexpected occurrences may be said to have acted as the trail of gunpowder that led straight to the tenurial revolution. Stonefield appears to have first brought forward at this time the idea of changing the existing tenurial system. He adumbrated it in a letter to the Duke on 5 September 1732 (SL 3: 28–30). The grant of leases to tenants would, he argued, remove them from their dependence on the tacksmen and transfer their loyalties to the Duke – 'It has been the misfortune of this country, and I might say all the Highlands, that the tenants depended upon other chiefs than the landlord.'[18] There was also the advantage 'that there is a greater reason to expect that the lands will be better improved if sett in smaller parcels'. On the other hand, he pointed out, rents from such tenants would be less reliably paid, and in some areas such as Tiree it was out of the question, for this reason, to dismiss the tacksmen.

In October 1732 he visited Mull and Morvern and reported the outcome to the Duke (SL 3: 46–50, 20 December 1737). The visit was significant not only because it gave him valuable first-hand information about these districts but also for bringing him into direct personal negotiations with the Morvern tenants whose petition had produced the new situation. The petitioners' grievances against the intended tacksmen he found exaggerated, but he agreed that they had grounds for apprehension if the Camerons received a tack. Moreover, he received information which for the first time established the complicity of the late Glendessary and other Cameron gentry in the theft of Craignish's rents in 1717, an act for which he was now able to demand full compensation. It was a discovery of crucial importance. It outraged Stonefield, who at once dropped all negotiations relating to the proposed tack to the Camerons. He recommended to the Duke that Morvern should be finally reduced to order by the appointment of a Campbell either as factor or as tacksman, and by prosecuting a methodical policy of colonisation by Campbell families and of policing by soldiers of the new Highland Companies, which were known as *Am Freiceadan Dubh*, 'The Black Watch', and were mainly officered in Argyll by Campbells. The choice between the two alternative systems of administration – a Campbell tacksman or a Campbell factor – was resolved by the fact that, because of the danger of reprisals, in Stonefield's words, 'no Campbell will take the half of the country', viz. the Camerons' half.

The period from late 1732 until the late summer of 1737 was one of waiting and uncertainty. Donald Campbell Yr. of Airds was appointed factor of Morvern in early 1733 but was given no power to grant leases, presumably pending a general settlement of the entire insular districts when the tacksmen's leases in Tiree and Mull should lapse in 1735. He was instructed that the Camerons were to be tolerated, provided they behaved well, and the Maclachlans were to receive favour (SL 2: 75–7, probably January 1733). Airds managed to let the farms advantageously on a year-by-year basis, but never attempted to collect rents unless accompanied by an armed posse. Cattle *houghing* and other acts of intimidation continued, and still no Campbell colonists dared to appear.[19]

Step by step a situation had thus developed in Morvern where the system of tacksmen had been in fact suppressed. It had come about, not through any deficiencies or oppressions of the system as such – for if a Campbell had been available, he would have been appointed tacksman – but as a result of a conflict of interests between chief and landlord. The only tacksman to be got represented the interests of Locheil, and had proved himself party to a criminal act against the representative of his landlord, Argyll. Rather than accept a manifest enemy to represent him, Argyll appointed a Campbell factor to collect his revenues and safeguard his interests.

That Argyll could do this, even if with only partial success, was significant of his growing power in a district so much under the influence of the Camerons. For the first time a group of tenants had emerged prepared to risk bringing charges against the dominant clan and to bid for farms against the Camerons. This perhaps would not have occurred had they not been emboldened by manifestations of the growing interest of the Government and of Argyll in establishing more effective control in this turbulent area. The work of General Wade, the forming of the Black Watch and Sheriff Campbell's recent tour of enquiry all assisted in this direction – and Campbell diplomacy too played a part by exploiting the rivalries of the clans in Morvern.

> As the possession of McLean's Estate, whereof this is a part, cost your Grace's predecessors no small trouble and expence', thus wrote Stonefield whilst negotiating the Morvern tacks with the Camerons and Maclachlans in 1732, 'I thought it for your Grace's interest rather to lessen than increase the power of any sett of people, lest some time or other they should become uneasy and render the possession troublesome and therefore thought it more advisable to divide the country between two clanns, since you have then a probable chance to have one of them always of your side (SL3:II, n.d. probably Mar. 1732).

Estate Management in a Period of Economic Depression

Stonefield had had considerable influence on the formulation of the new tenurial plans, but it was not to be left to him to carry them through. A latent tension existed between the 2nd Duke and his Chamberlain. In the thirties the Duke depended on receiving approximately £4,000 of his Scottish rents and feu-duties in late March and early April each year. Rent increases had evidently already begun to place a considerable strain on the tenants, especially in the islands. Early in 1728 James Campbell of Stonefield reported that the sub-tacksmen of Tiree 'give in a vast account of losses by broken tenants and other damages they sustain . . . more for a year or two than the Duke has sustained in the whole estate these 22 years that I have had the honour to serve him' (SL 1: 105–6, 14 March 1728). It was the Chamberlain's task to make the Duke's rents effectual in conditions that were increasingly difficult during the thirties. The Duke, residing at Adderbury in Oxfordshire, was quite incapable of understanding the problem. Being without any intimate knowledge of conditions in the Highlands, he was simply irritated by interruptions or delays in his supplies of money.

The Stonefield brothers, on the other hand, had, as Chamberlains of Argyll,[20] a close acquaintance with local conditions and daily experience of the immediate relationship between rents on the one hand and weather, harvests, cattle prices, drovers' failures and a score of other circumstances on the other. Moreover, they had the outlook of small lairds, depending as they did for most of their income on the rent of their lands in the north of Kintyre. Their chief concern as landlords was to realise a regularly-paid revenue, with as little arrears as possible, and they actively practised the article of faith expressed by Archibald Campbell of Stonefield in a letter to the Duke that 'a sure and well paid rent' was better than 'a high one ill paid' (SL 3: 195, 10 May 1737). In their view, the worst eventuality was for a laird to be left with part of his lands untilled and 'waste' through the insolvency of tenants.

From these basic principles it followed, first, that when lands were to be 'set' and agreements made with tenants, all the holdings must be occupied, without any waste land. At each period of letting, the Stonefields showed great anxiety to ensure that all the 'rooms' were taken. If need be, tenants in other districts were induced to come.[21] Secondly, it followed that honest and reliable tenants were preferred, though offering a lower rent, to tenants of uncertain credit and character offering more. High offers were treated with extreme reserve and might not be accepted. Finally, it was essential to prevent tenants from becoming insolvent, quitting their holdings and leaving the laird with his rents unpaid. Indulgence in time of need was therefore both wise and necessary. Archibald Campbell was only expressing practical wisdom when, in December 1731, he advised the Duke against charging interest on arrears of rent in Kintyre: 'By experience I find in your Grace's affairs as well as in my own little concerns that it is necessary for a landlord to give some indulgence to his tennent according to his circumstances, and I'm afraid there was seldom more occasion for it than will be this year' (SL 3: 1, 23 Dec. 1731). Stonefield's outlook and practice were by no means exceptional. During the depression of the 1730s Archibald Campbell of Knockbuy, laird of a Lochfyneside estate, allowed tenants' arrears to run from three or four years before being cleared. It might also be necessary to give a struggling tenant practical assistance.

The Stonefield policy is illustrated by James Campbell's handling of the situation on one of his farms, where two groatland holdings[22] were liable to become waste by tenant failures in November 1728. One groatland was, if possible, he instructed his overseer, to be taken over by the rest of the tenants: 'but whatever you doe you must take care that no more of the lands be waste, even tho some of the rents should be given down [lowered] and that I rather doe by giving it out of my pocket.' The other groatland was likely to become waste by a tenant 'having lost his labouring horses', and in this case Stonefield recommended to his overseer: 'If no better can be done you must provide him [with] a horse. You very well know he was obliged to labour that ground till Whitsunday if he has anything in the world, and this is no time of year to put off lands, and indeed if you allow them to run away 'twixt terms this way I may have enough of waste lands in a short time' (SL 1:184–4, 8 November 1728).

As Chamberlains of Argyll, both Stonefields attempted to apply these principles of estate management. It was no easy task. Economic conditions in the West Highlands appear to have been generally adverse in the decade preceding the Lord President's visit.[23] Most years saw the Duke's rents collected with difficulty in one district or more generally, arrears commonly high and tenants in frequent distress. Rents had never been higher, but the economy was extremely sluggish, owing, in particular, to the slackening in the demand for cattle, on which rents almost entirely depended. There was scarcely a year between 1730 and 1740 when low cattle prices were not mentioned, or when, for this or other reasons, farmers and landlords in the West Highlands were not in difficulties. In 1733–4, one of the worst years, the failure of the harvest aggravated the distress. The year 1735–6 was perhaps the only crop-year when the Chamberlain's task was reasonably easy (SL 3: 106, 14 April 1736), but the spring of 1736 carried off many cattle in Kintyre. It was immediately followed by one of the worst years of the decade and the beginning of an emigration movement from that district which greatly alarmed the Chamberlain (SL 3: 170, 19 February 1737).

The Chamberlain was in the unenviable position of having to press tenants for higher rents in a period of severe economic depression. He did so with as much consideration as possible and only as a last resort adopted the self-defeating policy of impounding the stock of tenants in arrears. In his letters to the Duke, Archibald Campbell had frequently to excuse the state of the remittances, as, for example, in March 1734 when he wrote to the Duke:

> As the expence of the work[24] is not now so heavy as in former years, His Grace might have expected a greater remittance at this time, but the

price of cattle has been so low that the returns have been small and late in coming to us. It is computed that in Scotland the price of cattle last year has fallen a crown a head. In Tiree and Morvern there is yet no rent come up. From the latter I expect to have some soon. Those countreys and Mull have not only suffered by the low price of cattle but likewise in their corns by the long drought last summer and the great shake in harvest, and they and other parts of the country are in a very lamentable condition at present by the death of their cattle, which they ascribe to the great rains that fell this Winter and yet continue' (SL 3: 74–6, 21 March 1734).

By mid-April 1734 he had sent only £3,000 to the Duke.

The rentals of the insular districts were due to be settled in 1735, when the tacks of Mull and Tiree expired, but Forbes of Culloden postponed the matter, probably hoping for an improvement in general conditions, which would produce better offers of rent. Although uncertainty continued, the shape of the future was becoming clearer. The tacksmen appear to have accepted the non-renewal of their tacks with reasonably good grace and to have complied with a request from Culloden to transmit to the Chamberlain, in Culloden's words, 'exact rentals of the districts that fall within their severall collections, which may be a rule to the factor to be employed, together with what they honestly take to be the rent of their respective possessions in which they are to be continued'. He went on: 'That will I think oblige the Duke, it will be a rule for the immediate collection and will give light to the Duke or me, or any other person that may go to the spot to set the lands next year' (CP 2968: 31, 14 October 1736).

To lighten the Chamberlain's task, Culloden arranged for the appointment of a factor for Tiree and Mull in October 1736 (CP 2968: 31–3). The person chosen was Archibald Campbell of Ballimore, a brother of Sir Duncan Campbell of Lochnell and a kinsman of Stonefield. He had previously been one of the tacksmen of Mull and had willingly resigned his tack when informed of the Duke's intentions. His having been a tacksman in fact commended him to Culloden since, as the latter wrote to the Duke, 'this man was perfectly acquainted with the condition of the estate and therefore able to controul the rentalls which the other tacksmen may offer if fallacious' (CP 2986: 32, 16 October 1736).

Ballimore began his rent collection in early February 1737, but made painfully slow progress because of the low price of cattle and the general poverty of these districts. In a report presented to Culloden in spring 1737, he detailed the problems facing him and offered certain advice. Tenants, he explained, in their anxiety to get land would make extravagant offers of rent which they could never pay. In Tiree, for example, the tenants had offered him sums totalling more than £400

Sterling, a large amount since this did not include the two ends of Coll. With cattle markets so depressed, and tenants so wholly dependent on them, he urged that in the future set of the islands, rents should be fixed at a moderate level, remarking: 'In my opinion if Tirrie, secluding the two ends of Coll, exceed much four hundred pounds sterling rent for some years, the tennants will not live happily'. He explained further that the tacksmen were at an advantage in collecting rents, since they could accept linen cloth and other produce or take young cattle which could be grazed for a year or two and then sold (CP 2970: 183–6).

Tenurial change had thus become virtually certain some months before the Lord President (Culloden) paid his visit to the west. His report in 1737 strangely ignored the important preliminaries that had already taken place, including the receiving of offers from bodies of tenants (for offers were coming in from Morvern as well as Tiree) and the appointment of factors (SL 3: 146–51, 3 December 1736; 191–5, 10 May 1737). Yet if Culloden had not made his visit, it seems certain that Stonefield would have granted leases to a larger body of tenants in all districts. That it was Culloden and not Stonefield who in the event carried out the tenurial reorganisation was the result of a widening of the gap between the Duke and his Chamberlain.

The Duke and Chamberlain in Disagreement

In the first half of 1737 it became clear that the Duke had become totally dissatisfied with the management of his rents and believed that the fault lay, not in the condition of the tenants, but in the misconduct of his officials and tacksmen. A series of letters from the Chamberlain in the early months of 1737 spoke of devastating mortality among the cattle in Mull and Morvern, of impoverished tenants in the insular districts, and of a new and marked decline in Kintyre, where an alarming interest in emigration had suddenly developed. 'There is a great change in that good country within these two years', he wrote to the Duke on May 10th, and to explain why he was able to remit only £3,700, he claimed that rents were 'much worse than ever I knew them'. Evidently to rebut the charges that had been made, he went on,

> I can venture to say your case is not singular, and that it is not for want of diligence in the persons I employ to collect the rents, but real want of money in the country. The factor of Morvern complains that the tenants are much impoverished there this year by the death of cattle in that country and that Mull has had the same fate, where as many are swept off as was in Kintyre last year. He likeways observes that it is a loss both to your Grace and the tenants in that country that they are so long in an uncertain state without leases and that it must affect the payment of

rents till once they are settled' (SL 3: 194, 10 May 1737).

The Chamberlain then made a proposal that was to be of great significance: 'If the Lord Advocat were to make a tour to those countreys as he once proposed, he might enquire into the circumstances of the tenants and the manner of payment of rents, discover the true cause of slow payments, settle with the tenants for new leases and give directions for the most prudent and speedy methods of collecting the rents.' He adds the wise counsel: 'That a sure and well paid rent is preferable to a high one ill paid must be allowed and deserves to be adverted to when these countreys are lett in lease' (SL 3: 193–5, 10 May 1737). Three weeks later, with only £258 received from Mull and Tiree, and £272 from Morvern, Stonefield defended the factor's zeal: 'I am perfectly persuaded if Airds had not exerted himself and had not, with some address, encouraged drovers to buy the tenants' cattle, it would not have been in his power to remit so much this year. I believe it will give him greater trouble that his Grace is not satisfyd with his management than that he should be discharged' (SL 3: 188, 3 June 1737).

His letter of 22 June is a reasoned statement of the causes of the general economic depression, as he understood them, with a series of comments on the prospects of improving the rents in each of the insular districts. In view of later events, his remarks are of unusual importance, for he was to prove vindicated in almost every detail. Conditions were bad on the mainland as well as in the remoter areas. 'Since ever I had occasion to know anything of the business of this country there were always before this time of year eight hundred or a thousand cattle sold off from Kintyre to people from the Low Country, Galloway or our dealers here. This summer there is not a man come to the country to buy one head.'[25] The crisis moreover was common to all areas and all estates:

> The circumstances of tenants in this shire is very much changed for the worse within these two or three years. This I have access to know not only from the payments by his Grace's tenants, who are still in a better condition than the tenants of other heritors, except those in the islands, but likeways from the collection of cess[26] and from my own small concerns where I sensibly feel it, and in short in the course of all payments whatsomever.

In Morvern, rents could not be raised any more, he argued, for he himself had augmented them considerably in 1732, and since then cattle prices had declined and the lead-mine, which 'made a circulation of money', had closed down.[27] 'As for Mull, if it be lett at the rent the under-tennents paid, I'm afraid it will be too high and that the payments may not be regular since substantial tenants cannot be got to take it at that rate, the consequence of which is that the tenants will not be able to stand above a year or two, and then several parts of it will be to lett again . . .'. Tiree was the greatest problem of all:

> What to say of Tiry I cannot tell. Most of the people are, and I believe ever were miserably poor since the first settlement of people there. What will it signify to give leases to people that will not be able to hold them above a year? Many of them do not pay above twenty merks Scots of rent, and several only ten merks, and how a family can be subsisted upon such a small proportion of land without any trade and pay the rent is not easy to conceive, nor is it possible to get good tenants to go and settle in that country without encouragement (SL 3: 202–5, 22 June 1737).

Stonefield evidently did not despair of influencing the settlement of these districts, for he wrote: 'These things I thought it my duty to take notice of that his Grace might have them in view when he gives directions for setting the lands.' And on the eve of the departure of the Lord President, he wrote to the Duke's secretary, reinforcing his views, urging the need for moderation in the rents and caution in granting leases. They should be given, he urged, only to gentlemen and men of substance – 'By gentlemen I do not mean lairds or landed men but persons having a stock of two, three or five hundred pound, for such are in these countreys so designed.' By leasing to gentlemen as much land as they could occupy with their own stock, and permitting sub-tenancy, he saw the best prospect of improving the rents. On this footing, he envisaged Tiree being leased to ten or twelve tenants, some of whom would be non-resident or, better still, to one tacksman (SL 3: 210–13, 4 August 1737).

Stonefield's credit had fallen low with the Duke and his advice had ceased to carry much weight. Nevertheless, his statements on the economic situation in the 1730s, and in particular the serious effects which he attributed to low cattle prices, are consistent and well supported. Reports by Ballimore and others authenticate what Stonefield said and show that he was not simply making excuses for bad management. Cattle were, after all, the lynchpin of the Highland economy. There was usually little else to pay the rents (Walker 1812, Vol. 2: 46), and a sharp fall in price or a severe winter that swept off large numbers of cattle could be disastrous to tenants – and lairds.

Archibald Campbell of Knockbuy (1693–1790), who dealt extensively in cattle at certain periods and who was an intimate of Stonefield's, recorded in his rent-books the prices which he allowed tenants for cattle given to him in payment of rents.[28] Whilst not providing a fully reliable index for cattle prices in this period – for the numbers bought vary from year to year from a handful to a score or more – Knockbuy's accounts do give a valuable guide to the movement of cattle prices in the West Highlands from 1728 to 1786. So far as they go, they completely substantiate the Chamberlain's reports. They show that cattle prices, though generally rising throughout the century, did so in a succession of waves with marked crests and troughs, and that the deepest trough did in fact occur between 1730 and 1740, and extended over most of these years (see Appendix and graph).

Tenants' cows bought by Knockbuy averaged £15 17s. Scots in the three year period 1729, 1730 and 1731, but in the eight years that followed (1732–9) they sank to an average of £13 3s. then climbed again to an average of £17 19s. in the ten-year period 1740–9. Bullock prices are a less useful guide, for the reasons given in the Appendix, but they indicate a similar pattern, with the thirties forming a trough between periods of fairly high prices (KP/R). This pattern is borne out convincingly by the prices paid by the Navy Victualling Board. Buying scores of cattle every week for barrelling, the yards were normally paying, during the first three decades of the century, between 20s. and 25s. per hundredweight. Prices dropped abruptly in the thirties and remained low, at an average of 16s., until 1740, when they recovered. For three years running, prices had fluctuated around 13s. 6d., their lowest point of the century: precisely at that crucial period for the insular districts, 1735–7 (see Appendix, and graph; Beveridge 1939: 568–71).

Scotland thus did not by any means wholly escape the agricultural depression that engulfed much of England in the period 1730–50 (Mingay 1955–6; Chambers and Mingay 1966: 40–2). Scotland's corn prices, in contrast to England's, remained steady (Mitchison 1965), but as a mainly pastoral country she would be seriously and generally affected by the depression of cattle markets in the thirties – how seriously in the West Highlands will have already become apparent.

The Lord President's Expedition and the New Rental

The expedition started from the home of Sir Duncan Campbell of Lochnell at the end of the first week of August. The party, consisting of the Lord President, Sir Duncan Campbell, Stonefield, a number of Argyll lairds and the Duke's Edinburgh lawyer, Ronald Dunbar, was accommodated in the Duke's capacious barge, along with a crew of twelve or thirteen men, 'twenty bolls [of meal] and some barrels of sea bisket, a little quantity of flour, some gallons of whiskie and some ship's beer', ordered by the Chamberlain before she sailed from the Clyde. Culloden himself, with his usual foresight, brought an additional supply of fourteen dozen bottles of wine to cheer the long and arduous weeks ahead (SL 3:207–9, 24 July 1737; and 230–2, 16 December 1737). Gentlemen came to pay their respects to the Lord President and his company wherever they landed and there would be much conviviality. With all its good cheer, however, this was a portentous visit, comparable in its ultimate significance for the West Highlands with the tour of Bishop Andrew Knox in 1609 to impose Lowland ways on the western chiefs. Here, in closest juxtaposition, facing each other across an unseen, unbridged abyss, were the representatives of a highly traditional military society and the redoubtable leader of the new commercial Scotland.

Stonefield was at pains to inform Culloden about all that related to the rents and conditions in these districts (SL 3: 216, Stonefield to the Duke, 27 September 1737). No man could have done more than Stonefield to set guidelines for this crucial reorganisation. The Lord President appears to have respected his views in leasing the bulk of the land to 'men of substance', but in two important respects this *legatus a latere* chose to override the Chamberlain's advice. In the first place, he encouraged unrestricted competitive bidding for the leases of farms and so realised a considerable augmentation in the rental. In the second place he created a multitude of small joint leaseholders from the body of former subtenants and common tenants.

Culloden's report, made to the Duke after the expedition was over, is almost the only source of information about the progress of the tour (CCR 1884: 380-94). In this he relates how he summoned the tenants together, first those of Mull and Morvern, then those of Tiree, 'and acquainted them with your Grace's favourable intention of delivering them from the tyranny of taxmen [sic], of freeing them from the oppression of services and herezelds, and of incouraging them to improve their farms by giving them a sort of property in their grounds for 19 years by lease, if they showed themselves worthy of the intended favour by offering frankly for their farms such rent as honestly and fairly they could bear.'

Culloden was surprised and offended when the inhabitants appeared to show no interest in the Duke's 'favour', and concluded that it was 'the effect of a combination' carefully prepared by the tacksmen and their kinsmen, the gentlemen. Some sort of tacit agreement not to bid up the rents there probably was, though not necessarily for the sinister reasons that he supposed. With the help of Campbell of Lochnell's brothers, Ardslignish and Ballimore, he managed to coax or threaten the inhabitants to begin to bid. Competition once started became keen and what Stonefield had most dreaded – a considerable addition to the rental – was realised. The rental of Tiree and the two ends of Coll was raised to £533 8s. (at the time of making his report, Culloden believed that £570 would be realised), compared with the old tack-duty of £325 (CCR 1884: 390; ICP/M-Ac). The rental of Mull was raised to £794, compared with £500 from the tacksmen,[29] and that of Morvern remained at £467 as it had been since it ceased being in tack, compared with £222 from the tacksmen prior to 1732 (CCR 1884: 390-1). The rental for the insular districts was thus 39 per cent above that of 1735 (viz. from £1,292 to £1,794) but the increase was rather over 60 per cent for Mull and Tiree. The actual increase to the tenants was smaller, since they had formerly paid the tacksmen a surplus; in Tiree, for example, it meant an actual increase of 26 per cent to the tenants.

The Lord President felt constrained to excuse his failing to produce a larger increase – quite unnecessarily – for the Duke's reply (CP 2968: 64) expressed the greatest satisfaction:

> I am sorry my endeavours have not answered your expectations or my wishes, but I am confident your Grace will not suspect the disappointment is owing to any want of care or patience in me. I have assigned, in the course of my narration, the true causes – the miserable poverty of the people, proceeding from the oppression of their late taxmasters, the badness of the seasons for some years and the sensible decay in the demand. for cattle (CCR 1884: 391).

In due course, as positive improvement got under way, the Duke would reap a richer harvest:

> Another advantage this expedition has brought you is that the view I have had of the grounds, and the knowledge I have gained of the condition and manners of the people may prevent future impositions, and put your Grace in a method of improving your estate, by bettering the condition of your tennents, which in a small time will bring you a secure rent, and put it in the way of yielding considerable augmentation, if or when a new set happens to be made (CCR 1884: 391).

His mood was one of optimism and sober satisfaction.

> Tho' your Grace's expectations or mine may not be answered as to the improvement of the rent, yet in this I have satisfaction, and it may be some to you, that the method you have taken has prevented the totall ruin of these islands and the absolute loss of the whole rent in time coming to your Grace. Had the taxmen [sic] been suffered to continue their extortions a few years longer, the islands would have been dispeopled, and you must have been contented with no rent, or with such rent as these harpies should be graciously pleased to allow you ... (CCR 1884: 391).

This, then, was only the preliminary stage to a great expansion of the revenue and of productivity; this was the convalescence after a near-mortal disease, in which the tenants must be 'tenderly dealt with'.

The Tenurial Reorganisation: Social, Economic and Political Aspects

The immediate consequence of the tenurial reorganisation was that the great tacksmen finally lost their control of patronage in land in the Duke's insular estates, and the powers of bailiary and other rights associated with it. In their place a large body of tenants emerged throughout these districts from the status of sub-tacksmen and subtenants.[30] Their leases guaranteed them secure and undisturbed occupation of their land, usually for nineteen years, provided that they kept the conditions of their leases. Their rents were payable in money, except for certain victual rents, and they were released (to quote the wording of the Mull leases) from 'all herezalds, caswaltys, and other prestations and services whatsomever . . . except the services of tennants for repairing harbours, mending highways or makeing or repairing miln leads for the general benefit of the island'.

On the face of it, these were immense advantages which could not but elevate the status and material conditions of the mass of the new tenants. They were now free to pursue their own interests, unimpeded by the demands of a tacksman, and since subletting was specifically forbidden in all the leases the whole elaborate pyramid of subordinate relationships, based on land, which linked together the various classes of society and culminated in the tacksman, would presumably disappear. Culloden expected that a benevolent landlord would bring the lessons of advancing agricultural knowledge within the reach of tenants, and as an earnest of this gave a lease of the farm of Ruaig in Tiree on advantageous terms to a Glasgow merchant born on that island, on condition that he introduced improved methods of farming (ICP/M–Ac 1743; V65 various papers). Culloden envisaged that as the experiments proved profitable and successful they would be adopted by neighbouring tenants, so raising the general standard of agriculture in Tiree and producing higher rents for the landlord.

To the 8th Duke, writing as the apologist of nineteenth-century landlordism in the high noon of the Victorian age, the events of 1737 represented a great leap forward, a manifestation of benevolent landlordism apparently justifying his assertion that in this island 'every single step towards improvement that has taken place during the last 150 years has been taken by the Proprietor and not by the people' (Argyll 1887: 271). For any progress to be possible, he argued, the landlord had first to resume the powers over his lands and tenants that had been 'delegated to men whose own possession was not permanent, and whose interests were therefore not identified with the growing wealth and permanent prosperity of the people' (Argyll 1887: 257). Having regained control over the land by dismissing the tacksmen, he was free to allocate it in such a way that tenants, enjoying modern conditions of security and freedom, would collaborate eagerly with the landlord in the fullest exploitation of the land and its resources. It is the contention of the 8th Duke that progress proceeded uninterrupted from this point, borne on the willing shoulders of a secure and liberated tenantry.

Whether this claim will prove well-founded or not, the 8th Duke rightly saw 1737 as a watershed in the history of these districts, indeed in the evolution of the Highland region in general. More than half a century of growing commercialism in the management of the Argyll estates lay behind it (and this the 8th Duke overlooked), so that the events of 1737 came less as a revolution than as a formalisation of practices in which the estate had already some experience. What was important was that in the leases granted by Culloden a new orthodoxy was announced, new standards of value were given the official seal, and a new framework of relationships, designed to be more favourable than the traditional system to economic development, was created.

The assumption on which the new system was based was that land should produce a revenue for the landlord like any other capital asset and that it should therefore be allocated, not as a token of kinship, as a reward for allegiance or as a means of maintaining a following, but in response to the operation of competitive bidding. It appeared fair that the value of land should be settled by the impersonal arbitration of the open auction. The implications of this new orthodoxy for the whole of the Highlands were far-reaching. Ultimately, as it gained ground, it would change the form of society and bring the whole region into the closest dependence on the industrial western world. As a direct consequence of the application of this commercial principle, classes of society would be transformed, whole populations would move and the political and military ebullience of the Highlands would become a thing of the past.

More immediately, it threatened the privileged position of the Campbell colonists and to some extent placed them at the mercy of the clans whom they had ousted and who now enjoyed equal opportunities of acquiring farm leases in open auction. A number of the former tenants recovered land, whilst some of the colonist families, like the Campbells of Auchinard on Iona, lost their holdings. In general, the colonists retained their dominant position, but their dominance was due to their competitive strength and not to their name. It was, to say the least, politically hazardous to weaken the morale of the clan Campbell in the insular districts at a period when Jacobitism, drawing on the genius of clanship for creating a devoted following, was becoming once again an active force. The Duke appeared to be denying himself the strongest weapon in his armoury and to be setting at risk the delicate political balance of the West Highlands.

Whilst accepting the great significance of 1737 as a watershed in the development of the West Highlands, one must enter a caveat. Attitudes and sentiments change slowly in the Highland region; there is an immense conservativism constantly moderating the forces of change and absorbing innovations into a traditional way of life. The announcement of a reform does not imply complete and immediate change in society; simply an attempt to influence society, which may be more or less effective. In general the 8th Duke appears in his writings to exaggerate the pace of social change and to underrate the forces making for continuity. It is important to correct this imbalance, and to emphasise that social changes, though they were far-reaching, took place within a society whose nature it was to shape the unfamiliar into familiar forms. Despite the shattering events that overtook the Highlands in the eighteenth century, it is possible to see organic links between the aristocratic society of the late seventeenth century and the crofter world of the early nineteenth century.

The destruction of the tacksmen's enormous holdings and the grant of leases did not totally revolutionise the social and economic bases of life. It did not, for example, radically alter the distribution of wealth in the insular districts, and so left unaffected much of the hierarchic social structure. Thus about a quarter of the new leaseholders were of the *daoine uaisle*, gentry of the clan Campbell or some other clan. This minority of tenants in fact occupied three-quarters of the total land in the Duke's insular estates. Competition had produced some changes in the occupying families, but by and large the resident tenants had succeeded in retaining their farms, though at much higher rents. The holdings of the large tenants were no longer the vast districts of the tacksmen, but they corresponded closely with those of the sub-tacksmen and ranged mostly between one and four extensive farms. In the first decades of the eighteenth century the Ross of Mull had been in tack to Archibald Campbell and Donald Campbell, belonging respectively to the closely related branches of Crackaig and Scammadill, who were also closely linked with the Campbells of Clenamacrie. After the tenurial reorganisation, six farms in the Ross district were occupied by small tenants (five of them probably on a lease), three were in the hands of single tenants named MacLean, and the remaining thirteen were in the occupation of large Campbell tenants. The Crackaig branch held three farms, the Scammadill branch four, and the Clenamacrie branch six (ICP/M–R 1742).

Such families, though deprived of the powers of tacksmen, remained leaders of local society, enjoying economic power and social eminence. Their households were large, with numerous men- and maid-servants, and formed the nucleus of busy rural communities of agriculturalists and rural craftsmen (Cregeen 1964: xxiv–xxv). This patriarchal order had by no means passed away when Johnson travelled in the Hebrides in 1773. Sub-tenancy was formally prohibited under the conditions of Culloden's leases, but because of the chronic shortage of specie [cash] it must have survived in some form in such rural communities. In practice it was virtually impossible to distinguish between a subtenant paying rent for his land in labour services and a married servant receiving part of his wages in a portion of arable ground and grazing rights for a few beasts.

The hierarchic structure of Highland society thus largely survived the tenurial reorganisation. Former tacksmen and their kinsmen maintained their social pre-eminence and much of their control over the people, and to a considerable extent succeeded in holding on to the lion's share of the land. Members of this class filled the appointments of district factors newly created to carry out duties formerly discharged by the tacksmen. The essential change was less in personnel than in function. The large tenants owed their position not to their name and ancestry but to their competitive strength and economic resources, and they could hope to survive only by enabling the Duke to gain the maximum return from his estates in terms not of fighting men but of money rents.[31]

One of the most significant innovations introduced by Culloden was the grant of leases to small tenants occupying a fractional share of a large farm. 'Common tenants' accounted for about three-quarters of the new leaseholders. The 8th Duke claimed the creation of this new class of petty leaseholders as one of the most significant achievements in the social development of the West Highlands. Once again he overlooks the continuities and presents too rosy a view. Their economic status was basically unchanged by their possession of leases. They were allocated no more than a quarter of the total land available. In certain important respects they were positively handicapped by a system which translated payments in labour or kind, both reasonably available, into cash, which was scarce. Former subtenants were deprived moreover of supplies of working capital and animals which their masters had provided under steelbow arrangements. The leases forbade the subletting of land and insisted on tenants grazing only their own stock. Thus, from an economic position that in some respects was weaker than before, small tenants were undertaking more exacting commitments, especially in the matter of rents.

What the 8th Duke dismissed as 'some little immediate increase of rent' (Argyll 1887: 259) amounted, as has been shown above, to a general increase of 40 per cent, and, for Mull and Tiree, an increase of 60 per cent over the 1735 level. Such an augmentation would annex not only all the tacksmen's profit but a large increment besides, which could only come out of the tenants' pockets. If the tacksmen had been avaricious tyrants, how then could the Lord President justify a level of rents substantially above that required by the tacksmen, especially in view of the Chamberlain's warnings and in a period of profound economic depression?

Culloden's report gives no satisfactory answer to this question, for the expansion of production which he envisaged was necessarily a long-term project whose success was in doubt. Instead he brought unsupported charges against the factors' management and made intemperate accusations against the tacksmen which contrast with Stonefield's reasoned statements about economic conditions. Unfortunately, Culloden's report was more acceptable to the Duke, who welcomed this evidence that he had been cheated of his proper rents by the mismanagement of his servants and representatives. The tacksmen were thus made the scapegoats for all the evils of the times and the way was prepared for an intensification of the very measures which had helped to impoverish the Duke's insular tenants. Culloden's report is to be taken, not as a dispassionate survey of conditions, but as a brilliant piece of special pleading. It was the kind of report to please the Duke, but it does more credit to Culloden the Lord Advocate than Culloden the Lord President, and it was in the end a great disservice to the Duke.

Stonefield expressed himself on the whole subject with quiet scepticism in a letter to the Duke written shortly after the expedition was over:

> The rents are augmented beyond anyone's expectations. Whether that augmentation will stand I cannot take upon me to determine. I heartily wish they may but shrewdly dread the contrary, especially if the seasons do not turn out better than they have for some years past. I now observe that there is no great difficulty to raise the rents of any countrey, expecially islands, as high as one has a mind. Poor people will keep their land at any rate [i.e. at any cost] as long as they can, and will rather beg in the land of their nativity than live tollerably elsewhere.

Offers, however, were no sure guide to what tenants could pay, 'for once a competition of bidding for lands happens, people will sometimes exceed the just value, so that upon the whole there is yet no certain evidence that this settlement with the tenants will prove effectuall, nor can there be till once they come to pay the augmented rents' (SL 3: 215–18, 27 September 1737).

Disaster Threatens the New System

It was perhaps not the most favourable period for innovations. Political instability, always present in the west, broke into open war in 1745. The islands were several times visited by disastrous seasons in the forties. General economic conditions were, nevertheless, vastly better than in the thirties and cattle prices were back to their earlier buoyancy. For the remarkable plight of the insular districts during the forties one must look as much or more to the human errors embodied in the new tenurial system as to political or climatic vicissitudes. The full extent of it is revealed in detail in factors' reports submitted to the second Duke's successor in 1747 and 1748. The intervening stages are not so clearly recorded, for the Stonefield letterbooks end in 1738, but estate accounts and occasional letters, memorials and reports indicate the main features.

The Duke's mood of satisfaction changed fairly rapidly into disenchantment. He had replied to Culloden's report in delighted terms (9 October 1737):

> I am very far from not having my expectations answered; for, upon my word, I took it for granted, from the Sheriff's way of stating the affairs of that country, that things would turn out as you found them; and believe me, I think myself well off on the foot that you have put them, and I am fully persuaded, if you had not given yourself the trouble you have done, some gentlemen had brought about their ends whose duty it was to serve me better. When you have time, my curiosity makes me wish to know your observations on Teree. I have strange notions of that island (CP 2968: 64).

Further details about the condition of Tiree effectively discouraged the Duke's curiosity. He wrote to Culloden in a more sober mood on 25 March 1738: 'I have received your letter with your state of the island of Tyrie, by which I find a young man who could hope for thanks from those who were to succeed him might take advantage of that place. You know I am not in that state; but however I am not the less obliged to you for your constant concern and anxious care for everything that in any degree relates to my interest or welfare' (Duff 1815: CLXXXVI). A commission in the Blues for Culloden's son expressed the Duke's gratitude to a loyal servant but for Culloden's brain-child there was clearly to be no endowment from the Duke. The more positive aspects of Culloden's new programme would be quietly forgotten. They would be revived later under successors more actively committed to improvement.

Intractable difficulties were early in appearing. Numbers of tenants in Mull and Tiree had 'resiled' from their leases (that is, had refused to conclude the agreements by signing them) and, on a technicality, could not be legally coerced (CP 2970: 173–7), Arrears were accumulating, especially in Tiree. One of the Duke's advisers wrote to him early in 1738: 'The arrear now due from that country is very great. If exacted vigorously it's probable the country would be laid waste. Every small tenant cannot be at the expense of coming into the continent in order to turn his effects into money' (*loc. cit.*). The same official warned the Duke that punctual rents could never be expected from the island until industry and improved agriculture were introduced.[32]

Petitions coming in from the islands at this time suggest that the failure of the new system to produce either revenue or contented tenants was due not only to high rents but to the lack of flexibility in the method of collecting them. One such petition was presented (evidently in 1738) by a number of substantial tenants in Mull and Iona. It runs:

> The petition of your submissive and obedient tennants in the Isle of Mull to His Grace the the Duke of Argyll.
>
> Humbly sheweth
>
> That we having made proposals for the lands that we now possess [i.e. occupy] are willing to adhere to the same, but that we dread very much the dangerous consequence of binding ourselves to pay our rents compleatly at Martinmass term by reason that our cowes and horses nowadays gives little or no price att all and that a great many among us may use severall shifts to get penies of money betwixt Martinmass and Whitsunday that they cannot do before Martinmas and therefore we begg that your Grace would consider our circumstances so far as if necessity did oblidge us to come short in making compleat payment at the Martinmas that the remainder may be taken from us in money at the Whit-sunday thereafter.
>
> May it therefore please your Grace to grant us our petition and your petitioners shall ever pray . . . (CP 2970: 182).

A petition presented to Culloden by a group consisting mainly of small tenants in Mornish in Mull (CP 2970: 177) complained that the factor was rigorously exacting interest on rents unpaid at Martinmass (as he was entitled to do under the terms of the tacks) and was forcing them to sell their cattle to him below the price offered them by drovers. For these reasons they declared: 'We shall never sign our tacks on stamped paper untill we have reason to believe that we shall not be dealt with after this manner for the future.' These and similar reasons, all reflecting a severely legalistic approach, caused the negotiations for many of the new tacks to break down at the final stage.

Ballimore, factor of Mull and Tiree, appears to have managed his districts in a somewhat ruthless manner. Airds, however, was restrained by more tender sensibilities in dealing with the Morvern tenants. In April 1738 he offered his resignation. Stonefield explained the reasons to the Duke: 'He said if he continued in his office he must either be the executioner of the people or disoblige his constituents, and that he would chuse rather to demit than do either' (SL 3: 246, 12 April 1738). He was, however, evidently persuaded to continue.

By the summer of 1739 the Duke's high hopes of better rents had totally faded. Even Kintyre was disappointing him. Mull and Tiree were in deep arrears and had, in fact, yielded none of the rents due at Martinmas 1738. The Duke wrote to Culloden on 14 July, deeply dejected.

> I have written to the Sheriff by this post and expressed some disgust at the treatment I meet with in the affair of payments. . . . He seems not to be displeased that Ballimore behaves so extravagantly ill as he does. I confess I did not think that man would have given the Sheriff such subject of triumph. I end my dissertation on my private affairs with telling you

that what I would faine obtain is to know what I can receive and when I can receive it. I will rather lessen my rent-roll than not be able to know what I have to depend on from your parts of the world (CP 2968: 117).

Thus already within two years of the great reorganisation, Stonefield's views were beginning to be vindicated and the Lord President's policies were losing the Duke's confidence. Nevertheless, so long as Culloden remained his principal adviser, there was no change in policy.

A list of annual revenue received by the factor of Mull and Tiree from 1735 to 1743 and presented in a memorial by the Deputy Chamberlain in 1747, provides a useful guide to the earlier years (ICP/M–Ac. 1743 'State of Tyrie and Mull'). The years given represent the crop-years. Thus the first year, 1736, includes the rent received from Martinmas 1736 to Martinmas 1737, and marks the first year after the expiration of the old tacks. The year 1737 includes the receipts for 1737–8, the first year of the new leases and higher rents. The list is as follows:

1736 [– 7] ... £514 18s 8d   1740 [– 1] ... £1,199 4s 5d
1737 [– 8] ... 624 6s 2d   1741 [– 2] ... 741 9s 2d
1738 [– 9] ... 931 10s 4d   1742 [– 3] ... 825 2s 11d
1739 [– 40] .. 1,071 0s 7d   1743 [– 4] ... 1,113 10s 7d

The rental (i.e. the rents due) for Mull and Tiree in 1736–7 was £994. It was raised to £1,323 in 1737–8 and remained at approximately this figure in the six following years. It will at once be apparent that receipts in 1736–7 and 1737–8 were abysmally low, undoubtedly reflecting the very low cattle prices prevailing. A marked improvement in revenue followed in the years 1738–9 to 1740–1, and this almost certainly resulted directly from the rising cattle prices – the long delayed emergence from the depression of the thirties (see graph, p. 63 and Appendix p. 98).

Receipts from the insular districts throughout the forties do not however reflect the generally much higher level of cattle prices, and this is significant. The years 1741–2 and 1742–3 yielded poor results, which contrast with remarkably inflated cattle prices. And, to anticipate the evidence somewhat, 1744–5 was the beginning of a prolonged crisis signalised by low receipts and heavy arrears; this continued until almost the end of the decade.[33] Had cattle prices been the only factor, one might have found the Duke's revenue in a healthy and improving state throughout the forties. Other circumstances were evidently exercising a prepotent influence, and these must now be considered.

The West Highlands appear to have escaped the terrible winter of 1739–40, when men, cattle and wild life suffered heavy mortality and extreme privations in the Lowlands of Scotland and throughout much of north-west Europe. At any rate neither the severe winter of 1739–40 nor the wretched harvest of 1740, with its aftermath of hunger riots, are reflected in the insular revenues, as one would expect them to be if cattle had died in great numbers and if large quantities of meal had had to be bought.³⁴ In mainland areas of the estate rents continued to come in fairly easily in the early forties, as the Chamberlain informed the Duke's Commissioner, Lord Milton, in December 1743 (SAL 401 Letter of 29 December 1743). In the islands, however, things were far otherwise. Despite buoyant markets the receipts dropped to a level suggesting widespread tenant difficulties in 1741–2 and 1742–3. There is no specific evidence about climatic conditions, but heavy mortality among cattle, combined with high rents, probably lies behind the crisis. This assumption gains support from evidence from Tiree in 1748 and from the fact that in 1744 the new Duke instructed his factor in Tiree to lower rents in certain cases, as the general level was too high (ICP/V65 'Instructions' 1744).

The Crisis Develops: The 3rd Duke's Counter-Measures

The improvement of 1743–4 shown in the higher receipts was short-lived. Not only the islands, but the whole mainland also, were by the spring of 1745 in the depth of a renewed crisis from which they were long in emerging. It ran counter to cattle markets, which were rising again after a fall in 1744 (a fall much less severe in Argyll than in England, to judge by the Knockbuy prices). The predisposing cause was the exorbitant level of rents, but more specific circumstances served to trigger off the crisis. Mortality among cattle was at a disastrous level in early 1745 and was evidently due to severe climatic conditions in the winter of 1744–5. One laird alone lost 510 cattle 'by mere want' in Glenorchy.³⁵ 'I cannot express the sufferings of this shire', Stonefield wrote to Milton in April 1745, 'Their loss of cattle is very great and universal, and corn is very scarce and dear, but now we have fine weather, I wish it may abate the mortality. We used commonly to receive £4,000 [Sterling] of his Grace's rents before this time of year, and we have not yet received £2,000' (SAL 403, Stonefield to Lord Milton, 18 April 1745).

Thus the months immediately preceding the Rising were a time of hunger and catastrophe in the West Highlands. What effects this had in producing a mood favourable to the Jacobite Rising can only be conjectured, but it may have played a significant part in the situation. One may follow the prolonged crisis through the estate accounts. Arrears of rent in 1743–4 for the whole Argyll estates in Scotland, with a gross rental of about £7,500 Sterling, were approximately £2,000, which was very much more than in the Duke's earlier years.³⁶ By 1744–5 arrears cannot have been less than £4,000; in 1745–6 they exceeded £5,000 and were still larger in 1746–7; they declined to a little under £4,000 in 1747–8.[37]

The Rising placed an added strain on the West Highland economy. Farms were burnt and cattle driven off by the Government forces in Morvern and neighbouring districts after Culloden.[38] Tenants were called away from their work or were burdened with the payment of a substitute. But these circumstances, and any temporary interruption that the Rising may have caused in the cattle-trade, only aggravated what was already a desperate situation in the spring of 1745. The rent of Morvern was better paid than that of some districts outside the area affected by the Rising, as for example Tiree, where neither government nor Jacobites recruited many men (ICP/M–Ac. 1745, 1746). The severe loss of cattle in early 1745 is probably the most significant factor, for its effects would be felt for several years after, until the losses had been made good, and would not be wholly compensated by the high cattle prices which followed the murrain outbreak in England in 1745–6 (Haldane 1952: 121; Reid 1942: 177–81). It seems most likely that the severe climatic conditions of winter 1744–5 were prolonged into the two years following and affected other parts of Scotland.[39]

The Lord President's optimistic rental of 1737–8 was revealed as so much wishful thinking in the succeeding ten years. The Duke's revenue gained little or nothing by the increase in rents in the insular districts. In the years from 1738 to 1743 the accounts for Tiree and Mull show that in no single year was the rental achieved, and that, in fact, annual receipts, on a rental of about £1,320, averaged only £980 (ICP/M–Ac 1743 'State of Tyrie and Mull'). Similarly, after Mull was joined to Airds' factory of Morvern in 1744, receipts for these districts averaged £978 a year, some £300 short of the rental (ICP/M–Ac 1744, 1745, 1746, 1747, 1748). The situation was even more catastrophic in Tiree after being disjoined from Mull in 1743. In the period 1744 to 1746 inclusive, the island, though scarcely touched by the Rising, yielded no more than £732 in all, viz. an average of £244 per annum on a rental of just over £500 (ICP/M–Ac. 1746). The rest simply formed a massive toll of arrears. Even allowing for what might be collected of the arrears, the average yield, on the Chamberlain's reckoning in 1748, had been no more than £300 a year in the ten-year period 1738 to 1747, whilst the Deputy Chamberlain estimated that more than £1,400 Sterling of the Tiree rents had been lost in that time.[40]

The succession of Archibald, 3rd Duke of Argyll, in 1743 produced important modifications in the tenurial system. More politically alert than his predecessor to the spread of Jacobitism in the West Highlands, he instructed his various chamberlains in the following terms in the autumn of 1744: 'I would have it made a condition of the tacks that every tenant should take an oath of allegiance and a promissory oath never to rise or encourage any rising in rebellion against the present government.' Loyalty moreover, would be rewarded: 'You are to use your endeavours to introduce tennants well disposed to the government and my family. And as I am informed that my lands are rather too high rented in those countreys, so that there may be a necessity for some abatement of rent, I do approve that these abatements be chiefly given in those farms where you bring in people well disposed to my interest.'[41]

This revival of political considerations in the management of the estate marks a significant retreat from the almost purely commercial principles which had recently controlled the choice of tenants. It must have heartened the Campbell colonists at this critical juncture. They proved the most reliable element in the west in 1745–6, and their presence was perhaps not without importance in limiting the areas of disaffection. The Prince gained many recruits from Morvern, which lay outside the area of Campbell settlement, in contrast with the islands of Mull and Tiree, where the Jacobite sympathies of the natives were counteracted by the activity of the Campbells. Tests of loyalty continued to be required of tenants through most or all of the 3rd Duke's time.

A second important modification in the tenurial system was made in 1747, when the Duke relaxed the total prohibition which his predecessor had placed on subletting and permitted the larger tenants to sublet land, 'provided the tacksmen [viz. the large tenants] be restricted from convenanting and receiving from their sub-tenants any further payment or prestation of any kind than six days' service of one man yearly ... over and above the rent payable by themselves for the lands subsett' (ICP/M 'Instructions' 1747). This relaxation may have been dictated in part by the growing extent of land lying waste through the failure of small tenants, and it restored a component of the traditional economy which could not yet be given up without loss of production. Significantly, too, it marked a reversion towards what Stonefield had recommended when he urged that leases should be confined to substantial men and not conferred on small tenants who would not survive bad seasons.

A third modification which the 3rd Duke was induced to make took the form of rent-reductions. These were not as large as the Chamberlains recommended, but they were significant of a more realistic and flexible approach. The rental of Mull and Morvern was reduced in 1748 by nearly 10 per cent, from £1,227 (as rentalled in 1744) to £1,104. Tiree did not benefit, however, in spite of her needy condition, though there had been some small reductions in that island in 1745 and 1746 (ICP/M–Ac annually 1744–8 inclusive). The situation had become serious to the point of catastrophe by 1747. For three years consecutively, arrears ran at an unprecedented level, for two years almost equalling the gross rental of the estate. Many tenants had failed and large areas lay uncultivated. Even the loyal Campbells were threatening to leave the islands, as Stonefield explained in a memorial to the Duke in 1747:

The condition of the tennants in every part of Argyllshire having declined much for two or three years backward, those of Mull and Tiry have suffered as much as their neighbours, tho' they could not bear it so well, as they were but weak and their rents dear. Many of them who, or their predecessors, have gone to settle in that country since my Lord Argyll got that estate, and who are most attached to his interest, are disposed to leave it and come back to the body of the shire. This will be a great loss to his Grace, and endeavours ought to be used rather to encourage them and engage others of that friendly disposition to settle there (SAL 405 'Memorial on the Duke of Argyll's Business' 1747).

Having a half-brother, Archibald Campbell, resident at Killichronain in Mull, Stonefield was likely to know the settlers' mind. The wholesale removal of Campbell colonists from the islands would be a disaster of the first magnitude, threatening alike the Duke's future revenue from those districts and their political security.

Other reports from his officials in 1747 and 1748 presented a distressingly similar story in all districts of the estate: cattle dead, tenants ruined, arrears high, land waste. After the death of their cattle, many tenants in Kintyre were removed (SAL 405 'Memorial on the Duke of Argyll's Business' 1747). Something like half the tenants were insolvent in the heartland farms around Inveraray and Loch Awe and had either failed to take up their tacks or been obliged by their circumstances to give them up.[42] In Mull the factor, Campbell of Airds, recorded twenty-six farms (out of a total of some ninety) 'which are now or likely to be waste in whole or part against Whitsunday 1747', and warned the Duke that these could not be rented at so high a rent after the insolvent tenants removed (SAL 405 'Remarks of several tenements in Mull' 1747). It was for these reasons that the Campbell gentry of Mull, many of them in arrears and recorded in this list, were seriously contemplating quitting the island and returning to the mainland.

Nowhere is the plight of the tenants more plainly revealed than in the factor of Tiree's report on the farms under his charge in Tiree and the neighbouring island of Coll. This report the Duke had himself ordered after receiving disquieting information from the factor about the state of rents and the poverty of the tenants. A combination of high rents and severe climatic conditions appears to have operated on the tenants to produce a quite exceptional level of failure and poverty. 'Were the arrears presently due out of that estate, with the current rents for cropt 1747 completely levyed, I may with assurance say it, there woud not remain thereafter of effects near what woud stock one fourth part of the island.' So the new factor Campbell of Barnacarry declared in 1747 (ICP/ V65 'Memorial by Archibald Campbell of Barnacarie' 1747). Misfortune struck large and small tenants, gentry and commoners, loyal Campbell colonists and disaffected natives. Great tracts of once fertile machair lay under blown sand. 'Traik of cattle' left the island understocked. An island which had recently been rentalled at over £530 sterling was now producing barely £300 a year (ICP/V65 'Memoriall by Stonefield concerning Tyree' 1748). Scarcely anything survived of the Lord President's new system of tenure except a handful of leases from which the holders implored release.[43]

Typical of this remnant of leaseholders was Alexander McIlvra, who had the farm of Hough:

> This farm was set in tack to Alexander McIlvra of Penighaill by the Lord President. This man is now in arrears to your Grace the sum of £1097:2:10 Scots. The present factor could ne'er receive payment of him as he had no effects in Tyrie and very little in Mule where he resides, only the mailling of Penighail and Carsaig, holding of your Grace. There is horning and caption against him for the greater part of this sum. He has petitioned your Grace more than once to get terms to clear up these arrears but had no return . . . 'Tis the factor's opinion, as this farm has and does yearly suffer greatly by sand-blowing, it would want an abatement yearly of £36.[44]

This sum represented 25 per cent of the rent of the farm.

Of the thirty-six farms in Tiree (some of which were normally combined), the Lord President had, it seems, successfully set twenty-five in tack in 1737. His negotiations for the letting of the remaining eleven had proved abortive (contrary to the expectations expressed in his report in 1737) and were simply let year by year to small tenants, whose condition is illustrated by Balevouline:

> The factor observes that this town was set by the Lord President at so dear a rent that he coud get no tennents to take the same in tack, the paying of which rent so reduced the tennents [i.e. the nine occupying without a lease] as that they became insolvent and a great part, almost the half, thereof became waste, which has been so these severall years past . . .

Of the twenty-five Tiree farms actually leased in 1737, only eleven remained in tack in 1748, and in almost every case the holders were pleading to be rid of the burden of the lease or to have the rent very much reduced, as in McIlvra's case. The lease of fourteen of the twenty-five farms (that is, 56 per cent of them) had lapsed by the tenants' falling into arrears. Numbers of the gentry are found in this condition. Hector MacLean of Gott and Vuill had fallen into deep arrears, become insolvent and so lost his tack. Donald McLarin, deputy factor, lost all his effects and gave up his tack of Barrapol and Kenvar, which then served to graze poynded cattle. Campbell of Ballimore, one-time factor, whose timely offer had assisted the Lord President to breach the opposition and get the island rented in 1737, had been so reduced that he gave up his farms there. John Campbell, who claimed that his grandfather had been the first Campbell settler in Tiree (Cregeen 1968: 170), received a lease of three farms in the west of the island in 1737, but 'in a short time thereafter became insolvent by reason of the dear rent he offered and is still considerably in arrears to your Grace'. His lands were occupied by eleven tenants, who 'are all in low circumstances except Archibald McDonald . . .'. The list could be prolonged monotonously.

The new tenurial system was thus virtually foundering by 1748. So far from fulfilling the Lord President's expectations that revenue and productivity would expand and greater security be conferred on tenants, the new leases appear rather to have been associated with widespread misery and insecurity among the tenants and chaos in the ducal revenue. Stonefield's summing up of the situation in Tiree in 1748 was pungent without being self-congratulatory:

> It was with intention to reform the country as much as the nature of the thing would admit of that the late Duke dismissed the tacksmen, imagining that they squeezed the undertennents by exacting high rents, but very unluckily my Lord President followed the same plan, by augmenting the rents beyond what the tacksmen ever exacted, a rent that the country was less capable to yield during the factory than in the tacksmen's time because they occupied severall of the farms with their own stock and when any of the lands could not be sett, they possessed it themselves' (ICP/V 65 'Memoriall by Stonefield concerning Tyree' 1748).

The restoration of the tacksman system was in fact being actively considered. Stonefield, reporting on Tiree in 1748, recommended that the first essential measure was to reduce rents to under £400 and to let the farms either to the existing tenants or to a tacksman: 'I have been making tryalls in that shape likeways, and the highest offer I could bring anybody was to £340' (ICP /V65 'Memoriall by Stonefield concerning Tyree' 1748). This was roughly the amount of tack-duty paid by the tacksmen of Tiree before the Lord President's visit. John Campbell, brother to Barnacarry and deputy-chamberlain of Argyll, even offered to become tacksman of the whole of the ducal estate in Mull, Morvern and Tiree, at a tack-duty of £1,333 6s. 8d. Sterling, but no more is heard of this breathtaking project (ICP/V65 'Memorial concerning Mull, Morvern and Tyree' 1747).

The Tenurial Reorganisation: General Assessment

A number of general conclusions emerge from this examination of the 2nd Duke's tenurial reforms. It is clear that the accounts which have hitherto been available, and have been very influential, are in need of drastic revision. Culloden's report cannot be taken as a dispassionate account but as the attempt of an astute politician to justify measures which he had carried out against the advice of the Duke's senior officials. He made the tacksmen, and to a lesser extent the Duke's officials, the butt of his main accusations, and in so doing diverted attention from what was most responsible for the ills of the tenants of the insular districts – the depressed condition of the cattle-markets, on which tenants depended to pay their rents, and the Duke's heavy demands upon the tacksmen.

The 8th Duke of Argyll's account of the tenurial reforms emphasises the humane and rational intentions of the 2nd Duke and his agent, and represents the new leases as the opening of a happy and secure era in the insular districts. His historical writings, brilliant though they were in many ways, had as their main object the defence of the landlords' record in the Highlands, and this he carried out with vigour and success but at some expense of accuracy. He disregarded, or was ignorant of, a great many relevant documents in the Inveraray Castle archives which shed a quite different light on the tenurial reform.

These documents have been extensively used in this investigation. Among the main conclusions which they suggest, the first is that the tacksmen in the insular districts were by no means so much to blame for the plight of their sub-tenants during the thirties as Culloden represented. It would appear that the Duke's management of these districts was governed in the main by his need for revenue, and that the increasing load of rent which he required of the tacksmen reacted seriously on the condition of the mass of the population, and was especially damaging to their economy in the period of depressed cattle-prices which immediately preceded the tenurial reorganisation.

This tenurial reorganisation had its humane and progressive aspects, as is apparent from Culloden's report. If it had been carried out in the way proposed by the Chamberlain, it could have become the turning-point in the development of the economy of the West Highlands. But the strong financial motivation behind the reform proved overwhelming, and in Culloden's hands the tenurial reorganisation turned into a disaster both for the Duke and for the tenants who were supposed to be its main beneficiaries. The following years witnessed, not the radical improvement intended by Culloden, but – in spite of the new buoyancy of cattle prices – chaos in the Duke's revenue, widespread distress and ruin on an unusual scale among the new tenants, and the virtual collapse of the new tenurial system over large areas of the estate.

This failure was as unnecessary as it was lamentable. Had the Duke trusted his Chamberlain he might have seen such progress in the development of agriculture as Campbell of Shawfield achieved in Islay through the agency of his tacksmen (MacDonald 1811: 75–7).

Stonefield's solution would no doubt have been biased in favour of his clan and would have restricted leases to substantial tenants of the *daoine uaisle,* but it would have had the advantage of developing out of the existing economic and social situation instead of running counter to it. His policy of moderate and flexible rents would have encouraged a real sense of security and trust in the tenants, basically more important that the grant of formal leases,[45] and would have led to a rapid growth of technological progress and an expansion of the Duke's revenues.

The Duke preferred to be advised by Culloden, whose abilities in the field of government were not matched by equal competence in the management of the Duke's West Highland estates. By rejecting the best available advice, Culloden established the new tenurial system on foundations which were unsound from the beginning. His most serious error was to stimulate competitive bidding for the leases and to produce, as a result, a rental that could only end by ruining the successful candidates and injuring the estate. The Chamberlain's warnings on this head should have been heeded. In these districts where the native clans had contended over land for centuries and where recently they had been deprived by the Campbells, competition for leases was simply a prolongation of clan warfare, and bids were used like sword thrusts to injure rival families and clans.[46] The auction of leases thus did not operate to establish a fair or realistic valuation of land; it reflected the candidates' desires and passions rather than their financial resources.

The greatly advanced rents were, as has been shown, the chief cause of the failure of the reform. Culloden was the director of the tenurial reorganisation but the ultimate responsibility must lie with the 2nd Duke, who set the objectives and chose the instrument. Like most men of his rank in eighteenth-century Britain, the Duke conceived of improvement in terms of magnificent building and the development of parks and domainal farm-lands (Habakkuk 1952). He showed extreme reluctance to divert any financial resources from these to the capital outlay on drains, dykes, fences and buildings that the estate in general required if any real progress were to be made. This would have to be left to 'a young man who could hope for thanks from those who were to succeed him'.

The effects of this unwillingness to carry through agricultural innovation by providing financial support became obvious in the island of Tiree. Here Culloden had shown a genuine interest in encouraging improvement and had granted an improving lease on favourable terms to a Glasgow merchant, Lachlan MacLean. As an experiment it proved completely successful. He succeeded in growing clover and sown grasses and showed the possibility of ending the mortality in cattle that was so frequent an occurrence in the spring months (ICP/M 'Description of the Island of Teree' 1748). The general adoption of his methods in the island would have transformed the economy, but fences were necessary to protect the crops from trespassing animals, and to build them, tenants required a great deal of practical assistance (Campbell 1965: 31). Such assistance was not generally available until almost the end of the century, in the 5th Duke's time. As a result, agricultural improvement had little real impact on traditional methods in the years following Culloden's visit.

The mass of small tenants had been economically too dependent on the tacksmen and sub-tacksmen for credit and working capital to stand long unaided, and were quite incapable of developing a more productive agriculture without generous treatment from the landlord when their masters had been removed. In the traditional system, with all its limitations, tacksmen had a real interest in maintaining their manpower and probably discharged their obligations faithfully until heavy demands began to crush them in the eighteenth century. Precisely at a time when the small tenants were deprived of their normal supports from the traditional system, they were required to pay considerably higher rents. Moreover, rents paid to the tacksmen had not only been lower but could also be partly paid in labour and agricultural products. These could not readily be turned into cash to pay the landlord's rents.

The grossly inflated rental which Culloden reported to the Duke as a triumph represented, in fact, no advance in technology, no expansion of production, and no widening of commercial outlets. It simply transferred the claim to non-existent wealth from the tenant to the Duke. When it failed to materialise the tenant lost his lease together with what stock he had. Essentially what was taking place in the forties was an intensification of the kind of management that the Duke had applied to these districts since his succession. The results were now more serious both for the tenants and for the landlord's revenue. Previously land left vacant by the failure of sub-tenants was not unproductive, since the tacksmen would make use of it. Now such land was truly waste and unproductive, and the revenue suffered.

The tenurial reorganisation of 1737 was certainly a turning-point in the history of the insular districts of the Argyll estate. It may fairly be asked whether, so far from representing a great leap forward, it did not in fact inflict irreparable injury on the inhabitants, damage social institutions of considerable value, and postpone the development of a healthy economic system for many years. The blame cannot at any rate be laid on those convenient scapegoats, the tacksmen.

A Summary View of the Tenurial Reorganisation and its Aftermath

The tenurial system of most Highland estates until the eighteenth century was well advanced rested on an élite of upper tenants known as tacksmen, who were usually close kinsmen or functionaries of the chief.

They occupied extensive holdings of land on a virtually hereditary basis, paid rents to the chief in money and kind at a privileged rate, and gained a profit-margin (amounting in the areas studied here to 30–35 per cent) by sub-letting part of their holding to sub-tenants at higher rents, paid in money, kind and labour. It became fashionable among writers and publicists in the eighteenth century to regard the tacksmen as an oppressive and parasitic class. In fact, however, as Dr Johnson perceived, they performed vital services within Highland communities, were leaders of the clan both in war and peace, patrons and not seldom practitioners of the arts, and middlemen in the processes of production.

In the insular districts of the Argyll estate, only recently forcibly acquired from the MacLeans of Duart, the tacksmen controlled larger areas than ordinary. Under them much of Mull, Morvern, Tiree and certain other islands was settled by Campbells and their friends in the late seventeenth and early eighteenth century. These colonies were of great political importance to the Whig Dukes of Argyll in maintaining control of the mainly Jacobite West Highlands, but they needed support and favour, threatened as they were by the deprived natives to whom the Jacobite cause offered not only a sentimental appeal but the hope of restoring the *status quo*.

A combination of political, economic and idealistic motives caused the 2nd Duke of Argyll to undertake a wholesale reorganisation of land-tenure in these districts in 1737. There can be little doubt that the Duke was chiefly motivated by hopes of increasing his revenues. Since his succession in 1703 he had applied to the management of his Scottish estates commercial ideas that ran counter to the Highland tradition of managing land to support a following of kinsmen and dependents. Steeply increased rents had begun to produce immense stresses in these districts long before 1737. Tacksmen were forced inevitably to pass heavier rents on to their tenants, and signs of distress and impoverishment were evident already by the end of the twenties.

The situation became more acute in the thirties, when the cattle markets on which Highland tenants depended to pay their rents sank to their lowest level for many years. The deepening poverty of the tenants seriously affected the Duke's revenues and made him suspect mismanagement or fraud in his officials and tacksmen. Meantime, in Morvern, the Camerons, who controlled the land in defiance of the Duke's ownership, had overplayed their hand and brought into existence among the lesser clans a resistance movement which the Duke's Chamberlain, Campbell of Stonefield, was not slow to exploit. Stonefield's conclusion that the time was ripe for change, chiming in with the Duke's dissatisfaction over revenue, led to the momentous tour of Duncan Forbes of Culloden, the Duke's business agent, to the insular districts in 1737.

The removal of the tacksmen was a foregone conclusion. The Chamberlain had already appointed factors in Mull and Morvern to take over the tacksmen's administrative duties. Culloden's reorganisation of tenures was much more radical than the Chamberlain had recommended. Not only were the tacksmen removed from all parts of the insular districts, but leases were granted to large numbers of small tenants of runrig farms as well as to the gentlemen of the clan. Further, by throwing leases of farms open to competitive bidding, Culloden was able to increase the rental by roughly 40 per cent.

Culloden described the favourable outcome of the tour to the Duke in a report that has become well known. He presented the most optimistic view of the future both for the new tenants and the Duke and laid most of the blame for the tenants' plight on the tacksmen, whom he roundly abused as 'harpies'. His report showed an awareness of the urgent need for agricultural improvement and help from the landlord in the insular districts, and he regarded the large increases in rent as a reasonable return for security of tenure and the abolition of praedial services. Nevertheless the report was less than a fair assessment of the situation, his accusations against the tacksmen and officials were supported by no evidence and were probably largely unfounded, and he disregarded the Chamberlain's strong advice to keep rents at a moderate level and to be cautious in granting leases to small tenants.

Events quickly proved the Chamberlain right and Culloden wrong. The Duke was soon disappointed of his hopes of increased revenue. Tenant insolvencies ran at a remarkable level in the forties; not only many small tenants but numbers of substantial tenants were reduced to poverty. Arrears accumulated and leases were given up. In Tiree, ten years after Culloden's tour, less than a third of the farms were still under leases. The Jacobite Rising of 1745–6 and a series of bad seasons aggravated the situation and were the precipitating cause of much of the insolvency, but in general the economic climate of the forties was more favourable than in the thirties and cattle prices were notably higher. The ultimate cause of the widespread distress among tenants and of the chaos in ducal revenues was evidently the exorbitant level of rents fixed by the Lord President and the inflexible way in which they were subsequently enforced. It further aggravated the rate of failure that many of the tenants had only recently emerged from the relatively sheltered condition of sub-tenants and were being exposed, without sufficient resources or working capital, to the chill air of the commercial world.

The 3rd Duke, who succeeded in 1743, appointed Andrew Fletcher, Lord Milton, as his principal agent in place of Culloden. He was more practical and humane than his predecessor and gave more weight to Stonefield's advice. Though he failed to prevent the ruin of a high proportion of the new tenants, he alleviated some of the worst effects of the new system. He was especially sensitive to the political dangers which it had created by unsettling the colonists, and took steps to restore their confidence and security. Tests of loyalty were incorporated in leases, and a brake was put on the unrestricted commercial management of the estate.

It was seriously proposed in 1747–8 that the system of tacksmen should be restored, but in fact the new tenurial system was to remain a permanent institution of the Argyll estates. There was no going back on the principle, finally established in the 2nd Duke's time, though developing since the seventeenth century, that the primary purpose of land was to provide the landlord with revenue, not to maintain his kinsmen and followers. This new attitude towards land would, as time passed, gradually eliminate the old aristocracy of the clan from their positions of privilege, leaving the Highlands rich in tradition but impoverished in leaders.

The gradual disappearance of this élite in general throughout the Highland region probably hastened the lairds away from their estates, as Dr Johnson had predicted. A social vacuum was left which the minister and the factor, whose consequence grew with the departure of the tacksmen, only partially filled. The tenants gained a new independence from the gentry of the clan but lost the protection which they had given them, and were exposed to new hazards. The landlord, released from obligations to his kinsmen, was free to develop his estate as he wished. He was bound, admittedly, by legal contracts but was less amenable than before to the rules of custom and kindliness. The triumph of economic individualism represented a new and disturbing force in the Highlands.

There was, however, on the Argyll lands, a prolonged period during which, after the initial shock and chaos of the tenurial reorganisation, elements of continuity reasserted themselves in the insular districts. The raw economic principles, so influential under the 2nd Duke, were tempered, under his successors, in the selection of tenants. The 3rd Duke replaced the open auction of leases by a system of private offers which made it possible to assess candidates for farms not only for their economic virtues but their political reliability and their attachment to the family of Argyll. Memorials submitted by candidates exemplify this fusion of traditionalism and modernity: they urge their claims as tenants by reciting improvements carried out or promised, and offering, usually, an increase in rent, and, at the same time, they reinforce their cause by citing the ancient ties between their forbears and the house of Argyll.

The ascendancy of the Campbell settler families in the insular districts had been severely shaken by the tenurial reorganisation. A privileged position would never again be awarded automatically to those who could claim descent from the founder of the clan Campbell. Nevertheless the dominance of the Campbell gentry in Mull and Tiree remained

THE TACKSMEN AND THEIR SUCCESSORS 99

formidable for longer than might have been expected, for it had a strong basis in their economic resources, their clan-consciousness and tightly drawn unity, and their influence over the administration. Moreover, the revival of Jacobite activity, capable of causing alarm to the Duke and his friends during the fifties, and the continuing hostility of the MacLeans and Camerons to the Campbells, still remarkable at the end of the eighteenth century, reinforced the dominant position of the colonists. It was brought to an end only in the closing years of the eighteenth century and the opening of the nineteenth century as a result of revolutionary economic and social changes, which affected the Highlands in common with the rest of Britain. In the rise of a new crofter class, compounded of diverse social elements, one may see the Highlands coming to terms with the industrial age. Half wage-earner, half agriculturalist, the crofter had a foot in both camps, and carried much of the essence of the traditional Highlands into the modern world.

APPENDIX

Note on the Knockbuy Cattle Prices

The cattle prices on which the lower line of the graph is based are prices which Archibald Campbell of Knockbuy recorded in his rentals as having been credited to tenants in payment of their rents. Stots (bullocks) have been excluded from the data, since their prices varied widely from one beast to another according to their age. To have any significance, it would have been necessary to base calculations on stots of a particular age, e.g. two-year olds, and thus exclude the bulk of the data. The problem was solved by omitting stots altogether, and using only the prices allowed for tenants' cows. This still left a reasonable amount of data, since the laird was taking approximately as many cows as stots from tenants. Prices of cows offer a more reliable basis for comparison. Cows were already fully-grown animals (the younger female animals are stated apart as heifers and queys) and thus formed a more homogeneous group, with smaller variations in price from one animal to another. (This is made apparent in a complete list and valuation of Knockbuy's animals contained in the rental in 1750.)

The accompanying list [below] shows the details on which the graph is based. Its value clearly varies from year to year with the number of animals entering into the calculation of the average price. For the purposes both of the table (p. 99–100) and of the graph (p. 63), prices have been allocated to their true year, which is not necessarily the year of the rental, since arrears of rent might be cleared several years after they were incurred. The average prices appear in the graph in the calendar year following the rental (or crop) year, since the rental runs from November to November, with most of the cattle purchased by the laird from January onwards.

The upper line of the graph shows prices paid for beef oxen by the Navy Victualling Board at their London yard (Beveridge 1939:568-71). They represent the average of prices for October, November and December each year, and the points on the graph are therefore marked slightly later than those on the lower line.

Comparison between the two lines shows a remarkably close similarity in the Argyll and English price trends. Both reveal high though fluctuating prices in the first three decades of the century, then severe depression in the thirties, followed by a return to more buoyant prices in the forties. After 1747 the Argyll trend diverges from the English trend rather more. The boom of 1749–51 in the Argyll prices (confirmed from independent sources) has no counterpart in the southern prices, and in the fifties the English series shows a buoyancy unmatched by the stabler Argyll price movements.

Crop Year	Calendar Year	Number of Cows	Average Price £Scots
1728	1729	11	14 18s. 0d.
1729	1730	2	15 18s. 0d.
1730	1731	3	16 15s. 7d.
1731	1732	6	13 0s. 0d.
1732	1733	13	13 5s. 4d.
1733	1734	8	14 10s. 10d.
1734	1735	4	12 15s. 0d.
1735	1736	8	13 2s. 2d.
1736	1737	6	12 6s. 8d.
1737	1738	27	12 13s. 11d.
1738	1739	9	13 10s. 4d.
1739	1740	13	15 14s. 5d.
1740	1741	–	
1741	1742	8	16 15s. 0d.
1742	1743	6	23 5s. 5d.
1743	1744	3	16 16s. 8d.
1744	1745	14	19 1s. 9d.
1745	1746	3	18 7s. 8d.
1746	1747	1	16 3s. 4d
1747	1748	5	17 4s. 4d.
1748	1749	–	
1749	1750	83	24 0s. 0d.
1750	1751	2	26 13s. 4d.
1751	1752	–	

1752	1753	1	17 6s. 0d.
1753	1754	–	
1754	1755	3	19 10s. 0d.
1755	1756	2	18 3s. 0d.
1756	1757	6	19 16s. 0d.
1757	1758	3	17 14s. 0d.
1758	1759	3	18 6s. 0d.
1759	1760	2	17 8s. 0d.
1760	1761	12	17 2s. 0d.

REFERENCES AND NOTES

References

I. Manuscript Sources

CP: Culloden Papers. National Library of Scotland.

KP: Knockbuy Papers. In the possession of Miss Campbell of Kilberry, F.S.A. KP/R refers to two volumes of rentals and accounts kept by Archibald Campbell of Knockbuy from 1728 to 1788.

ICP: Inveraray Castle Papers. Lack of a detailed catalogue makes precise references sometimes impossible, but the following abbreviations will be found useful as aids to identifying sources used here:

M and V preceding a number indicate a volume of papers in the Muniment Room and the Vault respectively. M is also used in combination with the following letters to indicate a volume or a type of material in the Muniment Room:

Ac: Accounts (in bound volumes). A date is usually added.

G: Genealogical material in box-files.

L: Loose papers awaiting classification.

R: Rentals (in bound volumes). A date is usually added.

*: This indicates papers temporarily in the keeping of the Glasgow City Archivist. As an illustration, ICP/M–Ac 1743 refers to a bound volume of estate accounts dated 1743 in the Muniment Room of Inveraray Castle.

SAL: Saltoun Collection. National Library of Scotland. Boxes of papers are identified by number.

SL: Letter books of James and Archibald Campbell of Stonefield. Scottish Record Office. G.D. 14/10. 3 vols.

TRANS: Transcripts made by the 10th Duke of Argyll from original papers and kept in black binders in Inveraray Castle.

II. Printed Sources

Anderson, James: *An Account of the Present State of the Hebrides*. Edinburgh, 1785.
Argyll, George 8th Duke of: *Scotland As It Was and As It Is*, 2nd edn. Edinburgh, 1887.
Arnot, Hugh: *The History of Edinburgh*. Edinburgh, 1818.
Beveridge, W.: *Prices and Wages in England*, vol. 1: *Price Tables*. London, New York and Toronto, 1939.
Blum, J.: *Lord and Peasant in Russia*. Princeton, 1961.
Bloch, Marc: *Caractères Originaux de l'Histoire Rurale Française*. Paris, 1931.
Buchanan, J.L.: *Travels in the Western Hebrides*. London, 1793.
Burke: *Burke's Landed Gentry*. London, 1952.
Cameron, Alasdair ('North Argyll'): 'The Lead-Mines of Strontian', *Transactions of the Gaelic Society of Inverness (1937–1941)* XXXVIII: 444-52, 1962.
Cameron, Alasdair ('North Argyll'): 'The Lead Mines of Strontian', *Oban Times*, 11 Jan 1958.
Campbell, J.L. And Thomson, D.S.: *Edward Lluyd in the Scottish Highlands*. Oxford, 1963.
Campbell, R.H.: *Scotland since 1707*. Oxford, 1965.
Chambers, J.D. And Mingay, G.E.: *The Agricultural Revolution 1750–1880*. London, 1966.
Clerk of Penicuik, Sir John: *Memoirs of the Life of Sir John Clerk of Penicuik, Baronet*. Scottish History Society XIII, 1892.
Crofters Commission Report. Report by Duncan Forbes of Culloden to John, Duke of Argyll and Greenwich, 1737. Appendix LXXXV: 380-94, 1884.
Cregeen, E.R.: 'Reminiscences of an Argyllshire Drover', *Scottish Studies* 3: 143-162, 1959.
Cregeen, E.R. (ed.): *Argyll Estate Instructions: Mull, Morvern, Tiree 1771–1805*. Scottish History Society. Edinburgh, 1964.
Cregeen, E.R.: 'The Role of the Ducal House of Argyll in the Highlands', *History and Social Anthropology*, I. Lewis ed. London, 1968.
Duff, H.R. (ed.): *Culloden Papers*. London, 1815.
Exhibits: *Exhibits in the Cause Allan McLean of Drimmin against John Duke of Argyll*. In the Brown Library, Inveraray Castle. n.d.
Fergusson, Sir James: *Argyll in the Forty-Five*. London, 1951.
Gille, Bertrand: *Histoire Economique et Sociale de la Russie*. Paris, 1949.
Grant, I.F.: *Everyday Life on an Old Highland Farm*. London, 1924.
Grant, I.F.: *Social and Economic History of Scotland*. London and Edinburgh, 1930.
Grant, I.F.: *The MacLeods: the History of a Clan*. London, 1959.
Gray, Malcolm: *The Highland Economy 1750–1850*. Edinburgh, 1957.

Habakkuk, H.J.: 'English Landownership', *Economic History Review*, 2nd series x: 2–17, 1940.

Habakkuk, H.J.: 'Economic functions of English Land-owners in the 17th and 18th Centuries' in *Explorations in Entrepreneurial History*, no. 6., 1952

Haldane, A.R.B.: *The Drove Roads of Scotland*. Edinburgh and London, 1957.

Hamilton, H.: *The Economic History of Scotland*. Oxford, 1963.

Handley, J.E.: *Scottish Farming in the 18th Century*. London, 1953.

Johnson, Samuel: *A Journey to the Western Islands of Scotland*. Glasgow, 1825.

Jones, E.L.: *Seasons and Prices*. London, 1964.

Lang, Andrew (ed.): *The Highlands of Scotland in 1750 from Manuscript 104 in the King's Library*. Edinburgh and London, 1898.

Lamont, W.D.: 'Old Land Denominations and "Old Extent" in Islay.' *Scottish Studies* 1: 183–203; 2: 86–106, 1957, 1958.

MacCormick, John: *The Island of Mull*. Glasgow, 1923.

MacDonald, James: *General View of the Agriculture of the Hebrides*. Edinburgh, 1811.

Mackenzie, A.M.: *Orain Iain Luim*. Edinburgh, 1964.

McKerral, A.: 'The Tacksman and his Holding in the South-West Highlands.' *Scottish Historical Review* 26: 10–24, 1947.

McKerral, A.: *Kintyre in the Seventeenth Century*. Edinburgh and London, 1948.

Macphail, J.R.N.: Highland Papers, vol. 1. *Scottish History Society*, 2nd series, Vol. 5. Edinburgh, 1914.

Menary, G.: *The Life and Letters of Duncan Forbes of Culloden*. London, 1936.

Mingay, G.E.: 'The Agricultural Depression 1730–50.' *Economic History Review*, 2nd series, vol. 8: 323–38, 1955–6.

Mitchell, D.: *History of the Highlands and Gaelic Scotland*. Paisley, 1900.

Mitchison, Rosalind: 'The Movement of Scottish Corn Prices in the Seventeenth and Eighteenth Centuries', in *Economic History Review* XVIII, no. 2: 278–91, 1965.

Morrison, A.: 'The Contullich Papers', *Transactions of the Gaelic Society of Inverness* XLII: 197–218, 1966.

Murray, Sir Alexander: *The True Interest of Great Britain, Ireland and our Plantations*. London, 1740.

Paton, Henry: *The Clan Campbell*. Vols. 1 and 3. Edinburgh, 1913–22.

Reid, R.C.: 'Some Letters of Thomas Bell, Drover, 1746', *Transactions of the Dumfriesshire and Galloway Natural History and Antiquarian Society* XXII, 3rd series: 177–81, 1942.

Robertson, James: *General View of the Agriculture of the County of Inverness*. London, 1808.

Scots Magazine 1740, Vol. 2.
Scots Magazine 1741, Vol. 3.
Sinclair, A. MacLean: *The Clan Gillean*. Charlottetown, 1899.
Sinclair, Sir John (ed.): *The Statistical Account of Scotland*. Edinburgh. Vol. IV, 1792; Vol. VI, 1793; Vol. IX, 1793.
Sinclair, Sir John (ed.): *General Report of the Agricultural State and Political Circumstances of Scotland*. Edinburgh, 1814.
Vernadsky, G.: *A History of Russia*. New Haven and London, 1961.
Walker, John: *Economical History of the Hebrides*. 2 vols. London and Edinburgh, 1812.
Warriner, D.: 'Some Controversial Issues in the History of Agrarian Europe', *Slavonic and East European Review* XXXII: 168–86, 1953–4.
Willcock, John: *A Scots Earl: The Life and Times of Archibald 9th Earl of Argyll*. Edinburgh, 1907.

Acknowledgements

I wish to express my sincere thanks to His Grace the Duke of Argyll for permission to carry out research into the archives at Inveraray Castle, and for much help and advice; to Miss Campbell of Kilberry F.S.A. for her generous assistance and for permission to use the Knockbuy rent-books; and to Dr I.F. Grant, Dr Christopher Smout, Mr T.W. Fletcher and my colleagues at the School of Scottish Studies, Messrs B.R.S. Megaw, John MacInnes and D.A. MacDonald for their valuable criticisms and suggestions. I have to acknowledge the kindness of the Scottish Record Office and the National Library of Scotland in granting permission to quote from documents in their keeping, and the expert assistance of members of their staffs. My thanks are also due to Captain K. Short, Chamberlain of Argyll, for his ready assistance at all times, and to Mr R.F. Dell, Glasgow City Archivist, for placing at my disposal Argyll estate documents temporarily in his charge.

NOTES

1. See Grant 1924 and McKerral 1947.
2. See Campbell, J. L. 1963: 18–21; MacCormick 1923: 113–15; Mackenzie 1964: 142–5; MacPhail 1914: 245–337; Mitchell 1900: 508–37; Sinclair, A.M. 1899: 178–253; Willcock 1907: 197–9. I have also consulted numerous documents in ICP.
3. ICP/V20–Rental 1706; Exhibits: 132 (where the tack to Cluanes is dated 1701).
4. The role of the tacksmen in providing intelligence and dealing with political and religious suspects is evidenced by many papers in SAL and SP.

5. ICP* no. 213 'A Representation of the Present State of Morverne', 30 Nov. 1719. Further evidence of the turbulence in Morvern between 1715 and 1745 comes from ICP/M–L 'Minutes of Business' 1744, and SL, particularly vol. 3: 10–12, a letter from Archibald Campbell of Stonefield to the Duke, n.d. but probably Mar. 1732. The anonymous author of *The Highlands of Scotland in 1750* gives an account of the acts of terrorism used by the Camerons to force a minister out of a farm in the neighbourhood of Fort William which had been previously in the hands of a Cameron. '... throughout all Lochaber and the adjacent wild countries, the farms have been always given to the cadets of the lesser families that are the heads of tribes, which they possess for ages without any lease, and look upon them as their right of inheritance, and when they are not able to pay their rent and are turned out, they look upon the person who takes these farms after them as usurping their right. These people have often refused to take a written lease, thinking that by so doing they give up their right of possession' (Lang 1898: 91–3).
6. Tacksmen in the South-West Highlands normally held between one and four large farms, but very much bigger holdings were to be met with in Kintyre in the seventeenth century as a result of the Marquess of Argyll's plantations (McKerral 1947: 13–14; 1948: 135).
7. Braglen's tack was recorded 25 September 1716 (TRANS. XIX, no. 13). His predecessor as tacksman of Torosay was the head of Braglen's branch of the clan, Campbell of Lochnell, whose tack commenced in 1964 (TRANS. XVII, no. 96).
8. The judicial rental of 1715 defined the pennyland in Mull as equivalent to a 16/8 land of Old Extent, the pennyland in Morvern as equivalent to a 6/8 land.
9. McKerral 1947: 13–14. For a lucid summary of the confusing land denominations in use in the Highlands see McKerral 1948: 179–81. Lamont 1957 and 1958 deals more specifically with land denominations in Islay.
10. For details of rents in money and kind payable in the barony of Ardnamurchan at the same period see Murray 1740: Plate VI – 'The Anatomie of the Parish and Barony of Ardnamoruchan and Swinard'.
11. Blum 1961: 394 ff., 414–33; Gille 1949: 118–20; Warriner 1953–4: 168 ff.
12. Grant 1930: 518–19; Gray 1957: 20–1; Morrison 1966: 211–12. The Knockbuy rentals provide abundant evidence of arrears of rent running for several years before being cleared.
13. Gray 1957: 17–18; McKerral 1947: 20–1; and 1948: 135–6; Robertson 1808: 249.
14. Habakkuk 1940 shows that large landowners in the English midland counties in the late seventeenth and early eighteenth century were buying up smaller properties in the neighbourhood of their estates and then letting farms to improving tenants at substantial rents.
15. From 1703 to 1712 inclusive £10,050 Sterling was paid to creditors of the 2nd Duke of Argyll. In this period the total revenues of the Argyll estates amounted to £52,493 (ICP/M *Abbreviats of Accompts*).
16. 'The sett of the country 1692 expired 1710, and severall proposals were made to the Duke, but still with a view to lessen the rents, but the sub-tacksmen in generall offered if the Duke would accept of them for their severall possessions they would enter into tack 19 years and pay the same rent they payed their masters, which proposals the Duke accepted' (ICP/

M–L 'A Particular State of the Lordship of Kintyre').
17. The main source for events in Morvern at this time is a series of letters from the Chamberlain of Argyll, Archibald Campbell of Stonefield, to the 2nd Duke and other persons in SL 2 and 3.
18. This conflict in interests between chiefs and landlords, which was found in many parts of the Highlands at all periods is discussed by I. F. Grant 1930: 507 ff. It is forcibly illustrated by the annotated map of Morvern and neighbouring districts in Murray 1740 (Plate 2), which shows the considerable areas in the actual occupancy ('possession') of the clan Cameron though owned by a different proprietor.
19. SL 3: 58, a letter dated 11 May 1733; also a letter dated 9 May 1748 from Airds to Lt. General Bland in SAL 406; ICP/M – L 'Minutes of Business' 1744.
20. James and Archibald Campbell successively held the post of Chamberlain of Argyll, James from 1706 to 1729, Archibald from 1729 to 1748. Both also held the appointment of Sheriff-Depute of Argyll (which was normally given to the Chamberlain of Argyll) and were commonly referred to as 'the Sheriff.' They were half-brothers, their father being Revd Alexander Campbell of Auchincloich, who lost his charge of Kilmore in Lorne in 1689 for his refusal to pray for William and Mary. James's mother was a Campbell of Dunstaffnage; Archibald's mother was of the Campbell of Breadalbane family. They traced their descent to the 2nd laird of Lochnell, who flourished in the late sixteenth century. The name of their estate in Lorne, Auchincloich, was rendered into English as 'Stonefield' and attached to their lands at Kilchamaig when the family removed to Kintyre in the seventeenth century. In contrast to their father both the sons were staunch anti-Jacobites (ICP various papers; *Burke's Landed Gentry* 1952).
21. James Campbell wrote to Lochnell in 1729 asking him to direct to him certain of his people who could not get a holding in Ardnamurchan (SL I: 195 n.d. but probably 27 Jan. 1729). About the same time he wrote to some inhabitants of Glenorchy, inviting them to settle on his lands: 'It is well known you are as responsable and as good payers of rents as any there, and I should be very sorry that a people so friendly to the name of Campbell and who, as I am informed, are as true Campbells as any of us should meet with such bad encouragement' (SL I: 195 n.d. but probably 27 Jan. 1729) See also his letter to David Campbell, 12 Feb. 1729 (SL I: 222–223).
22. A groatland was equivalent to a 4/2 land of Old Extent, that is, rather less than a third of a merkland (McKerral 1948: 181).
23. See SL 2 and 3 *passim*, but particularly letters written by Archibald Campbell on 5 Feb., 6 and 23 Mar. 1732; 22 June and 25 July 1733; 21 Mar. 1734; 6 and 14 Mar. 1735; 18 Dec. 1736; 19 Feb., 10 Apr., 10 May and 3 June 1737.
24. He is referring here to improvements being carried out in the policies at Inveraray.
25. From the Knockbuy rentals it appears that cattle prices continued at rock-bottom until 1739–40. Ballimore's report from Tiree in spring 1737 states that prices were low (CP 2970: 183).
26. The Chamberlain of Argyll was normally appointed, by virtue of his office, Collector of Cess for the county of Argyll. The profits of this appointment, which were considerable, compensated for the low salary he received as

Chamberlain and for the fact that as Sheriff-Depute he received no fees or sentence-money (SAL 406. 'Memorial... concerning the manner of levying the cess in Argyleshire' 1748). Archibald Campbell, after his resignation from his offices in 1748, came under heavy attack from a number of the landowners in Argyll and the Commissioners of Supply investigated charges that both he and his deceased brother had levied more cess than was legal over a long period of years. They were exonerated in 1754 but Archibald Campbell accepted the Duke's advice to offer £600 to pay for a new tollbooth and court house at Inveraray, an offer which was cheerfully received by the shire (SAL 407, 412, 413, various papers).

27. There were lead-mines at Strontian, operated first by a company formed in 1724 by Sir Alexander Murray of Stanhope, proprietor of Ardnamurchan. Murray made grandiose claims for this and other mining projects in this district, describing them as 'the Greatest National Improvements this Age has produced' (Murray 1740: Plate IX). His company sold out in 1730 to the York Building Company, but it had no better success and eventually closed down in 1740, though the mines continued to be worked from time to time until the end of the nineteenth century and finally closed in 1904. At this early period they suffered badly from plundering raids by the Camerons. The miners' settlements of New York near Strontian, and that at Liddesdale in Morvern, associated with the Glendow mines, created a demand for farm produce. (Murray 1740; Cameron 1958 and 1962; SL 3 : 14 Mar. 1737; ICP/M – L 'Minutes of Business.' 1744.)

28. Further details about this enterprising laird appear in Cregeen 1959: 144–6.

29. What the sub-tenants of Mull paid the tacksmen was almost certainly the same, or nearly the same, as the rental of £669 settled for 1736–7 after the tacks came to an end, since the factor appears to have based it on rentals given in by the tacksmen (CP 2960: 31–3, Culloden to Sheriff Campbell and the Duke).

30. There were possibly as many as 400 tenants holding land in the insular districts under Culloden's 'sett'. A Morvern rental exists for 1738, but the earliest post-1737 rentals of Mull and Tiree which I have traced date from 1742 (ICP/M). They do not show, however, which tenants have leases. Information about the Tiree leases comes from ICP/V65 'State of the Farms in Tyrie', 1748. In fifty-one extant Mull leases given in 1737–8, there were approximately three small tenants to one substantial tenant (ICP/M – A29).

31. It appears that tacks may have been given in earlier times to the candidate offering the highest tack-duty (see above), but if so it was on a much-restricted scale and certainly was not such a threat to the colonists as it later became.

32. This memorial (CP 2970: 173–7) is unsigned and undated. Internal evidence indicates a date in early 1738. The author was evidently one of the inner circle of the Duke's officials or advisers, and may have been Culloden himself. If so, he was becoming aware of some of the problems the reorganisation had brought.

33. Fairly complete estate accounts exist for the Argyll lands from 1742, but not for 1720 to 1741, nor do they lend themselves, for the years 1742–8, to being used to give a comparative series of receipts from the insular

districts. This is because of the method of keeping accounts (as for example combining several years together), and also because until 1744 Mull and Tiree were under one factor, but in that year Mull was placed under the factor of Morvern and Tiree under a separate factor, so that the system of accounting was basically altered.

34. See particularly Arnot 1818: 161; Clerk 1892: 149–51, 159; Hamilton 1963: 7; Jones 1964: 138–9; Mitchison 1965: 283–8; Sinclair 1790–8, IV: 300; VI: 131–4; IX: 151–2 and 498 f.; *Scots Magazine* 1740, II: 42, 59, 191, 482–4, 577; III: 45–6, 142–3.
35. Sinclair 1790–8, VIII: 339 f. This event is described (fifty years after the event) as occurring in 1744. I take it to mean the Winter of 1744–5.
36. Arrears on the Argyll estates from 1703 to 1712 inclusive averaged £404 per annum (ICP/M *Abbreviats of Accompts*) but this did not include Kintyre. In the next ten-year period, years of fairly high arrears were 1716 (£892) and 1720 (£1,120).
37. These totals are approximations. Arrears of mainland districts are given year by year in the accounts. Those of the insular districts are aggregated for the years 1744–6 inclusive. I have assumed insular arrears to be about the same for 1744, 1745 and 1746 (known figures from the Mull and Morvern accounts suggest that this is a fair assumption), and have added to the mainland arrears for each year a third of the aggregated total of insular arrears.
38. Fergusson 1951: 207–15; Haldane 1952: 121; SAL 404 'Memorial by Airds to the Earl of Albermarle', 10 August 1746.
39. It is significant that arrears in the Duke of Argyll's lands in the parishes of Dollar and Muckart (known as 'the Campbell estate' in the accounts) were three times as great for the period 1744–7 as for the period 1741–3 (SAL 405 'Abstract of the Duke of Argyll's Accounts 1744–8').
40. ICP/V65 'Memoriall by Stonefield concerning Tyree' 1748; 'Memorial ... concerning Mull, Morvern and Tyrie', 1747.
41. Quoted from the Tiree instruction in ICP/V65. A similar instruction went out to the other factors.
42. ICP/M – L 'State of Farms in Argyll Collection that are not in tack' n.d. but *circa* 1748.
43. The factor submitted a rental in 1747 'at the rate he thinks the country may be lett reasonably' (ICP/V65). His rental amounts to £370 19s. 4d. in contrast to Culloden's rental of £533 8s. 2d., which, despite certain reductions, was still the one in use.
44. These and following details of the state of Tiree are based on Barnacarry's survey of 1748 (ICP/V65 'State of the Farms in Tyrie ...').
45. 'Except ... for its use in areas of large-scale and progressive farming like Norfolk, it does not seem that in general we can regard the lease as a very important instrument in agricultural improvement, nor its absence as a great obstacle to efficiency.'
46. The effects of clan and family rivalries in causing offers for farms to soar to unrealistic heights was noted by one of the 5th Duke's chamberlains in 1771, with reference to Mull and Morvern, 'where offers for the same land came from different people, keenly incensed against each other on account of old feuds and animosities still subsisting between their clans which, on principle of pique or revenge, carried offers beyond the real value of the subject' (Cregeen 1964: XVII, where the subject is further discussed).

7
ORAL SOURCES FOR THE SOCIAL HISTORY OF THE SCOTTISH HIGHLANDS AND ISLANDS[1]

Oral History, Vol. 2, No. 2, 1974, pp. 23-36

The School of Scottish Studies is primarily concerned with the collection and study of the oral traditions of Scotland. Its approach is very wide and comprehensive and we record many aspects of cultural life, including songs and music, beliefs and customs, tales, reminiscences and other kinds of traditional material which are characteristic of Scotland. This broad comparative approach and the field methods we use link us closely to folklore institutes like the Irish Folklore Commission, which had an important influence on the School at its inception in 1951. (Our first [Gaelic] field-worker, the late Calum MacLean, was trained by the Irish Folklore Commission before coming to work in Scotland, and several of us have been associated with it for many years.) Most of the School's research workers, however, although they represent a variety of disciplines, have a strong interest in the social and economic, as well as more specifically cultural, features of Scottish life, and thus the Sound Archive contains a great deal of material of use and value to the social historian.

Apart from this, incidental historical background and some of the other traditional material which has been recorded both in the Highlands and the Lowlands can be of immense value to historians. From the standpoint of someone whose research work in the School depends on the investigation of oral traditions and of written sources, I would like to speak about a few of these categories.

Musical traditions are, perhaps, the most fundamental in Scottish life. Music in all its forms – piping, fiddling, psalm-singing, unaccompanied songs – was much more than recreation. It was a necessity of life, indulged in not only on special occasions but at all times. Songs are crucial to understanding life at all times in the Highlands and Islands, far more so than in England, and are one of the prime sources for the historian, for they mirror the concerns of everyday life – the courtings and weddings, feuds and disasters, work and recreations, evictions and clearances which people experienced personally. Songs consoled them in their daily hardships, and were continually being sung in the home, among neighbours and at work. Many, in fact, were work-songs, and their rhythm matched the pulse of the task. One old man told me, 'In the old days that's the only thing they had, songs, and the old ones was learning the young ones'.

The bard was consequently greatly respected in the Highlands and his influence was enormous. Fear of being satirised by one of the poets was one of the characteristics of early Celtic society, and it has survived into the lifetime of old men and women of the present day. As one old man said recently:

> Well, a poet is allowed – he is not blamed for whatever he would compose. And if you're a wise man you'll never say a word to the poet in case he'll make poems to you. The sensible men, they were keeping on the poet's side, so as not to expose themselves.

Some of the bards had a keen sense of political and social satire, and their comments on contemporary events and personalities in the nineteenth century have considerable interest. More than any other source, it is the orally transmitted songs which revive much of the social scene for us – the foibles of individuals, the popular indignation felt about evictions, the hatred and scorn harboured against cruel factors and their agents, the sorrows of emigration, the humour and camaraderie of the rural township. Often the bards were far more than journalists; some were men and women of art and genius, vital to the creation and transmission of the knowledge and ideas and values of a largely non-literate society. The recording of many hundreds of their compositions, many of them unprinted, has been one of the School's major tasks.

The way in which the poets served as a kind of power-house in Highland society is illuminated by Donald Sinclair, an outstanding tradition bearer, in discussing his own township in the island of Tiree about a century ago:

> DS: But of course at one time this very township that we're in here, they were the wittiest people on the island of Tiree. And there were so many poets among them. There was sixteen poets in Balephuil at one time. But no wonder they were witty when they would sit together at night. A song was composed in five minutes. Aye, you would make your own verse and I would make a verse and inside five minutes the song was completed. They were all poets. That's why Balephuil over there is called 'the town of the poets', *Baile nam Bard* . . . Aye. And some of the houses, there were five or six poets in the one house.
> EC: Did you compose songs yourself, Donald?
> DS: Many's a time I've composed a song here and there . . . .

EC: Do you still compose?
DS: I'm too old now, too old now. But my sister was a very good poetess.

A great part of the School's collection consists of the kind of tales that Sean O'Sullivan and Alan Bruford have alluded to.[2] I do not propose to say very much about these. Some are of great length and antiquity and deal with legendary figures. Others are short anecdotes of purely local interest, and others again give an account of historical incidents and personalities which may be of great value to the historian. In each case, the story has to be evaluated critically. It may be that, though the facts presented are largely fictitious, the story conveys a great deal about contemporary popular beliefs and attitudes. The distortions which occur in a story may be very significant. A story I have recorded in Tiree tells that at one time it was the custom for the man who arrived last to pay his rent to be hanged to provide sport for the notables [?nobles] and people. On one occasion an old man arrived last, delayed 'by old age and feebleness', but he escaped hanging by denouncing one of the MacLean notables, who was in charge of the proceedings, for having failed to take vengeance for the slaying of his own grandfather by the Campbells. The notable was hanged instead.

The historical setting of this story would seem to be the 16th or 17th century, when the two clans, Campbell and MacLean, were often at feud, but before the late 17th century when the Campbell chief, the Earl of Argyll, gained possession of the island. Thereby he created a permanent legacy of resistance among the islanders, for he planted it (as well as other MacLean lands) with Campbell chieftains and their sub-tenants. They performed a similar role to that of the Scots colonists in Ireland and helped to create similar problems for the future. The intense resentment which the Campbell takeover produced in the islands has lasted up to the present, even though that clan has lost its dominance. A Mull man said to me recently: 'The Campbells are still with us but it is different. They are subdued now.' It may be impossible ever to separate the folkloristic and historical strands in this story and it is possible that no such historical incident happened in this precise way. Nevertheless, the story-teller assumes that his audience would appreciate that kinship ties demanded that a killing must be ruthlessly avenged, and for the historian it provides a fascinating glimpse into Scotland in the age of the blood feud.

The School has collected a great deal of personal reminiscence and family and local tradition. Family tradition in the Gaelic areas is remarkable for its depth and accuracy. It has often been said that most Highlanders are genealogists by nature. It is probably due not so much to nature as to the fact that in their traditional kind of society, where one's claim to status and wealth depended largely on heredity, it was vitally important to preserve one's genealogy. Even today it is quite normal to use a person's patronymic and most informants have no difficulty in tracing their forbears back five, six or seven generations. Some have inherited accounts of their forbears dating back three hundred years and more. This family lore opens up tremendous possibilities to the historian. One's informant's grasp of the patronymics of his ancestors and of those of his neighbours frequently gives easy access to very early data indeed, enables one to identify individuals who are named in 17th- and 18th-century records and vastly reduces the labour of investigating written records. Indeed it is an indispensable research tool in Highland areas where parish records may not be available until the end of the 18th century. Thus, in talking of his great uncle Malcolm MacDonald, who fought in the Peninsular War [1808–14], one of my informants normally refers to him as *Calum mac Iain 'ic Nìll,* that is 'Malcolm son of John son of Neill', and often adds [in Gaelic] for good measure 'of the black MacDonalds of Caolas'. And another old informant, speaking of his great-grandfather, John MacDonald, who suffered eviction about a century ago, called him *Iain mac Nìll 'ic Dhòmhnaill 'ic Eachainn Mhòir,* or [translated] 'John son of Neil, son of Donald, son of big Hector', and traced the history of these forbears from one farm or croft to another over a period of two centuries. One of these same informants, asked to comment on the names of sixty-seven heads of households listed in the 1851 census of his township, had information about sixty-two of them. He knew the name of the individual's father in thirty-two cases, and was able to give a great deal more detail for a considerable number. For example, [he gave] the names and occupations of grandparents and great grandparents; details of their children, their occupations, appearances and abilities – whether for example they had the second sight or composed songs, and frequently he could sing their songs, which were otherwise unknown.

One woman, recorded in the 1851 census at sixty-three years of age, was dead long before my informant was born, but by recalling her name and patronymic, he took one back to a period around 1700. [I began by citing] the name of the woman to my informant as it appears in the 1851 census:

> EC: A crofter, a widow called Mary MacDonald, aged 63; she was a widow and had one child? (PAUSE)
>
> DS: Aye, but that Mary MacDonald, it was not over here she was living. On the island, we call it Slieve, that's where her house was.
>
> EC: Was it far from here?
>
> DS: Not very far, just when you're going back home when you leave along your road, there's two houses, there's a big house. When you reach this big house on your right-hand side, down the road on your left-hand

side there's another house. Well that's where her house was. Her house was on the right-hand side where the big house is today.
EC: Do you know what her father would be called?
DS: Let me see. John.
EC: Do you know what his father's name was?
DS: James. She took the smallpox and her face was freckled owing to the smallpox. There were at that time a lot of people who had taken smallpox. And she used to be scratching her face, and her face was pockered, and they used to call her '*Màiri Bhreac*, the daughter of John James'. I've never seen the woman but I heard about her.

That is, 'speckled Mary, daughter of John, son of James', so that James must have been born about 1720. If one is studying land tenure, and the influence of kinship in land tenure, all this adds enormously to what one can get from documents such as the Parish Records, which become very sparse in the eighteenth century.

I have been making a special study of the island of Tiree in the Hebrides from oral traditions and written sources. It is fascinating to compare the different kinds of information that the written sources and oral tradition provide. The written sources are mostly connected with the administration of the island by the Duke of Argyll, and tend to reflect the attitudes of the landowner and his agents. They throw light on the progress of agricultural and general economic improvement; on the system of landtenure; on the creation of the crofting townships in the early nineteenth century and the alarming growth of the population in this period; on such events as the potato famine in the late 1840s and the heavy overseas emigration that followed, and the land troubles of the later decades of the century. Sometimes they throw a very clear light on social practices, but in general they do not reflect the attitudes and behaviour of the great mass of the population.

The oral traditions of the island record the customs and beliefs of the islanders in considerable detail, and serve to complement the written record. They provide reliable data on the history of families and communities of occupations and industries and many other aspects of life. But one has to handle oral traditions as critically as written records and be aware of their bias and omissions and distortions. So far I have found oral tradition in this island very reticent about physical suffering and poor material conditions. Remarkably little has come down about the harsh years that followed the potato famine. On the other hand there are many traditions about oppressive acts by the Duke's factors (resident officials), such as evicting blind men, requiring unpaid labour services, putting their favourites in the crofts of evicted families, and so on. It would seem that oral tradition has operated selectively to transmit lore which accorded with the islanders' ancient hostility to the Campbells for dispossessing the old lairds, the MacLeans. One is reminded of a piece of written evidence from 1771:

> The small tenants of Tiry are disaffected to the family of Argyll. In this disposition it's thought that long leases might render them too much independent of them and encourage the people to that sort of insolence and outrage to which they are naturally prone, and much incited by their chieftains of the Maclean gentry.

This undercurrent of resistance to the Campbell rule is one of the continually recurring themes found in the documents. It showed itself in the '45, when the factor was forcibly prevented from recruiting soldiers for the Government, and again in the Seven Years' War, when a company of new recruits defected when they were marched through the island of Mull. It simmered during the rest of the century but broke out again in the nineteenth century, when it combined with other social and economic ills to cause land riots. Oral tradition gives us many illustrations of this ancient hostility to the Campbells. One informant recalled a story about a certain Archie MacDonald, who flourished at the end of the 19th century and who carried his hatred and contempt of the Campbells to the limit. He rarely spoke to anyone who was not a MacDonald. When the 8th Duke of Argyll visited the island and wished to greet him, he refused:

> 'Me going to shake hands with him? Nothing of the kind!' he says. 'I'll no shake hands with a Campbell with a good heart and I'm no going to shake hands with him with a bad heart.'
>
> So he walked away. He wouldn't shake hands with a good heart . . .

He could not, he felt, make any kind of peace with the head of a clan which had massacred members of the MacDonald clan at Glencoe two hundred years before. (In another version it is the Duke's son, later the 9th Duke, whom MacDonald snubbed, but the substance of the story is the same.)

It seems sometimes that the sufferings of the people of the island in the last century have been remembered and passed on, not for their own sake but as an illustration of the wickedness of the clan Campbell. The Duke's factors are cast in the role of the arch-villains of the piece. One indeed, Malcolm MacLaurine, who flourished at the beginning of the nineteenth century, is represented in stories still current as a practitioner of the black arts. Another, John Campbell, who was in charge during the potato famine, is the most hated of all. Scurrilous songs were composed about him, and I have recorded at least one of them. Published collections of songs rarely include materlal of this kind, but popular satire constitutes one of the most important and interesting branches of oral tradition.

It is not, however, easy to use, for it contains allusions to local events, persons and customs. One Gaelic song was composed by John MacLean, Balemartin, to ridicule those of the islanders who turned out to celebrate the birth of a son to one of the factors. Part of one verse (sung here) runs, in translation:

> The factor has a strong rope coiled behind his back
> And a bundle of oats in his left hand
> As he makes for the hill
> He will put a lead on every horse with his crafty eyes.

The imagery was obscure but my informant was able, after singing the song, to explain it.

> Especially at the end of October they used to let the horses roam on the common, and when they were digging potatoes or anything like that, when the carts were full on the field, they were getting a bit of rope and they were going to catch their horse to bring the potatoes home. The *bàillidh* (factor) was just the same about the crofters. He got his own rope in his hand behind his back and the poet was meaning that he would put a halter on the crofters. They were that much under his thumb, they were only like horses in his eye. The north end people up there, they were looking up at the factor like looking up at God, but the rest of the Tiree people, they didn't care much about the factor. But the factor got all the northern people in Tiree under his thumb and they would do anything at all for the factor. And when Hughie MacDiarmid was born, that was the factor's first son, the Balevullin people and Kilmoluag people, they made a bonfire in Beinn Hough up there, rejoicing that the factor had a son. But the other townships in Tiree never bothered their arse about it.

As historical records the stories and songs are not to be taken literally – they belong after all to the realm of creative literature and art – whereas much of family history, genealogy and 'non-political' tradition can be relied upon as exact. Yet the stories are important to the historian trying to understand the society in which they were current, partly because the way in which they present events casts light on underlying attitudes and beliefs of great significance. In detail, the record of events in Tiree, given on the one hand by written sources and on the other by oral tradition will often differ; but on the basic fact of the undying hatred of many of the islanders to the Campbell regime established three centuries ago, there is basic agreement.

The written sources say a great deal about religious movements and the profound influence of evangelical forms of religious belief in the nineteenth century in Tiree. This is also apparent in oral tradition, but tradition gives greater prominence to phenomena which rarely appear in the documents – the activities of witches and supernatural beings, the visions of seers and the use of talismans and charms. So pervasive in the oral tradition of the island are stories of this kind that one can scarcely separate them as a category apart. In 1856 a sudden storm brought disaster on the fishing boats that had sailed on a fine morning from Balephuil. At least nine men were lost, and the bard, Alasdair Mòr Macdonald, composed a moving lament, only a part of which is now known. My informant, the only person who can sing this lament, in telling of the storm went on to say that it was blamed on the machinations of two local women, whom he named, one of them being a relation of his own. There was no doubt in his own mind that the accusation was true and that their motive was to rid themselves of their husbands, both of whom were drowned in the disaster.

> DS: Oh, in my time, though I'm old enough but I'm not a great age, in my time there was witches here too. Aye . . . I'm sorry to say some of my lady ancestors, they were witches too.
> EC: What kind of things could they do?
> DS: They could do anything . . . but they were blaming my great-grand-aunt here and another lady from the village down there that it was them that made the drowning disaster.

Most historians would not accept this as the true explanation of the disaster. But oral traditions of this kind perform for us the service of bringing to our attention the role played in everyday life by beliefs about the supernatural and by non-rational behaviour in general.

I have found that the oral traditions of this small island are far from uniform and undifferentiated. Some strands of tradition are much less hostile to the house of Argyll than those mentioned and tend to represent the dukes as innocent of the misdeeds of their factors, who are seen as the real villains of the piece. Again, though some stories and songs are widely known, there are traditions confined to individual little communities and families. There are differences, too, due to distinctions of status, wealth and education. The traditions of the better-off crofter class differ significantly from those of the fishermen and other cottar families. Our best tradition-bearers nowadays are usually drawn from the crofters and landless cottars, simply because theirs was a less literate culture, but it is important to maintain a balance, and to interview people whose forbears were of a higher social status.

The School of Scottish Studies has recently branched out into undergraduate teaching, and is pressing forward with the publication of archive material, both in printed form and on discs. But priority is given to collecting, since oral tradition is very much on the wane. The decline of oral tradition in the Highlands and Islands is linked with the general process of social and cultural change over the past century. The standards of industrial society have been more and more adopted by the Highlands. Customs which kept alive the inherited lore of the past, such as meeting in one another's houses to sing and talk and tell stories, have virtually died out. In this change of attitudes and customs the influence of a system of public uniform education, unresponsive to local needs, has been of great importance, and so has that of the religious movements of the nineteenth century, which frowned on secular amusements. The pressure of such powerful moral and educative forces left the poets and storytellers bereft of an audience, or, sadly, deprived them of a sense of performing a valuable function in their community. Here an old informant [Donald Sinclair] describes the change which overcame a poet in his own township:

> DS: An old poet that was in Balephuil here called Alexander MacDonald, I remember him too. Aye, he used to be going rock fishing, and I remember the way he was carrying the fishing rod, right across on his back, and his hands in his pocket. I fancy I see the old man coming from the *cairidh* [fish-trap usually built in the form of a stone wall to catch fish at the ebb tide]. And he had seven cats. It was for the sake of the cats he was going rock fishing, to get fish for the cats. And he was a good poet too. But of course in his old age he was a Christian man . . .
> EC: Did that change him at all? Did he stop writing poetry?
> DS: Oh yes, yes, he was a good man at the last.
> EC: Yes, and did he give up making poetry then?
> DS: Oh yes, yes. He was a Christian man, aye.
> EC: And did he think that it was wrong then to make songs?
> DS: Well, he was not complaining at all as long as you would compose decent songs, but he was against vulgar songs. Well, a poet can compose vulgar – it's easier for him than decent poetry.

Well, Donald should know, being a poet himself and that is perhaps why he has only on rare occasions consented to record any of his own compositions.

CONFERENCE DISCUSSION

Paul Thompson, University of Essex: We have seen this impressive range of material presented, which is much wider than the normal concerns of historians; it deals with work, domestic arrangements, inheritance, religious customs, sometimes sexual customs and so on. Clearly this is the kind of folklore material which social historians ought to use. However, when I have gone to printed folklore sources such as the County Volumes [published by The Folklore Society, London] (which admittedly go back to the 1890s), I have been frustrated to find that they do not give the basic sociological information that one needs about the social background of the informants – what their occupation was, their father's occupation, the size of their family and so on. If other social historians were going to use the School's collection, could they quite easily get at those facts?

Alan Bruford, School of Scottish Studies, Edinburgh: Usually the best way to find out your facts is to find the informant, and then look up his repertoire.

Raphael Samuel, Ruskin College, Oxford: One possible way in which stories could be used as a part of social history would be this. Although it may be the case that the storyteller has a very definite place in only a limited number of communities in Ireland, in Scotland, and in England, I think that in fact there are many more storytellers than we are aware of. Taking a quite stray example, the village postman at Norton near Banbury composes a poem I am told once a day, perhaps about something that has happened in the village in the last twenty or thirty years, and he recites these poems as he goes up and down the village street. I suspect that if the sociologists who studied the motorcar workers in Luton, as well as being interested in the affluence or otherwise of workers, were interested in factory stories, a fourth volume could have been added to their study, a volume of factory stories. Similarly, when Christopher Storm-Clark was going round from coalfield to coalfield to ask miners about work and the community, he could have simply collected stories and then printed them at the back of the book.

Again, if you want to try to find out what people thought about common rights, many stories which are apparently quite archaic, for example, about village witches, actually do have to do with issues like common rights. There are a number of stories of people who were bewitched because they refused to give an old woman some faggots. So, although the communities of your study have a much more developed storytelling tradition, nevertheless storytelling is probably universal, and should be available to anybody if they look for it. Perhaps folklore itself is much more general than folklore is sometimes made to seem, not something for which one necessarily has to go to Scotland or Ireland.

Paul Thompson: I wonder, as we have Tony Green from Leeds here, whether in fact he feels that the material that they have is comparable to what has been collected in Scotland?

Tony Green, University of Leeds: Well, yes and no. It is not comparable in bulk though we do have the advantage of that – at least our catalogue is up to date. Neither in fact is it comparable in content. You simply do not find in England the great international folktales that Sean O'Sullivan was talking about as having been collected in Ireland and Scotland. What you do find are stories of different kinds. Stories of witchcraft, jokes, anecdotes of various kinds, about work situations, about things that have happened at home – these exist in enormous numbers. The point is that the storyteller in England is in a much less socially structured position than in Ireland or Scotland and he may not necessarily be recognised. There is some limited kind of recognition in the sense that if you go into a pub, shall we say, and simply ask the barman or the landlord who is a good storyteller, he will usually be able to tell you, 'Well, probably the fellow in that seat would be.' But the whole situation is much more informal. In England it is broadly true that everyone is their own storyteller. I do not doubt that everybody in this room could quite easily tell a story of their own personal life experience. We concentrate in fact increasingly much more on urban rather than rural traditions because in our situation that seems a sensible thing to do. The oral traditions (whatever that means) began to die out in England much faster than they did in Ireland and Scotland, and it consequently seems quite logical to concentrate on new traditions that have been produced by the dynamic growth of the urban cities. We do a lot, for instance, on rumour. We have a large number of scurrilous stories, which we cannot yet publish, on the sexual proclivities of various members of the Royal Family! We have stories about hauntings, about bewitching, from urban communities too. These certainly could very well be exploited for social history, but you will not find the type of story that adds to one's documentary evidence of the rather distant past, such as Eric Cregeen has talked about. You will find much more evidence that relates to the last 50 or possibly 100 years, and certainly evidence that relates to unofficial culture today. Basically what we are concentrating on is unofficial culture today, and to that extent our collecting is sociological rather than historical.

Paul Thompson: Do you again record facts such as the occupation and family background of your informants?

Tony Green: Yes. However, one of our difficulties is the actual process of documentation. Most of our fieldwork is by students, both graduate and undergraduate, because the staff of the Institute are teachers, so the work is rather patchy; but, yes, we do attempt to insist on full documentation of informants and usually we get it.

Robin Page Arnot, University of Wales Swansea[3]: Surely there should be a clear distinction in people's minds between the folklore of England, which is the folklore of a subject class, and the folklore of Scotland, Wales and Ireland which is the folklore of a whole people that had to suffer from English chauvinism.

Tony Green: I am afraid I qualify what you are saying about English folklore. It seems to me that middle and upper class have their folklore just as the lower classes do. We have tended to concentrate on it rather less, but that is a fault of our concentration and not a fault of the informants. We ought to collect more about the middle classes.

Robin Page Arnot: There is an element of 'resistance' in the folklores of the Welsh, Scottish and Irish and there is no element of resistance of that kind in England.

Eric Cregeen: A more important distinction here is that in the countries that you have named there is probably much less in the way of a written literature, a written tradition, much more in the form of an oral tradition.[4] It was the fact that this oral tradition was dying out and threatened by the influence of modern Anglo-American culture that I think stimulated the founding of these various institutes. A sense of doom, if you like, as much as resistance.

Charles Parker, BBC: You have assumed that oral traditions in England are dead, but the fact is that they are not. For instance, working on a documentary programme on miners without any special effort I recorded 97 stories. Quite half of these dealt with death, and a superman concept of the big hero. And in the Black Country, at the moment, we are discovering an abundance of singing, which relates stylistically to the most traditional English folk music.[5]

Paul Thompson: Certainly, I understand that at Leeds Stewart Sanderson has been collecting material on department stores, and the extraordinary beliefs of their shop assistants. Wherever you get work communities you can expect this kind of lore to develop, as a new manifestation of the basic processes which produced the old traditions.

D.J. Steel, Berkshire College of Education, Reading: I myself am primarily a biographer. Can I quote one example from my own experience? I have done a certain amount of work in Ayrshire, and one of my informants gave me a complete run-down of all the farming families in the district, back to the 1750s, complete with kinship links, and a lot of which I had very painfully constructed from parish registers. Then she went on to talk about a story that her mother had told her, that *her* grandfather had told her of how, when he was a boy, his grandfather had told him that one of the origins of their family name was from the Arran name from MacMurch, Curr, Currie. The Curries had been in Ayrshire: the oldest documentary evidence was 1513 and I had a consecutive pedigree for this family in fact to about 1620. But there was oral tradition in this family that each year the Ayrshire Curries went to their Arran kinsfolk, to collect an annual consignment of whisky. Well now, working this out in rough chronology, I would imagine this must have died out about 1790, so here we have kinship links being kept up between Arran and Ayrshire from perhaps the 1400s, up to the late 1700s, and then an oral tradition of this surviving right up to nearly the present. So I wonder if this kind of memory is at all common?

Eric Cregeen: I think you were lucky in finding a MacMhurich descendant. They are perhaps the most celebrated family of *seannachies* in the Highlands, having come from Ireland originally and become seannachies [historians/tradition-bearers] to the Lords of the Isles and then later up in Uist and Skye. This is one of the very few families in Scotland from whom you could expect to find anything remotely as comprehensive as that in terms of family history. As for the comprehensiveness of our collecting on family history and land tenure, only a limited number of families have been covered in Tiree and their genealogies have been traced back to the 17th or the beginning of the 18th century in some cases. It is possible to do this, to use this technique with regard to emigration to the Lowlands, but not enough has been done yet. I think that tracing migration through families is an extremely important facet of social history that has not been anything like sufficiently stressed.

In the Lowlands, Hamish Henderson is mostly responsible for our work. He has collected a fair amount on seasonal work, particularly the work of tinkers and other travelling families.

Professor John MacQueen, School of Scottish Studies: There simply is not enough material of this kind on the Lowlands in general to be worth speaking about. We have not got a quarter as much as we would like to have, because we have only had the one field-worker.

Dr Stephen Fisher, Exeter Centre for Maritime Historical Studies: I think there might well be some discussion of this claim, or this statement, of the need for urgency. In a sense, traditions have been lost for a long time back and they are continually being lost, and continually being transmitted. However, one can see some of the arguments for saying that some of the traditions are being lost more rapidly now. You yourself said that your informants are dying out rather fast, down to the last 10 or so. Is it really as bad as that?

Eric Cregeen: There is transmission, certainly, yes, in an informal kind of way. But when the *céilidh*, this institution of meeting in the evening and talking and swapping songs and talking stories, passed away about 50 years ago, the social focus of tradition ceased.[6] You get some sort of transmission taking place, but it is not so disciplined and it loses something very much more in each generation.

George Ewart Evans, University of Leeds: Traditions have survived in Ireland, because in many parts of Ireland the material culture has remained essentially the same. You have the same methods of cultivation and the village has not broken up. But in somewhere like East Anglia there was a very dramatic changeover in 10 to 15 years, from 1950 on to 1960. All the horses went off the farm as the old horsemen retired, and you had a complete change in material culture. There is now no transmission of stories in the stable on a wet day. You get one man working a tractor now on a 200-acre farm. He and the farmer are the only people at work on the farm where previously there were 12 or 14 men. The break in tradition has been quite dramatic in East Anglia, but I think where the material culture remains the same then you can still get the retention of tradition.

Christopher Storm-Clark, University of York: Can the speakers help us on the chronological perspective that the social historian gets from the oral tradition? Clearly if you were to record, for sociological purposes, the fifty least dirty stories of Leeds commercial travellers, it would have a chronological perspective, because their stories would concern motor cars and road-houses. But we are really talking about recording the 'traditional way of life'. Is this oral tradition about the way of life in the late 19th century, or have there been distinctive changes in ways of life such that some of the tradition can be generalised back to the early 19th century?

Alan Bruford: It depends on your informant. Some of our informants pass on pretty reliable things that they have heard straight from their grandparents. One of my best informants in Orkney, whom you heard talking about the shipwreck, can go back to things that he heard from his father in the 1900s. He is about 70 now, and his father was about 70 then. He was born in 1837, so that takes you back well into the 19th century. It just depends on the age of the informant and how far back their own family tradition goes.

NOTES

1. This paper was originally presented at the 1974 conference of the Oral History Society. The proceedings were edited and published by the Society's founder, Paul Thompson, of the Department of Sociology, University of Essex. Cregeen's presentation was preceded by a paper entitled 'The Archives of School of Scottish Studies' by Alan Bruford, who gave examples

of songs and stories that related to specific historical events, concluding with a comment that linked both papers: The 'relevance to Social history I leave to Eric Cregeen'. [Ed.]
2. At the time of this conference, O'Sullivan and Bruford had attained international recognition for their seminal works on the folk-tale: Sean O'Sullivan, *Folktales of Ireland,* (London & Chicago) 1966, and Alan Bruford, *Gaelic Folk-tales and Mediaeval Romances,* (Dublin) 1969. [Ed.]
3. Robin Page Arnot, born in Greenock (1890), co-founded the University Socialist Federation as a student in Glasgow University. During the Great War was imprisoned as a conscientious objector and on release became Secretary to the Labour Research Department. He was a founding member of the Communist party in 1920 and a prolific writer on the social history of the miners. [Ed.]
4. The focus of the discussion seems to have been on legend (i.e., stories told as true) rather than folktale (stories told entirely for entertainment). Possibly, because of this, there is no mention of John Frances Campbell's *Popular Tales of the West Highlands,* the remarkable four-volume collection published by Edmonton and Douglas in Edinburgh 1860–62, or of the fact that, by the turn of the 20th century, England lagged behind most of Europe in its lack of any comparable collection. [Ed.]
5. Charles Parker, along with Ewan McColl, created the groundbreaking series of documentary radio programmes 'The Radio Ballads'. [Ed.]
6. As this would suggest it had died by 1924, this is probably overly pessimistic for many parts of Gaelic Scotland. The coming of electricity in the 1950s was a significant factor in changes in lifestyle, yet, even in my own childhood and adolescence in the 1950s and 60s, the informal house-visit or *céilidh* was widespread. It was becoming evident then, however, that the focus was more on anecdotal storytelling and memorates rather than on the long tales that had once characterized these gatherings. [Ed.]

8
ORAL TRADITION AND AGRARIAN HISTORY IN THE WEST HIGHLANDS

Oral History, Vol. 2, No. 1, 1974, pp. 15-33

In thinking of historical source material, it is as well to remember that written sources and oral tradition are not necessarily mutually exclusive categories. There is an element of recorded tradition in many written sources and conversely a literary component in much tradition. The printed Minutes of Evidence taken down by the Napier Commission in 1883 from the testimonies of Highland crofters and others are a record almost entirely of oral traditions and reminiscences. Similarly, original material recorded for the School of Scottish Studies by tradition-bearers over [several] decades now exists in written publications, *Scottish Studies* and *Tocher.* Moreover, for many centuries (*pace* Dr Johnson[1]) Gaelic manuscripts have existed in the Scottish Highlands and have influenced traditional accounts, and the penetration of written material into oral tradition has grown apace during the last century of universal literature in English.

In spite of this interaction between written and unwritten accounts, it nevertheless remains true to say that, in general, in the Scottish Highlands, as in the other Celtic-speaking areas of the British Isles, oral tradition has a character of its own, markedly distinct from written sources, and leading to a conception of history in some respects fundamentally different from that produced by the records. In the past two centuries, if one excepts the publications of Gaelic scholars and folklorists, the written records have been in English, composed by people literate in that language – lawyers, officials, merchants, factors, ministers, lairds and travellers. They reflect the Highland scene as viewed and understood by observers and actors who were usually outside the community or somewhat detached from it by their status, education and outlook. Oral tradition, handed on in successive generations in the native tongue, reflects the same scene as viewed from within the community by people who shared its attitudes and values.

Until the twentieth century, society in Gaelic areas was predominantly non-literate and preserved its traditions with care. In the days of the chiefs these were transmitted by historians (*seannachies*) and bards and other men of skill in the arts, and since they were part of the retinue of chiefly families much of this lore concerned the deeds of the ruling class. The breakdown of this aristocratic society in the eighteenth century brought an end to patronage and to the existence of a privileged class of scholars and poets, but did not destroy the vigour and creativeness of native tradition. This lived on to flourish in the nineteenth and twentieth centuries at a more popular level and by more informal methods among communities of crofters and cottars. Sometimes the best tradition-bearers of recent times, whether of historical lore or of music and poetry, are found to be descended from the bards and seannachies of earlier times. In other cases, where there is no genetic inheritance, a direct personal link with members of bardic and scholarly families can be traced.

The richness and variety of this inherited lore can be appreciated even today, when it is disappearing rapidly. The efforts of a small number of scholars working on their own over the past century have ensured that a good deal will survive. More recently, the work of individual scholars like J.L. Campbell of Canna has been increasingly supplemented by collecting based in university departments, museums and other bodies. The most active body in Scotland has been the School of Scottish Studies, set up by Edinburgh University in 1951 to investigate and record such aspects of life and culture as tales, instrumental music, songs, customs, place-names and material culture. Its archive now [by the mid-1970s] contains well over four thousand hours of original recordings.

Whilst historians have had little to do with pioneering the study of oral traditions, it is clear that they have much to gain from them, for they complement the written sources in a number of ways. In the Highlands, the written sources are, on the whole, deficient in what concerns the day-to-day lives of ordinary people; oral tradition excels in precisely this kind of material. Written sources offer little biographical material about farmers, crofters, fishermen and others of minor economic standing; oral tradition preserves personal details about such individuals which may go back a hundred, or possibly two or three hundred years. A further important consideration is that the wealth of stories and songs that exists already in written form and illumines the cultural life of the Highlands can be greatly expanded from still surviving oral tradition.

Recent historians, especially perhaps those most sensitive to the claims of social justice, have banished the romantic aura in which Highland history has been so often shrouded. This is all to the good, but it seems that some of the most distinctive features of Highland life have been obscured by the darker tone which they have introduced into the picture. If one relies wholly on written sources it is easily possible to come to the conclusion that non-literate communities, living in the Highlands under material conditions so starkly depicted in government reports and the like, could not sustain a civilised lifestyle. Moreover, because of the deficiencies of the sources, one begins to think of the Highlanders after the eighteenth century as an anonymous mass of featureless peasants, passively suffering the blows of fortune and the injustices of the powerful, without sufficient initiative to comment on or react against them.

The study of oral tradition tends towards different conclusions and different emphases. The facts of poverty, eviction and emigration remain, but these same communities are seen to possess style and dignity in the midst of poverty, a rich and widely shared culture, and a complex and well-organised society which preserves the fundamental decencies of life and, as far as possible, protects the sick and aged. They frequently suffer extreme hardship and injustice, but in oral tradition they react to events in individual and positive ways. They satirise lairds and factors in song, they organise riots and demonstrations, plan emigrations, head for the Lowland harvests in hard times or the east-coast fishing, and in day-to-day affairs regulate communal activities and settle internal disputes.

The argument presented here could be supported by oral evidence drawn from a variety of Highland districts. I have chosen to use material from the outer islands of North Uist and Benbecula for a number of reasons: that it was recently collected, with specific problems in mind, that these islands have excellent tradition-bearers, some of them quite outstanding, and that I had the guidance of my colleague, Donald Archie MacDonald, who has an intimate knowledge of these islands.[2]

The broad outlines of past social and agrarian life in the Highlands emerge clearly enough from the literature. The population normally occupied one or other of two types of agricultural settlement before the nineteenth century. One type was held jointly by a number of co-tenants and was cultivated in runrig, their arable holdings lying in a number of scattered strips, which were periodically re-allocated among the tenants. The other and originally more widespread type of settlement was that associated with the farm of one of the clan gentry or tacksmen. Himself a tenant, and often a kinsman of the laird, the tacksman sub-let part of his holding to sub-tenants. These, however, rarely appear in the rentals, and the literature leaves some aspects of the system obscure: whether, for example, sub-tenants practised runrig on their arable holdings, whether and to what extent they co-operated in grazing arrangements, and whether the land in the tacksman's own possession was always separate from that of the sub-tenants. The runrig farms of the co-tenants are more fully reported on in the written sources, but even here there are important aspects of their social and agricultural organisation which are ignored in estate papers and the literature of improvement. Here I wish to illustrate the sort of contribution that traditional material can make to the study of some of the problems of each type of community.

Donald Alex MacEachan is a man in his late fifties, reared in the township of Aird in Benbecula. He acquired a remarkable amount of traditional lore from old people, notably from two old men in his township who were grandsons of the Uist bard Angus Campbell (*Aonghuis mac Dhòmhnuill 'ic Eoghainn 'ic Dhòmhnuill Ruaidh*) who was tailor to the Clanranald gentry. They used, he said, to talk of the clan battles and the local men who fought in them 'as if it was yesterday'. He has, moreover, inherited family traditions reaching back over three centuries, and although he himself is an avid reader, he has preserved intact this orally transmitted lore.[3]

> MacE: Well, my name is Donald Alexander, son of Alexander, son of Donald, son of Alexander, son of Eoghainn, son of Ian Bàn, son of Eoghainn Mòr of Drumandaraich . . .

Eoghainn Mòr came to Uist in the seventeenth century from Arisaig, to serve the chief of Clanranald. Among the forbears mentioned in his patronymic, Donald Alex said of one of them:

> MacE: There was Eoghainn, who was a soldier. He was at Culloden . . . He survived Culloden but he passed two miserable years in England after Culloden . . . in prison. And it was through Clanranald that he got out of there, that he got home. And he was slightly wounded at Culloden field and he was either taken to Leith or taken overland to London. . . I've heard that he was stripped even of his under-garments on Culloden field. And Clanranald paid some money, a kind of ransom, to get him back here to Benbecula, and he got the land free of rent from Clanranald till the day of his death. That was the pension he got, the croft that I reside on today.
> EC: The same land?
> MacE: The same land.
> EC: Is it common to find that kind of long-continued connection with a particular piece of land here?
> MacE: Oh yes, yes. There's folk in the islands here that their forbears have been in the same land for generations.
> EC: Did you hear your people talking about these traditions?
> MacE: Oh yes.
> EC: As far back as that?
> MacE: Oh yes. They knew it.
> EC: Without reference to books, or did they use books as well?
> MacE: They didn't use books.
> EC: I see. It's a family tradition?
> MacE: It's a family tradition, and all the family traditions in the islands are

the same. In my younger days, the old folk that were living at that time, they could trace their families back for generations. (SA 1973/34)

One of the most significant things to emerge from this account is the continuance of certain families in the same holdings for two or three hundred years. Eviction and emigration were familiar to the people of the Uists and Benbecula in the nineteenth century. Some townships were entirely cleared to make way for sheep farms, and the events are commemorated in oral tradition as well as in written sources. One becomes predisposed to accepting a wholly catastrophic view of Highland history as one reads, for example, the Minutes of Evidence taken by the Napier Commission in 1883. Indeed it is clear that the Commissioners themselves regarded continuity in the occupation of land as rare and had to be reminded, as we are reminded by Donald Alex MacEachan, that there were numerous families still established on the land which their ancestors had held.[4] Had there not been stability of occupation in some of the townships one could not well explain the existence of such a wealth of tradition or the survival of much of the customary way of life.

There have been large farmers known as tacksmen in the Outer Isles into the 20th century, but the old system in which sub-tenants depended on the tacksman disappeared in the middle of the nineteenth century. Donald Alex MacEachan must be one of the few [in Benbecula] who have inherited traditional lore about the way in which it operated. The farm of Nunton in Benbecula had a portion called Balfinlay which was held in this fashion by a member of the Clanranald until 1836. The sub-tenants emigrated shortly after this, evicted by Gordon of Cluny, the new laird. Donald Alex MacEachan is familiar with the names and forbears of these sub-tenants and can identify the location of their houses, and in a recently recorded account he threw light on some of the obscurities of the system, particularly in regard to the management of the arable land:

MacE: . . . the northern part of Nunton here known as Balfinlay. Balfinlay moor was cut out between fifteen or sixteen sub-tenants. And they emigrated, it was more or less a compulsory emigration about 1843.
EC: About how much land each did they have?
MacE.: They would have from twelve to twenty acres.
EC: And were they paying rent for this?
MacE: They were paying rent. They would pay the rent in cash or in labour, whichever suited.
EC: Have you any idea how many days' labour they might owe for those acres that they had?
MacE: Oh, taking the whole acreage like that, oh maybe from twenty to thirty days, a whole month.

EC: From each man?

MacE: From each man, for each holding.

EC: And this would be at certain times of the year, would it?

MacE: Mostly at the harvest time and the potato picking.

EC: Now their pieces of land, were they scattered about in a sort of runrig fashion or – ?

MacE: No, they weren't. No. It was the *machair* land that was in runrig fashion, *imirean*.

[*Machair* is grass-covered sandy land behind the shore-line.]

EC: But they had holdings that were – well not enclosed but separate?

MacE: Oh you can see them, still see them, distinguish where the boundaries were, where the marches were, by boulders of stone and remnants of sod walls.

EC: As well as these separate holdings which they had, had they also got strips down on the *machair*?

MacE: On the *machair*, yes they had.

EC: And they worked this in a runrig fashion?

MacE: In a runrig fashion.

EC: And did this mean that they would keep a certain number of pieces for one year only or for several years?

MacE: For three or four years at a time and it was changed over and new ground, well old lea that was maybe four or five years old, it would be broken up and sub-divided again.

EC: What crops were they growing on the *machair*, these sub-tenants?

MacE: Mostly barley.

EC: How many animals would they have?

MacE: About two cows per share.

EC: I see. And any sheep?

MacE: Sheep? Eight sheep per share.

EC: And horses?

MacE: They had more horses in some instances than of cattle because during the summer months they used to be working at the kelp. (S.A. 1973/38)

Written sources give much greater detail about the runrig townships than they do about the tacksmen's farms, but for comprehensive accounts of the internal organisation of such townships one has to turn to the descriptions based on fieldwork reports from oral tradition. Such are the accounts given by Alexander Carmichael in Skene's *Celtic Scotland* and in the *Crofters' Commission Report* and the unpublished report by Trefor Owen made in 1953 for the School of Scottish Studies.[5] Both deal with North Uist and particularly with the Paible district on the west coast. Carmichael's account, with a wealth of folkloristic material, is a composite one, which sometimes ignores differences in custom between one township and another. Owen's modern survey is a valuable contribution to the sociology of the Hebrides and examines the economic and social organisation, as well as the religious life, of the Paible district, focusing on the township of Kyles Paible. More recently, D. A. Macdonald and the present writer have carried out fieldwork in this and neighbouring townships, and have made a good many hours of recordings, now in the School of Scottish Studies Archive.

One of the outstanding tradition-bearers in North Uist is John Macdonald, who until his retirement in 1970 was a crofter at Kyles Paible. He is a man of wide experience in local affairs, is township clerk and serves as an assessor to the Crofters' Commission. His great-grandfather was known locally as 'the seannachie', and he himself has a remarkably retentive memory, an instinctive respect for the facts, and a gift for lucid expression both in Gaelic and English. His reminiscences and traditions concerning the township form the basis of the following very much summarised account.

The township was in the hands of a tacksman, Dr Macdonald, until 1852, and sub-tenants occupied about a quarter of the farm. From then until 1948 it was occupied jointly by six co-tenants, who were technically crofters but held their arable in runrig. In 1948 the bulk of the arable land was parcelled out in separate holdings among the co-tenants but the *machair* continued to be worked on the runrig system until 1959. John Macdonald's account embraces a period from the early 19th century until the present, but its focus is on the later 19th century, when his father was young. At this time the population of the township included the six tenants, two cottars and several squatters, with their families, a total of around a hundred people.

Like many Highland townships, Kyles Paible had arable land, grazing land, peat moss[6] and access to the sea, which gave it a basic economic autonomy, though this was never total. There were rents to be paid in money, and articles of consumption such as tea, sugar, tobacco and whisky, and raw materials such as iron and tar, which had to be imported and bought from a merchant. This expenditure was met by sales of cattle at the Lochmaddy market in July, and also, at certain periods, by the manufacture of kelp from seaweed. The rest of the community's needs in food, drink, implements, housing and labour could be largely met from its own economic resources. Extra grazing was paid for by labour, and the wintering of the township bull on the farm of the neighbouring laird of Balranald was paid for by thirteen days' labour given by each tenant at harvest-time as and when the laird required it.

Labour was no problem. The cottars rented their house-sites from the estate but had no land. In return for a sub-let of around two acres of arable land from the tenants, and grazing rights for two cows and two yearlings, a horse and ten or twelve sheep, they provided labour for herding the township animals and seasonal work at peat-cutting and harvest-time. Further labour was provided by the squatters (who also were landless but paid no rent of any kind to the estate) in return for similar arable and grazing accommodation from the tenants. The squatters too were economically important, having special skills. They included a blacksmith, a weaver and a turner who was descended from a shipwrecked Swedish sailor and whose spinning-wheels were famed over a wide area.

Kyles Paible was part of Lord Macdonald's lands until 1865, when Sir John Campbell-Orde acquired them. Rents of £10 per annum due from each tenant were reduced by the Crofters' Commission to £8 in the 1880s and remained at this level until recently [early 1970s]. The tenants gained security of tenure under the Crofters Act of 1886, but, in fact, there have been no changes in the personnel of the tenant community from 1852 until very recently, when two of the crofters gave up their holdings. John Macdonald speaks of them as 'shareholders' in English (but *cruitearan*, crofters, in Gaelic) and in some ways they resembled a company of business partners, with a joint stock of land and other assets. But the parallel is not an exact one, for, although the co-tenants co-operated for certain purposes, each had his own animals, implements, steadings and working capital, and a share of the arable land made up of strips which were distinct from those of his fellows during the growing season. It is the fine balance between the communal and the individual rights and duties, and the tension between them, that lend the greatest significance to the study of the development of such townships in the 19th and 20th centuries.

In the 18th century the communal aspects were stronger in relation to the individual. (In the township of Aird, Benbecula, there had been a township stackyard, *iodhlann*, where each tenant knew his own stacks. Today they are overshadowed, indeed eclipsed, by the individual aspect. The whole trend of 19th-century political and economic thought with its enthusiasm for individual effort and for competition was against them, and the creation of separate crofts by landlords in the early 19th century was a practical expression of this philosophy. John Macdonald's account catches the township at a stage before the claims of individualism had overpowered those of the community completely.

The settlement at Kyles Paibles consisted of a cluster of thatched houses occupying much the same site as that occupied by the tacksman and his sub-tenants in the early 19th century. John Macdonald's own house embodies, in fact, the tacksman's one-storey house. The stance of the houses was immediately south of the arable, which was sandy *machair* land fringing the seashore. There were over 250 acres of arable among the six co-tenants, though little more than a quarter would be cropped in any one year. To the south a long sea inlet, with Bayhead at its inner end, lay between the township and its inbye grazing (*gearraidh*), 240 acres of rough, peaty land, where many of the horses and cattle were grazed in summer and autumn. Beyond this, and separated from it by a stone and sod wall (the *gàradh-crìche* or *gàradh-slèibhe*) was the general hill-grazing (*sliabh* or *monadh*), ten thousand acres of rough moorland shared among ten townships, including Kyles Paible. The peat-cutting allocations and the summer pastures lay in the hill.

These, with the shore where the wrack came in, formed the natural assets of the co-tenants, and they made Kyles Paible incomparably better off than the crofting townships to the south and east, where the land was poorer and the shares smaller. It was more fortunate, too, than the neighbouring townships in the west, like Knockaline, with its twenty crofts and Balmore, with eighteen. Because of this, Kyles Paible could concentrate on agriculture and grazing, whereas the poorer townships had to gain much of their livelihood from the sea. It is noteworthy that no grievances were presented by the crofters of Kyles to the Napier Commission in 1883. Many others complained of overcrowding, insufficient land, and a lower standard of living than had existed fifty years earlier.

These assets were managed by the six co-tenants in accordance with rules laid down by the estate and conventions inherited from their forbears. The arable land was held at any one time in six separate shares made up of scattered strips or rigs, each ten to twelve yards wide and containing a quarter to half an acre. Each share was cultivated and harvested by the individual tenant for his own use and profit. His barley sheaves, for example, were tied by a distinctive band, so that, if they were scattered by a gale, he could recover them. But the method of sharing out the arable, the periodic reallocation of the rigs, and, above all, the fact that after every harvest the arable land became common grazing, open to all the township cattle, emphasised the paramount interest of the community of co-tenants. Voluntary co-operation and mutual aid were marked features of agrarian life at Kyles, as elsewhere, and help was always given by neighbours to tenants who needed it, especially at harvest-time.

John Macdonald's description of the allocation of the runrig strips is an example of the value of reminiscence to the historian, supplementing as it does the accounts given in earlier agricultural printed surveys and estate papers.[7]

> J.M.: Well, there was say about six acres of land taken in, in the one plot. Perhaps each crofter would have about two or maybe three rigs, which would amount to about eighteen rigs, maybe at times twenty-four rigs. It was shared out by marking an equal share, even they had a piece of rope measuring the width of the ground, so that each crofter

would have his equal share. And when it was measured out, a man was following the constable or the clerk or whoever it happened to be, and he was turning a sod up at every mark the constable would make. Then lots were drawn by the constable. One of the crofters just turned away for a wee while and they all put down their own ... token, and the crofter who turned his back to the remainder was called then and he was handed over the tokens, and he was placing a token on each of the rigs so that each crofter knew his own rigs. And then immediately it was done like this, each crofter was marking his own rigs with a letter, which would be maybe the first, initial letter in his surname or in his Christian name, letters A, C, D or whatever it happened to be ...

EC: Was the land variable on the *machair*?

J.M.: There's parts of land on the *machair,* say now where there's about three acres of land, you'll find that the one half of it is very good land, the other half of it is not nearly so good. This was divided up into twelve equal shares. When lots were drawn, lots were only placed on six shares, and this meant that when the six shares were marked out the crofter whose rig came right up to the centre of the area of land, he then was given the next rig beside it, and so on, and the crofter that was on the outside of the area that had been marked out was on the outside of the other area as well, which was giving them an equal share of the good and bad land ... The herdsman always had a share, but this share was usually left on the outside of the rigs altogether. The reason for doing this was to ensure that the herdsman would attend to the corners. He would not let the cattle run through the corn because his own share was on the outside. (S.A.1968/73)

This same interaction between individual and communal claims characterised the management of the animals. The sheep were marked by the crofter's proprietary ear-mark. But since the bulk of the grazing land was common grazing, the tenant's souming (*sumachadh*) or quota of animals, was laid down by the township. It was fixed at eight cows, twenty-six breeding ewes, two horses and their followers (viz., their young), but some variation in the tenants' stock was allowed by substituting one type of animal for another according to an agreed scale of equivalents (thus one horse was taken to be the equivalent of two cows, and eight sheep the equivalent of one cow). A tenant was responsible for the normal management of his animals, and his womenfolk took sole charge of the milking and dairying, but the summer and autumn grazing was managed to a large extent communally under the surveillance of a herd or *buachaille*.

Herding the township animals was made necessary by the unfenced state of the land. There was, indeed, the boundary wall made of stone and turf, delimiting the township from the general hill-common, but it could be scrambled over by the sheep and even by horses or cattle. There were sod-enclosures in the inbye common for special purposes, as for example for the lambs after they were separated from the ewes in August, and for the horses in summer and autumn, and a fold near the houses for milking on the *machaire*. But the arable was entirely unprotected. Accordingly the tenants appointed a town shepherd, *buachaille nan caorach,* to tend the sheep on the hill common from May to November and to prevent them from trespassing on to the inbye-common, as they were apt to do, especially in the day-time. A house was provided for him on the inbye common, at Ardheisker near the boundary wall, and in addition he received a small portion of arable and modest grazing rights. The appointment might continue in one family for generations. A town-shepherd was a common feature in Benbecula also, though here he was termed *coimheadach,* literally 'a watcher', and in the written sources the name 'grasskeeper' is often applied, though in older times it implied less a shepherd than a custodian of the township marches.[8]

Herds for the cattle were also appointed.[9] At Kyles there were regularly two, one for the cows and one for the calves. John Macdonald described part of the herds' duties:

> J.M.: The duties of the *buachaille*? They used to have more than one *buachaille,* especially in this township. They used to have a *buachaille* for their cows and they used to have a *buachaille* for the calves. And the calves were kept separate from the cows. And this was going back say seventy years ago. Now the cows were taken into the fold round about ten o'clock in the morning, then the *buachaille* or the herd of the calves, he was taking over the calves on to the cattle fold. And each crofter had a small gate on the side of the cattle fold and each crofter's calves would go straight to their own gate with the result that the cows were waiting on the other side of the gate for the calves. And all the crofter and his wife had to do was to let in the calves, one by one, to have their share of the milk, turn it out again and bring in another one and milk the cows then. They were only getting one half, one side of the udder to milk.
> (S.A. 1973/36)

Like the shepherd, the herds received payment in kind (a house and some arable land and grazing) and the appointment might continue for many years in one family, though the herds were engaged only for six months in each year, approximately from May 28 to November 28 (or such time as the corn and potatoes were harvested and the arable was thrown open to all the animals). At Kyles the commencing date roughly coincided with the return of the cattle from the hill pastures, where they were taken in April to be under the care of the girls of the township at the *àirigh* (sheiling). Sometimes they remained longer, well into June, if the grass was late on the *machair*. In townships without *machair* the *àirigh* period went on longer.

This system gradually broke down in the twentieth century. The shepherd's appointment ceased in 1910 when the Board of Agriculture fenced off the inbye common from the hill. The cattle-herds continued to be engaged, but the practice of paying them in money wages, which began just after the First World War, and the rapid inflation of their wages subsequently, and especially in the Second War, brought the system to an end.[x] John Macdonald here discusses the cattle-herd:

> J.M.: In the old days his wages were more or less in kind. He was given so many, so much land from the crofters to work for himself, to get so much corn and potatoes. He kept maybe a couple of cows and a horse. That was more or less his wages for the six months, up until the beginning of the first World War, that's when they started paying out money, and wages were very low and very small in those days. The cattleman usually wasn't getting more than £12 for the six months, £2 a month anyhow. But it's entirely different nowadays, crofters couldn't possibly manage to pay a cattleman to attend to their stock.
> EC: That was one of the reasons, wasn't it, for – ?
> J.M.: Oh yes, one of the reasons for stopping. The wages were getting that high. (S.A. 1968/72)

The crofters assumed the duties themselves, but finding them too burdensome, they applied in 1948 to the Land Court for apportionment, and after experiencing the convenience of separate holdings they finally, in 1959, divided the *machair* and abandoned the runrig system. It is significant that the dissolution of this traditional arrangement can be traced, at least in part, to the penetration of ideas of monetary payments into an area of the township's economy where previously payment in kind had been the rule.

Did the runrig system work well or was it as inefficient as much of the literature on improved agriculture suggests? This is a problem to which oral tradition and surviving practice can contribute. In point of productivity, the rigs at Kyles Paible, though demanding in labour, gave excellent yields. According to John Macdonald, barley sown on the *machair* normally yielded crops thirty to forty times the sowing (viz., thirty to forty hundred-weight of barley from the acre, sown at the rate of seven pecks, which is roughly one hundred-weight). Since apportionment and the consequent change in ploughing methods, the arable is now less good. Remarkably, the North Uist estate factor, in his evidence to the Napier Commission, gave it as his opinion that the runrig townships were better cultivated than the divided townships.[11]

So far as the wider social implications of runrig for the effective working of the townships are concerned, it emerges from traditional accounts that the system worked smoothly as a rule, and that any disputes which arose were usually settled without recourse to law.

The tenants and their families observed the township conventions and collaborated cheerfully. In May, when the whole community went to cut peats, the task was done together in an atmosphere of gaiety. Each household's supply of peats was cut in turn by the whole labour force. There was no scarcity of peats to sharpen the edge of rivalry. In the varied obligations which the runrig system imposed on its members, the individuals normally behaved responsibly. The pressure of public opinion, the desire for a good name and the real fear of being satirised by a local bard, were usually effective.

There were certain areas of life and work which appear to have been more sensitive and dangerous, and more productive of disputes. The exploitation of seaweed was one such area. Storms would deposit tangle and other seaweed on the shores in the winter and spring, and throughout the Hebrides it was assiduously gathered by the inhabitants and used to manure the ground. Seaweed was in fact the chief source for renewing the fertility of the soil and as such indispensable to the crofters and tenants. When it was scarce the inhabitant would cut *feamainn dubh* (black seaweed) from submerged rocks with long-handled sickles, and scour the shores in the early morning. But to ensure that crofters did not outreach their neighbours, the townships in the Paible district had a well-organised look-out system to give general warning that wrack had been washed ashore. The precious weed was then divided into shares and allocated among the crofters of each township by casting lots, under the supervision of the township constable. Years of scarcity might lead to bitter disputes and even violence. In such cases it was the duty of the township constable to try to settle matters.

The office of township or grazing constable (*maor a' bhaile*) is little noticed in histories of the Highlands, yet it is of great significance. How far back its origins go is uncertain, but it plays an important part in the time-frame illumined by oral tradition. In some areas he was appointed by the landlord to control and supervise the affairs of each township under the general eye of the ground-officer (*maor-dùthcha*). In others there were two constables, one appointed by the estate, one chosen by the crofters.[12] At Kyles Paible, the constable was elected by the co-tenants themselves and held office for three years with the possibility of being re-elected. John Macdonald, whose father was constable for many years at Kyles Paible, gives an account of the office:

> J.M.: There was a constable in the township of Kyles, a constable in the township of Knockline, Balemore and all the townships in the district of Paible in my younger days. But since then they have been changed from constables to grazing committees...
> EC: What were the duties of the constable?
> J.M.: The duties of the constable were exactly like the duties of a ground

officer, or even a policeman. You can say he had to look after all the affairs of the township and he could order the crofters to do whatever he thought was fit for doing and all the work that was needed to be done in the township. He just called a meeting and told the crofters, 'Well, you've got to go on such and such a day and gather the sheep in. You've got to go on such and such a day and attend to this fank and build it up, put it in better order', or 'attend to the cattle fold' or 'attend to the roads', the peat roads they used to have in these days. And everything like that.

EC: Was he appointed by the estate?

J.M.: He was appointed by the crofters.

EC: Oh was he? One of themselves?

J.M.: One of themselves... In this township it was more or less a constable up to shortly before the last World War.

EC: Then if there were any disputes would he settle them?

J.M.: Oh yes... If he failed to settle them the ground officer was called in. And the ground officer represented the estate and the ground officer's word was final. (S.A. 1968/73)

The constable was in effect the manager of township affairs and his authority extended over every part of its communal economic activities. Yet he was without powers of enforcement and, where he was appointed by the township, depended wholly on the consent and support of the co-tenants. The fact of tenants or crofters participating in a form of agrarian democracy, however modest, which emerges from oral testimony is a valuable corrective to the impression given by estate papers and most written sources that the whole of society in the Highlands was controlled by laird, factor and minister. Moreover, since this participation in self-government appears most clearly in runrig townships, themselves a species of survival, it may well be that it was much more widespread and fundamental before the nineteenth century swept most of the runrig system away.[13]

This account of Kyles Paible, based entirely on recorded reminiscence and tradition, is necessarily much abbreviated but probably sufficiently indicates the added depth that such sources can give to the study of Highland life. Kyles represents only one type of township. There were also crofting townships where crofters held their arable land separately but grazed their animals in common, and these were the more numerous type in the late nineteenth century. There were large farms like Nunton and Balranald, combining a market-orientated economy with a semi-feudal system of management. Material [from oral tradition] has been gathered from examples of both types of farm, notably by D.A. Macdonald at Balranald, but further investigation is needed into such aspects of social organisation as the family and household, succession and inheritance, and provision for the aged. It will be interesting to see what local divergencies occur within the more general conformities in social custom.[14]

Kyles, for example, was virtually a kinship group in which all the tenants and cottars were closely related.

> EC: When there were cottars as well as crofters did it often happen that the cottars were related to the crofters?
> J.M.: Most of them were. In fact if you go back a hundred to two hundred years, or even less than that, you will find out that even most of the crofters were related to one another.
> EC: In a township?
> J.M.: Yes. Even in this township itself. They were more or less first and second cousins, say fifty or seventy or eighty years ago. (S.A. 1973/36)

One would not necessarily find this typical of most Hebridean townships in the late nineteenth century, though it is a feature always potentially present and of great importance in earlier times. One would probably find the custom of allocating land among all one's married children to be widespread, and also that of leaving holdings to be divided among all one's children. And the joint household, combining under one roof the aged parents and one or more of the married children, with their families, may very likely turn out to be not at all the *rara avis* that some historical sociologists imagine. It is described as very common by John Macdonald and Donald Alex MacEachan, and was part of the everyday scene in Barra in the 1940s, as the parish minister, the Revd Donald Mackenzie, recounts.

The greater part of this paper has been concerned with a limited range of material referring to a historical context not too remote and vouched for by informants of proved reliability. The body of information, in each case, shows a high degree of self-consistency. But this is not always the case in the investigation of oral traditions and recollections, especially with new informants and on unfamiliar ground. Oral testimony has to be evaluated as critically as written sources. Some of the problems involved were discussed by the writer at the Leicester conference in March 1972,[15] with special reference to a project which has been in progress at the School of Scottish Studies for about three years. It has now received a generous grant from the Social Science Research Council, to enable research to be carried to completion over a further three-year period.[16]

The object of this project is to gather material for a comprehensive history of the small Hebridean island of Tiree from the late eighteenth century to the early twentieth century, and to do so by investigating both the island's oral traditions and the unusually abundant written material. It presents many problems, both practical and theoretical, but the combination of approaches and methods will, one hopes, produce a more valid history than either approach singly could possibly do. A constant process of interaction takes place as one combines, for example, the study of census lists with enquiries into family traditions and genealogies, or the use of rentals with traditional lore about the history of crofts and farms. Moreover, by juxtaposing written accounts and oral sources, it becomes possible to isolate more clearly the characteristics of the history which emerge from one and the other. There is little point in asking which is more 'true', for not only does each have its own validity and use, but in written sources and unwritten alike one can make out strands that can be described as objective and others which are interwoven with the values, beliefs and myths of a community or class, and the latter are fully as rewarding of a historian's study as the former. In the final illustration, which follows, the account given by a North Uist crofter of a land-raid made by returned soldiers shortly after the First World War on the estate of Balranald, which caused the Government to intervene and divide the estate among some fifty crofters, Donald Ewen MacDonald unconsciously reveals as much about second-sight and its influence on the community as he does about the events of the raid:

> D.E.M.: And then it was our Member of Parliament that made the start of it; he was Dr Murray. He was from Lewis. And he said, 'Well boys', he said, 'till you break the law you'll never get the land.' The land was promised to the boys when they joined the First World War; when they would come back they would get land. Anybody who had so much, the land would be taken from him and given to the ex-servicemen. So at that time there was no much going on in the whole country, work or anything, but you had to turn your hand to something. And so the boys made up to raid, as there was a raid over in Raasay before that. Yes, well, but this was the biggest in Scotland. And so we made up our mind, and I was very young at that time; I was only about twenty. So I was first to cross the border, playing the bagpipes for the boys. And I was seen twenty years [before I was born] by an old weaver before we came across. And when she saw us coming across, 'That's the very one that was leading them,' she said. 'That's the piper. And this place, the estate is finished today,' she said. And she was called Catherine MacInnes, the weaver. She could see funerals and the like of that. She saw that twenty years before I was born, and she noticed, she heard it again in 1917 and she saw the men going. She was wondering what was going to happen. And today there's fifty that got land – it was the biggest raid in Scotland.
>
> E.C.: How many took part in it?
> D.E.M.: Oh twelve altogether.

E.C.: And you were at the head of them?
D.E.M.: Aye, the piper at the head.
E.C.: What were you playing?
D.E.M.: It was a, they wanted a local tune and it was composed by an old schoolmaster at Bayhead, Donald MacLean. It was a – I could put the tune on the chanter just for a, for you . . . *[Tune played on chanter]*
E.C.: Was the laird at home at this time?
D.E.M.: Oh yes. Oh he knew we were coming; we told him that we were coming. And 'Och,' he said 'they'll do just what the other people did.' They [viz. the Raasay raiders] manured the ground you see and the first summer they got they retired and he had the place manured and he got the good of it. He [Balranald] was told when the Paible boys would come they would never give up. So they did. They went to prison for it'.

NOTES

The writer of this paper, who is on the staff of the School of Scottish Studies' has been carrying out research on the history and oral traditions of the West Highlands since 1954, but acquired his first professional experience of investigating oral tradition in the Isle of Man from 1948 to 1950, when the Manx Museum, at the instigation of the Irish Folklore Commission, began to collect the oral traditions of the island systematically. This archive now forms a very complete record of island life.

1. In his book A *Journey to the Western Isles of Scotland* (London, 1775), Samuel Johnson, who had no knowledge of the Gaelic language or literature, made erroneous, dismissive statements about Gaelic, misinforming generations of readers. [Ed.]
2. Donald Archie MacDonald was born and brought up in North Uist. He was fieldworker and lecturer at the School of Scottish Studies from 1962 to 1994. Remarkably, he recorded over 800 tapes for the archive and, specializing in traditional narrative, he set up the Tale Archive, which is an outstanding testimony to his life's work. He died in July 1999. [Ed.]
3. The excerpts given in this paper are verbatim transcripts from recordings in the School's archives. Dots indicate words omitted which do not materially affect the sense. The sound archive (S.A.) references, which are given, include the year of the recording and the serial number.
4. The following quotation is taken from the *Crofters' Commission Evidence* (Parliamentary Papers, Edinburgh 1884), vol. I, p. 823.

    Cameron:. . . surely if so many acres have been thrown out of cultivation, must it not follow that the produce of grain has decreased?

    Factor: No, not from that cause. A crofter who was a crofter fifty year ago has the same holding today. There has been nothing taken from that croft His father and grandfather had it at the same size. He had plenty of grain in the days you speak of. He has the same amount of land today, but he has not the grain.

Cameron: But I don't think we have found any man who is in the same spot and in the same circumstances as his father and grandfather?

Factor: There are a great many here.

[To head the commission the British Government selected Lord Napier whose professional life was served in India. The fact that he had no previous experience of the Highlands of Scotland may be not unrelated to an occasional lack of understanding of the Gaels or their cultural norms. [Ed.]

5. See Skene, *Celtic Scotland,* vol. III, p. 370 ff. (Edinburgh, 1880), and *Crofters' Commission Report.* Appendix, pp. 451–73 (Parliamentary Papers, Edinburgh 1884). Trefor Owen's typescript *Fieldwork in North Uist* (1953) is in the library of the School of Scottish Studies.
6. The general usage in Scotland is 'peat banks', while 'moss' is the more common expression in Ireland. [Ed.]
7. One such account is given in 'Report on Nether Lorn' (1766) in the Breadalbane Collection at the Scottish Record Office, and summarised in Malcolm Gray, *The Highland Economy,* p. 20 (Edinburgh, 1957).
8. See *Statistical Account of Scotland,* Vol. xiv, p. 197.
9. Crofting townships like Aird, with numerous crofting families and plenty of man- or child-power, did not need to engage a town-herd in the nineteenth century. Some townships appointed teenage boys as town-herds, as Kyles did for a period.
10. Trefor Owen notes that the appointment of the calf-herd ceased in 1902, when six enclosures were made in the *machaire*.
11. *Crofters' Commission Evidence* (1884), Vol. I, p. 818.
12. *Crofters' Commission Report* (Edinburgh 1884), pp. 452–454.
13. The principle of democracy among the Hebridean people was, perhaps, most evident among the St Kildans. Until they were evacuated in 1930, they held a daily 'parliament' where their elders met to discuss the concerns of their island. [Ed.]
14. At the annual meeting of the Society for Northern Studies held at Sabhal Mòr Ostaig, Skye, in 2003, a paper discussing this area was presented [Ed.]
15. This was the Oral History Conference at which this paper was originally presented.
16. This research grant enabled Cregeen to appoint a team, which, under his leadership, would eventually record, document and publish this detailed investigation. He gives more detail in 'Oral Tradition and History in a Hebridean Island', published posthumously here and in *Scottish Studies,* vol. 32. See p. 14 and his acknowledgement, p. 35. Tragically, Eric did not live to fulfill his aim. [Ed.]

9

DONALD SINCLAIR: ORAL TRADITION OF TIREE

Eric Cregeen with D.W. MacKenzie,
Tocher, No. 18, 1975, pp. 41–65

Donald Sinclair – *Dòmhnull Chaluim Bàin* as he was usually called – was born on 6 August 1885, at Balephuil in the island of Tiree, and died less than a mile from his birthplace on April 3 this year [1974]. The intervening eighty-nine years were spent, apart from his service in the navy in the first World War, almost entirely in his own island, 'low-lying Tiree of the machairs', and mostly in and about Balephuil. His father was a fisherman and tailor, and he himself would have liked to follow the sea, but family ties and the care of aged relatives kept him at home and unmarried. After schooling at Hilipol and work at herding and farming, and a spell on road- and pier-building, Donald took up the shoemaker's trade and later inherited a croft in West Hynish on the south boundary of Balephuil. He remained here until the death of his brother and an operation on his face caused him to go to live nearby with his nephew Donald Archie Kennedy and his wife Mary and their family. Here he died, and with him the island lost its strongest link with the older tradition of Gaelic song and story, and Scotland one of the finest tradition-bearers of this century.

When you first met this small, compact man with the old man's stoop, you little suspected the riches of his mind, though his eyes, which were an intense blue, conveyed intelligence, humour and reflectiveness. By 1968, when I first met him, his mind ranged less freely over the older tales he had recorded for my colleague, John MacInnes, but I was amazed by his knowledge and his tenacious memory, and fell under the spell of his songs and story-telling. Sitting beside the fire, pipe in hand, he would while away the hours for anyone willing to listen. There were tales of the *Lochlannaich* and of Finn and his warriors, of former chiefs and their feuds, and of the legendary witch, the *Cailleach Bheur* and more recent stories of the dukes and the factors and the Land-League; songs of *Donnchadh Bàn* and *Ailean Dall* and *Iain mac Ailein* and great poets from the whole Gaelic world as well as songs composed by little-known poets from his own island and township; traditions about ancestors and vanished customs, and reminiscences of his early days.

It was often Balephuil township and its people he talked about. So many poets inhabited the place, he would recall, that it was known last century as *baile nam bàrd*, 'the township of the poets'. I came to know most of these people, long dead though they were: Donald the Cooper, poet and crofter, whose brother was the famous bard, *Iain mac Ailein*; *Calum mac Iain 'ic Nìll*, Donald's colourful ancestor, who was known as 'Lancer' from his having picked up a knowledge of blood-letting in the Peninsular War; the poetess who was believed to be a witch and whose spells were blamed for the fearful storm of July 1856; and *Alasdair Mòr* MacDonald, the fisherman who taught Donald many things as a boy and who had composed the elegy on the fishermen drowned in that storm; above all, his father, *Calum Bàn*, the gentle storyteller whom Donald worshipped. And there were many others in the history of this island he told about – crofters and weavers, ministers and seers, chiefs and robbers, smugglers and shebeeners.

It was more than superb entertainment; it was true art. When he was telling of the great storm, you were there on the shore, watching the boats founder, and felt the terror and the pity of it. Then the melancholy would go from his voice, and his face would light up and his eyes shine as he recounted some wild escapade of one of his ancestors. The width of his sympathies and the rich complexity of his nature were part of his greatness as a *seanchaidh*. Within the space of an evening you saw him as the devout Christian, wondering about life and death and the judgement; as the humorist who loved to tease and outrage and mock at the *unco' guid*; the believer in charms and spells; the man of reason deprecating 'old superstitions'; the singer of songs and teller of tales; the satirical bard, reluctant to sing his own songs; the affectionate and dutiful son, recalling his parents; the boisterous, warm-hearted friend.

Such individual genius cannot be explained wholly in terms of the environment, but one cannot imagine *Dòmhnull Chaluim Bàin* except as the heir of a family tradition and family gifts shared by many of his kinsfolk dead or alive. It is worth recalling that his father, *Calum Bàn*, was one of the tradition-bearers whom the folklorist the Revd J. Gregorson Campbell, visited frequently and collected from.[1] Nor can he be thought of except in relation to a gifted island community passionately attached to song and to tradition, and still unsubjugated in his day by a rigid and unsympathetic educational system. Donald, and others who are still alive and remarkable as *seanchaidhs*, were in time to save a great part of the lore of their island and of the Highlands for posterity. I wonder if he realised this when he said: 'Isn't it queer? My voice will be heard when I'm a goner.'

Folklorist Calum Maclean visited Donald in 1953, and although

Donald was unwell and the recording was brief, he made a great impression on Calum. Donald was still living at his own croft with his brother Hector when John MacInnes recorded him in 1960. By 1966 he had moved from his house, and the later and more numerous recordings were made in his nephew's home. The care and understanding of the Kennedy family were important to Donald in these last years, and also made the task of recording him immensely easier.

The material now published has been selected by John MacInnes and myself to illustrate the main *genres* of Donald's lore – the ancient tales of a kind that were formerly common in the Highlands and Ireland; Tiree songs and songs from the general body of Gaelic composition; traditions about island life at a remote period as well as more recent ones; personal reminiscences that illuminate the more immediate scene of work and leisure, family and neighbours. Donald recorded historical information and reminiscences for me mainly in English – he was proficient in it, possibly because of his service in the navy – but the songs and much of the best of the traditional material are in Gaelic. In two of the following excerpts, we give Donald's own English version, in preference to a translation, along with his Gaelic version. It is interesting to compare them. [Any major differences in the content of the versions are pointed out in the note that follows the texts]. Revd Donald Mackenzie has helped me greatly in preparing this material for publication and my wife has provided a drawing of Donald, based on a photograph taken a few years ago. A fuller account of the man and his lore is in view, but in the meantime this brief selection is presented as a tribute to the memory of Domhnull Chaluim Bain.

All recordings unless otherwise stated were made by Eric Cregeen; transcriptions and translations by Eric Cregeen and Revd Donald Mackenzie, and revised by Donald A. MacDonald.

    E.C.: What do you usually get called in Tiree?
    D.S.: *Domhnull Chaluim Bàin.*
    E.C.: That was because your father was –
    D.S.: Was a fair man. His name was Malcolm and he was fair in the hair. *Domhnull Chaluim Bain*, that's what they call me to this very day, aye, the neighbours anyway. Some polite people call me *Domhnull Singleir* or *Mac na Ceardaich. Ach Domhnull Chaluim Bàin*, that's the name I'm more under. My father was a fair man and his name was Malcolm . . . Oh, I remember my father well and I'm not praising. He was a very nice man, aye very good-looking. He got fair hair and blue eyes and a bonnie face . . . and he was a very refined man, my father. But my mother was a big healthy woman. She would wring your neck like the neck of a hen. Oh, she was a big strong woman.

E.C.: When you were punished at home, was it your father or your mother?

D.S.: Aye, it was my father that was punishing us, and he was strapping my bottom. Aye, 'down with your trousers'. Many's a time I had to lower my trousers. But I was not a bad boy all the same. I was not often in trouble. But I was more scared of my mother than what I was of my father because she was a strong hefty woman. But she was not so refined as my father. My father was very refined. And he was always trying to help youngsters to be merry and happy. That's the style of a man he was.

– *SA 1968/248/A* Recorded by Eric Cregeen

Blar Nan Sguab

E.C.: Did you ever hear tell of the Battle of the Sheaves?

D.S.: Oh, that was at Balephuil, aye, at the beach over there . . . *Sin a' latha bha sguaib choirce gu crios a' dol ann a' cridh' an Lochlannaich. Bha na Lochlannaich an uair sin, 'nuair a bha iad a' tighinn do na h-uile dùthaich 's a' creachadh 's a' goid. Ach air an traigh sin thall, a' latha seo, chunnaic iad na Lochlannaich a' tighinn agus 'dol a' thighinn air tìr air an traigh. Ach chaich an coinneachadh. Agus 's e foghar a bh'ann agus thòisich am batal air an tràigh agus cha deach Lochlannach do na bh'ann, cha deach e as. Chaich am marbhadh air fad. 'S a sguaban coirce a bh'aig feodhainn dhiubh a's a bhatal agus bha iad 'cur na sguaibe a dh'ionnsuidh na bann ann a corp a' Lochlannaich. Nach b'e na daoine foghainteach iad? . . . Bha e 'na chleachdadh aca roimhe sin a bhith tighinn 's a' goid 's a' toirt leotha a h-uile nì a gheibheadh iad greim air, ach cha d' thàinig gin dhiubh do Thiriodh as déidh a' latha ud . . . . Dé an uine ach a bhios bhuaithe sin? Bheil tri cheud bliadhna bhuaithe sin, tha fhios gu bheil, bho'n a bha na Lochlannaich a' tighinn do na h-eileinean seo a ghoid 's a spuinneadh?*

At this time the Northmen were coming to every country to plunder and steal. But this day, on the shore over there they saw the Northmen coming and getting ready to land on the shore. There was a fight. It was harvest time and the battle began on the shore. Not a single one of the Northmen got away. They were all killed. Some of them had sheaves of corn with them in the battle and they were thrusting the sheaves right up to the band into the Northmen's bodies. Weren't they mighty men? . . . Up to this time it was their custom to come and steal and carry off everything they could lay hands on, but not one ever came to Tiree after that day . . . How long will it be since then? Will it be three hundred years – it will, surely – since the Northmen were coming to these islands to steal and plunder?

– *SA 1968/240/B*

This story is well-known in Tiree still and the setting of the battle is usually Kilmoluag on the northside of the island. J. G. Campbell collected a version of the story in 1865 in Tiree in which the Fenian warriors were the principal actors and used sheaves of corn to defend themselves whilst their weapons were brought from a dun at the other end of the island. (*Waifs and Strays of Celtic Tradition.* Argyllshire Series, no. IV, 'The Fians', 172–74). A very similar Irish version, given in the *Duanaire Finn* MS., makes Tara the setting of the battle and prefaces the battle by an account of the *Féine* hunting. When the fawn hides in a cornfield, the warriors cut the corn to find it, and when the Northmen appear in force they send Caoilte to bring their weapons and meantime slay the enemy with sheaves of corn.

> D.S.: Lord Archibald Campbell . . . was coming this day to the township and he was calling at every house. He could talk the Gaelic too . . . And he happened to come into my uncle's house and my uncle was, he was at his dinner. It was potatoes and fish he had . . . Lord Archibald says . . 'Will I have a spit of potatoes?' 'Yes, yes,' says the old fellow, 'yes and two of them. Take as many as you like.' And he lifted two spits of potato and a bit of fish. And he ate it out of his hand. 'No wonder,' he says, 'you're strong and healthy, the food you're taking.' 'I'm strong enough,' he says. 'There's not a Campbell in Argyll, I'll put the best Campbell in Argyll, I'll put him down wrestling.' 'Well,' he says, 'I'm very pleased to meet a man of your age, so hardy and healthy, in the Island of Tiree.' And he was that. He was a healthy old man.
>
> – SA 1968/247/B
>
> E.C.: Where did you hear this story about the Lochlannaich?
> D.S.: From my father. Oh, if you were living in my father's time you would get stories. He was a storyteller. He got all, every old history. And I'll tell you what sort of man my father was. He was a very pleasant man and always doing his best to entertain anybody. And down in Balemartin there, the next village, behind that hill, there was a lot of sailors and they would be away at sea during the summer and autumn. And they had small crofts you know and then they had to come home. They would come home today and tomorrow night they would be ceilidhing with my father, they were thinking that much of him.
> But of course I had a long spell in the service of certain MacNeills in Tiree, up at Greenhill, and they were not Tiree men at all. They were from Jura or Colonsay, but their father came as a schoolteacher, Gaelic and English, to Tiree. And they settled down over there and he got a croft and a house there and it was in this township that he died. Well, the family moved after that to Vaul in Tiree – that's at the east end. And later on this township up west, Greenhill is the name, was vacant and it was under offers, and the MacNeills they sent in an offer and they

got Greenhill. And seeing that I was from Balephuil they were thinking the world of me, and I was two or three years with them, and they were the best Gaelic scholars on the island . . . I was living in the house with them. Seeing that I was from Balephuil and they knew my people so well, I was like one of themselves. I got the four ends of the house, do what you like with it . . .

I was only about fifteen years of age. And there was a library of books the size of that wall, most of them Gaelic and old Gaelic. I used to be out herding cattle – they had a lot of cows – and I could bring any book at all with me out of the library to keep me going when I was herding the cows. That's where I learn my Gaelic [reading]. I might say I picked up the Gaelic myself, I learned it myself.

E.C.: Yes, because you wouldn't be taught in school?

D.S.: Oh no, I was not taught in school. And I can write the Gaelic too.

E.C.: How did you learn that?

D.S.: Oh, I pick it up like the rest. I believe it is not boasting, I believe I am the best Gaelic scholar in this township. I can read and write my own letters . . .

E.C.: And were you taken on as the herd, as the herd-boy?

D.S.: Yes, as the herd-boy . . . the pay was not much, three pounds in six months for the herd-boy and his keep. [But he received no clothing or shoes] . . . I was not handicapped as regards clothes. My father was a tailor to trade, and out of old trousers he would make me a new one. But I'm not praising my mother. He was a tailor to trade and she was not a tailoress at all, but she was better than my father at the job. She would make a far nicer job than my father. Oh, my father was full of old histories.

E.C.: Where did he get his stories from?

D.S.: Oh, from old people I suppose . . . Aye, and he used to be at the herring fishing in Mull and all over where the herring fishing was to be plentiful. Especially in Mull. And he would be there at the winter herring fishing. That's where he got most of his old stories, among the old Mull men . . . but my uncle that used to be with him, he was a Christian and he was, he didn't care about old stories nor songs or anything like that. He was a wise man, he was a Christian[2] . . . but he was not that much better a Christian than my father though he was collecting all the old folklore. And there was a man round here not very long ago, and he called on me and he said, 'Where did you get all your folklore?' 'Oh, well,' says I [winding him up[3]], 'seeing that you ask about it I'll tell you that. In every *machaire*,' says I, 'there's knolls, but there is a *machaire* over there and there's a big, big knoll, and they call it 'The Fairies' Knoll'. Well, I happened to be six months in that knoll along with the fairies. That's where I got all my information.'

– *SA 1968/240/B*. Recorded by Eric Cregeen.

A' Bhanarach Agus A' Meirleach

Tha mi dol a dh'innseadh dhuit mu'n cuairt air 'nuair a bhite 'goid a' chruidh. Bha 'ghoid sin a' dol air aghaidh aig taigh agus bho thaigh. Agus 's ann a mhuinntir Lathurna bha cuideachd mo mhathar-sa air taobh a h-athar agus a seanamhar. Agus aig an am shònraichte bha seothach bhiodh iad a' goid crodh air Diùc Earraghaidheal. Agus thachair gu robh mo shìnn-sinn-seanamhair, gu robh i 'na banaraich aig Diùc Earraghàidheal. Agus chan fhanadh na gillean a dh'fhaire dé, bha gabhail àite ach thubhairt ise an oidhche seo, 's e boirionnach sgairteil a bh'innte, 'Fanaidh mise' ars ise, 'nochd a dh' fhaire chruidh ach dé chi mi.' Agus thilg i oirre am breacan – 's e bh'aig cailleachan an àite pleidichean an uair sin, breacain a bh' aca – chuir i oirre am breacan 's rinn i air a' bhàthaich.

Shuidh i fo cheann mairt. Cha robh i fada fo cheann a' mhairt 'nuair a thàinig na mèirlich, dithis, 's bha iad a' feuchainn a' chruidh ach có'n fheadhainn a bu reamhra. Agus cà' na chur fear de na mèirlich a chorrag ach ann am beul na té bha fo cheann a' mhairt. Agus 'nuair a fhuair i greim air a chorraig, le aon *snap* thug i dheth bàrr na corraig. Theich na mèirlich. Agus as a' mhaduinn 'nuair a bha h-uile nì gu gasda thubhairt an Diùc rithe, 'Ciamar a chaich dhuit a raoir?' – 'se Seònaid a bha oirre- se cuideachd – 'a Sheònaid?'

'Chaich gu math,' thubhairt ise. 'Sin agaibh pios de mheur a' mhèirlich agus faighibh fhéin a' chòrr.'

Agus s'e tuathanach nach robh brùideil fada air falbh a bha goid a' chruidh, chionn fhuaradh e. Cha b'urrainn dha chorrag fhalach agus bha e air a bhrath. Bha sgonn eile de'n chorraig aig a Diùc. *Well*, chan eil fhios agam an deach an duine sin a' pheanasachadh. Tha mi cinnteach gun'n deachaidh.

Ach 'nuair a phòs, mo shinn-seanair Nic Chaluim seo, nighean na té a rinn ... bha 'n Diùc a sineach, 'nuair e phòs e [nighean] Seònaid Nic Chaluim, an té a thug a mheur far a' mhèirlich. Thainig e dhachaidh do Thiriodh comhla ri fear do na baillidhnich, agus ma tha mo chuimhne-sa ceart, 's e am bàillidh MacLabhruinn a thainig e dha chaidh comhla ris. Agus bha 'taigh aige thall ann a sin anns a' mhachaire lamh ri ... glé dhlùth air Taigh an Eilein mar a bheir sinn ris, *Island House*. Agus tha e tiodhlaicte ann a Sórobaidh, 's tha' chailleach a rinn an gniomh, tha i tiodhlaicte ann a Sórobaidh cuideachd.

The Dairymaid and the Cattle-Thief

I am going to tell you about the time they were stealing cattle. It was going on far and near. And my mother's people were from Lorne on her father's and her grandmother's side. And at this particular time they were stealing cattle from the Duke of Argyll. And my great-great-grandmother happened to be a dairymaid to the Duke of Argyll. The boys wouldn't stay on the look-out to see what was happening, but this night she said – she was a hardy woman – 'I'll stay tonight,' she said, 'and keep watch on the cattle and see what happens.' And she put her tartan plaid on – the women were wearing tartan plaids instead of plain ones in those days – she put her tartan plaid on and made for the byre.

She sat herself down at the cow's head. She wasn't long there before the thieves came, two of them, and they were feeling the cattle to see which were the fattest. And where did one of the thieves put his finger but in the mouth of the woman sitting at the cow's head. And when she got hold of his finger, with one snap she took off the end of it. The thieves fled, and in the morning when everything was in order the Duke said to her, 'And how did you get on last night, Janet? – she was called Janet too.

'Oh, I got on well,' she said, 'here's a piece of the thief's finger and you can find the rest of it for yourself.'

It was a farmer who lived not fearfully far away who was stealing the cattle, for he was found. He couldn't hide his finger and he was given away by it. The Duke had the other bit of the finger. Well, I don't know if that man was punished but I'm sure he would be.

But when my great-grandfather married this MacCallum woman, the daughter of the one who did . . . the Duke was present, when he married [the daughter of] Janet MacCallum, the one who bit off the thief's finger. He came home to Tiree with one of the factors, and if my memory is right it was factor MacLaurine he came home with, and his house was over there on the *machaire*, very near Island House, as we call it. And he is buried in Soroby, and the old woman who did this deed, she is buried in Soroby too.

SA 1968/247/A There may well be a folkloristic element in this story, but the details of the story are quite consistent with conditions in Argyll in the eighteenth century. Elsewhere Donald says that the Duke's name was John; 'Diùc Iain'. It is possible that Janet MacCallum as a girl was a dairymaid to John, 2nd Duke of Argyll, who died in 1743, and in whose time cattle- and horse-stealing was rife, even in the neighbourhood of Inveraray. The next Duke John was the 5th Duke, who succeeded his father in 1770 and sent factor MacLaurine to Tiree in 1800.

Marbhrann do Mhrs. Noble[4]

'Se seo bliadhna mo chlisgidh,
An ochd ceud diag, an dà fhichead 'sa trì,
'N darna miosa de'n t-Samhradh
'S an treas latha thug teann orm sgriob.
O'n a chàirich mi, ghaoil, thu
Ann an lèine do chaol-anart grinn,
'S tu gun chlaisneachd gun léirsinn
Sin an saighead tha reubadh mo chrìdh'

Leam is duilich do phàisdean
Bho'n is lag iad 's gun mhàthair ri'n cùl.
'S iad mar luing air a fuadach
Ann an anradh a' chuain far a cùrs'
Ann an cunnart gach stuaghach
Bhrist i ceanglaichean 's dh' fhuasgail an stiùir
A' chairt-iùil air a sracadh
Dh'fhalbh a' chombaist, na slatan 's na siùil.

'S i do shùil bu ghlan sealladh
'S cha robh gruaim orra mhalaidh no sgraing
'S tu bha fiughantach fialaidh
'S tu bu shìobhalta briathran is càinnt
'S i do làmh nach biodh dìomhain
'S bu ghlan obair do mhiaran gun mheang
'S ann an nochd tha mi cianail
'S e do bhàs rinn mo liathadh ro'n àm.

Thainig dìth air an fhàrdraich
Agus dh' éirich muir-bàite na còir
Thuit crann-ubhal mo ghàraidh
Agus fhroiseadh a blàth feadh an fheòir
Chaidh mo choinneal a smàladh
Bu ghlan solus a' deàrrsadh ma'n bhòrd
'S bhrist an gloin' ann am sgàthan
'S dh' fhalbh an daoimean á m' fhàinne glain òir.

Chan eil feum bhi 'g ad ionndrainn
A nis o'n a dh' fhalbh thu 's nach till
Cleas an t-seann-fhacail dhearbh-te
Dh' fhiosraich cuid gum bu shearbh e bhi fìor
Gum biodh sùil ri beul fairge
Ach cha bhi sùil ri beul reilgeadh a chaoidh
'S dh'fhàg sin mise mar bhalbhan
'S bidh mi tarruinn le m' sheanchas gu crìch.

Elegy for Mrs Noble

This year I was shaken rudely –
Eighteen hundred and two-score and three,
In the mid-month of summer
On the third day dark doom fell on me,
When I laid you, my darling,
In the shroud of the fair linen-lawn:
You there without speaking or hearing,
That's the arrow that tears at my heart.

Woe is me for your children!
Weak without a mother's support,
Like a vessel storm-tossed
In a turbulent sea off its course,
Threatened by every billow
The couples and rudder are sprung.
Torn is the chart; the masts,
The sails and the compass are gone.

Bright your eye, clear and shining,
And your brow was unlined and serene.
You were generous, kindly;
In conversing how mild was your speech.
And your hand was not idle,
Your handiwork fine and without flaw.
Tonight I am pining
Turned grey too early by your death.

The home was despoiled
When the waves all around overwhelmed.
The apple-tree in my garden has fallen
Its bloom scattered in the grass;
Extinguished my candle
That once shone so bright round the board;
The glass of my mirror is broken;
Gone the gem from my ring of bright gold.

It is useless to mourn you,
You have gone and no more will return.
The old proverb is proven
Although bitter its lesson to learn –
'Though there is hope for the missing sailor,
To hope by the graveside is vain.'
And since therefore words fail me
I shall bring my sad tale to an end.

SA 1966/107 Recorded by John MacInnes. Text transcribed and translated by Revd Donald Mackenzie [with minor amendments – ed].

Music transcribed by Alan Bruford. This elegy by John Maclean (*Iain mac Ailein, Bàrd Thighearna Chola*) for the wife of another Tiree settler in Nova Scotia has been called 'perhaps the finest in the Gaelic language' (see Cameron, *Na Bàird Thirisdeach* pp. 80–85).[5] Donald Sinclair's tune varies considerably in rhythm from verse to verse, but the notes of the basic chant vary little.

A' Chailleach Bhuana

> D.S. Am bad mu dheireadh a tha iad a' gearradh tha iad 'g a dhreasadh suas ann am paipear rìomhach. Tha iad 'g a chrochadh air a bhalla 's tha e ann a sin fad na bliadhna gus an ath bhliadhna. Tha: *good luck* ... Nuair a tha mart a' dol a bhreith tha i faotainn caigeann do na suip a bha 'sa chaillich, 's tha sin *luck* air a mhart. Ach tha moran do na rudan sin, chaneil iad ga chreidsinn an diugh. Tha 'saoghal air fas cho Gallda an diugh, cha chreid iad a's na rudan sin ann.
>
> E.C. A's an robh iad a' toirt a' chailleach do na h-eich nuair a bha iad a' dol a mach a treabhadh anns an earrach?
>
> D.S. O bha. Bha iad a' toirt rud do'n chaillich a cheud latha a thòisichadh iad air treabhadh, bha iad a' toirt leotha bad beag do'n chaillich agus bha iad 'g a toirt do na h-eich a bha 'dol a thoiseachadh ri treabhadh. Nach iad bha *superstitious*? 'S iad. Ach bha iad a' creidsinn a's na rudan sin. Tha.
>
> O bha iad air an uamhasachadh ro'n chailleach. Chaithriseadh iad an oidhche a' buain airson nach biodh a' chailleach aca. Nach iad a bha gòrach?

– SA 1971/85/A

The Harvest Maiden

> D.S. The last handful [of corn] they cut, they dress it up in pretty paper. They hang it up on the wall and it stays there all year till the next year. It's good luck ... and when a cow is going calve she gets a handful of straws from the *cailleach* and that's luck on the cow. But there's a lot of those things they don't believe in today. The world has grown so Lowland today they don't believe in those things.
>
> E.C. And were they giving the *cailleach* to the horses when they were going out in the Spring to plough?
>
> D.S. Oh yes, they were. They would give some of the *cailleach* the first day

they began ploughing, they would bring a wee bit of the *cailleach* and give it to the horses when they were going to start ploughing. Weren't they superstitious? They were that. And they were believing in those things. Yes.

Oh, they were terrified of the *cailleach*. They would stay up all night reaping so as not to have the *cailleach*. Weren't they foolish?

Donald has been talking of what he calls 'a' chailleach bhuana', the last handful of corn to be reaped on any farm or croft, and she brought good luck. But he also uses the word 'a' chailleach', for 'the carline' who brought bad luck to the last man in the township to finish his harvest. There are interesting parallels in Banks, *British Calendar Customs/ Scotland*, vol. 1, pp. 68 ff. His next story concerns the *cailleach* people were afraid of. The English version comes first, followed by a Gaelic version recorded on the same occasion which is substantially the same, apart from a few points which are noted afterwards.

Niall Og's Harvest

E.C.: And were there any sayings about the *cailleach*?
D.S.: Well, the only saying I heard about it was that everybody was doing his best so as not to have the *cailleach*. It was the last man that was finished, that man was to keep the *cailleach* . . . in his house, and he was to feed that *cailleach* the year round till next year. So if you had the *cailleach*, if you were the last finished with the harvest, that was meaning bad luck to you. So everybody was doing his best so as not to have the *cailleach*, aye. They were even, some of them, up through the night getting the harvest finished so as not to have the *cailleach*. But that was foolishness, old superstition, old superstition . . .

I remember, well it's a good many years back, and this man, he was all alone and more than likely he was to have the *cailleach*. I remember this well. And this night three boys, it was a clear moonlight night, and they were *ceilidhing* in one of the houses over there. This was the time this township was broken up into holdings and so many of the cottars they got a holding. Oh, I remember it as well as last night. This man, he was all alone, he was an old man and his family was getting old and they were married in different parts of the world. But the old man was very superstitious and he didn't like to be on the tail-end . . .

This night three or four boys got together and they said to themselves, 'Anything against going and finishing the harvest for such and such man?' 'No.' Well, when everything got quiet those three lads got away with a scythe – there were two lads and a young maid, the maid was with them – and they started cutting this plot of their neighbour and in an hour's time the job was finished, and it was tied up and made into stooks.

So the old man, he was believing in the old things and he didn't like to have the *cailleach*. So he got up early, him and his wife, and he was not going to have the *cailleach*, he was going to try and finish it himself. So off he went before his wife. When he arrived at the field it was in stooks, every straw in his croft. He looked at it. 'Well,' he says, 'the fairies were out last night. There was some good fairy behind me.' . . . He came home and his wife says to him, 'Are you back already?' 'Yes,' he says, 'the fairies were out last night. When I arrived at the field all my corn was in stooks, nice and tidy, so there was some friend behind me last night.' But he was a liberal man, he had a good idea who did his harvest home, he gave them a dram each.

A Gaelic version was recorded from Donald on the same occasion:

Bha 'm bodach seo, bha e leis fhein, cha robh aig' ach e fhein 's a bhean. Bha pairt de'n chloinn aig' ann a difir àiteachan de'n t-saoghal. 'S ann a bha, bha e pòsda dà uair 's bha dà theaghlach aige. Bha gu leòr de'n chloinn aige beò, feadhainn dhiu 'n Glaschu 's feadhainn dhiu'n Sasunn's moran dhiu 'n Ameiriga. Bha e air a chur thuige air a shon sin, bha sean chleachdadh a tighinn fainear dha, cha bu mhath leis a' chailleach a bhith aige ged a bha e sean. Ach dh'fhalbh mise an oidhche seo, mi fhein agus dà ghille eile agus bha gealach gheal ann. Aon ghille bha comhla rium agus nighean. Agus 'se 'nighean a fhuair a' speal dhuinn, a' nighean a bha seo, fhuair i dhuinn a' speal. Tha i marbh, 's tha fear a bha comhla rium marbh cuideachd. Agus rinn sinn air a' chruit aig a bhodach seo, bràthair m'athar. Agus cha robh daoine bhos an uair sin ann a seo-ach ann, cha robh taigh no nì ann. Aite fas, cha robh an t-aite ach air a bhristeadh na cruitean. Bha sinn ann a caraibh na buain aig bràthair m'athar agus chaich a buain agus a buain gu math cuideachd. Agus thainig sinn dhachaidh rathad cùil nach fhaiceadh duine sinn. Agus bha a' bhuain, bha i na h-adagan ann a siod.

'S bha seo a' cur dragh air a' bhodach, bha sean chleachdadh a' cur dragh air, cha bu mhath leis a' chailleach a bhith aige, a bhith air dheireadh. Ach dh'fhalbh e glé thrath a' s a mhaduinn agus bha e fhéin dol a dheanamh na buain. Agus nuair a ràinig e bha 'bhuain aig' ullamh agus i na h-adagan. Agus thill e dhachaidh. Agus thubhairt a bhean ris, 'An do thill thu cheana?' 'Thill,' ars esan, 'a luaidh. Bha na sibhirean a mach a raoir,' thubhairt esan. 'Dh'fhosgail a' Stalla Dhubh a raoir agus bha na sibhirean a mach,' ars esan, 'agus tha a' bhuain agam air a deanamh,' ars esan, 'cho glan agus a chunna tu riamh agus i na h-adagan, cha robh agam ach tilleadh dhachaidh. Bha,' ars esan, 'caraid agamsa an àit-eigin a raoir a sheall as mo dheigh.' *Well*, bha ùineach mór mu'n d' fhuair iad a mach có rinn a' bhuain.' Bha e co toilichte ri balach beag gun deachaidh a' bhuain a' dheanamh's nach robh' chailleach aige. Agus fhathast 's e duine beannaichte bh'ann, bha e creidsinn a's na sibhirean, ach bha e creidsinn a's a' chailleach cuideachd.

– SA 1971/85/A

[Not surprisingly, the Gaelic version adds colour and gives more detail: Donald himself was actually with the two lads who were the 'good fairies'. It was the girl who got them the scythe and the unnamed 'old man' was actually Donald's paternal uncle, Niall. The youngsters took an alternative route home so nobody would see them. There is no Gaelic reference whatsoever of 'superstition' but instead Donald points out that it was the implications of the old *custom* that bothered his uncle. The dialogue concerning the fairies is juxtaposed by Donald's comment about 'some friend' looking out for him – the tone does not give away any indication that he believes or disbelieves in fairies. English equivalents are found in remarks that allude to good fairies, guardian angels, or 'Someone up there watching over you', none of which reflect the actual faith of the speaker. Finally, as is still very common among 21st century Gaels, Donald makes a remark about the fact that his uncle's strong Christian faith was not at odds with Celtic cosmology that embraces fairies within a range of otherworldly concepts [Ed.][6]

An Corp-Creadha Mu Dheireadh

An corp-creadha mu dheireadh a chaich a dhèanamh ann an Tiriodh 's ann aig Cumhang dubh Bhaile-pheadrais a bha iad ag obair air a dhèanamh. Agus bha bodach mór làidir a sin bha aig an aon tuathanach mhór a bh'ann an Tiriodh, ann an Còrnaig. Bha e aig Iain Mac Alasdair Oig ann an Cornaig ri fasdadh. Iain Mac Alasdair Oig *was a Maclean*. Agus bha a *chousin* comhla ris aig an tuathanach sin cuideachd ann an Còrnaig. Agus aig an am a' bha sineach treud sam bith a bh'aig na tuathanaich a bu mhotha ann an Tiriodh 's ann a dh'ionnsuidh na h-Eaglais Bhric a bha iad a' dol gan creic. Agus bha 'm bodach a bha seothach, tha cuimhne agamsa gu math air, bodach làidir, thilgeadh e dheth an dà bhròig agus chuireadh e na brògan an ceanghal mu amhaich agus hdh'fhaodadh gur an leitheach eadar Tiriodh agus an Eaglais Bhreac a chuireadh e air iad. Bodach làidir, tha dùileam gu bheil mi 'ga fheitheamh.

Well, bha iad e fhéin 's a *chousin* a' falbh leis an treud a' latha seo, a *chousin* 'dol gan fhaicinn air bòrd a 's na bàtaichean comhla ris aig Sgairinnis. Agus chaidh e suas agus chunnaic e na cailleachan 's dh'aithnich e iad 's bhruidhinn e riutha 's bhrist e 'n corp' creadha. 'S thubhairt e riutha, 'Nis,' ars esan, 'ma chluineas mise nì de'n t-seòrsa seo gu bràth tuilleadh, bidh sibhse agam,' ors esan, 'agus tha fhios agaibh

Poster by Lily Cregeen, 1960

TOP. Peel Harbour, Isle of Man, with Peel Castle in the background

LEFT. Eric's grandfather, Allen Radcliffe
RIGHT. Elizabeth Radcliffe, school-teacher

TOP. Eric's brother Allan at the Old Smithy, The Cronk, Isle of Man

BELOW. The Rev. James Pentland Cregeen and his wife Elizabeth (née Radcliffe) with their children, Allan (left), Eric and Sheila on her mother's lap. (Early 1920s)

SOME OF THE AUTHOR'S MANX-SPEAKING FRIENDS IN THE ISLE OF MAN

TOP. Left to right: Zillah Sayle, Lola Kinvig, Mr & Mrs John Kinvig, Margaret Hall, 1949

BELOW. Left to right: Herbert Collister, Arthur Radcliffe, Arthur Kneale, Dennis Christian with their horses, 1941

TOP LEFT. J.F. Cowley repairing wall at Harry Kelly's cottage, Cregneash, 1949

TOP RIGHT. Esther Kaighin holding Kirsty, daughter of Eric and Lily Cregeen, 1959

BELOW. Thatched house near Sulby Bridge, 1972

TOP LEFT. 'Such men are the salt of Extra-Mural education in the Highlands ...' Tradition bearer and enthusiast, Angie Henderson, blacksmith, Isle of Mull, 1958

TOP RIGHT. Argyllshire drover Dugald MacDougall, aged ninety

RIGHT. Drove road, just above the medieval church of Kilinevair leading up and over the Leckan, 1959. The author, centre, having crossed the river by stepping stones.

TOP. Keills jetty, with Islay and Jura under snow in the distance

MIDDLE. Drove road leading from Keills jetty, Argyll

BELOW. Buttertubs, part of the drovers' route on the Rest and Be Thankful, 1959. The new road is in the foreground.

TOP. Glen Douglas, the road sometimes used by Argyll drovers

MIDDLE. Opening of Glasgow to Garnkirk Railway, 1831. By 1880 it extended to Oban and the coast, gradually resulting in the decline of droving.

BELOW. Carron Ironworks viewed from Falkirk (painting, c. 1824)

TOP. The modern era: driving Highland Cattle, Cairndow, 1957

BELOW. Eric and Lily Cregeen with their younger daughter Nicola, Auchterarder, 1966

TOP LEFT. The author, Ardura, Mull, 1959

TOP RIGHT. Working on a manuscript, early 1970s

BELOW. Eric Cregeen kept a meticulous record of fieldwork notes such as these, illustrated from one of his many notebooks.

TOP. Flailing in Argyll: John MacKinnon, Tiree, 1959

BELOW. John, 5th Duke of Argyll, 1771–1805 (by Gainsborough) is remembered in Tiree as 'the good duke' (reproduced by kind permission of Argyll Estate Trustees)

LEFT. Eric Cregeen interviewing Lachlan MacLeod, Grimsay, North Uist, 1969

BELOW. Lachlan MacLeod working with the *cas chrom*, fertilizing lazybeds (*feannagan*) with seaweed, at home in North Uist, 1970

TOP. John Macdonald, township clerk, Kyles Paible, North Uist, with his wife and Donald Archie Macdonald on the right

MIDDLE. Harvesting seaweed below. Bringing the seaweed ashore by boat, North Uist, 1979

Cutting peat, North Uist, 1979, taken during the filming of the STV production, 'The Clearances'

LEFT. Donald Ewen Macdonald, Balranald, North Uist, 1973, with the pipes with which he led the land raid

BELOW. Ploughing the *machair*, South Uist, 1979

TOP. Thatched houses, South Uist, 1979, reminded Cregeen of Manx cottages

BELOW. Burning kelp on the shore at Gribun Head, Mull (from William Daniell: A Voyage Round Great Britain, vol. III, London, 1818)

TOP LEFT. The kelp industry – 'Oral Tradition and History in a Hebridean Island'

TOP RIGHT. The drawing of Donald Morrison is based on a photograph taken in June 1976 by Mrs Anne-Berit Borchgrevink from Oslo (*Tocher*)

BELOW LEFT. Hynish West and Donald Sinclair's house, Tiree, 1971

BELOW RIGHT. Donald Sinclair, Domhnull Chaluim Bain

TOP LEFT. 'Cutting Corn in Tiree', an oil painting by Duncan McGregor Whyte, 1924

TOP RIGHT. Hector Kennedy, Hilipol, Tiree, June 1973

BELOW. Clunary weaving factory, Bridge of Douglas (south of Inveraray), was set up by the 5th Duke of Argyll to relieve hardship gu dé théid a dhèanamh oirbh – theid ur losgadh.' *Well*, riamh roimhe no 'na dhéidh cha chual' mis' iomradh air corp-creadha a bhith air a dhèanamh ann an Tiriodh.

   Ach chunnaic mi té de na cailleachan a bha 'dèanamh a' chorp-chreadhaich ach chan fhaca mi 'chailleach eile ged is ann a muinntir a' bhaile seo a bha i. Chan fhaca mi ise riamh. Bha 'n taigh aice thall mu Bhaile-pheadrais a sin. Ach a' chailleach eile, bha mi cho eòlach oirre 'sa ghabhainn. Boirionnach beag bòidheach, ach bha fìor choltas an donais oirre air a shon sin. Bha iad a' cur as a leth gur e buidseach a bh'innte. Agus 's e 'bhuidseach a bh 'innte cuideachd. Agus an call a chaidh a' dhèanamh ann am Baile-phuill, 'nuair a chaich na daoine 'bhathadh 's a thàinig a' latha mosach, bha iad a' ciallachadh gur e 'chailleach seo agus piuthar do'n té a bha comhla rithe ann an cumhang dubh Bhaile-pheadrais a' dèanamh a' chorp-chreadha, gur e sin an dà bhoirionnach a rinn a' fuadach latha Bhaile-phuill. Có dhiu bha iad 'ga chur as a leth, bha 'h-uile té dhiubh coma dhe 'n fhear a bh'aice pòsda, 's bha iad airson faotainn . . . dèanamh air falbh leis na fir . . . . Agus bha iad a' tilgeil air an dà chailleach seo gur iad a rinn a' ghaoth, chionn tha buidseach comasach cha mhór air rud 'sam bith a dhèanamh. Ni i gaoth 's ni i fiath mar is miannach leatha fhéin.

– SA 1968/245/A

The following is Donald's English version. Donald gives the identity of the man for whom the women were making the clay body as Lachlan MacQuarrie, the ground-officer in Tiree. As this English version lacks the details concerning the part played by the witches in the drowning disaster of Balephuil, the final paragraph of the Gaelic version is given in translation.

The Last Clay Image Made In Tiree

   Yes, I've seen that man. Aye, I've seen him, I remember him well. And I've seen the man that smashed the clay body too. Maclean was his name. And his cousin, MacArthur, was with him and they were going to – with a drove of cattle to Scarinish. That was the place they were shipping their cattle at the time, and a very hard job too before you would get the cattle shipped in a small boat. So they were away early, say about three o'clock in the morning. It might have been the late summer or the beginning of autumn. And when they came to this narrows at Balephetrish – there's rocks on the left-hand side when you're coming this way and there's parks and a fence on the other side, and there's a road, a good road leading beside the rocks down – well, they saw the two women and they were up among the rocks above the road.

And this old Maclean, he was a very brave man, he says, 'I wonder what are they doing up there at this time of the morning. But I'll find out,' he says. And up he went and he knew the two women, and I'm sorry to say one of the women was from this township here, and I've seen the woman, I remember her. But I've never seen the other woman but she was related to this township, though her house was over at Balephetrish. He saw what they were doing. They were making a clay body. And he asked them, 'Who you were making the clay body to?' 'MacQuarrie,' they said. 'Ah well,' he says, 'I'll sort that.' And he got hold of the clay body and he made smithereens of it. 'Now,' he says, 'if I hear anything from now on I've got my witness down here below me. You two will be burnt at the stake, so don't let me see or hear any more of this.'

Well, I believe that was the last clay body that was made on the island. But old Maclean made smithereens of it. A hardy old *bodach*, there's not his like on the island of Tiree nowadays; he was not scared of anything.

– SA 1968/245/A

The following is a translation of the last paragraph of the Gaelic version:

I have seen one of the old women who were making the clay body but I haven't seen the other woman though she was of a family that belonged to this township. I've never seen her. Her house was over at Balephetrish. But the other old woman, I was as familiar with her as I could be. A little pretty woman, but she had a really evil look about her all the same. They were saying that she was a witch, and so she was – a witch. And the disaster that befell Balephuil, when the men were drowned and the day turned bad, they were believing that it was this old woman and a sister of the one who was with her in the black narrows of Balephetrish, when they were making the clay body, that they were the two women who caused the Balephuil drowning disaster. Anyway they were blaming her. Neither of them had any great love for their husbands and they wanted to get rid of them ... And people were casting it up against these two women that it was them who caused the wind, because a witch is able to do just about anything. She'll make wind or calm just as she pleases.

– SA 1968/245/A

The Loss Of The Fishing Boats

Donald tells of the '*Fuadach*', the storm which brought disaster to the fishing boats from Balephuil on 8 July 1856.

Yes, there was a good many lost. The boat, this boat in which Maclean died of exposure – that was the husband of my grand-aunt, he died of exposure . . . the boat took a very bad sea and she took away the helmsman and the rudder and the helm. He took the helm and the rudder with him. And there was an old navy man aboard the boat and the boat was filled to the gunwales with water as you will find out in the history of this book here. This old navy man, he turned round and he says, 'Take courage men. All that was to go is gone. Bale the boat as quick as you can.' They started baling the boat and he rowed with an oar because the helmsman took the helm and the rudder when he went [overboard], and he steered the boat to Islay with the oar. And they were for a week in Islay before they came home, till a suitable day came.

And my mother remembered that day. She was a girl, a big girl at the time. And she saw two of the boats, they nearly made it. These two boats, they nearly made the harbour but it was two old men and boys that were aboard and the boys was tired pulling at the oar, so they took the wind after them and made for Islay. But a good many were – there was two boys from Sliabh up there, two brothers, they were drowned, that's two. And there was Campbell, the steersman of this boat, three. And Maclean, the father of the people that was here, that's four, and two from Moss, that's six. There was about twelve or fourteen drowned.

My grandfather, he was a very sensible man. I heard my father talking about it often. They had a boat too. The old boy got up early and he looked at the sky and he says to the boys – my father was only a boy at the time, 'I don't think we'll go fishing today at all. The day is not promising and I have a message [errand to do] up with the [wood-]turner at Sandaig, and I think I'll go up there today and I'll give the fishing a miss.' So my father and uncle and grandfather didn't went out. Well, he made up where the turner was at Sandaig, something the turner was making for him, a spinning-wheel. He got to Sandaig before the day changed and he was there till late at night before he could manage to come home. The gale came just suddenly.

– SA 1968/243/B

I heard my mother telling me that she was over here as a girl seeing the boats that was battling to come home. And outside, somewhere there, one of the boats capsized and she told me the storm was so strong if you didn't watch yourself the storm would knock you down. And wasn't it queer? They landed on a beach in Islay and there was a big house above the beach. And they went up to this big house and, oh, they were welcomed there. There was a big peat fire on and they got every comfort. And an old grey lady came up to the house and she says, 'Where are you from, poor men?' she says. 'We're from Tiree,' *thubhairt* – it was Gaelic they were speaking. 'We're from Tiree.'

'Do you know,' she says, 'a place in Tiree called the *Port Mór*, the Big Port?'

'Yes, it was the Big Port we left this morning.'

'Well,' she says, 'I knew Big Port all right. My uncle was factor in Tiree and his house was above the Big Port at Balephuil.' And she told the housekeeper, 'Now see and be good to the Tiree men. And you'll no leave here until a day comes suitable to take you home. I will no let you away till it is a good day.' And they were the best part of a week dining with the old lady.

– SA 1969/161/A

... but my uncle told me, and I'm not telling lies behind him and he's dead long ago, told to me, 'If I was there with my own boat she was quite capable of coming home, but the rig,' he says, 'that they had with the boats they wouldn't go through the wind at all.' The big sail was in the middle and a small sail was forrit. Well, in my time the big sail was forrit and the small sail aft. That's what my uncle said to me, 'My boat,' *ars esan*, 'would come home easily.'

– SA 1969/161/A. Recorded by Eric Cregeen

Oran An Fhuadaich[7]

Refrain: Tha mi fo chùram, fo mhóran cùraim
G'eil fear na stiùrach 'sa ghrunnd gun éirigh.

Seachad Colbhasa' dh'fhàs i dorcha,
Bha uisge 's stoirm ann 's bha'n fhairge beuchdaich

Tha fleasgaich 's maighdeannan taobh Beinn Hoighnis,
Cha chulaidh aoibhnis a bhi 'gan éisdeachd.

Song of the Loss

My heart is laden, so heavy laden,
The helmsman's grave's in the ocean floor-bed.

Passing Colonsay, the sky grown surly,
The rain came squalling, the sea was roaring.

The youths and maidens beside Ben Hynish,
No cause of joy was to hear them mourning.

This fragment of the song, composed about the disaster by a fisherman at Balephuil, Alasdair MacDonald, is all that Donald had of *Oran An Fhuadaich*.

D.S.: I remember him too. He used to be going rock-fishing and I remember the way he was carrying the fishing-rod, right across on his back, and his hands in his pocket. I fancy I see the old man coming from the point. And he had seven cats. It was for the sake of the cats he was going rock-fishing... And he was a good poet too, but of course in his old age he was a Christian man...

Apparently no-one else had Donald's version which adds a verse to the fragmentary song printed in Cameron, *Na Baird Thirisdeach*, with a different refrain.

– SA 1968/243/B Recorded by Eric Cregeen. Transcribed and translated by Revd Donald Mackenzie.

Traditions about the Fiann Warriors

> D.S.: 'Se Oscair an gaisgeach bu mhotha bha 'san Fhéinn riamh ach 'se Diarmad fear-claidheimh a b'fhèarr.
> JMI.: Agus an cuala sibh dad ma Dhiarmad? An cuala sibh naigheachd...?
> D.S.: Nach eil Uamh Dhiarmaid thall ann an sin an Ceann-a-Bharra?
> JMI.: A bheil?
> D.S.: Tha gu dearbh, 's a' leab' anns an robh e laighe.

> D.S.: Oscar was the greatest warrior ever in the Fiann but Diarmad was the best swordsman.
> JMI.: Did you ever hear anything about Diarmad? Did you ever hear a tale...?
> D.S.: Isn't Diarmad's cave over there in Ceann-a-Bharra?
> JMI.: Is it?
> D.S.: Yes, indeed; and the bed where he slept.

Diarmad agus Gràine

> Nach do phòs... 'se mac peathar Fhinn a bh'ann an Diarmad agus phòs Fionn a rithist agus 'se boireannach òg a phòs e, agus bha iad thall ann an Ceann-a-Bharra ann a sineach. Sin far a' robh iad,... chuid ma dheireadh de'n bhanais aca agus gu dè ach ghabh a' bhean òg aig a' rìgh, ghabh i gaol air Diarmad, agus bha i deànadh a h-uile rud a b'urrainn dhi air Diarmad 'g iarraidh air teicheadh comhla rithe. Bha Diarmad 'n a dhuine ceart 's cha teicheadh e leatha. Ach le comhnadh bean-shìdhe fhuair i ma'n cuairt air Diarmad agus dh'fholbh Diarmad leatha agus bha iad a's an Uamhaidh Mhóir ann an Ceann-a-Bharra, 's tha leabaidh Dhiarmaid a's an Uamhaidh Mhóir gus a' latha 'n diugh. Agus có gheibheadh 'g a h-ionnsaidh, mharbhadh e leis a' chlaidheamh uiread 's a thigeadh air ma faigheadh iad a stigh, chionn tha Uamhaidh, sin an doigh a's a bheil

i. Agus an oidhche seo bha e fhéin 's i fhéin – Gràine 's e sin an t-ainm a bh'air a' bhoireannach – Gràine Nighean Charmaig a' Chuilein . . . Agus thàinig an Gaisgeach seo stigh do'n Uamhaidh Mhóir an oidhche seo agus gu dé fear a bha seo-ach ach Ciuthach mac an Doill agus e air tighinn a' Eirinn agus chunnaic e solus an teine a's an Uamhaidh Mhóir agus rinn e air. Agus thòisich e air tarruinn as a bhoireannach a bha còmhla ri Diarmad agus far a chéile chaidh iad agus mharbh Diarmad e leis a' chlaidheamh.

Ach thànaig na Lochlannaich a' latha seo agus bha 'm batal ag obair air Traigh Bhì agus bha fìdeag aig Fionn ris an abradh iad An Gurra Fiugha agus cha robh aige ris an fhìdeag seo sheinn nas lugha na bhiodh e ann an éiginn mhóir, agus duine 's am bith a chluinneadh i bha aige ris a' ghairm a bha seo-ach tighinn thuice. Agus chuala Diarmad a's an Uamhaidh Mhóir an fhìdeag air a seinn agus thuirt e, 'Tha Fionn 'na éiginn,' thuirt esan, 'Bràthair mo mhàthar, agus tha mi fo chrosan 's fo gheasan gu feum mi 'n glaodh ud a fhreagairt.'

'Marbhaidh iad thu,' thuirt ise.

'Chan'eil sin go deifir,' thuirt esan, 'Feumaidh mi folbh.'

Agus dh'fholbh e agus cho luath 's a thàinig Diarmad cha robh iad fada cur crìoch air na Lochlannaich, chionn bha e math leis a' chlaidheamh – 's e duine treun a bh'ann. Ach cho luath 's a bha 'm blàr seachad dh'iarr Fionn (?iodhlach) dheanamh ma'n cuairt air ach bha ' chompanaich a' deanamh bealaich agus lig iad air folbh Diarmad, agus chuir Fionn, chuir e Bran as a dhéidh, agus chuir e Caoilte as a dhéidh an toiseach ach rachadh Caoilte dlùth do Dhiarmaid* ann – bha fhios aige gu marbhadh e e ged a bha e luath, ach chuir e seo, chuir Fionn, chuir e air folbh Bran. 'N uair a chunnaic Diarmad Bran a' tighinn sheas e agus rug iad air Diarmad, agus thog iad orra as a dhéidh sin agus 's ann do Liosmór a chaidh iad.

Agus bha gleann ann a sin agus bha torc fiadhaich a's a' ghleann nach d' thàinig duine riamh uaithe beò. Agus chomhairlich Fionn, chomhairlich e do Dhiarmad gu'm b'fheàrr dha dhol a shealg an tuirc. Agus cha robh aig' ach sleagh, agus mharbh Diarmad an torc, agus thàinig e fhéin bhuaithe beò. Agus bha Fionn air a shéideadh agus thuirt e ris, 'Tomhais an torc,' thuirt esan, 'A Dhiarmaid.' Agus thomhais Diarmad an torc. Agus fhuair e sia troighe deug ann de'n fhìor thomhas. 'Chan e sin an tomhas idir. Tomhais e rithist, a Dhiarmaid. Tomhais e,' ors esan, 'ann an aghaidh a' chuilg.' Agus bha casan Dhiarmaid ris, agus bha fhios aig Fionn gu math *spot* a bh'air bonn coiseadh Fhian [sic] na rachadh bìor 's am bith ann a sin gum biodh Dhiarmaid* marbh. 'S ann a seo a bha galair a' bhàis. Agus chaidh aon de na frioghain a bh'air an torc anns a' *spot* a bha seo – ach ann an cas Dhiarmad* 'n uair a bha e 'ga thomhas agus thuit e.

J.M.I.: Ann an cas Dhiarmaid?

D.S.: Ann an cas Dhiarmaid, agus dh'iarr e air Fionn, 'Thoir thugam làn do bhoisean,' ors esan, 'de dh'uisge a's an t-sruth agus bidh mi sàbhailte gu leòir.' Agus a h-uile uair a bha Fionn a' tighinn, 's an t-uisg' aige 'na bhoisean, bha e cuimhneachdh air Gràine agus bha e ligeil as an uisge. Agus bhàsaich Dhiarmaid.*

'Nach e siod,' ors esan ri Gràine,'bas as duilghe leat a chuala tu riamh na glaodh?'

'Chan e,' thuirt ise, 'Cha do laigh,' ors ise, 'Fionn comhla riumsa ... cha do laigh Diarmad comhla riumsa riamh nach do shìn e 'n claidheamh eadrainn. Ach 's e 'n oidhche a mharbh e Ciuthach mac an Doill as an Uamhaidh Mhóir ann an Tiriodh, sin an glaodh a bu duilghe leamsa chuala mi riamh. Mharbh thu,' thuirt ise, 'nis Diarmad agus bha e neochoireach.' Agus dh'iarr i 'n toll a chladhaich domhain agus 'n uair a bha Diarmad air a chur ann leum i fhéin ann comh' ris. Agus sin 'n uair a thuirt Oisean:

> Thiodhlaic sinn aig bun na tulaich
> An ám suidheachadh na muice fiadhaich
> Gràine, nighean Charmaig a Chuilein,
> Dà chuilean agus Diarmad.

An cuala tu sin riamh?

J.M.I.: Cha chuala riamh.
D.S.: *Well*, ' fhios aig an t-seann Tirisdeach air.

Diarmad and Gràine

Didn't he marry ... Diarmad was a son of Fionn's sister, and Fionn married a second time, he married a young woman and they were over there in Ceann-a-Bharra. That's where the latter part of their nuptials was. And it so happened that the King's young wife fell in love with Diarmad and she did everything in her power to make Diarmad elope with her. But Diarmad was an honourable man and he refused. However, with the help of a fairy woman she got round Diarmad and he went off with her and they were in the big cave at Ceann-a-Bharra, and Diarmad's bed is in the big cave to this day. And whoever would come to attack it, he would kill with the sword everyone that came upon him before they managed to enter – the cave was made like that. This night they were there, himself and herself – Graine – that was the woman's name, Gràine, daughter of Carmag of the whelp ... And this warrior came into the big cave one night, and who was this man but Ciuthach Mac-an-Doill, just come from Ireland, and he saw the firelight in the big cave and he made for it. And he began pestering the woman that was with Diarmad, and they quarrelled and Diarmad killed him with the sword.

But one day the Lochlannaich came and the battle was waged on Traigh Bhì, and Fionn had a whistle called *An Gurra Fiugha*, and he only had to sound it if he was in dire straits, and anyone who heard it, he had to rally to the call. And Diarmad in the big cave heard the whistle being sounded and he said, 'Fionn is in trouble,' he said, 'my mother's brother, and I am bound by oaths of obligation to answer that call.'

'They will kill you,' said she.

'It matters not,' said he, 'I must go.'

And off he went. And no sooner had Diarmad arrived than the Lochlannaich were despatched because he was an able swordsman – he was a valiant man. As soon as the battle was over Fionn asked them to form a (ring?) round about him, but his companions left a gap and they allowed Diarmad to escape. And Fionn set Bran after him. He sent Caoilte after him first but Caoilte would not come near Diarmad* at all – he knew that he would kill him, swift as he was, and then Fionn unleashed Bran. When Diarmad saw Bran coming he stood and he was seized. And afterwards they set off and went to Lismore.

And there was a glen there and in the glen there was a wild boar which no-one encountered and came back alive. And Fionn advised Diarmad to go and hunt the boat. Diarmad was armed only with a spear but he killed the boar and survived. Fionn was incensed and he said to him, 'Measure the boar, Diarmad,' he said, and Diarmad measured the boar. He found it measured sixteen feet exact length. 'That is not the way to measure it at all. Measure it again Diarmad. Measure it,' said he, 'against the bristles.' And Diarmad was barefooted and Fionn well knew there was a spot in the sole of Diarmad's* foot and that if any prickle were to enter it Diarmad* would die. Thus he was to receive his death blow. And one of the bristles of the boar entered the spot in Diarmad's* foot when he was measuring and he died.

J.M.I.: In Diarmad's foot?

D.S.: Yes; in Diarmad's foot, and he asked Fionn, 'Bring me the fill of your palms,' said he, 'of water from the stream and I will be quite safe.' And every time Fionn was coming with the water in his palms he was remembering Graine and he was spilling the water, and Diarmad died.

'Was not that,' he said to Graine, 'the most doleful death or death-cry that you ever heard?'

'No,' said she, 'Diarmad never lay down without placing a sword between us. But the night he slew Ciuthach Mac-an-Doill in the big cave in Tires, that was the most doleful cry I ever heard. Now you have killed Diarmad and he was innocent.' And she asked that the grave be dug deep, and when Diarmad was placed in it she leapt in along with him. Thus, as Ossian said:

We buried at the foot of the mound,
When the affair of the wild boar was settled,
Graine, daughter of Carmag of the Whelp,
Two whelps and Diarmad.

Did you hear that?

J.M.I.: No; I never did.

D.S.: The old Tiree man knows it!

*Donald says Fionn here instead of Diarmad.

– *SA 1960/70* Recorded by John MacInnes.
Transcribed and translated by the Revd Donald Mackenzie.

NOTES

1. The Revd John Gregorson Campbell was minister in Tiree from 1861 to 1891. He was born in Argyllshire in 1836, and in 1846 was sent to school in Glasgow, the only Highland boy in his class. He studied law at Glasgow University and later divinity. His correspondence with the great folklore collector, John Francis Campbell of Islay led to his association with the Duke of Argyll, who then appointed him to the parishes of Tiree and Coll, requesting that he should interview his parishioners, and write down as much as possible from living oral sources. John Gregorson Campbell is best remembered for his books, *Superstitions of the Highlands and Islands of Scotland* (Glasgow, 1900) and *Witchcraft and Second Sight in the Highlands and Islands of Scotland* (Glasgow, 1902). [Ed.]
2. 'Christian' in this context implies the experience of a spiritual conversion, rather than reference to a nominal religion. [Ed.]
3. *Editor's note*: there are numerous instances where folklorists have been spun a yarn by interviewees with a sense of sport, and clearly this was the case with Donald Sinclair. [Ed.]
4. The melody is transcribed in *Tocher,* pp. 50–51. [Ed.]
5. Though there is a slight overlap in the verses selected by E.Cregeen and D.W. MacKenzie for *Tiree Bards and Their Bardachd* (1978), the verses sung by Donald Sinclair reflect his tradition of the song. (Ed.)
6. Editor's note replaces the original in *Tocher,* which leaves readers to identify the differences and the cultural nuances implied by this account. [Ed.]
7. The melody is transcribed in *Tocher,* pp. 60–61. [Ed.]

10

DONALD MORRISON: ORAL TRADITION OF MULL

Eric Cregeen with D.W. MacKenzie,
Tocher 24, 1976, pp. 289–319

Donald Morrison is one of that diminishing race of *seanchaidhs* and storytellers who have for centuries carried on the traditions of Highland Scotland. Born at Ardtun in the Ross of Mull on 29 January 1885, his lively appearance and vigour of mind belie his ninety-two years. Although he is now a resident at 'Dunaros', the old folks' home at Salen in Mull, he seems in many ways still to be a man in the prime of life and continues to record songs, stories and other traditional lore for the School of Scottish Studies. As recently as December 1976 he recorded a fuller version of a song he first recorded in 1953 for Calum Maclean.

Donald's deepest roots are in the Ross of Mull. Here his father was a crofter and five generations of Morrisons have paid rent to the Argyll Estates. Before them a long line of Morrisons had been in the service of the Maclean chiefs. Donald was schooled at Bunessan until the age of thirteen and by then had received a good grounding in the basic curriculum and had developed a passion for literature. His schoolmaster, a Mr MacMaster from Onich, unlike many of his contemporaries, encouraged the use of Gaelic in the school and playground. Any further education Donald had was by his own efforts and by his wide reading of prose and poetry, both English and Gaelic, and, perhaps more significantly, from close contact with the living oral tradition of the older generation.

When Donald was a boy, his township of Ardtun was – despite earlier emigrations – still populous, supporting many crofter-fishermen and their families. In his lifetime on the croft he saw the scene change. The whole district of south-west Mull, with its sea lochs, bold headlands and fertile townships, was drained of its younger people and of its busy life. This island of marvellous grandeur, a land fit for the Fingalian heroes the old people spoke of, could no longer retain its children. Donald himself married a Skye girl, Kate MacRaild, and had four sons and two daughters. All his sons went away to make their way in the world. This is the usual pattern, and has been since the first World War.

Donald himself stayed in the Ross and managed the croft. Had he gone away, his natural abilities would have carried him far, for few of his generation in the Highlands have had such a combination of qualities – mental and physical vitality, a prodigious memory, a fine command of language and a sensitivity to it, a generous and independent character. But we would have lost the most outstanding living tradition-bearer in the south of Mull and Scottish studies would have been the poorer.

To meet Donald Morrison is to know that his is a unique personality. His eyes sparkle in a face full of humour and character; his conversation is racy and original without any hint of offence. He prefers to speak in Gaelic but, when he uses English, he speaks it forcefully and elegantly, often with the cadences of the Victorian stylists, but with great economy of words. He is modest, but there is an old-world dignity in his manners and bearing, and he has a sense of occasion. When the late Duke of Argyll invited him to Inveraray Castle to entertain his guests at a gathering, Donald accepted the role of *seanchaidh* as to the manner born, and won great acclaim.

The Morrisons to whom Donald is related were known as 'Clann na h-Oidhche', Children of the Night, and several generations of them served as *seanchaidhs* to the Macleans of Duart. The older form of the surname is *O Muirgheasáin*. In Donald's own account of how they first came to Mull, his ancestor was one of a band of warriors picked by *Murchadh Geàrr* to assist him in recovering the castle and lands of Lochbuie from the intruding Macleans of Duart. He acquired the nickname 'Mac na h-Oidhche' during the expedition. Donald recalls that the chiefs of Lochbuie kept up a close connection with the descendants of the original warrior-band, and, until his grandfather's time, would regularly invite the Morrisons to a great week-long New Year feast at Lochbuie.

There were other men and women of character and ability among the Morrisons. They included Mary MacDougall, composer of the hymn, *'Leanabh an Aigh'*, ['Child in a Manger'], a Morrison on her mother's side, and her brother, Duncan, hymn-writer and poet, and the more famous David Livingstone, missionary and explorer, who was the grandson of Niall Livingstone from Ulva and his wife, Annie Morrison. There were good pipers as well as poets and *seanchaidhs* among the 'Clann na h-Oidhche'.

Donald's mother was a MacDiarmid, and her father, Donald, had been evicted from Islay and took a croft at Bunessan. According to Donald, it was from the MacDiarmids that he inherited his retentive memory, remarkable in being both aural and visual. Having read a long passage of prose or poetry two or three times, Donald has it for life, and we have often heard him recite, without faltering, several hundred lines of poetry he learned in his middle age and whole pages of prose he read as a child. He delights in the sound of words, especially the rolling periods and sonorous phrases of the Land-League orators and the epic poetry of the Islay Gaelic poet, William Livingstone. He recalls, too, much of what he heard in his early years under the smoky rafters of the old black houses, where the long winter evenings were filled with songs and stories. It was when the old-style houses went, he says, that the custom of *ceilidhing* disappeared: *nuair a dh'fholbh na tighean tugha agus na cabair dhubha dh'fholbh a' chéilidh.* [When the thatched house and the blackened rafters went, so did the céilidh.] But if the old way of life has gone, we owe it to Donald Morrison and his like that a vital part of the traditional lore has survived.

Donald was first recorded for the BBC by Hugh MacPhie, before the late Calum Maclean of the School of Scottish Studies made a splendid recording of some of his songs and stories during a visit to Mull in 1953. In the past decade or so, other members of the staff of the School have added to this collection of Donald's traditional lore, which now amounts to some fifteen tapes. Most of them are in Gaelic and relate chiefly, but not exclusively, to the Ross and other parts of Mull. There are tales of clan feuds and forays, family traditions, and stories and anecdotes about illicit stills and excisemen, *bàillidhs* [bailiffs], drovers, fugitives and other colourful personalities. There are brief versions of Fenian tales, including a story of *Fraoch* in *Tìr a' Ghoill*, which he heard from his mother. He had heard stories of the frightening *each-uisge* [water-horse] and the *bòcain* [hobgoblins] but usually he deprecates such things as 'superstition'. He speaks with knowledge and passion about the Highland Clearances, and he remembers meeting the Land-League leader, John Murdoch, when Murdoch was an old man.

Donald's repertoire includes unpublished songs composed by Mull bards who were popular in his youth but are now rarely heard. Among these, the song 'Sìoman donn, fada, donn', by Mary MacDougall (*bean Lachainn Néill*) shows the bard teasing the local menfolk as they suffer the pains of a temporary tobacco shortage. One of the earliest songs he has, 'Mo rùn air a' ghille dhubh', was composed by a local bardess, Màiri na h-Uamha, of whom little is known. Although Donald has not recorded many waulking songs, he heard them as a boy and he sings in a fine traditional style.

We owe a special debt of thanks to the matron and staff of 'Dunaros', who have been unfailingly helpful. The atmosphere of the home is delightfully informal. It is always a pleasant experience to meet Donald Morrison. With true Highland courtesy he vacates his chairs for his guests, seats himself on the bed, or more often reclines on one elbow like a seaman in his bunk, and launches almost at once into the recital of a story or poem. When he begins, his eye kindles and his voice gathers strength and resonance. He is a superb storyteller, and from time to time he casts an appraising glance at his audience to measure the effect of his words. It is clear that he is in his element and that we are in the presence of a past-master.

What follows is a representative selection from Donald Morrison's material in the School's archives. The earliest examples date from 1953 and the latest from December 1976. Unless otherwise stated, the transcriptions and translations from the Gaelic are by the Revd Donald W. Mackenzie, Auchterarder, who spent much of his own boyhood in the Manse of Ulva. The notes are by Eric Cregeen, Donald W. Mackenzie and the Editor [Alan Bruford]. We are grateful to D.A. MacDonald and other colleagues for many helpful suggestions, which have been incorporated. The drawing of Donald Morrison is based on a photograph taken in June 1976 by Mrs Anne-Berit Borchgrevink from Oslo.

– *Eric Cregeen and Donald W. Mackenzie*

Murchadh Geàrr Agus Clann Na h-Oidhche

> DWM: Ciamar a thàinig na daoin' agaibh do Mhuile an toiseach – Clann Mhoireastanach?
> DM: Thàinig iad as Éirinn, as Anntruim. Bha iad 'na saighdearan a's an arm aig Iarl' Anntruim. Agus nuair a chaill Murchadh Geàrr an caisteal agus chaidh e nunn a dh' iarraidh comhnadh air Iarl ' Anntruim . . . . mu ám na bliadhn' ùir' no'n Nollaig agus bha iad ag iomain, agus dh' iarr e trì-diag de dhaoine air Iarl ' Anntruim a thigeadh leis a nall feuch an toireadh e mach an caisteal a rithis . . . . Caisteal Loch Buidhe . . . . Agus thuirt Iarl' Anntruim ris, 'Tha iad ann a sin agus pioc fhéin a mach asda an fheadhainn a chòrdas riut.'
> Agus thàinig e agus trì-diag aige leis de dhaoine a chluich . . . . a bha math air claidheamh, agus thàinig iad air tìr aig *Java*, taobh shuas thall de Chreag-an-Iubhair far a bheil an *hotel* ùr sin suas an dràsda – an àiteigin a sin, agus thàinig iad air aghaidh ann an Creag-an-Iubhair agus rinn iad air Loch Buidhe. Bha fear dhiubh, dh' fhuirich e air deireadh, agus feumaidh gu robh amharus air choireigin ac' air: thachair duin' air agus thuirt e ris, 'Co ainm tha ort?' Thuirt e, 'Bu Mhoireastanach an diugh mi, ach 's e Mac na h-Oidhche th' unnam a nis.' Agus 's e Clann na h-Oidhche theireadh iad riutha an déidh sin . . . . .
> Ach có dhiubh, ghabh iad air aghaidh agus nuair a ràinig iad Loch Buidhe, a réir mar tha 'n eachdraidh a' dol, agus fhuair iad bruidhinn – chunnaic iad a' bhanarach agus chaidh Murchadh Geàrr a bhruidhinn rithe, agus dh' aithnich i Murchadh – dh' innis e có e – agus thuirt i riutha, ' 'S e rud a nì sibh, tha 'n crodh a 's an darna pàirc agus tha na laoigh a 's a' phàirc eile, agus ligidh sibh mach na laoigh agus ligibh a

stigh am measg a' chruidh iad agus leanaibh an crodh, agus . . . gus an tòisich iad air ràicich, agus bidh an fheadhainn a's a' chaisteal, thig iad a mach nuair a chluinneas iad a' gheumraich a bhios seo.' Agus 'se sin a chaidh a dheanamh, agus sheall a h-uile duine bha 'sa' chaisteal – bha e mach air a' mheadhoin-oidhche feuch gu dé bha cearr, agus nuair a thàinig àsan a mach, chaidh na h-Éireannaich a stigh 's fhuair iad an caisteal . . . . Fhuair iad an caisteal – sin mar a tha 'n eachdraidh air a h-innse có-dhiùbh.

- SA 1971/79B. Recorded from Donald Morrison by Eric Cregeen and Donald W. Mackenzie. In place of a translation an English version of the same story told by Donald Morrison follows.

Murchadh Geàrr and 'The Children of The Night'

D.M.: But they got strong, Lochbuie, you see, and they ousted out the MacFadyens. And then it came to the point when Lochbuie and Duart were fighting one another and .the head of Lochbuie was Murchadh Geàrr or 'Dumpy Murdoch' they called him. And he lost the castle and he hooked it off [?*thug e air* . . .] to the Earl of Antrim for assistance.

And the mother of the first Earl of Antrim was a daughter of MacDonald of the Isles, that's Islay. And his mother was over there with him and she was always asking him to put Highlanders over there. And at last he gave her that but not in one year. The story says, the *traditional* story says, that he filled the seven glens in Antrim with Highlanders from the Butt of Lewis to the island of Arran. And that went on for a long time.

But at this time he [Murchadh Geàrr] lost his castle – Duart got a hold of Lochbuie and he fled to the Earl of Antrim for assistance. And he asked for assistance and Antrim said to him that he would give them thirteen big swordsmen and a boat, a *currach*, and they had to row. Now a *currach* is a boat made of skins, with a wooden frame. They were common in these old days. And they rowed her from Derry up to Craignure there, to Java, and they came ashore there. It was getting near to the night. And they dodged along by Craignure. And there was one of them that loitered behind. And some of the Mull men were dubious about them and they asked this man, 'What's your name?' He said, 'Today I was a Morrison but now I am a Son of the Night.' – He didn't know where he was going.

But it passed like that and they went on to Lochbuie to the castle and Dumpy Murdoch got in touch with the dairymaid, she knew him. And her opinion was that – The cows were in one park on this side of the castle and the calves were in the other . . . They had shielings in these days, you know. And she told them, 'Let the cows and the calves among one another and chase them, two or three of you, and make them roar till they make a big noise, and then the people in the castle will come out to see what's wrong, and when they come out, you rush in.' And it worked and they got a hold of the castle and they had it ever since until it was sold by – well, by the last chief of Lochbuie that I remember. And now it belongs to a Lewisman, it's sold. Ay, that's the way. And the castle's there yet, the ruins of it. I was never in Lochbuie.

E.C.: And is that how the first Morrison came to Mull?

D.M.: Yes, that's how the first Morrison came to Mull. He was a soldier in the army of the Earl of Antrim.

E.C.: And when did they go down to the Ross of Mull first?

D.M.: Through succeeding generations. The friendship was kept up by Lochbuie till the time of my grandfather. He used to send [for] him to a party at New Year and he came from the Ross of Mull on a pony to Lochbuie, and they had a big spread, all the descendants of them that came from Antrim . . . . But it dwindled, my father was never asked to go there. Yes, but I heard my father say when he was a wee boy he remembered his father going on horseback away to Lochbuie . . . . They had a big spread, it lasted for days, aye.

E.C.: And who were the other families that came at that –?

D.M.: MacCormicks, MacFadyens, they came, some of them, too, and various other names that are not found here now, yes.

E.C.: So you are of Irish descent then?

D.M.: Yes, pure Irish descent and I'm proud of it that I have got Irish blood in my veins.

– SA 1976/54B. Recorded from Donald Morrison by Eric Cregeen

Donald Morrison tells this as a tradition handed down in his own family, those Morrisons nicknamed *'Clann na h-Oidhche'*. There seem to be at least two families using the surname Morrison (*Moireasdan*) in Mull, but there is reason to suppose that in this case it is an adaptation of the Irish name O *Muirgheasáin*. This bardic family also used the alias *'Mac na h-Oidhche'*, and members of it served as seanchaidh to MacLean of Duart before 1660 (see Derick Thomson in *Scottish Studies* XII pp. 71, 73). The basically historical account of the return of the dispossessed *Murchadh Geàrr* (c.1496–1586) has been mingled in oral tradition with migratory motifs common to clan legends of this sort. The Earl of Antrim seems to be taken in such tales as the representative of the Irish nobility in general, perhaps because of his descent (in the male line) from the MacDonalds of Islay, but in this case there is a connection, since *Murchadh Geàrr* seems to have married a daughter of Sorley Buy MacDonald, whose son eventually became first Earl of Antrim. In the Gaelic [version] Donald says that *Murchadh* chose his Irish followers from the men who were playing the seasonal game of shinty at New Year when he arrived, and in an earlier recording (SA 1953/100) he adds that his own ancestor was steersman of the boat. The retaking of the castle appears to date from about 1540 (see Burke's *Landed Gentry*, 18th edn) A version of the story – not including the '*Mac na h-Oidhche*' tradition – is printed in John MacCormick's *Island of Mull*.

It may be worth adding two other brief historical traditions connected with this story: the tale of how the MacFadyens were pushed out of Lochbuie, and the legend, still quite well known in Mull, which tells of the birth of *Murchadh Geàrr*. Though the latter is a fiction with worldwide parallels among tales of the birth of avenging heroes, it has some slight factual basis in the uncertainty of the Lochbuie succession on the death of John, the 5th chief, in 1539, leaving his natural (though recently legitimated) son *Murchadh* as heir. His two legitimately born brothers John and Eoghan (*a' Chinn Bhig*) had died violent deaths, though not as in the legend before his birth, and the rival claimant was in fact his uncle Murdoch MacLean of Scallastle. There seems really to have been a smouldering feud, if not open warfare, between the MacLeans of Lochbuie and Duart in the time of *Murchadh Geàrr*'s father, which provides the background against which the legend must have grown; possibly indeed Duart favoured Scallastle's claim.

An t-Ollamh Muileach, who appears in this and many other tales in the Western Isles, means any member of the family of Beatons who served as Physicians to MacLean of Duart, holding the lands of Pennycross in return.

Alan Bruford recorded, transcribed and translated the next item [SA 1973/67 A6]:

> AB: Cha chuala sibh có bh'ann an Loch Buidhe romh linn Chloinn Illeathain?
>
> DM: Bha, Clann Phàidein ... Seo beul-aithris ... Bha e aig Clann Phàidein, agus thuirt MacIlleathain ri Clann Phàidein, nan toireadh e seachad liad seiche mairt – craiceann mairt – a's an togadh e – air creagan na air àiteiginn a bha shìos ris a' chladach. Agus thuirt e gun toireadh, agus dh'fholbh iad agus ghearr iad an t-seiche ... mar gum biodh ann barriall bròige, caol, agus chuir iad an ceann a chéile i, agus thòmhais seo pios mór do ghrunnd. Agus thog iad an caisteal ann a seo. Agus nuair fhuair iad astaigh ann a sin bha iad làidir, fhios agaibh, agus ri ùine phùt iad Clann Phàidein amach. Sin agad an naghachd a chuala mise.

Translation

> AB: You didn't hear who was in Lochbuie before the time of the MacLeans?

DM: ... Yes, the MacFadyens ... This is the tradition ... The MacFadyens had it, and MacLean said to the MacFadyens, would he [sic] let him have the breadth of a cowhide – a cow's skin – to build on, on the rocks or somewhere down by the shore. And he said he would, and they went and cut up the skin ... just like a shoelace, narrow, and set it end to end, and it measured out a big piece of ground. And they built the castle there. And when they got a foothold there they were strong, you know, and in time they pushed out the MacFadyens. There you have the story I heard.

A version of the international legend AT 2400, told of many places in Scotland and Ireland, including Inveraray Castle (see *Tocher* 17, pp. 37–8). Other traditions add that MacLean aimed an arrow at MacFadyen from the top of the new castle and shot out of his hand the bone he was picking, at which point he decided to leave quietly. The MacFadyen clan then became a family of goldsmiths (*'sliocbd nan òr-cheard'*) in Mull.

Breith Mhurchaidh Gheàrr

Tha cuid ag ràdh a réir beul-aithris gu robh 'rud mar seo: bha 'athair, 'se bu Tighearna air Loch Buidhe, agus bha e'tighinn air aghaich ann am bliadhnachan, agus fhuair fear Dhubhairt greim air. Agus chuir e ann an eilean amach ann a sineach e, cùl Stafa, ris an abair iad Cearnaborg. Agus .... chuir e a's a' phrìosan ann a sineach e agus chuir e 'm boireannach a bu ghràinne 'm Muile còmhla ris, a' deanadh biadh dha, agus tha fhios gu robh h-uile h-uidheam aca a réir na timeannan a bh'ann. Bha seo a' dol gasda, ach dh'atharraich a' chùis: dh' fhàs an té bha leis ann am Cearnaborg – nach robh i cumail gu math, agus chaich a cuir – toirt as a sin, agus a toirt do Thorrloisgt' – shìos ann a seo, Clann Illeathain a rithist. Agus bha 'n t-Ollamh Muileach, bha e thall taobh Loch Sgrìdain a sin, Peighinn a' Ghàidheil, agus 'se bu dotair aig MacIlleathain Dhubhairt. Agus chaich am fear seo, chaich fharraid dheth 'n tigeadh e shealltainn air a' bhoireannach nuair a bhiodh feum air, agus thuirt e gun tigeadh. Agus thuirt fear Dhubhairt ris, 'Mas e mac a bhios ann, tachdaidh tu e, ach mas e nighean a bhios ann, ligibh leis [sic] a bhith beò.' Agus 'se mac a bh'ann, agus chaich, tha e coltach, an t-Ollamh Muileach air ais, agus 's ann thubhairt e gur e nighean a bh'ann. Agus chaich a ghléidheadh a' falach gus an d'fhàs e 'na dhuine; bha e shuas ... àite shuas ann a seo ris an abair iad Gleann Cainnil, bha e aig feadhainn do Chloinn 'Ic 'Ille Bhràth a' falach ann a sin, gus an d'fhàs e suas 'na dhuine, agus thog e 'cheann a sin. Agus, bha, fhios agaibh ... mar am biodh duine ann an déidhich an fhir a bha 'sa phrìosan, do theaghlach aige – ann an Cearnaborg – bheil sibh faicinn, bhiodh Loch Buidhe aig Dubhairt còmh' ris a' chòrr! .... Sin a' naghachd a chuala mise le beul-aithris.

The Birth Of Murchadh Gearr

Some say, according to tradition, that it happened like this: his father, he was laird of Lochbuie, and he was getting on in years, and Duart captured him. And he put him on an island out there at the back of Staffa, which they call Cairnburg. And . . . he imprisoned him there and he left the ugliest woman in Mull with him, to prepare his food, and I suppose they had all the facilities available in those days. That was going on fine, but events took another turn: the woman who was in Cairnburg with him grew – she wasn't very well, and she was sent – taken away from there, and taken to Torloisk – down here, MacLeans again. And the Ollamh Muileach [the Mull Doctor], he was over by Loch Scridain there, Pennyghael, and he was MacLean of Duart's doctor. And this man, he was asked to come and see to the woman when it was needed, and he said he would. And Duart said to him, 'If it's a son, strangle him, but if it's a daughter, let her live.' And it was a son, and apparently the Ollamh Muileach went back, and he said that it was a daughter. And he was kept in hiding until he grew up; he was up in a place up here they call Glencannel, with some of the MacGillivrays in hiding there, until he grew up to be a man, and then he came to the fore. And, yes, you know . . . if there hadn't been anyone to succeed the man who was in prison, no family – in Cairnburg – you see, Duart would have had Lochbuie along with the rest! . . . That's the story I heard handed down.

– *SA 1973/67 A5*. Recorded, transcribed and translated by Alan Bruford. According to MacCormick's *Island of Mull* the mother, a MacPhee, gave birth to twins, a boy and a girl, and showed only the girl to the doctor; but Donald's version is more usual.

Blar Phort Bheathan

Bha, rithisd, bha cath fuathasach shuas a seo, àit' ris an abair iad Port Bheathain a's a' Ros Mhuileach, eadar Cloinn Illeathain agus Cloinn a' Phì Cholbhasa. Bha MacIllebhràigh an Gleann Caineil, bha e leanachd Dhubhairt, agus thàinig duine, latha, rathad an tigh aige agus dh'fharraid e airson MhicIllebhràigh. Thuirt iad ris gu robh MacIllebhràigh a' sealgaireachd a's a' Ghleann Mhór, agus thuirt e, 'Ciamar a dh' aithnicheas mi e?'

'Tha cu leis agus cluas gheal air.' Agus ghabh e air folbh agus thachair e air . . . . MacIllebhraigh 'sa' Ghleann Mhór agus mharbh e e. 'S ghabh e sin a nuas do Pheighinn a' Ghaidheil, agus bha bràthair do MhacIllebhràigh á Gleann Caineil a' fuireach ann a sin, agus 'se rud a rinn e, chuir e teine ris an tigh aig an duine sin. Agus thachair cuideigin air a bh' air a chois tráth 's a' mhaduinn agus thuirt e ris, 'Bheil thu 'faicinn an tigh ud a tha ri theinich?'

'Tha.'

'Abraidh tu ris an fhear a tha fuireach a's an tigh ud gu bheil cù marbh a's a' Ghleann Mhór agus e dh' fholbh agus g'a thiodhlacadh.' Agus theich a' fear seo a rinn seo, theich e do Cholbhasa, agus dh' iarr Dubhairt a chur air ais agus gun toirte breth air a réir lagh aca fhéin airson a' ghnìomh a rinn e. Dh' fholbh na Colbhasaich agus mharbh iad e, agus chuir iad gad seilich throimh'n dà shùil aige, agus thilg iad air tìr air cladach a' Rois e. Agus rinn seo aimhreit.

Ach goirid as a dhéidh thàinig na Colbhasaich a nall a thogail creach, agus birlinn – bàtaichean – aca, agus thàinig iad go àite ris an abair iad Port Bheathain agus thàinig iad air tìr. Agus thruis garbh-bhratach a' Rois 's fir dhubha Bhròlais 's Cloinn Illeathain Thorrloisgte (thainig àsan air muin each); agus thuirt an t-Eòlachan – se bha 'facal Eòlachan a' ciallachadh, duine bha fìor eòlach far an robh 'n cath a' dol a bhith: bha fhios aige air gach glac is cùil is fròg – 's e seann duin' a bh' ann, agus thuirt e, ' 'Se 'rud a nì sibh,' thuirt e ri Cloinn Illeathain, 'teichidh sibh a suas do 'n mhonadh. Tha'n tràigh a' tighinn agus gheibh sinn cothrom orra aig a' chladach mas faigh iad a' stigh 'sna bàtaichean.'

Agus theich Cloinn Illeathain agus chaidh iad a suas do'n mhonadh, agus chuir iad buidheann dhiubh fhéin ann an tom-falach as an fhraoch eadar iad 's an cladach agus thuirt an t-Eòlachan, ' a chì sibh a' sgailc agam – a' sgall no sgailc agam-s' – a' tighinn ris, nuair a bheir mi dhiom mo cheann-aodach, an fheadhainn a tha eadar iad 's an' cladach éirichidh iad a sin.'

Agus bha iad a's an àm seo ann an àite ris an abair iad Cille Chaoibein agus thòisich an cath ann a sin. Agus nuair a thug an t-Eolachan dheth a' rud a bha m'a cheann, na feadhainn a bha falach dh' éirich iad, ach thòisich an cath dà-rireadh a sin. Ach bhris na Colbhasaich thrompa gu cladach agus lean iad iad, agus nuair a ràinig iad an cladach bha na bàtaichean tràighte agus thòisich iad air am putadh a mach, agus thòisich muinntir a' Rois orra leis a' chlaidheamh agus thruis iad, an déidh do'n bhlàr a bhith seachad, thruis iad naoi naoidheannan de làn an taomain de dh' òrdagan chas 'us làmh nan Colbhasach.

Agus bha aon fhear a phut am bàt' a mach agus cha robh 'm pinn' idir innte agus 's e 'rud a rinn e – dhe na Colbhasaich – chuir e 'mheur ann an toll a' phinne agus ghabh e 'n claidheamh agus ghearr e 'mheur dheth fhéin. Agus cha chuala mi gun tàinig Cloinn a' Phì Cholbhasa a thogail creach do'n Ros Mhuileach tuilleadh.

Fhuair mi'n naigheachd bho sheann duine bha 's an uair sin suas ri ceithir fichead bliadhna, nuair a bha mise ma cheithir bliadh' deug de dh' aois, agus tha mi nis ochd agus trì-fichead. 'Se *Blacach* a bh' a's an duine agus bha e 'na mhaighstir-sgoil' aig aon ám, agus bha móran de sheann naigheachdan aige. Ach siud agaibh mar a chaidh latha Blàr Phort Bheathain – Clann Illeathain a thug buaidh.

The Battle of Port Bheathain

There was also a terrible battle in a place up here which they call Port Bheathain in the Ross of Mull, between the MacLeans and the MacPhees of Colonsay. MacGillivray of Glen Caineal was a follower of Duart, and one day a man came by his house inquiring about MacGillivray. They told him that MacGillivray was hunting in Glen More and he said, 'How will I recognise him?'

'He has with him a dog with a white ear.' So he set off and he met MacGillivray in Glen More and he murdered him. He then went down to Pennyghael where a brother of MacGillivray of Glen Caineal was staying, and what did he do but set this man's house on fire. And someone who was afoot early in the morning met him and he said to him, 'Do you see that house which is on fire?'

'Yes.'

'Well, tell the man who stays in the house that there is a dead dog in Glen More, and he is to go and bury him.' And the man who did this, he fled to Colonsay, and Duart demanded that he be sent back to be tried according to their own laws for the deed that he had done. The men of Colonsay went and killed him, and they put a withy of willow through his eyes, and threw him ashore in the Ross. This gave rise to a vendetta.

But shortly afterwards, the Colonsay men came over on a cattle-raid in galleys – boats – and they landed at a place they call Port Bheathain. And 'the rugged banner (?) of the Ross and the black [haired] men of Brolas' and the Macleans of Torloisk (they came on horseback) gathered together. The *Eolachan* said, – the word *Eolachan* meant a man who was well acquainted with the lie of the land where the battle was to be fought: he knew every hollow, nook and cranny – he was an old man, and he said, 'What you will do is this,' he said to the Macleans, 'you will retreat to the hillside. The tide is ebbing and you will have the advantage of them at the shore before they get on board their boats.'

And the Macleans withdrew to the hillside, leaving an ambush party in the heather between them and the shore. And the *Eolachan* said, 'When you see my bald head appearing when I take off my headgear, those who are between them and the shore will rise to the attack.'

And they were at that time at a place they call *Cille Chaoibein* (?) and the battle began there. And when the *Eolachan* took off his headgear, those who were hiding rose and the battle was joined in earnest.

But the Colonsay men broke through towards the shore, and they pursued them. And when they reached the shore the boats were high and dry and they began to launch them, and the men of the Ross attacked them with the sword, and they gathered up, after the battle was over, they gathered up nine times nine baler-fulls of fingers and toes of the Colonsay men.

And there was one man who was launching a boat that was without a bung, and what he did – a Colonsay man – was to thrust his finger in the bung-hole and take his sword and cut off his own finger. And I never heard that the MacPhees of Colonsay ever came again to the Ross of Mull on a cattle raid.

I got this story from an old man who was then upwards of eighty years old, when I was fourteen years of age, and I am now sixty-eight. He was a Black, who had been a schoolmaster at one time, and he had many old stories. But that was how the day of the Battle of Port Bheathain went – the Macleans were the victors.

– SA 1953/101. *Recorded from Donald Morrison by Calum MacLean*

An English version of this story is printed in John MacCormick, *The Island of Mull* (1923), but Donald Morrison's version, with its interesting terms and allusions, clearly represents a very old tradition passed down orally in the Ross. Embedded in this account of what is surely an historical incident, or series of incidents, are various folkloristic motifs. The cutting off of the fingers and toes of the Colonsay men recalls a similar motif in the story of the Battle of Bloody Bay, where one Neil MacLean received the nickname '*Niall nan Ordag*' (Neil of the Thumbs/ Toes), and the tale of the man who plugged the boat with his own finger is told of the first Macintyre, who got his epithet of '*Saor na h-Ordaig*' (the Wright of the Thumb) in this way. We cannot throw any light on the terms '*garbh-bhratach an Rois*' and '*fir dhubha Bròlais*', evidently slogans or epithets for the MacLeans of Ross and Brolas respectively. The historical setting of the battle is probably late in the sixteenth century, when the feud between the MacLeans and the MacDonalds was at its height, and the MacPhees of Colonsay sided with the MacDonalds. In a version recorded in 1976 Donald identified the '*Eòlachan*' as *Lachainn Odhar*. He was a chieftain of the MacLeans of Ross in the late 16th and early 17th centuries.

Mo Run Air a' Ghille Dhubh

> DM: Seo agaibh, an t-òran a rinn Màiri na h-Uamha do dh' fhear Loch Buidhe:

'S mo rùn air a' ghille dhubh
'S mo luaidh air a ghille dhubh,

'S mo ghaol air a' ghille dhubh,
'S chan ann do d' chinneadh tha mi.

'S taitneach leam an sgeula
Thàinig moch an dé oirnn –
Tha Murchadh an Dùn Eideann
Is dh' òrduich m' eudail bàl dhuinn.

'Se seo am bàl as docha leinn,
'S an t-Oighre fhéin a' cosg oirnn;
'S chan eil gill' òg no bodach
Nach òl toileach do dheoch-slàinte.

Gur fiùran anns an deisidh thu,
'S i bualadh air bac-iosgaid ort.
Có theid an danns' is deiseile
Na shiubhal chreag is mhàm riut?

'S bu shunndach anns a' chòmhlan sinn;
Bu ghleadrach, greadhnach, ceòlmhor sinn.
As a' Sgùrr bha'n Còirneal ann
Is oighre Bhròlais làmh ris.

Bha mise agus Nic Lachainn ann,
'S bu mhath air na *Country Dances* sinn;
Is fhuair mi'n t-urram, 's math leam siud,
O Mhaighstir Caimbeul Chàrsaig.

(Chorus repeated at the end)

CM: Dé'n cinneadh a bh'aig Màiri na h-Uamha?
DM: Cha chuala mi riamh . . . Thuirt Fear Loch Buidhe rithe, 'Nach mise fear as fheàrr a chunna tu air Loch Buidhe riamh, a Mhàiri?' Thuirt Màiri, ' 'S tu as miosa de na chunna mi, ach 's tu as feàrr de na chì mi.'
CM: Bheil fad ann o bhiodh seo ann?
DM: O, tha linntean is linntean . . . Seallaibh an ùin' o'n a thàinig an *Capitalist System* a stigh, o'n a chaidh an *Clan System* a mach a *date* . . . Màiri na h-Uamha, bha i fuireach ann an uamhaidh shuas a sin.

– SA 1953/100 Recorded from Donald Morrison by Calum Maclean.

My Dear One is the Black-haired Lad

DM: Here you are, the song composed by Mary of the Cave to the Chief of Loch Buidhe:

My dear one is the black-haired lad,
My beloved is the black-haired lad,

My darling is the black-haired lad,
Although I am not of your kin.

Joyful to me was the news
That came to us early yesterday –
Murdoch is in Edinburgh
And my darling commanded a Ball for us.

That is the Ball that pleased us most
Seeing that the Heir is providing it for us;
There is not a young lady or old man
But would drink your health with good-will.

You are a gallant in [Highland] dress,
[The kilt] swinging behind your knee.
Who is more ready than you to join in the dance,
Or to range the crags and passes?

We were joyful in that company,
Noisy, festive, full of music.
The Colonel was there from Scour,
And beside him was the Heir of Brolas.

I was there with Miss MacLachlan
And we excelled at the country dances.
I got a commendation, to my delight,
From the Revd Mr. Campbell of Carsaig.

CM: What *was* Mary of the Cave's surname?
DM: I've never heard . . . Lochbuie said to her, 'Am I not the best chief of Lochbuie you ever saw, Mary?' Mary said, 'You're the worst of all I have seen, but you're the best of all that I shall see.'
CM: Is it long since this would have happened?
DM: Oh, yes, centuries and centuries. Look how long it is since the Capitalist System came in and the Clan System went out of date. Mary of the Cave, she used to live in a cave up there.

We owe the following information (based on the Maclean of Drimnin Papers) to James Maclean, younger of Glensanda:
This song was composed by '*Màiri na h-Uamha*' in proxy for Christina, daughter of Donald Maclean of Drimnin, one of the Barons of the Exchequer, who married Murdoch Maclaine, 18th chief of Lochbuie, in March 1813. Her father, referred to here as 'heir of Brolas', organised a ball in the Edinburgh Assembly Rooms on 30 October 1812 to celebrate the couple's engagement and the homecoming of Murdoch, wounded, from service with the Black Watch. The 'Colonel of Scour' (celebrated in Mull tradition for his strength and courage) is Archibald Maclean,

a colonel in the 79th Regiment. *'Maighstir Caimbeul Charsaig'* is probably the assistant minister who lived at Carsaig. *'Nic Lachainn'* is Christina's best friend, Janet, daughter of Ewen MacLachlan of Laudale and Auchnacraig. *'Màiri na h-Uamha'* herself was a natural daughter of Charles Maclean of Killunaig, and may then have been housekeeper to the Revd Mr Campbell. She never married. She may have got her nickname by resorting to the cave at Carsaig where the *Ollamh Muileach* is said to have collected curative herbs.

The tune is better known in Mull to the song *'A mhàldag a' bhrollaich ghil'*. In the last verse the poetess may be speaking for herself rather than Christina. The last line of the chorus presumably refers to the distinction which was felt between the line of the Maclaines of Lochbuie (*'Sìol Eachainn'*) and the branches of Clan Gillean descended from Lachlan of Duart: *cinneadh* therefore means 'kindred' here rather than 'surname'.

Sìoman donn

Refrain:

Sìoman donn, fada, donn,
Sìoman donn, 's beag mo thlachd dheth;
Sìoman donn, fada, donn,
Sìoman donn, 's beag mo thlachd dheth.

Siud an luibh a bha dhuibh daor,
'Chum sibh bho adhradh na maduinn:
'S mur tig cobhair bho Dhiardaoin,
Fo na taoid theid do cheangal.

'Ille, ma tha agad pìob,
Thig a nìos, dean do gharadh.
'Chan eil agam ach rud crìon:
'S beag dhomh fhìn e gu maduinn.'

Nuair theid cearc, an 'Doll', gu feum,
Bheir i leum air an fharadh:
Beiridh i 'n t-ubh bòidheach, réidh,
'S air an fhéill nì i passadh.

B'fheàrr leam fhéin na mìle crùn
Gu robh do dhùrachd bhith agad –
Sgiobadh làidir 's bàt' fo 'siùil
Bheir a null thu do Reachlainn,

Far a' faigh thu 'sìoman donn
Thogadh fonn air do mhala,

'S nuair a thilleadh tu do'n tìr
Gum biodh sìth aig a' bhaile.

'S duilich leam thu bhith cho gòrach
'S a' spliùcan ròin rinn thu chagnadh
A bha agad ann ad phòc'
Le cìocras mòr air son tombaca.

> – SA 1953/91/8. Recorded from Donald Morrison by Calum Maclean. The first line only of the refrain is repeated after every verse. [The melody, transcribed by Alan Bruford, see *Tocher*, No. 24, p. 304]

Brown Twist

Refrain:

Brown twist, long brown twist,
Brown twist, I care little for it. [twice]

That was the weed that cost you much,
That kept you from morning worship:
And unless relief comes by Thursday
You will have to be restrained by ropes.

Man, if you have a pipe,
Come up [to the fire] and warm yourself.
'I have nothing but a tiny bit –
Little enough for myself till morning.'

When the hen, the 'Doll', proves herself useful,
She will hop up on to the roost:
She will lay a fine, smooth egg
That will be bartered at the fair.

I would rather than a thousand crown pieces
That you had your heart's desire –
A sturdy crew and a boat under sail
To convey you over to Rathlin,

Where you would get the brown twist
That would leave your brow unfurrowed,
And when you returned to land
There would be peace about the place.

It grieves me that you were so foolish
As to chew the sealskin pouch
That you kept in your pocket,
So great was your craving for tobacco.

The above song is one of the few surviving songs composed by Mary MacDougall, who is better known for her carol *Leanabh an Àigh* ('Child in the Manger'). She is also variously known as *Màiri NicLùcais* (since her MacDougalls had changed the surname from MacLucas), or *Màiri Dhòmhnallach* or *Màiri Nèill Lachainn*, as Donald Morrison usually calls her, after her husband. She was born, according to the monument erected to her by the main road through the Ross of Mull near Ardtun, in Brolas in 1789 and died in Ardtun in 1872; the Morison MSS. (see *Tocher* 17, p. 24), however, give her date of birth as 1800. She married Neil Lachlan MacDonald, and the early years of her marriage were spent in the adjacent townships of Siaba and Ardalanish in the Ross; according to the Morison MSS. they were evicted from Ardalanish, and settled in Ardtun, where they were neighbours and kinsfolk of Donald Morrison's family. She was active in the Baptist movement, as was her brother Duncan in Tiree, but this song shows that she also had a talent for light-hearted satire.

The song was composed, according to Donald, in Ardalanish, when they ran out of tobacco. The poetess shows her contempt for tobacco by using '*sìoman*', the Gaelic for 'simmons' or rope made of twisted straw (or hay or heather), for the tobacco twist her menfolk were smoking. Leaves of various wild plants were used as substitutes for tobacco: in Mull, according to Donald, one substitute was bog-myrtle browned on the girdle and mixed with a little crotal lichen. The translation of the third verse departs from the apparent meaning of the Gaelic, to follow Donald's explanation that 'Doll' was the hen's name and her eggs could be bartered for tobacco among other goods. Rathlin Island seems to have been a staging-post for smugglers taking whisky out to Ireland or the Isle of Man and bringing tobacco in.

Oran Luaidh

I hao rithill hóireannain
O ho call éileadh
Oho hì hóireannain.

Chunnaig mise mo leannan
'S cha do dh'aithnich e 'n dé mi
Ho hóho hì hóireannain.

'S ann a mharcaich e seachad
Air each glas nan ceum aotrom.

Ach bha mis' anns an uair sin
Ceart cho suarach m'a dhéidhneadh.

'Se mo rùn-sa Clann Dòmhnaill:
Siud an còmhlan nach tréiginn.

Luchd giùlan nam biodag
Air criosan nan éilidh.

Luchd giùlan nam biodag
Dheanadh milleadh is reubadh.

Thug iad mionnan air a' Bhìobull
Aig sruth ìseal Allt Éireann

Nach rachadh claidheamh an truaill leo
Gun a' bhuaidh aig Rìgh Seumas.

Sin na tha cuimhn' agam air.

Waulking Song

*I hao rithill hóireannain
O ho call éileadh
Oho hì hóireannain.*

I saw my sweetheart
and he didn't recognise me yesterday
Ho hoho hì hóireannain.

He just rode past
on the light-stepping grey horse.

But at that time I felt
just as much indifference to him.

My favourites are Clan Donald:
they are the company I would not desert,

The ones who wear dirks
on the belts of their plaids

The dirk-wearers who
would wreak destruction and havoc.

They swore upon the Bible
beside the low stream of Auldearn,

That they would not sheathe their swords
until King James had won [the victory.

– That's all I can remember of it.

SA 1969/141 A6. Recorded, transcribed and translated by Alan Bruford.
The refrain of meaningless vocables is shortened to one line by Donald,

except at the beginning, but would have been sung in full throughout at a waulking. This is one of the most widely-known waulking songs, and was also sung in mainland Inverness-shire. The reference to the battle of Auldearn seems to date at least this part of the song to the time of Montrose's campaign in the seventeenth century – 'King James' is Charles (*Seurlas*) in other versions. There are texts of over 30 waulking songs or songs of similar form in the Morison MSS., including 17 couplets of this one, and a few unusual Mull waulking songs were recorded [in the 1950s] by Calum Maclean from the late Capt. Dugald MacCormick, but it is remarkable to find someone in Mull [in the 1970s] who, as the next passage shows, actually remembers seeing a waulking. Waulking cloth – stretching the damp new-woven web by hand on a board or table to thicken it and raise the nap – is still widely remembered in Skye and the Outer Hebrides (see the Scottish Tradition disc 'Waulking Songs from Barra' and J.L. Campbell and Francis Collinson, *Hebridean Folksongs*) but is usually only a vague memory now in mainland areas and all of Argyll.

Luadh anns a' Ros Mhuileach

DM: Bha sin ann ri linn dhomhs' 'ith beò; chunna mi iad a bhith aige sin cuideachd . . . Chunnaig . . . bhiodh iad a' gabhail òran . . . 's an té bh'aig ceann a' chleith, 's ise bha gabhail nan òran, 's bha na h-igheanan eile bha mun cuairt a' togail an fhonn . . . Oran luaidh: sin agad òran luaidh, 'Hao rithill hóireannain, ohó call éileadh, ohó a rì hóireannain,' 's òrain shunndach mar sin . . .

Agus bha iad an déidh sineach, bhiodh iad 'gam paidhreachadh, gillean is nigheanan, rud ris an abradh iad 'A' long Eireannach' –

Hó có bheir mi liom air a' long Eireannach,
air an fhidheall, air an tromb,
air a' long Eireannach?
Mórag a bheir mi liom air a' long Eireannach . . .

Cha robh iad a' seinn sineach, ach 'se 'n té bh'aig ceann a' chleith-luaidh a bha deanamh seo: bha i 'gan cur còmhla, fhios agad – bhiodh dannsadh ann an déidh a' luaidh, bheil thu tuigsinn. Agus thigeadh sibhse – cha robh e ach air son dibheirsean, a' rud, a bheil thu faicinn, 'gam chursa 's a' nighean seo eile còmhladh, 's thusa 's a' nighean ad eile, 's 'gam paidhreachadh mar sin . . . Cha robh fonn air a . . . siod ann, ach 'se rann a bh'ann, *prose* mar a their thu ris 'sa Bheurla:

O có bheir mi liom air a' long Eireannach,
Air an fhidheall, air an tromb, air a' long Eireannach?
Mórag a bheir mi leam air a' long Eireannach

Agus, ma 'se, 'Iain a bheir mi liom air a' long Eireannach,' a rithist, bha iad 'tighinn còmhla.

Agus bha iad a' cuir car dheth leis a' ghréin trì uairean, agus: 'Cuiream car le –' chan eil cuimhn' 'am air air fad –

Cuiream car le 'Guidheam sìth,
Beannachd nan Trì,
Sian an Àrd-Rìgh,
A dhìonas còmh' ribh.
Air chranna na long
A shiubhal nan tonn
'S a h-uile taobh an téid thu.'

Seo Beannachadh a' Chlò. Bha sin a' dol 'sna sean làithean – O, bha 'n clò aca, dìreach, 's iad a' cur car dheth, trì uairean leis a' ghréin.

AB: Ai, ach nuair a bha iad a' luadh, 'se bòrd a bh'aca – ?

DM: O, bòrd a bh 'aca, 'se, 's iad 'na suidhe mun cuairt air, agus aig a' cheart am a' gabhail nan òran. Gu math tric bhiodh an té bh' aig ceann a' chleith-luaidh, bhiodh i 'gabhail nan òran, agus bha na h-igheanan a' togail an fhonn; bhiodh na gillean mun cuairt an taighe na dh'fhaoidte mach mu'n dorus. Sin agad mar a bha. O, chluinneadh tu air astar iad a' gabhail nan òrain – chluinneadh shìos aig a' chladach as a seo. À, ach dh'fholbh na cleachdainnean sin, gach fasan bh'aig clann Earraghàidheal dh' fholbh e . . . [Bha an clò air a dheanamh] le beart-laimhe, ach chan eil sin an diugh ann: dh'fholbh sin mar an còrr. Bha iad ann ri – nuair a bha mis' òg, bha h-aon, a dhà . . . bha dhà na trì ann shuas a seo do dh'fhigheadairean, agus dhianadh iad aodach gu math cuideachd, agus . . . dh'fholbh sin cuideachd . . .

AB: Agus an ann an taigh an fhigheadair a bhiodh a' luadh, no – ?

DM: O, gu math tric bhiodh e ann a' sabhal . . . [aig] na daoine leis am bu leis an clò; agus ged nach robh thu 'ga chreic idir, bheil thu faicinn, ma bha mise deanamh aodach a bha dhìth orm, plaideachan na dé 'n t-aodach a bh'ann, bha mi trusadh nan coimhearsnach, bheil thu tuigsinn, 'ga luadhadh, 's cha bu ruith ach leum leotha sin a dhianamh, gu sònruichte an òigridh.

Waulking in the Ross of Mull

D.M. That went on in my lifetime: I've seen them doing it too . . . Yes: they used to sing songs, and the woman at the head of the board, she was the one who sang the songs, and the other girls round it took up the refrain . . . A waulking song: one waulking song is 'Hao rithill hóireannain' [etc.: see above], and cheerful songs like that.

And then after that they would pair them off, boys and girls, [with] something [a match-making song] they called 'The Irish ship' –

Ho, who will I take with me on the Irish ship,
on the fiddle, on the trump [Jews' harp],
on the Irish ship?
It's Morag I'll take with me on the Irish ship.

They didn't sing that, but it was the woman at the head of the waulking-board who did that: she was giving them partners, you know – there would be a dance there after the waulking, you see. And suppose you came – this was just for fun, this business, you see, partnering me with this other girl, and you with that other girl, and pairing us off like that . . . There was no tune to that, but it was a rhyme, 'prose' as you call it in English:

Oh, who will I take with me on the Irish ship,
On the fiddle, on the trump, on the Irish ship?
It's Morag I'll take with me on the Irish ship,

And, say it was, 'It's John I'll take with me on the Irish ship,' next, then they became partners. And they turned it [the cloth] round sunwise three times, saying: 'Let us give [it] a turn with – ' I can't remember it all –

Let us give [it] a turn with 'I pray for peace,
The blessing of the Three,
The spell of the High King
Who will give protection with you,
On the masts of the ships
To sail the waves
And everywhere you go.'

That's the Blessing of the Web. That went on in the old days – Oh, they had the web, exactly, and they turned it three times with the sun.

AB: Aye, but when they were waulking, it was a table they had – ?

DM: Oh yes, it was a table they had, and they sat round it, and sang the songs at the same time. Very often the woman who was at the head of the waulking-board, she sang the songs and the girls took up the refrain; the boys were round [the walls of] the house or maybe out by the door. That's how it was. Oh, you could hear them singing the songs from a long way off – you could hear them down at the shore from here. [This was recorded in his daughter's house at Uisken, quarter of a mile or more from the shore.] Ah, but these customs have gone, all the ways that the folk of Argyll had, they've gone . . . [The cloth was made] on a hand-loom, but there isn't such a thing now: that's gone too. They were there when – when I was young, there was one, two . . . there were two or three weavers up here, and they made good cloth too, and . . . that's gone too . . .

AB: And would the waulking be in the weaver's house, or – ?

DM: Oh, very often it would be in a barn . . . [belonging to] the people who owned the cloth [having provided the wool and paid the weaver]; and though it mightn't be for sale at all, you see, if I was getting cloth made that I needed [myself], blankets or whatever cloth it might be, I would get the neighbours together, do you understand, to waulk it, and they would jump at the chance to do that, especially the young ones.

– SA 1969/141 A5. *Recorded from Donald Morrison by Alan Bruford*

Lament For The Factor Mór

DM: There was this old man, according to traditional story, he was evicted from his croft, and then he got a small 'rookery' beside a burn or a small river. And he was there all his days but he always regretted that he was evicted from his croft. And the Factor died. *Uisdean Ros* they called him and he said, when the Factor died:

Tha sgeul anns an dùthaich, 's tha sinn sunndach 'ga h-éisdeachd,
Gu bheil am Bàillidh 'na shìneadh, 's e gun trìd air ach léine,
'S e gun chomas na bruidhneadh, gun sgrìobhadh gun leughadh;
'S gu bheil cùl-taice nan Ileach 'na shìneadh 's chan éirich.

'S nuair a théid iad do'n bhàta nì sinn gàir a bhios éibhinn;
'S nuair a chruinnicheas sinn còmhla bidh sinn ag òl air a' chéile
Uisge-beatha math Gàidhealach, fìon làidir is seudar;
'S cha bhi sinn tuilleadh fo chùram o'n a sgiùrsadh a' bhéist ud.

Gum bi a' Factor air thoiseach a's an t-slochd 's a bheil Sàtan,
'S Aonghas Mór as a dheaghaidh, 's lasair theine ri mhàsan,
Leis na rinn thu de dh' ainneart air mnathan 's air pàisdean,
'S a' sluagh bha 's an dùthaich rinn thu sgiùrsadh far sàile.

'S nuair a chualaig iad an Canada gun do chaidil a' bhéist ud
Chaidh an tein-éibhinn fhadadh is chaidh bratach ri geugan.
'S ann a sin a bha làn-aighir, 's iad a' tachairt r'a chéile,
'S chaidh iad uil' air an glùinean 's thug iad cliù gun do dh' eug thu.

There is news going around that we rejoice to hear –
That the Factor is laid low without a stitch of clothing save a shroud;
That he is bereft of speech, unable to read or write.
The champion of the Islay folk is stretched out never to rise again.

When they go to the boat we will laugh with glee,
And when we foregather we will toast one another
In good Highland whisky, in strong wine and in cider,
And we will no longer be anxious now that the monster has been routed.

The Factor will be foremost in Satan's pit,
With Big Angus next in line, fiery flames about his backside,
On account of the women and children that you oppressed,
And the people of the country that you evicted overseas.

When they heard in Canada that the monster was asleep,
The bonfires were lit and bunting was strung on the branches.
There was great celebration as they met one another,
And they all fell on their knees giving praise that you had died.

– SA 1976/54A. *Recorded from Donald Morrison by Eric Cregeen*

The *'Factor Mór'* of this mock-lament was John Campbell of Ardmore. He was factor of the Argyll estates in Mull from 1845 until his death in 1873 and combined the post with the management of the Tiree estate, where he was known as the *'Bàillidh Mór'*, from c.1846 to 1864. He figures in songs and anecdotes recorded in both islands (see *Tocher* 17, p. 27). Most of them attack him bitterly for his oppressive acts, and he was undoubtedly harsh and arbitrary in nature. There are, however, other songs and traditions which show him a good husband and employer. Indeed, one of the chief causes of resentment among the people of Mull and Tiree was the preferential treatment which he gave to natives of his own island, Islay; he is described in this song as 'champion of the Islay folk'. When he died in 1873, his body was conveyed by boat to his native island; this is alluded to in the second verse. In the final verse, the poet imagines how the news of his death will be received in Canada among the islanders whom he had evicted. *'Aonghus Mór'* (Big Angus) in the third verse is probably the Factor Mór's ground-officer.

The composer of the song, Uisdean Ròs, had suffered at the factor's hands. He is to be identified with the Eugene Rose who held part of a croft at Ardtun in the 1840s.

Murchadh MacCarmaig agus na Gàidseirean

DM: Bha Murchadh MacCarmaig, bha e fuireach ann an àite ris an abair iad Port Uisgein agus bha e deanamh uisge-bheatha, nì a's an àm a's a robh e làthair a bha 'n aghaidh a' lagha, agus air là àraidh 's e tughadh an taighe, thàinig na gàidseirean air, ach mhothaich e iad a' tighinn, agus bha dà chasg uisge-bheath' aige air ùrlar a' chitsin a' feitheamh ri chur le bàta a null do dh' Éirinn nuair a thigeadh an oidhche. Agus nuair a chunnaic e iad a' tighinn dlùth, thuirt e ris a' bhean, 'Tilg fear . . . an darna casg dhiubh sin a stigh do'n leabaidh agus leum fhéin a stigh do'n leabaidh leis, agus cuir an t-aodach thairis ort agus gabh òran do'n chasg agus cuir a chadal e mar gum biodh ann pàisde. Agus bidh mi fhéin 'sealltainn as déidh an fhir eile.' Agus chuir e an t-slabhruidh a bha tighinn á mullach an taighe timchioll air a' chasg seo agus rol e suas e gus an do chuir e do mhullach an taigh' e agus an do dhùin e 'n toll air a robh 'n toit a' dol a mach. Agus thàinig na gàidseirean a stigh agus bha 'm boireannach 'sa' leabaidh agus i 'gabhail òran do'n chasg 'ga chur a chadal, ma b'fhior gur e pàisde bh' ann. Agus 'se 'n t-òran a bh' aice:

> Bà, mo leanabh, bà,
> Uist! agus dean tàmh.
> Ciod, a ghaoil, a nì mi riut
> 'S gun bhainn' agam a bheir mi dhuit?
> 'S tha 'n t-eagal orm gun gabh thu 'n gliug
> Le flichead a' bhuntàta.
> Bà, mo leanabh, bà,
> Uist! agus dean tàmh.

Thàinig na gàidseirean a stigh agus bha iad fhèin agus fear an taighe a' cracaireachd. Agus thuirt a' bhean ri fear an taighe, 'Dé na daoine a thi' agad a stigh a sin?'

'Tha, gillean a' Rìgh.'

'Gillean a' Rìgh', ors ise, 'na gillean an Diùc,' ors' ise, 'mur a fuirich sibh sàmhach 's ma dhùisgeas sibh ormsa am pàisde tha dona le fiabhrus na fiaclan, gabhaidh mise 'n clobha dhuibh.'

'S nuair a chualaig iad sin dh' fholbh iad a mach agus cha d'thàinig iad 'na chòir a' là sin tuilleadh. Agus fhuair Murchadh na buideil a chur sìos do'n chladach agus an tiodhlacadh ann an gainmhich gos an tigeadh aimsir a gheibheadh e 'n togail a rithis agus a chur 'sa smac. Agus cha do rug iad riamh air Murchadh agus bha seann daoin' ag ràdh gun d'thug e leis a' phoit-dhubh 'sa h-uile nì eile bha freagarrach air an uisge-bheatha dheanamh do'n Choille, do Chanada agus nach do rug iad riamh air thall a sin.

ERC: C'ùin' a bha Murchadh beò?

DM: O, bha e fada mu'n d'thàinig na *Clearances*. Bha e ann ro ám nan *Clearances*.

> – SA 1974/20 B1 *Recorded by Eric Cregeen and Donald W. Mackenzie*. [A translation is not given here as they also recorded this English version from Donald on SA 1974/19A]:

Murchadh MacCormick and The Gaugers

DM: Uisgean was a great place for that. There was a man, his name, history records it, Murdoch MacCormick, he made whisky and he made it at the end of the house, in the barn – it was connected with the house. And some way or another he had the fire there and the smoke was coming into the chimney of the house and they were going up, you see, and they couldn't detect it. Everything was closed during the night. However one day he was thatching the house and he had two small kegs on the kitchen floor for to send away to Ireland. Well, they would be leaving with the sailing smack about one o'clock in the morning. It was during the night, you see, that they had to sail away. But the cutter, the cutter men were after them – that was the excisemen. And he got a sign. They had a sort of sign language. If you would see the cutter men coming – they were afloat and they were ashore – I would warn you by some way. That [sign with fingers] that was one man, and if it was like that [different sign] it was a crowd.

However they came and he seen them coming and the two kegs were on the floor . . . And it was in these days the fire was in the centre of the floor and a hole at the top to let out the [smoke] and a chain coming down to hold the pot. And he said to his wife, 'Take one of them kegs and jump into the bed there and throw the clothes over you, and put the keg between you and the wall, and hum away at it, croon to put it to sleep, and I will manage the other.' And he got a hold of the other and he rolled the chain round it, whatever way, and he put it up till it reached – the roof wasn't very high – and he choked the hole and then the house was all smoke. And the men came in and she was lying in bed and she was humming – I'll tell it to you in Gaelic [translated here] – a crooning song to the keg and she was saying:

Ba, my baby, ba!
Hush, and be at peace!
What, my love, will I do with you?
I have no milk to give to you.
I fear that you will become sick
Through eating wet potatoes.
Ba, my baby, ba!
Hush, and be at peace!

And the woman faced the wall and she turned to her man, and the exciseman was sitting and talking, and she asked him, 'What man have ye got in there?'

He said, 'The king's men.'

She said, 'It doesn't matter whether you are the king's men or the duke's men. If you don't shut up, if you waken on me the child, that's bad with teething fever, I'll take the tongs to you.' And then the gaugers, they walked out, and they [Murdhadh] got free, they didn't ask. And they [Murdhadh and his wife] took the black pot with them to Canada, according to history, if it's true, and he was making whisky in the woods in Canada.

Also on SA 1974/19A Donald Morrison speaks about his grandfather having a [whisky] still (*briuthais*):

> DM: 'My grandfather was making it, – over, just beside the people I'm talking about, the other side of the stream. And he had it, he had stones down at the bottom and then he piled it up with sods and put some sticks below, you see, and it was like part of the hill. There was a wee opening at the end, where you could crouch in. They were making it at night in winter-time. When the whisky was made, you had to hide it, bury it, or put it out under the sea water if there was a sandy beach or the like o' that . . . and cover it with sand and put a stone on the top of it, a small stone. This was the mark so that you could get it. When the sea would come in, you see, it would smoothe the sand and you couldn't mark it without the stone being on the top of it. Then you would take it up again and send it to Ireland. Uisken was a great place for that.

Murchadh MacCarmaig lived, according to Donald Morrison, 'before the Clearances', evidently early in the nineteenth century when illicit stills were still operating. There is documentary evidence of a 'widow Murdoch McCormack' in a croft at Uisken in 1845. The Gaelic makes it clear that Murchadh buried the kegs in the sand as described above after the excisemen had gone, though the general descriptions of the English recording are lacking. For other stories of illicit distillers in Mull and elsewhere see *Tocher* Nos. 2 and 3. 'Flichead a' bhuntata' probably refers to potato blight, which began to appear early in the 19th century.

Domhnall Dròbhair

> DM: Air an uair seo, nuair chaidh e null fhuair e sàbhailte, e fhéin 's an treud gos 'n do ràinig e 'n Eaglais Bhreac, agus bha duin' eile leis, companach, agus chreic e ' sreud agus fhuair e am pàidheadh, agus bha e ' tighinn dhachaidh agus dh'fhàg e'n Eaglais Bhreac, e fhéin 's a 'fear seo, a chompanach, agus còta mór air agus bat' aige. Agus 'se sporan a bh' aige – mogan stocain, 's bha 'n t-airgiod air a phutadh sìos ann a sin – sin agad a' sporan a bh' aige. Agus thàinig iad a seo air aghaidh 's an oidhche agus bha iad air coiseachd. Ach nuair a bha e tighinn anmoch bha fhios aca far a robh taigh-òsda 's gu faigheadh iad fuireach ann.
>
> Agus mar a bha iad tighinn air aghaidh ghreas iad an ceum agus bha aca ri dhol thromh àit' a's a robh beagan coille air gach taobh de'n rathad mhór. Agus nuair a bha iad ann a seo, thàinig fear a mach as a' choille, agus gunn' aige, agus thuirt e ri Domhnall, 'Do bheatha na do sporan!'
>
> 'Chan eil,' arsa Domhnall, 'sporan agam-s' ann ach cuid dhaoin' eile.' O, chan éisdeadh e ris a sin agus thog e'n gunna agus chuir e air làn-ghleus i – sin gu robh i deas airson falbh – agus nuair a chunnaic Domhnall siud,

chuir e' làmh 'na achlais agus thug e mach a' sporan a bh' aige agus thilg e air a' rathad mhór e. Agus chrom a' robair a' dol a thogail a' sporain agus thàinig Domhnall air leis a' bhata agus rinn e coileach-dubh dheth agus fhuair e greim air a' ghunna 's thilg e stigh 'sa' choillidh e. Agus dh' fhalbh e sin agus rannsaich e agus thug e as a phocaid trì sporain dhe na fhuair e agus ghabh e air aghaidh do'n taigh-òsda.

Agus a ràinig e'n taigh-òsda bha dà dhuine stigh roimhe, fear air gach taobh de'n teinidh, fear dhiubh a' caoineadh, 's a' fear eile 's a làmh fo leth-cheann. Agus thuirt Domhnall ris an fhear a bha' caoineadh, 'An d' fhuair thu droch naigheachd, a dhuine?' Chan fhacaig e riamh e.

'Fhuair,' ars' an duine, 'Thachair a' robair orm agus b' fheudar domh 'sporan thoirt dha. Thog e'n gunna. Bha e dol a chur a' ghunna rium.'

'Thachair a' cheart rud dhomhsa,' arsa Domhnall – as a' fear eile air taobh eile 'n teinidh.

Agus thuirt Domhnall ris a' chiad fhear, 'An aithnicheadh tu do sporan fhéin na faiceadh tu e?'

'Dh'aithnicheadh,' ars' an duine.

''S an aithnicheadh tus' e?'

'Dh'aithnicheadh, ach dé math tha sin?' Chuir Domhnall a làmh 'na phòca 's thug e mach trì sporain 's thilg e air a' bhòrd iad. Agus thuirt an duine, 'Seo m' fhear-sa,' 's thuirt a' fear eile, 'Se seo a' sporan agam-sa.'

Ach bha'n treasamh sporan ann agus ochd notaichean ann agus cha robh fhios có bu leis seo na dé bha ri dheanamh ris. Thuirt Domhnall ri fear an taigh-òsda, 'Nis, gleidhidh tusa do shùil fosgailte seo, a h-uile duine thig ad rathad air astar, agus forfhaisidh tu bheil duine 's am bith a chaill sporan-airgid, ach chan innis thu dé na bh' ann ach farraid dhe a bheil fhios aige dé na bh' ann de dh' airgiod, agus ma their e ochd notaichean' 'se chuid e.' 'S ann mar seo a bha 's cha chualas riamh gun d' thàinig duine a dh' iarraidh a' sporain.

Agus dh' fhàg Domhnall an taigh-òsda agus e air a' rathad a' tighinn dachaidh, agus bha bùth a sin taobh a' rathaid agus bhiodh iad a' ceannach briosgaidean ann 's crioman càise a bhiodh iad ag itheadh air an turus dhachaidh. Bha e eòlach air fear a' bhùth, Domhnall, agus thuirt e ris, 'Bheil thu 'leughadh paipear-naigheachd an dràsda?'

'Tha.'

'An do mhothaich thu, ghràidh, a bheil mort a bhos a seo air a dheanamh – duin' air a mharbhadh?'

'O, chan fhaca mise nì,' ars' a' fear eile.

'Well,' ars' esan, 'tha sin gasda.' Bha e cur air, bha e smaointinn gun do mharbh e 'robair agus gum biodh na maoir as a dhéidh, bheil thu faicinn? 'S gum bu shuarach dha an t-airgiod seach an duine mharbhadh, bheil thu faicinn?

Có dhiubh, chùm e roimhe 's cha d' éirich dad tuilleadh dha gus 'n do ràinig e 'Ros Muileach. Agus chaidh e dhachaidh agus dh' innis e mar a thachair dha do 'n duine bha pòsd' air Màiri Dhomhnallach, a' bhana-bhàrd, Niall mac Lachainn a theireadh iad ris. Agus dh' innis e do Niall mar a bha, agus thuirt Niall ris, ' 'S gu dé tha thu ' smaointinn a thachair do'n fhear a bhuail thu le leithid sin de smùid?'

'Hó, laochain,' arsa Domhnall, 'laigh e far an do thuit e, 's mur an do thog neach eil' e, tha e sin fhathasd.'

Agus bha latha 's uair aige ri 'n coinneachadh – na daoine o 'n do cheannaich e 'sreud – ann am Bun-easain shìos, 's e 'g am pàigheadh. Agus chruinnich iad, agus bha móran dhaoin' ann 's an ám sin, agus bh a cuid a' seasamh a mach 's iad a' cracaireachd 's cha robh iad a' dol a stigh luath gu leòir le Domhnall. Ach mu dheireadh thàinig Domhnall a mach do 'n dorust agus thuirt e riutha, 'Domhnall Dróbhair, broke, broke! Anybody that won't be here at one o'clock will not get a farthing!'

– SA 1976/54B. Recorded from Donald Morrison by Eric Cregeen in June 1976

The English version that follows was recorded on the same tape.

DM: Donald MacGillivray . . . used to buy a tremendous lot of cattle down in the Ross of Mull in these days and he paid them when he came back from Falkirk Tryst. And sometimes, not always, he had the largest number of cattle going across . . . the Sound of Mull. But on this occasion he reached Falkirk without any mishap and he sold the cattle. And there was another man along with him, a companion, and he put the money in his purse. The purse was a *mogan-stocain*, that's the end of a stocking. And he had that in his oxter in the big pocket of the big coat.

And they were coming on the road during the night and as they were passing through a place where there were some trees on both sides of the road, a man came out and stood in the middle of the road in front of them and he said to Donald, 'Your money or your life.'

Donald said, 'I have no money, it's other people's money that I've got.' He wouldn't listen to that and he lifted the gun and I suppose put it at full cock as we call it. And when Donald seen this he took out the money from his pocket and he threw it on the road. And the robber bowed down to lift it and when he bowed down Donald came on him with the stick on the head and he knocked him out. And Donald searched him and took three purses out of his pocket.

And he kept on that night another distance and they turned into a hotel beside the road. They were put into a room. There were two men there before them. He never seen them and one of them was crying and the other had his chin in his hand and staring in the fire. And he said to the man that was crying, 'Have you got bad news?'

'Yes,' he said, 'the money that I had, I had to give it away to the robber or he would shoot me.'

'Aye, and,' the other man said, 'the same happened to me.'

And Donald said to them, 'Would you know your purse if you seen it?'

'Yes.' And he said the same to the other and he said he would know it too. And Donald put his hand in his pocket and he took out the three purses which he took out of the robber's pocket and pitched them on the table, and each man picked his own purse. But there was a purse containing eight pounds and they didn't know to whom this belonged. But it was made between them that the landlord was to keep his eye on everybody that came and went and ask them did anybody lose a purse containing money. But nobody turned up. But it was made up, the confidence he had, in the event of not anybody coming to claim the money, Donald was to keep it for his own bravery.

Here the English version was cut short, and what follows is a translation of the corresponding final part of the Gaelic text.

DM: And Donald left the hotel on the road for home. And there was a shop beside the road there where they used to buy biscuits and a bit of cheese to eat on their way home. Donald knew the shopkeeper, and he said to him, 'Do you read the newspaper nowadays?'

'Yes.'

'Did you notice, my friend, if a murder has been committed hereabouts – a man killed?'

'Oh, I've not seen anything,' said the other.

'Well, that's fine,' said he. He was worried, thinking that he had killed the robber and the police would be after him, you see. And the money was of little consequence to him compared with killing the man, do you see?

Well, he kept on his way and nothing else happened to him till he reached the Ross of Mull. And he went home, and he told what had happened to him to the husband of Mary MacDonald, the bardess, Neil *MacLachainn* as he was called. And he told Neil how things stood, and Neil said to him, 'And what do you think became of the man you hit so hard?'

'Ho, man,' said Donald, 'he lay where he fell, and if nobody else has picked him up he is there still.'

And he had fixed a day and a time to meet them – the men he had bought the cattle from – down in Bunessan, and pay them. And they gathered together, and there were a lot of people around in those days, and some of them were standing outside having a crack and they weren't going in quick enough for Donald. And at last Donald came out to the door and. said to them [in English], 'Donald Drover, broke, broke! Anybody that won't be here at one o'clock will not get a farthing!'

Donald MacGillivray, 'Donald Drover', was a well-known figure in the Ross of Mull in the early and mid-19th century. He appears in the historical record and had a croft at Ardtun as late as 1856. Donald Morrison describes him as *'duine onorach agus Gàidheal smearail'* – 'an honourable man and a doughty Highlander.' As was common at this time, Donald operated on credit, paying the farmers and crofters for their animals on his return from the sales at Falkirk Tryst. Drovers in general were regarded as unscrupulous, but Donald seems to have been an exception. Donald Morrison tells us that the drover had no schooling. Drovers were a natural subject for Highland tales about robbers, and the exploit related here is ascribed to several other drovers from Uist and elsewhere.

11

TIREE BARDS AND THEIR BARDACHD: THE POETS IN A HEBRIDEAN COMMUNITY

Eric Cregeen and Donald W. Mackenzie

Society of West Highland & Island Historical Research, Breacachadh Castle, Isle of Coll, Argyll, 1978[1]

Tha muran, luachair, is biolair uaine
Na lagain uaigneach far 'n goir an smeorach;
Is tric a fhuair sinn a' mhil 's na bruachan,
Bho sheilein luaineach breac-ruadh a' chronain.

Bent grass, rushes and wild water-cress
Are in secret hollows where the thrush sings.
Often we found honey in the banks
From the restless, russet-brindled humming bee.

– John Maclean, Balemartin[2]

The bards of Tiree deserve a place in the study of the Western Isles if only because of the commanding influence which they exercised on the life and society of the island. They had many merits, some of which we hope to discuss, and their productions, or *bardachd*, were characterised by features which were in many ways peculiar to Tiree. But the feature that is of most significance is one shared by Gaelic song in general, that it was widely practised and enjoyed by all ranks of the community. The history of the island cannot be understood without some appreciation of the immense influence wielded by the poets and their poetry.

The bards' compositions are remarkably abundant. The Revd Hector Cameron's collection contains, under the title, *Na Baird Thirisdeach*[3] works of no fewer than forty-eight native poets, who flourished for the most part in the eighteenth and nineteenth centuries. Even so, his collection represents only a fraction of their compositions and entirely omits a large number of known poets. A considerable number of unpublished poems have been recorded, mainly in song form, by the School of Scottish Studies since about 1960,[4] but it must be acknowledged that Cameron's collection fairly represents the various genres of bardachd composed in Tiree and that he salvaged an immense amount of poetry that would otherwise have vanished completely. He does not preserve the melodies to which the poems were sung, but, considering his lack of any mechanical recording aid, his collection was a considerable achievement.

In a brief introductory essay such as this, we cannot offer any detailed assessment of this body of songs and poetry or enter far into considerations of prosody. Our aim is to bring out some of its salient features, to relate the bardachd to its social setting and to discuss the role played by the bards in the life of the community. It is of first importance to consider the social and political milieu in which the bardachd developed.

The island lost its links with the Maclean clan organisation when Argyll dispossessed the chief of Duart in, or shortly after, 1674.[5] Something of the traditional social fabric and its hierarchy of upper tenants and sub-tenants survived through the eighteenth century, but few of the older families of tacksman status, whether Campell or Maclean, long outlasted the cold economic climate of the early nineteenth century.[6] While they did exist they evidently gave encouragement to bards and pipers in the island. It seems, too, that Maclean tacksmen might be attached by more than commercial ties to their landlord, the Duke of Argyll. A tombstone in Kirkapol kirkyard bears the inscription: 'Neil Maclean, in memory of his father Archibald Maclean, tacksman, Greenhill, died 17th Decr. 1885, aged 67 . . . He faithfully served the Duke of Argyll 44 years . . .' This, the last of the tacksman families, emigrated to New Zealand shortly afterwards, so bringing to an end the connection of the Macleans of Cornaig with their native island.

The place of the tacksmen had been taken by large tenant farmers whose operations were controlled by the markets, and who had no sentimental ties with the landlord, the island or the mass of the population. Thomas Barr, for example, managed his farm of Balephetrish with great efficiency and profit, purely as a large business concern, from the mid-1860s. From such entrepreneurs the bards could expect no patronage.

In the first decade of the nineteenth century, however, communities of crofters and cottars emerged in the island. Their material conditions appear gradually to have declined in the years of agricultural depression and soaring population which followed. Yet they embodied many of the traditional values and attitudes of older Gaelic society, giving pride of place to poetry, song and story in their everyday life. When chiefs and tacksmen disappeared, it was the crofting townships which fostered and developed the traditional culture and contributed to the renaissance of bardachd.

Bards must have been composing in Tiree in the clan period. None are known by name, but there is written evidence that in the middle of the seventeenth century, Maclean of Duart had his winter residence in the island.[7] In Tiree he was usually accompanied by a large retinue of kinsmen, falconers and servants, and his castle on an island in Loch an Eilein must have known lavish entertainment, with songs and harp music from skilled bards and musicians. Whether or not it was owing to the violent break in the social and political system brought about by the Argyll conquest, and the loss of the Macleans' presence and patronage, nothing has survived of bardachd in Tiree from before the eighteenth century. The heritage of classical songs enjoyed by some other parts of the Highlands is hardly represented in Tiree.

The earliest surviving example of native bardachd bears, however, the hallmark of an old tradition. It is a song addressed by Neil Lamont, Balevullin, to Sir Allan Maclean of Brolas and to the deceased laird of Coll, on the occasion of Sir Allan's sailing with his wife, a daughter of Coll's, to Jamaica in 1757.[8] The strophic metre is one associated with rowing songs and laments, as was appropriate for a song meant both as a blessing on a sea-voyage and an elegy on the dead Hector. In content and style, too, it is highly traditional as it recites the deeds of valour and the splendid entertainment of the heroic age of the Macleans. (H. Cameron, pp. 1–3):

Mo rùn an t-Ailein a chaidh thairis
Air luing chrannag thar chuan aineoil
Leis na fearaibh; cha b' e d' fhearann duthchasach.

Gur bochd a dh' fhàg thu na dearbh chairdean,
Bean is màthair gun fhiamh gàire,
An deigh an sàrach, 's iad a ghnath gad ionndraichinn

Mu'n aon pheugaig bh' aca fèin a
Thoirt air èigin do Shemeuca
Cul na grèine – sgeul tha dèurach dhuinne sud.

Ach guidheadh iadsan air an Ard-Rìgh,
Bho 'n 's e 's fheàrr a bhi mar gheàrd air,
A sgiath laidir anns gach àite cunnartach.

Air muir 's air tìr, gach àit' am bi thu
Bhi gad dhion am blàr nan rìghrean,
Bho d' luchd mì-ruin, 's tigh'nn a nios gun chunnart as.

Cha bheag a' chreach leam nighean Eachuinn
Dhol air astar leis a' Chaiptein ('s i ro mheata)
Air chuain farsuing: 's e 'n gaol pailt a dhubhaich i.

C'ait 'n robh aca coltas Eachuinn,
Am fiamh no 'm faicinn, cumadh pearsa?
Bha gach mais' ort; mo cheud chreach nach duisginn thu.

Gun togte bratach nan laoch gasda,
'N am do dh' Eachunn dol air each, 'na
Chulaidh mharcaich: shil an fhras gu dubailt oirnn.

B' ann diu Bròlas, 's Tòrloist còmhla
Bhiodh g' an coir an teaghlach mòr bha'n
Ros g' an comhnadh; chaisgeadh toir is ionnsaichean.

Nam b' eol dhomh aireamh air fear d' abhaist,
Gheibht' a' d' bhabhunn piòb is clarsach,
Mòran daimh, is bhiodh e lan de chuirt-fhearaibh.

B' e sin an tigh's am biodh a' mheadhair
Mhòr, 's an gleadhar anns gach seileir,
Aig luchd feitheamh, 's gloin' an laimh gach aoin-duine.

Nuair thigeadh Màiri nam flath àluinn
'G iarraidh iadsan chur gu tàmh ann –
A ghaoil, na saraich aon duin' aca.

Ge math a bruidhinn, b' fheudar suidhe,
Le'n ceann-uidhe, dh'ol na dibhe,
'S bhiodh fuigheall aig na cuairt-fhearaibh.

'S tu chitheadh dreach mu m' cheann 's mu m' chasan:
'N am tigh'nn dachaidh 'n deigh bhi d' fhaicinn,
Mar b' ait leam, gruag air dhath an fhudair orm.

'S aonta chorach bhuineadh dhomhsa
Bhiodh i d' phoca: fath mo bhroin thu
Dhol fo'n fhoid, mo sgiath mhòr 's mo chulanach.

Translation

My beloved is that Allan who sailed with the stalwarts over the foreign main on the ship of the tall cross-trees to an alien land.

In sad plight you left your kith and kin. Your wife and mother are unsmiling, oppressed, forever missing you.

Missing their own true peacock, who must needs sail to Jamaica – A place at the back of beyond – for us a matter of tears.

But let them supplicate the High King, Who best can defend him, And may His strong shield, in every place of peril,

On land or sea, wherever you are, protect you from your foes In the king's wars. May you return without mishap.

It is no small distress to me if Hector's daughter – poor gentle creature –

should accompany the Captain over the broad ocean, thus doubly proving her generous love.

Where among them all is Hector's peer in hue or appearance or presence? You were comely in all respects. Chief among sorrows is the fact that I may not sound your reveille.

The banners of the splendid warriors would be hoisted as Hector mounted his steed in his knightly attire – A double tragedy had deluged us.

Brolas belonged to that ilk, so too did Torloisk. The great family of the Ross were their allies – They who were wont to check both the rout and onset.

What can I say of one of your quality? Pipe and harp would be sounding within your ramparts. There would be many kinsfolk and a household of retainers.

That was the house where there used to be great joy With servants bustling about noisily in every cellar [To ensure] that every man had a glass in his hand.

When Mary of the fine chief's household would come requesting that they would retire for the night 'My dear,' [she would say] 'Do not exhaust any of them.'

Although she would speak them fair, they must sit it out, With their host, quaffing the dram, And there would be something left over for the dependents.

It was yourself that saw to it that I was bravely equipped from head to toe. After I returned from visiting you, to my great delight I even had a full, powdered wig.

And the title-deeds to my rights? Why they were there in your pocket. My grief! You are lying under the sward, my great shield and support.

Some kind of patronage relationship is indicated by the stanzas in which the poet bewails the chief's death and alludes to the finery Coll had given him, evidently the *bàidse*, the customary reward, which a bard received from his patron.

This is possibly the only song of Tiree provenance now surviving that uses the strophic metre which is found in the works of such seventeenth century bards as *Màiri nighean Alasdair Ruaidh* and *Iain Lom*.[9] The songs of the next generation of bards date from the end of the eighteenth century and the early nineteenth century. They display new features in their metre and treatment, but often hark back to the older tradition in subject-matter and imagery. The songs of Archibald MacPhail,

Balephuil, and Archibald Maclean, Kilmoluag, both of whom flourished in this period, dying *circa* 1830, are typically praise-songs or elegies composed for men of social standing like Campbell of Barmollach and Maclean of Kilmoluag. (H. Cameron, pp. 4–24). Such patrons might encourage a bard or a piper with occasional gifts and hospitality, but could not afford to maintain a professional bard in their household. In this connection it is interesting to find a John MacDonald listed as a 'musician' (presumably a piper) at Balephetrish in 1779.[10] It seems likely enough that the Barmollach family, who were then in Balephetrish, rewarded him with gifts in return for his services as a piper.

In a song typical of the genre of praise-songs composed about the turn of the century, Archibald MacPhail eulogises the factor, Donald Campbell, and his two sons, Duncan and Archibald, who were both destined to die in the Napoleonic Wars. (H. Cameron, pp. 6–8). There are frequent echoes of the earlier tradition as he extols the prowess of the sons, the benevolence of the father and the ancestry of the family:

> Small wonder it was to me that you achieved peace with victory everywhere./ Worthy the crop from which the noble and most amiable heroes were garnered./ Lochnell of old was of your stock and the Duke of Argyll too./ You adhered to the Crown as faithfully as ink to paper.

It was not long after that MacPhail composed a lament for the sons. Sung, or rather chanted, by the late Donald Sinclair, it is perhaps the oldest Tiree song to be sound-recorded in the island. (H. Cameron, pp. 13–15).

Early in the nineteenth century, Maclean of Hynish appears to have taken an interest in piping. According to the family tradition of John Maclean, a crofter in Cornaigbeg whom we recorded, Alan Maclean, one of his kinsmen and a fine piper, won the Pibroch Society's medal in 1810, as his father Neil had done in 1783. Alan was said to have played before Maclean of Hynish, and among the tunes he played were 'Blue Ribbon' and 'Bratach Bhàn'.[11]

It is in the compositions of John Maclean (1787–1848), or *Iain mac Ailein* as he is commonly known, that the transition is most clearly seen from chief's bard to popular poet. A shoemaker and son of a small tenant at the east end of the island, he derived in direct line from the Macleans of Hynish, a cadet branch of the Treshnish family, who were themselves sprung from the Macleans of Ardgour.[12] Bardachd existed in the family, and he was related to the Neil Lamont already mentioned as composer of the oldest surviving Tiree song, as well as to Archibald Maclean, Kilmoluag. It may be that the title, *Bàrd Thighearna Chola* – 'the laird of Coll's bard' – was largely honorific, but it is interesting as being the latest example of the use of a traditional style of this kind in the Highlands. It is noteworthy, too, that it was Neil Lamont, his great-grandfather on his mother's side, who received the bard's *'bàidse'* from the 11th laird of Coll.

Many of John Maclean's early compositions are addressed to the laird and his family and to other Maclean chieftains. They were composed on all kinds of occasions – marriages, deaths, accidents and the like, and in extolling the ancient virtues of *cruadal* (hardihood), *gaisge* (heroism) and *fialaidheachd* (liberality), which his patrons and their forbears exemplify in his songs, he ensured that the poet and his merits were kept in mind. In a song addressed to the young heir of Coll, on his marriage, his praise is combined with a timely warning:

B'i mo chomhairle ghraidh dha
Ma's e duin' e 'ni tamh am measg Ghall
E bhi fuathach air doighean
Cuid de dh'uachdarain òg tha dol ann.
Bidh iad amaideach gòrach,
A sior chluich an cuid oir 's a cur gheall'
'S furasd storas a ghleidheadh
Seach a bhuannachd an deaghaidh a chall.

– (H. Cameron, pp. 56–57)

My loving advice to him, if he is to be one of
those who live among the Southerners, is that
he disdain the habits of some of the young
lairds who go there. They are wont to be
foolish and stupid, continually gaming away
their gold and gambling. It is easier to
hold on to one's wealth than to win
it back once it is lost.

Patronage, alas, was not what it had been. In 1818 *Iain mac Ailein* published at Edinburgh a collection of his own and other Gaelic songs under the title *Orain Nuadh Ghaidhealach*. It was time, in other words, to appeal to a wider public for support. Economic circumstances compelled him to emigrate to Canada in 1819, where he found *A' Choille Ghruamach* ('the gloomy forest') which depressed his spirits but inspired a masterpiece of composition.

His genius blossomed in the congenial company of neighbouring families of Highland stock and speech. Already, before he left Tiree, he had shown himself capable of composing well and wittily on purely local subjects, comic as well as serious. He had made humorous ditties of the kind which were to become so typical of the bardachd of Tiree in the later nineteenth century. His laments had been composed to ordinary Highlanders as well as to chiefs. It is true that until the end of his life Maclean continued on occasion to apostrophise the Highland chiefs in praise-songs and elegies of more traditional style. But increasingly he cultivated a popular type of poetry, inspired by the people and scenes around him. In later life, deeply influenced by contemporary religious movements, he composed hymns of great excellence. Nothing could make him more representative of his age than this.

Iain mac Ailein's *Marbhrann do Mhrs. Noble* ('Lament for Mrs Noble'), composed for a Tiree woman who died in Canada in 1843, shows the bard using a time-honoured form to commemorate a friend. (H. Cameron, pp. 80–5). The song, composed as if it were by the husband, is replete with traditional imagery but it has fresh and genuine inspiration and remains one of the most beautiful laments in the language:

An nochd 's luaineach mo chadal
'S mi ri ghluasad 'am leabaidh gun tamh;
Leas a' bhruaillean s' th'air m'aigneadh,
O, cha dualach dhomh fada bhi slan.
Chuir mi cèile mo leapa
Ann an ciste chaoil, ghlaiste nan clar;
'S trom a' chis thug an t-èug dhiom –
Bidh mi cumhadh mu d' dheidhinn gu brath.

'S i do ghnuis a bha aluinn –
Gu'm b'e teisteanas chaich ort gu'm b'fhior;
Bha do phearsa gun fhailinn
Bho do mhullach gu sailtean do bhuinn:
Bha do ghruaidh mar na ròsan,
Slios mar eala nan lòn air na tuinn;
'S e bhi d' chumhadh mo chomhradh,
Is cha tèid thu ri m'bheò as mo chuimhn'.

Leam is duilich do phaisdean,
Gur a lag iad 's gun mhàthair ri'n cùl;
Sinn mar luing air a fuadach,
Ann an anradh a' chuain thar a curs';
Tha i'n cunnart gach stuaighe,
Bhrist na ceanglaichean, dh'fhuasgail an stuir;
Tha'n chairt-iuil air a sracadh:
Dh'fhalbh a' chombaist, na slatan, 's na siuil.

Thainig dhith air an fhardaich
Nuair a dh'èirich muir-bhaite fo choirc;
Thuit craobh-uabhal mo ghàraidh,
'S gu'n do fhroiseadh a blath feadh an fheòir;
'Bu ghlan solus a' dearrsadh mu'n bhòrd;
Bhrist an gloine 'bha 'm sgàthan,
Dh' fhalbh an daoimean a m' fhàinne glan oir.

Restless tonight is my sleep
As I ceaselessly toss on my bed.
So bemused is my spirit
I cannot remain long in health.
I have laid my dear wife
In the narrow sealed casket of deal.
Death exacted his levy,
Forever for you I will grieve.

How lovely your face.
All paid you this tribute sincere.
How flawless your form
From your head to the soles of your feet.
Your cheek like the roses,
Your skin like the swan on the wave.
I shall speak only to mourn;
I shall grieve as long as I live.

Woe is me! Your poor children
Are lacking a mother's support.
Like a vessel storm-tossed
In an angry sea off course,
Threatened by every billow,
The couples and rudder are sprung,
Torn is the chart; the masts,
The sails and the compass are gone.

The home was despoiled
When the white-crested wave overwhelmed.
Laid low in my garden
The apple-tree, scattered its bloom.
Extinguished my candle
That once shone so bright round the board.
The glass of my mirror is broken,
Gone the gem from my ring of gold.

The bards of the nineteenth century in Tiree achieved their transformation into popular poets with apparent ease and without any obvious hiatus. In the absence of any early surviving examples one cannot be positive, but it is highly probable that a popular song-tradition always existed alongside the more formal, aristocratic tradition, and was sustained and transmitted by local bards in informal ceilidhing and work-processes.[13] Gradually one sees the more formal tradition recede and give way to the popular. The praise-song and the elegy find their subject, as the century advanced, less in the chiefs and their kinsmen than in a popular member of Parliament, a local merchant or a skipper. The heroic panegyric is transformed into the mock-heroic as in the Calum MacArthur songs of the Balemartin bard. The titles of some of the typical songs of the later decades of the century suggest that poetry was reflecting social change. Among the subjects of such songs are: The Wedding Song, Song of the Storm, The Crimean War, Song to Tea, Lament for Neil Lamont, The Postman, The Fishing Song, and The Old Age Pension.

The slowness of the change is reflected in the elegy, which remained one of the most characteristic forms of poetic expression in Tiree into our own time. The highly stylised structure and imagery of the earlier elegies are only gradually shed. In elegies of the late nineteenth century, like those of Donald MacDonald, Caolas, and his sister Euphemia, there are echoes of the language and treatment of the eighteenth-century elegies with their long rehearsal of the virtues of the deceased, their reference to the relations and foster-folk who will mourn, and an almost morbid preoccupation with the funerary trappings of death. Hope of an after-life comes almost as an after-thought. The prevailing mood is one of resigned fatalism – *nos habebit humus*. In John MacPhail's lament for his brother, the poignancy of his emotion is expressed in language that has an almost classical spareness and control. Although thought, mood and treatment are so highly traditional that it might have been composed a century before, the poem has an unusual freshness and immediacy. (H. Cameron, pp. 237–9):

> Nuair thig am dol a laighe
> Is tigh'nn dhachaidh bhar cheilidh –
> 'S ann a bha thu, luaidh, cleachd-te
> A bhi mach as mo dheigh-sa –
> Ar leam g'eil ni ann a m' chridhe
> Aig eil fiuthair riut,'eudail;
> Ach cha chluinn mi thutighinn;
> 'S fada, ruighinn do cheilidh.

> When it comes to bedtime
> And time to go home from ceilidhing –
> [When I remember] that you whom I loved were always later out than I was,
> I am aware that there is something in my heart
> That still expects you, my loved one, to appear,
> But I cannot hear you coming.
> It is a long way to go to ceilidh with you.

The lament composed by the crofter-fisherman, Alexander MacDonald, for the men lost in the disaster which overwhelmed several fishing-boats in July 1856, survives only in a few verses published by Hector Cameron, supplemented by verses recorded from the singing of the late Donald Sinclair.[14] Composed in the old elegiac structure, its stark lines are deeply moving, especially when they are sung by a traditional singer.

It may be plausibly argued that the passing of the old patronage helped to develop a freer, more lyrical poetry, and that the crofting townships of the nineteenth century provided a most congenial milieu for bardachd. The bard's new patrons were men and women of similar status to himself, that is to say crofters, fishermen, seamen and occasionally men of wider education. There was indeed a danger of local inspiration producing banal and trivial verse, but there were compensations in the harmony of the bard with his subject and in the fresh immediacy of his emotion. Moreover, in the decline of the old social order and the rise of the new, there were elements of continuity that safeguarded poetic standards.

Among these elements of continuity one must place first the remarkable passion for bardachd which has always been widespread in Highland communities and which manifested itself in almost every aspect of work and social life. Laborious tasks such as rowing and cloth-waulking were accompanied by singing. Songs were composed to celebrate birth, marriage, love and death, and to record the incidents of everyday life. The most characteristic form of recreation was to meet in the *taigh ceilidh* (céilidh-house) in the evening to pass the time in talk, story-telling and song. So much did song pervade life in the township that it appears to have been as essential as eating and sleeping.

It was not simply a passive enjoyment. The passion for songs was accompanied by an ability to sing and often to compose songs. The gift for composition was remarkably widespread in Tiree. Every township had at least one practising bard in the nineteenth century (and probably, indeed, in the previous ages). A family called MacDonald at Caolas, who were crofters, was wholly characteristic in producing three successive generations of practising poets, including Mrs Archibald MacDonald, her son Donald, her daughter Euphemia, and two grandchildren, Alasdair MacDonald and Joseph Hardy. (H. Cameron, p. 288 ff.). It is likely that there were other members of the same family who made songs that were not published. Families with a long tradition of bardachd, in some cases demonstrably reaching back to the eighteenth century and to the age of patronage, were an essential element in the creation and transmission of poetry, and recall the bardic dynasties discussed by Derick Thomson in relation to Gaelic poetry and lore in the clan period.[15] They performed, too, something of the same function. In the age of the popularisation of the song-tradition, and the decay of chiefly patronage, such families must have mediated ancient skills and aesthetic standards to give discipline and form to the widespread creative ferment of the new age.

The MacPhails at Cornaig were evidently such a family. They were possibly related to Archibald MacPhail, Balephuil, whose compositions at the end of the eighteenth and the beginning of the nineteenth century have already been noticed. During the course of about a century, members of this family were active in composition, and included Archibald (d. 1889), a nephew, John (d. 1909), a niece, Mary Flora MacDonald, the Rev. William Macphail and an unpublished and very popular poet also called William MacPhail. John MacPhail, a highly gifted poet mentioned earlier, was conscious of the place his family held in the island's bardachd, and ends his song '*Moladh Thiriodh*' (Praise of Tiree) with the resounding claim:

> Chan e far an robh na baird, ach am bheil 's am bi gu brath,
> Fad 's a chluineas sibh Clann Phail a bhi 'n Cornaig.
>
> – (H. Cameron, p. 243).
>
> It is not a case of there having been bards in Tiree, but of bards being there now
> and for always as long as you will hear of a MacPhail in Cornaig.

It is reassuring to know that the bardic tradition continues today in that family.

The prime example of a bardic family, with a known record of two centuries of composition, is that of the already mentioned John Maclean, *Iain mac Ailein*. He and his brother, Donald the Cooper, were among the island's most gifted poets in the early nineteenth century. They were great-grandsons, on their mother's side, of Neil Lamont, Balevullin, referred to earlier as the author of the first surviving Tiree song. On their father's side, they numbered the poet, Archibald Maclean, Kilmoluag, among their close kin, and their father, Alan, could compose a little. A son of *Iain mac Ailein*, Charles, displayed poetic talent. Of Donald the Cooper's children, Anne is known to have composed, as well as three grandchildren (Archibald, Dugald and Angus Maclean) and a great-grandchild, John Macmillan. Siblings of John and Donald remained at the east end of the island. Their brother Neil's descendants include the well-known poets Neil Maclaine and John Maclean, Urbhaig. Their sister Mary's sons, Duncan and Lachlan MacDonald, Caolas, both possessed poetic gifts. The list of Maclean bards is impressive, though, for lack of information, far from exhaustive, and one could expand it to include highly-gifted representatives of the family alive at the present day in the island.

Certain of the townships contributed in a special way to the development of the island's bardachd. Balephuil, a crofter-fishing township in the south-west was pre-eminent and was generally referred to as '*baile nam bard*', 'the township of the bards'. The names of over thirty men and women known to have composed songs there in the nineteenth century have been recorded and there must have been many others of whom there is no record.[16] This, for a township of crofter-fishermen and cottars, rarely exceeding thirty or forty families, is remarkable, though in the context of the Highlands is perfectly credible – as it would be in many non-literate societies as well as in such literate villages as the Hungarian writer Gyula Illyes describes in his *People of the Puszta*. For something more than a century after the creation of the crofts in 1805 the astonishing ferment went on. Every other house seemed to have its poet. Macleans, MacDougalls, MacDonalds, Sinclairs, MacPhails, Browns, MacArthurs and Blacks all contributed to the cultural activity as poets, story-tellers and *seanchaidhs*. Present-day recollection and tradition speak of the constant gatherings at the *greusaiche*'s house (the shoemaker, Alasdair MacArthur) or some other *ceilidh-house*, for evenings of entertainment. A new song might be launched, and one hears of the bards vying in feats of extempore composition and wit.

Most of the Balephuil songs have vanished without a trace. Some we have recorded, and a number appear in Hector Cameron's collection. Whilst some are unremarkable, most of the Balephuil songs which we have come across have skill and merit. The early praise-songs of Archibald MacPhail, the songs of Donald the Cooper, Alasdair MacDonald's lament for the fishermen, Duncan MacDougall's hymns' represent no ordinary level of composition, but talent schooled in tradition.

What is perhaps most significant about Balephuil in this period is that it was accepted as normal and natural for men and women of little or no formal education to resort to songs to express their own emotions and opinions and to comment on the passing scene. An accident, a death, a marriage, an intrigue, a humorous incident or a piece of eccentric behaviour was enough to prompt a poet to compose a song. Widow Maclean, observing a bird singing on a rock on the shore, was moved to meditate on human life, and contrasts her own destiny with the bird's, in a spontaneous and touching song:

> 'S a smeòrach bheag air bhàrr nan creag
> gur taitneach leam do chomhradh.
> Cha chluinnear olc 'na gniomh na cainnt
> a bhios 'na nàimhdeas dhomhsa,
> Ach smaointean dlùth air Rìgh nan Dùl
> 'gam stiùireadh is 'gam sheòladh:
> Glòir do'n Athair 's cliù do'n Mhac
> a mhath an tìr nam beò mi.

> Little thrush, perched on the rocks,
> Your conversation is pleasant to me.
> In her word and deed, no evil to my hurt
> may be construed;

But only thoughts intent upon the King of the Elements
To guide me and direct me:
Glory to the Father and praise to the Son
Who forgave me in the land of the living.

'S dìlleachdain sinn a 's an t-saoghal
'us sinn as aogais tròcair;
'S ma dh' iarras sinn ni tha i saor,
's tha Rìgh nan neamhan beò dhuinn.
Urnuigh dhlùth a chur g'a dh' ionnsuidh
's cùl a chur ri dò-bheairt,
Sàtan cealgach theid air chùl
's a lùban dhuinn cho neònach.

We are but orphans in the world
If we are excluded from mercy;
But if we ask anything, it is freely given
Since the King of Heaven is alive for us.
Let us direct our earnest prayer to Him
And turn our backs on evil,
And deceitful Satan will be set behind us
However strange his wiles against us.

Nach sona dhuit aig ám do bhàs
cha sàsuichear gu mòd thu.
Tuitidh tu sios air a' làr
's gu bràth cha tig ort feòirich;
Ach 'n uair a laidheas mise sios
's a dhinnichear o 'n fhòd mi,
Mur bi mi beò an Iosa Criosd
gun dìtear aig a' mhòd mi.

You are fortunate at the time of your death
That you will not be dragged before the tribunal.
You will fall down upon the ground
But there will be no investigation of your life.
But when I lie down
And am pressed beneath the sward,
Unless I am alive in Jesus Christ
I will stand condemned at the judgment seat.

– (S.A. 1968/144A, School of Scottish Studies Archive).

Listening to such songs as these from the local poets, one is rewarded with impressions of everyday life, not superficially observed but as experienced by gifted and sensitive people.

The genesis of this rich local culture goes back to the very early years of the last century, when thirty or forty families from different parts of the island were settled on newly-created crofts in the township by the Duke's factor. Among them were the poet, Archibald MacPhail, and Iain mac Ailein's brother, Donald the Cooper. Soon after 1820 they were joined by Duncan MacDougall from the Ross of Mull, a Baptist missionary but also a member of a talented and poetic family. (It was his sister, Mary, who composed the well-known hymn, *Leanabh an Aigh*, 'Child in the Manger', as well as excellent secular verse.). Of MacDougall it is said that he acted as a sort of preceptor to the township bards, and certainly all his children were given to composing. Of his sons John MacDougall is remembered for the song *'Pilot Bàn'* (which tradition says was jointly composed by the household of poets), and Donald continued to compose after emigrating to Canada in the mid 1880s.[17]

From this conjuncture of a variety of bardic families, and the constant interaction of the members, the township evidently developed its vital tradition. From the power-house of these bardic families, the whole field around was influenced, and the potential of other families and individuals was raised to a new level. Neighbouring poets from other townships were attracted and would come to céilidh with the Balephuil bards. The Balemartin bard, John Maclean, who died in the 1890s, was a constant visitor in the house of the fisherman-tailor, Malcolm Sinclair, who was not a poet but a fine story-teller and acted, in his son's words, as 'patron' to the bard. The cultural ferment went on until almost the first World War and some elements survived into the inter-War period. The last of the bards was Colin Macdonald (*Cailein Fhearchair*), who died in 1943.

Bardachd in Balephuil shows the same development as the rest of the island as the clan tradition evolves into the popular. The subject-matter is drawn from everyday life – a flitting, a fishing expedition, a shipwreck, a love-affair, a whisky-still. Songs about wretched horses and amusing sea-journeys are typical products. Love songs and, later in the century, emigrant songs and nostalgic songs in praise of Tiree, are all found, but what are perhaps the most characteristic genres are humorous songs and satires. Much of this kind of bardachd may seem lightweight, but the songs are very skilfully made and extremely witty. This aspect of Balephuil bardachd is balanced, however, by a deeply serious note which becomes more dominant in the late nineteenth century. It may well be that the polarisation between mocking humour and salvationist brooding revealed strains in the culture and impending breakdown.

This religious mood is characteristic of the whole Highland area, as also of much of northern Europe and America in the nineteenth century. It is typical of much of Iain mac Ailein's later compositions. In Balephuil the new preoccupation with salvation is perhaps traceable first to Duncan MacDougall, the Baptist missionary. It left its signature in the solemn note which sounds through the compositions of many of the Balephuil bards, like '*S a smeòrach bheag air bhàrr nan creag* ('Song to the Thrush') already quoted. It proved itself hostile in some senses to the tradition and practice of bardachd, and caused Alasdair *Mòr* MacDonald to forsake composition. It is interesting, however, to find people of bardic gifts turning to the making of hymns, as did Donald Sinclair, Barrapol.[18] In the Cooper's family, two members, Duncan and Angus Maclean wrote hymns and in fact became ministers.

Duncan MacDougall's own hymns were published in *Laoidhean Spioradail a chum cuideachadh le Crabhadh nan Gael* in 1841.[19] Within the confines of a somewhat narrow theology, they show a mastery of language, felicity of style, and rich imaginative gifts that ought, when fully evaluated, to ensure him a place in the first rank of Gaelic hymn-writers alongside Peter Grant and *Iain Gobha na Hearadh*. His familiarity with the old praise-poetry is apparent in the imagery in which he describes the state of Adam before the Fall:

> Bha e fiorghlan na sholus,
> Mar an lochran as 'soileire: 'Ghrian.
> 'S mar an t-or as ro-ghlaine,
> Gun fhòtus, gun choire, gun ghiomh.
> 'S mar chrùn anns a chruitheachd; –
> A' cur mais' air an uighean le rian,
> 'Se mar cheannard an teaghluich,
> 'S 'h-uile nith ann am fonn mar a mhiann.

> 'Se mar ròs anns a Ghàrradh,
> A' cur mais' air na blàthaibh mu'n cuairt;
> Binn mar theudan na clarsuich,
> Togail fonn anns an nàdur le buaigh.
> Gràinne-mullaich gach poir e.
> Bh'anns a chruitheachd 's bu mhò dhiu an luach,
> Oir bha chridhe gun ghò ann,
> A chorp is anam gun mhór-chuis gu'n uaill.

He was clear-shining in his light/ like the clearest of all lights – the sun;/ He was like much refined gold/ without dross, without flaw, without fault/ He was as the crown of creation/ enhancing the elements by his control./ He was like the chief of a household;/ all things were harmonised according to his desire.

He was like the rose in the garden,/ shedding lustre on the surrounding plants./ Sweet as the harp-strings/ triumphantly creating melody in nature./ The crowning glory of every growing thing/ in creation and most precious of them all,/ because his heart was guileless,/ His body and soul without false pride or vainglory.

The bard had a secure and respected place in the community, at any rate until the end of the century. In the earlier clan period, the bard, together with the chief's *seanchaidh* and piper, was charged with the important function of magnifying the clan and its chief, and diffusing a sense of solidarity among all those attached to the chief. His position in the nineteenth century community in Tiree, even without the éclat of being the official bard, remained influential. A bard whose songs were on everyone's lips wielded more real influence than minister or schoolmaster. He was able to express the mood, the emotions and the opinions of his community because of his involvement in local life from its most trivial aspects to its most significant. He was at once the recorder of the passing scene, the entertainer, whose songs mocked the drolleries and peccadilloes of his neighbours, and the high priest charged with the serious business of upholding morals and customs.

It was the bard who, in praise-songs and laments, commended the virtues that the community cherished, presenting the ideal of the man of courage on the battlefield, of independent and principled character, loyal to his relations and friends, charitable and given to hospitality. The old fashion of using an accumulation of epithets in praising one's subject is found in nineteenth century praise-songs at Balephuil: 'You were peaceable, kind, friendly, humane, affectionate, hospitable and of good temper.'

It was equally the bard's place to condemn vice and anti-social behaviour. This might be achieved by light, bantering satire, intended to make the victim the object of laughter, as when Malcolm Black in West Hynish, in an unpublished song, rebuked his neighbour's meanness in feeding fodder, which was not even fit for bedding, to the township bull. Another of the Balephuil poets ridiculed the vanity and physical appearance of an unpopular factor.

'S o'n fhuair thu 'n deise philot
Tha fiamh agad ri saighdear,
Le iosgaidean mar choinnleir
'S an fhoill ann am bun do mhuineil.

Since you got the suit of Pilot cloth
You bear a faint resemblance to a soldier.
Your shanks are like candle-sticks,
And treachery lurks at the back of your throat.

– (SA 1968/143A in the School of Scottish Studies Archive)

The good-humoured mockery, which is characteristic of many of the Balephuil songs, can, however, turn into the most biting satire when grosser vices and outrageous conduct are its object. Some of the Tiree bards were masters of satire. In the best tradition of truly venomous satire, Duncan MacKinnon, Vaul, attacked James Shaw, the Lochnell bard, for criticising the 3rd Argyll Regiment (H. Cameron, p. 134).

> Ge math do mhaighstir gur nar ri aithris air
> 'Bhi gleidheadh cù air a dhùn cho sgaiteach riut;
> Gu criomadh chnamhan, 's gu gearradh shailtean –
> 'Se sin do ghnaths anns gach aite'n tachradh tu.

> Good as your master is, it is a disgrace to
> recount of him that he keeps on his dung-hill
> such a malignant cur as you, nibbling at bones and snapping at heels –
> that was your habit wherever you happened to be.

Not all who composed songs were bards in the same sense. In the highly creative period of Tiree bardachd which we are discussing, there were individual poets who were known in their locality as *Am Bàrd*, ('the Bard'). This was clearly the case with *Iain mac Ailein* during his Tiree years. It may have been true of his brother, Donald the Cooper, at Balephuil, in the first half of the century. In the latter half of the century this position and style certainly belonged to John Maclean, usually known as 'the Balemartin bard'. In the north-west of the island, the unpublished poet, Willie MacPhail, had a similar status and esteem early in the present century. The personal characteristics and witticisms of such bards have come down in anecdotal form to the present, and the older generation does not tire of reciting them.

No Tiree bard of the latter half of last century appears to have enjoyed greater regard in the community or wider fame outside it than 'the Balemartin bard'. Such of his compositions as *'Manitoba'*, *'Breacan Mairi Uisdein'* and *'Oran nam Priosanach'* won him widespread acclaim in the Gaelic-speaking world. He lived on a croft on the boundary of Balemartin and Balephuil, and, with the bard's distaste for steady industry, he spent much of his time céilidhing with the bards and neighbours of Balephuil, where he played a crucial role in the flowering of bardachd. It was events and personalities in his immediate locality that inspired his poetry and produced the series of humorous songs about his neighbour, *Calum Beag*, as well as his more serious songs. His genius raised him well above the level of a local poet, and his published verse reveals a fertile mind, a masterly command of language and an excellent ear.

His compositions range from the drolleries of the *Calum Beag* songs to savage satire, and from love-songs and laments to political songs. His love-songs are perhaps too facile, and are not as good as the best of John Maclean, Urbhaig's, but when his feelings were genuinely involved, he had no match in the island in expressing them in powerfully controlled language. His song, *'Manitoba'*, composed on the occasion of his friends John and Charles Maclean emigrating from Balephuil in 1878, conveys his personal sense of loss and then widens beyond the island's horizons to lament the changed Highland scene, with its empty glens and scattered people, unvalued by landlords who preferred money to brave soldiers. (H. Cameron, p. 165).

> Tha 'n oigridh ghrinn uallach, an diugh air am fuadach;
> Tha deas agus tuath tighean fuar agus fas:
> Chan fhaic mi a' ghruagach 'dol feasgar do'n bhuaile,
> 'S cha chluinn mi a duanag 's i cuallach an ail.

> Luchd fhéileadh is osan is bhoineidean coc-te
> Bha riamh air am moladh air thoiseach 's na blair;
> Tha iad ga'n cur thairis gu duthaich mhi-fhallainnn;
> 'S gun ni air an air' ach am fearann 'chur fas.

> The proud, handsome youths today are evicted,
> To north and to south, cold and empty the homes;
> I see not the maid of an evening go milking:
> I hear not her lilting when herding the droves.

> The folk of the kilt and the hose and cocked bonnets
> Were ever renowned as foremost in fray.
> They are sent overseas to climates unwholesome
> With no end in view but to lay the land bare.

It is not surprising to find the bard espousing the Land-League cause in the 1880s. His was the voice of those who stood to gain least from a ducal estate policy that, with all its benefits (and they were not inconsiderable), aimed consistently at creating larger, more viable croft-units, which were out of the reach of the cottars and small crofters. The songs which he composed at this period were not mere political propaganda, but were inspired by a passionate love for his native island, which found expression in sensitive and memorable verse. It contrasts with much of the sentimental and nostalgic versification which others were pouring forth at this time. *'Oran nam Priosanach'*, composed in 1886, a year of agrarian rioting in Tiree, begins with a paean in praise of the island, and the third verse continues:

> 'S a' mhaduinn shamhraidh nuair chinneas seamrag,
> 'S i geal is dearg air a' machair chomhnard,
> 'S lurach, blathmhòr a lusan sgiamhach
> Fo dhriuchd na h-iarmailt 's a' ghrian ga'n oradh.

> On a summer day when the clover burgeons
> Red and white on the level grass-land,

> Lovely the plants with their many blossoms,
> Fresh with the dew and shining in the sun.

It is not long before he harks back to former times, when the clans were powerful:

> Mu'n d'thainig Diuc ann, no aon d'a shinnsear,
> No Deòrsa riòghail a rioghachd Hanobhair,
> Bha'n t-ealan iosal, 'bu lionmhor airidh,
> Aig Clann nan Gaidheal 'na aite comhnuidh.

> Before a duke came or any of his people
> Or a kingly George from Hanover's realm,
> The low-lying isle, with its many shielings,
> Belonged as a dwelling to the Children of the Gael.

Now the people are dispossessed and their leaders in prison but the struggle for the Highlanders' rights will go on. (H. Cameron, pp. 168–9).

The bard's mastery shows in his command of language, achieving its aim in a vigorous and pithy style. This is well illustrated by the mock-heroic elegy on his horse, *'Cumha a' Ghluineinich'*. Although it is slightly ironical and – like much Gaelic poetry on the subject of animals – quite unsentimental, it achieves a powerful and moving effect.

> Dh' eug an de mo ghearran fhein
> Bha laidir, treubhach, luthar.
> Gu ruith 's gu leum bu math a ghreim,
> 'S e cur na creadh gu dubhlan
> 'Ach 's mòr mo dhoilich a chrith-reòta
> Tharruing sgleò mu 'shuilean,
> 'A dhaoine 's grannda 'n rud am bàs
> Nuair gheibh e'n aird air bruidean.

> Bha uair de'n t-saoghal 's cha b'fhear faoin
> A chuireadh taod, 'an cuil ris;
> Ri uchd an aonaich, luthar, aotrom,
> Sit'reach, sgaomach, siubhlach:
> 'S e 'n diugh gu fann aig fithich ghleann
> Le'n gob crom g'a chiurradh.
> Ach theid fear ùr a chur 'na ait'
> Nuair thig am Baillidh 'n dùthaich.

> Chi mi cocaire nan rocais
> 'Tigh'nn le òran tuchain;
> Luchd an sgainidh, 's rac 'nam braighead,

'Tigh'nn bho aird nan stuc-bheann;
'Gabhail cothruim air 's an dig,
O'n fhuair iad innte lubt' e;
Le'n an-iochd baobhaidh 'n cridhe shlaod iad
Mach air taobh a chuil as.

(H. Cameron, p. 173)

Yesterday my gelding died
That late was nimble, playful,
In leap and canter sure of hoof,
The clods of earth disdaining.
Great my sorrow that the hoar-frost
Now his eye is veiling.
Ah men! Death is an ugly thing,
Over the beasts prevailing.

There was a time when no mere lad
Could halter him in stable.
He'd breast the braes, with snorts and neighs,
So lithe and fleet and gamesome.
But now today he feebly lies
Rent by bent beak of raven.
(I'll get another in his place
When next I see the Baillie).

I see the scullion of the rooks
Come near with husky singing,
The spoilers of the throaty croaks
From lofty crag come winging.
He's at their mercy in the ditch,
Where crumpled, limp, they find him,
With savage ruthlessness they filch
His heart from out behind him.

The bard was ruled more by his head than his heart, and though he felt strongly for causes, the satire rather than the elegy was his forte. He was undoubtedly a master of controlled invective and devastating satire, and his use of these weapons follows a well-beaten track in Gaelic tradition. His intelligence and wit gave him an ascendancy over other bards, which he was prepared to exploit quite ruthlessly. It was no doubt with the Balemartin bard in mind that the late Donald Sinclair, Balephuil, said: 'A wise man would keep on the poet's side so that he would not expose them.'

The bard was typical of much of Tiree bardachd in its later phase; the strong sense of the comic, the flights of fancy, the sharp observation and gift of satire, skill in words and a fine control of metre, political awareness and a passionate love of his island and the Gaelic Highlands. He shows an uncharacteristic freedom from the influence of evangelical religion, however, and indeed expressed his contempt for neighbours who cloaked their greed under professions of religion.

Contemporaries or later poets in Tiree who could not match the Balemartin bard in skill and versatility, could nevertheless surpass him in certain fields. Neil Maclaine (d. 1919) was an excellent elegiac poet and is of considerable interest as a social poet, expressing the grievances of the cottars in contradistinction to the crofters. John MacPhail, Clachanmore, who was his contemporary, shows a depth of feeling in his elegy on his brother which is lacking in the Balemartin bard. John Maclean, Urbhaig, was perhaps given to protesting a broken heart too much in his love-songs, but he sings sweetly and uses considerable skill in composition.

Too little has been saved of the women-bards of Tiree. The love-songs of Mary Flora MacDonald, Caolas, composed as it were by a man to his beloved, are among the best of this genre. To the talent which she may have inherited from her MacPhail ancestors was added an acquaintance with South Uist. This very likely explains why her '*Rann Challuinn*' is one of the rare songs composed in Tiree in the form and metre of a waulking song. (H. Cameron, pp. 309–310). It is remarkable that, although waulking of cloth survived until at least the end of last century, and was accompanied by songs, this genre is practically unknown in the native songs of Tiree. The favourite waulking song used at Balephuil in his youth was, according to the late Donald Sinclair, Alasdair mac Mhaighstir Alasdair's '*Agus hò Mhòrag.*'

If one wished to illustrate the influence of religion on the bardachd of Tiree, it would be hard to better a short lyric, deceptive in its simplicity, composed by Mrs Archibald MacDonald, Caolas, on receiving the Old Age Pension. (H. Cameron p. 288). After speaking of her failing powers and her hopes of heaven, she completes this telling, epigrammatic song:

Fhuair mise crùn airgid
A tha dearbh-te bhò'n rìgh dhomh;
Ach cha dèan e bonn stath dhomh
Nuair bheir mo chàirdean don chill mi:
An Tì a dh'fhuiling nam àite,
Mur dèan mi tàir air an fhìrinn,
Bheir E Crùn a bhios buan dhomh
'S oighreachd shuas ann an Sion.

Mine is this crown of silver
By the king guaranteed me.
What's it worth when my kinsfolk

To the kirkyard will bear me?
He who for me suffered anguish,
If His truth I despise not,
A true Crown shall give me
And my birth-right in Zion.

The bardachd of Tiree has been almost entirely transmitted by oral methods. Poets composed their verse to be sung, and in the nineteenth century the céilidh-house, where neighbours met informally, provided a focus for bardachd in every township. In addition weddings and wakes, waulkings and harvest-work, nights at the kiln, and other such times were occasions for songs. The disappearance of the chiefly hall and the old warrior-society led to changes in the tradition of bardachd, but its flow remained copious and strong through the nineteenth century.

The written word is not to be ignored in the process of transmission. Largely as a result of schools founded by the S.P.C.K. (Society for the Propagation of Christian Knowledge), the Society for the Support of Gaelic Schools and also the General Assembly, literacy in Gaelic, though not in English, became common in the early nineteenth century. Apart from *Iain mac Ailein*'s collection of 1818, there was, however, little native poetry available in print, though religious works and hymns must have had an important influence through the printed word. There is evidence that manuscript versions of songs composed in the island were in circulation and reached emigrants in Canada, whilst emigrant songs like those of *Iain mac Ailein* and John Maclean, Balephuil, were transmitted in manuscript form to friends in Tiree.[20] Evidently John Maclean, Balemartin, would make written versions of songs which he had composed, and Hector Kennedy recalled the tradition that 'the Balemartin bard would write the songs down on the door [of the house] and his sisters would read it for the boys when they would come along. *He* was out céilidhing. Aye, and the old ones was learning the young ones.'

Oral transmission has undoubtedly played the most vital role in the continuance of the Tiree tradition of bardachd. It has operated informally in the family, in the township and in céilidhs which drew together people from different townships. In general our informants learned most of their lore from relations and neighbours. But bardachd in Tiree did not develop in isolation. The tradition has been influenced by songs introduced from other areas in the course of the islanders' travels and seasonal work, and by incoming settlers and travelling folk. The song-traditions of the neighbouring island of Mull are likely to have had the greatest influence, and several of the bardic families originated there. Few of the older generation of seanchaidhs nowadays can read Gaelic, and owe all their lore to hearing it spoken or sung. The late

Donald Sinclair was an exception, for he had read widely and knew a vast number of Gaelic songs from the whole Highland area either from reading or oral tradition.

The bardachd of the island was composed for singing, as is the case with nearly all Gaelic poetry. Most of the songs we have recorded belong to the nineteenth century and are mainly variants of tunes well known in the rest of the Gaelic area. A single tune will serve for a variety of different songs with the same metre. Donald Sinclair informed us that he would know what tune a song would be sung to, even if he had not previously met the words. Thus he sang Archibald MacPhail's song to Colin MacNiven, 'Do Chailein Mac Naoimhein, Fear-Ghrianail', (H. Cameron, p. 4) to a tune which *Donnchadh Bàn* used for one of his poems with which Donald was familiar. The Tiree style of singing is without the elaborate decoration found in Lewis, but performers such as Donald Sinclair and Hector Kennedy show the superb control and flexibility which was typical of the older Tiree singers.

Oral transmission has ceased to operate with any vigour in the island. Public *cèilidhs* are held, where native songs may be heard, but the informal *cèilidh* which sustained the tradition disappeared early in the twentieth century. Largely through the effects of a system of compulsory education which was conceived in English terms and which was established in 1872, respect for the older tradition and values has disappeared. The new generation has adopted many of the values of the English-speaking Lowlands, where indeed, for the most part, they now live and work. The bard has no patron and no easily available audience. It is perhaps no wonder that the late Donald Sinclair was called *am bàrd tosdach*, (the silent bard).[21] Yet the 'quick vein of poesy'[22] still exists in the island and among its emigrants, and is perhaps only awaiting a rekinding of interest in the language and the tradition to flourish once again.

ACKNOWLEDGEMENTS

We wish to express our sincere thanks to the Director and Staff of the School of Scottish Studies in the University of Edinburgh for their generous assistance, and in particular to Dr Margaret Mackay, Miss Morag MacLeod, Mr Donald A. MacDonald, Mr B.R.S. Megaw, and Dr John MacInnes for their valuable criticisms and suggestions. We also would like to record our indebtedness to the School's transcribing and secretarial staff for their valued help. Mrs Hector Cameron and Miss Edith Cameron kindly supplied information about the Revd Hector Cameron. To the many islanders who have recorded their oral traditions for us over a long period we owe a debt of gratitude that we can never repay, and in preparing this essay we are especially conscious of the wealth of tradition which has been placed at our disposal by Hector Kennedy, Hilipol, and by the late Donald Sinclair – *Dòmhnull Chaluim Bàin* – of West Hynish, who was first recorded extensively by Dr John MacInnes.[23] Much of the recent work carried on by Eric Cregeen and Margaret Mackay of the School of Scottish Studies, with assistance from the Revd Donald W. Mackenzie, in recording oral traditions in Tiree was sponsored by the Social Research Council, and here we express our appreciation for this support and interest.

The translations included in this essay are by the Revd Donald W. Mackenzie, with the exception of the verse of John MacPhail's elegy, which Donald A. MacDonald translated for us.

NOTES AND REFERENCES

1. This paper was published as a booklet by the Society of West Highland & Island Historical Research, Isle of Coll. The publication contained only English translations of the Gaelic poems quoted from Hector Cameron's *Na Bàird Thirisdeach*. The original Gaelic verses have been restored here and given precedence. [Ed.]
2. From *Oran nam Prìosanach*, Cameron, p. 168.
3. Revd Hector Cameron (ed.), *Na Bàird Thirisdeach* (Stirling 1932). Hector Cameron was born at Cornaigmore on the Island of Tiree in 1880 and was educated at Cornaigmore School and subsequently at Kingussie, Glasgow High School and the University of Glasgow. After being licensed to preach by the Presbytery of Glasgow in 1906, he served as minister successively in three Argyll parishes, Cumlodden, Kilmartin and Oban, between 1907 and 1932, when he became minister of the parish of Moy, Tomatin and Dalarossie. He married Edith Agnes Ross, the daugher of a parishioner at Kilmartin, in 1916, and had four sons and a daughter. He died in 1940. His volume of Tiree songs, which was published by the Tiree Association in 1932, contained some published material but consisted chiefly of unpublished songs collected by himself and other natives of Tiree who collaborated in the wrok. A bard himself, he included some of his own compositions. His own collecting and editing were carried out whilst he was parish minister at Oban between 1922 and 1932. References to this work in the text appear as H. Cameron, followed by the page number. [Ed.]
4. Particular mention must be made of the late Donald Sinclair, Hynish West, and Hector Kennedy, Hilipol, among the singers recorded, in that they have recorded many songs, some of them unpublished or variants of published versions.
5. J.R.N. MacPhail (ed.), *Highland Papers*, vol. 1, p. 242 ff. (Scottish History Society, Second Series V, 1914). Also E.R. Cregeen, 'The Tacksmen and Their Successors' in *Scottish Studies*, Vol. 13, part 2 (Universtiy of Edinburgh, 1969).
6. No comprehensive history of Tiree exists, but some aspects of the eighteenth and nineteenth centuries are dealth with in E. R. Cregeen (ed), *Instructions*

of the Fifth Duke of Argyll to his Chamberlains of Mull, Morvern and Tiree 1771–1805 (Scottish History Society 1964), and in 'The Changing Role of the House of Argyll in the Scottish Highlands' in Phillipson and Mitchison, *Scotland in the Age of Improvement* (Edinburgh University Press 1969). Noel Banks, *Six Inner Hebrides* (David and Charles 1977) contains some useful historical material about Tiree.

7. *Scottish Historical Review* (1912), pp. 343–4. We are indebted to B. R. S. Megaw of the School of Scottish Studies for this reference.
8. H. Cameron pp. 1–3. Brief biographical details of some of the poets appear in this volume. [The description in the poem of the Laird of Coll's hospitality is the earliest description to have survived of life at Breacachadh Castle].
9. The metres that these seventeenth century bards used were themselves innovations in the classical Gaelic praise-poetry tradition of unstressed verse. See J. MacInnes, 'Gaelic Songs of Mary MacLeod' in *Scottish Gaelic Studies* vol. XI, part 1 (1966), pp. 3–25, and also 'The Oral Tradition in Scottish Gaelic Poetry' in *Scottish Studies*, vol. 12, part 1 (1968), pp. 29–43. See also Introduction in W.J. Watson, *Bàrdachd Ghàidhlig*, (Stirling, 3rd ed. 1959).
10. E.R. Cregeen (ed), *List of people on the Argyll Estate, 1779* (Scottish Record Society, 1963).
11. John Maclean died in January 1978. An excellent piper, he had some of the oldest traditions in the island. His ancestors were the Macleans known as 'Diurach' ('of Jura'). His death is an irreparable loss for the traditions of Tiree.
12. For Iain mac Ailein's songs and some details of his life see A. Maclean Sinclair, *Clàrsach na Coille* (Glasgow 1881) and H. Cameron, pp. 38–114. His ancestry is traced in A. Maclean Sinclair, *The Clan Gillean* (Charlottetown, 1899) pp. 337–8.
13. J. MacInnes argues this in the papers already referred to and quotes Martin Martin's reference to the widespread practice of verse-composition among the common people of the island.
14. See *H. Cameron*, pp. 125–6, and for the tune and an additional verse see *Tocher*, No. 18, (University of Edinburgh 1975), p. 60.
15. See Derick Thomson, 'Gaelic Learned Orders and Literati in Mediaeval Scotland' in *Scottish Studies*, vol. 2, part 1 (1968).
16. The section on Balephuil is largely based on oral traditions and recollections recorded in Tiree since 1968. Excerpts from the recollections of the remarkable *seanchaidh*, Donald Sinclair, are printed in *Tocher*, No. 18 (1975).
17. Some details about this family of MacDougall (or MacLucas) appear in *Tocher*, No. 24 (1975).
18. Donald Meek discussed the hymn-writer, Donald Sinclair, Barrapol, in a radio talk broadcast in the Gaelic service of the BBC on February 7th, 1974.
19. *Laoidhean Spioradail a chum cuideachadh le Cràbhadh nan Gael* le Donnchadh Dughallach ann an Eilein Thiridheadh. (Printed by John Niven and Son, Glasgow, 1841).
20. This John Maclean is not the same as the Balemartin Bard, but both composed songs under the title 'Manitoba.' A manuscript version of the emigrant's poem on the subject, probably written in his own hand, was

recently found in Canada by Dr Margaret Mackay of the School of Scottish Studies.

21. *Editor's note*: Dr John MacInnes, who first met Donald Sinclair in the late 1950s, points out that this phrase was *only* known within Donald's own family. Dr MacInnes recalls that it was during one of their many recording sessions that Donald's nephew used the phrase, *am bard tosdach*:

> JMacI: One day he [Donald Sinclair] began to sing a song, [one] completely unknown to me, and then suddenly he stopped and said, 'I can't go on. It's renewing sorrow.' So I said 'Who made it, Donald?' He said, 'I made it myself.' And at that moment, his nephew Donald Archie came in. And I said, 'I didn't know that Donald was a bard.' He said, 'Yes he is, and he's made quite a lot of songs but he won't let them out. He says that they're not good enough, and what we call him here is *am bard tosdach* – a silent poet.' And, so far as I am concerned, and from what I was told by that family, *that* was why Donald was called the silent poet. He thought the quality of his work wasn't good enough for these songs to be circulated generally.
>
> [Tape-recorded interview with Margaret Bennett, 1999]

22. This commonly quoted expression is from Martin Martin's *A Description of the Western Isles of Scotland, circa 1695*. [Ed.]

23. Dr John MacInnes's fieldwork, entirely in Gaelic, produced many recordings of Donald Sinclair. (One visit, for example, added over twenty tapes to School of Studies Archives, SA1965/19–40 inclusive). Looking back on these visits he recalls events:

> J.MacI.: I went to Tiree first in the late '50s . . . I set out to find the site of my great great grandfather's house . . . my great grandmother was Mór MacKinnon, the first cousin of Donald MacKinnon, the skipper of Taeping . . . And I had heard about this man, Donald Sinclair, known in the island for being a *seanchaidh* . . . he lived with his unmarried brother Hector. I recorded historical lore and stories such as the stories about Fionn and Ossian and some fragments of Ossianic ballads, Fenian ballads, and I got from him what was pretty well unique in the whole record that has been recorded for the archives in the School of Scottish Studies – some stories about Cù Chulainn. Now these are extremely rare in Scotland – some very interesting stuff. Now the next time I went, I said, 'Do you sing?' because he had already on previous occasions given me stories. And he said, 'Yes, I do a bit,' and in fact, it turned out that Donald Sinclair had a very melodious voice. He was old by that time, but he had a beautiful voice – a very good ear I woud say, and a lovely sense of rhythm and overall, tremendous style. And in subsequent visits, he turned out to have such a fund of knowledge, local knowledge, genealogy, that sort of thing, which was very interesting to me, yet was somewhat on the edge of what I was aiming to get. And I felt no one person can cope with all this. So I told Eric Creegan about him.
>
> [Tape-recorded interview with Margaret Bennett, 1999]

12
ORAL TRADITION AND HISTORY IN A HEBRIDEAN ISLAND
written 1983, published posthumously in
Scottish Studies, Vol. 32, 1998, pp. 12–37

The Gaelic-speaking Highlands of Scotland are rightly regarded as possessing unique oral traditions of great interest and immense antiquity.[1] The songs, tales, proverbs, clan traditions and music have been intensively collected and frequently published in works of folklore, literature and history. But, with a few notable exceptions, almost exclusively found among scholars versed in Gaelic, professional historians have seldom in modern times looked to this body of oral tradition as a serious historical source.[2] To date [1983], among the multiplying works on the history of the Highlands, there has been little major critical assessment of oral tradition as a historical source.

It is not surprising to find historians chary of hazarding their reputations in a field in which they are untrained.[3] Nevertheless, there is a strong *prima facie* case for approaching the history of the Highlands with a mind alert to the claims of oral tradition. It is a region where general literacy in English arrived only in the last hundred years, where written sources are relatively scarce, and often quite absent, and where the transmission of knowledge has depended very largely on oral methods. Families of hereditary *seanchaidhs* once existed under chiefly patronage to recall and recite the history of the clan. Since the eighteenth century there has been no professional class of clan historians, bards or musicians, but oral traditions have flourished at a popular level, and have been passed on both within the family and in the informal evening gatherings or *ceilidhs* where songs and stories were sung and tales recited. It is this lively popular interest in and passion for the arts that has chiefly preserved the music, poetry and narrative lore of the Highlanders up to the present.

Professionalism had gone from the scene, but the transmission of stories and songs and other lore still depended in every part of the Highlands on story tellers and singers and *seanchaidhs* with natural gifts and tenacious memories. The early collectors on the staff of the

School of Scottish Studies recorded, a generation ago, tales that required several evenings for the recital, and repertoires of individual singers (like the late Nan Mackinnon of Vatersay) that numbered several hundred songs. All these items, with few exceptions, had been acquired, and were recalled, without the intervention of writing. The historical knowledge and powers of recall of such natural *seanchaidhs* as the late Donald Alex MacEachan in Benbecula were equally impressive. He had traditional knowledge, which frequently threw light on important aspects of social and economic life in the islands which are left obscure in written records. His genealogical knowledge included virtually every family in Benbecula and ranged over three to four hundred years with ease and certainty. He described himself[4] as 'Donald Alexander, son of Alexander, son of Donald, son of Alexander, son of Eoghainn, son of Iain Bàn, son of Eoghainn Mòr of Drumnadaraich', and he was able to quote traditional accounts concerning events in the lives of his remote forebears. An example taken from one of the few recordings which he made in English may be quoted:

> There was Eoghainn, who was a soldier. He was at Culloden... He survived Culloden but he passed two miserable years in England after Culloden... in prison. And it was through Clanranald that he got out of there, that he got home. And he was slightly wounded at Culloden field and he was either taken to Leith or taken overland to London... I've heard that he was stripped even of his under-garments on Culloden field. And Clanranald paid some money, a kind of ransom, to get him back here to Benbecula, and he got the land free of rent from Clanranald till the day of his death. That was the pension he got, the croft that I reside on today. (SA 1973/34A)[5]

How accurate and valuable are such oral traditions to the historians? Granted the good faith and marvellous faculties of one's informants, how strong and reliable is the chain of transmission? William Matheson, an outstanding authority on Gaelic oral tradition, indicated in a paper given at Edinburgh in 1977, that the influence of folkloristic *motifs* and of other distorting factors has to be reckoned with. In general, however, little work has been done in the crucial area where storytelling and poetry interact with historical tradition. For that matter, we know little about the influence of political events and pressures on clan traditions, though it is a century since Skene showed how, with their land under the threat from central government, clan genealogies were revised to incorporate more acceptable forebears.

Historians and anthropologists, faced with a comparable situation in non-European societies, have examined oral traditions more critically. Some of the early optimism felt about the reliability of African historical tradition became modified as a result, notably in Vansina's work.[6] The conclusions of anthropologists such as Willis and historians such as Roberts and Law make it clear that whilst historical traditions may be of considerable value to the historian, the influence of myth, political interest, written texts and human frailty is constantly present, and operates overwhelmingly on traditions that trace back to a period before the nineteenth century.

We do not know without careful investigation whether similar conclusions are true of oral traditions in the Highlands of Scotland, where social and cultural conditions were different. The present article discusses some aspects of an investigation recently carried out at the School of Scottish Studies, which affords a firmer basis to judge the historical validity of oral tradition in the Hebridean island of Tiree. If the conclusions formed only partially agree with those reached by Africanists, it should be pointed out that our investigation was more limited in time scale, reaching back into, but hardly before, the eighteenth century. It was also based on very different types of oral material, being concerned primarily with the traditions of ordinary island families and settlements in contrast with those of ruling groups and tribal entities, as is mainly the case in African studies.

The Tiree investigation developed from a series of field-trips commencing in 1968, made with the purpose of recording from the lips of the islanders such oral traditions as survived on topics already familiar to me from earlier documentary research. The interest and abundance of the traditional lore led first to limited but detailed local studies where methods and techniques were gradually improved, and finally to a fully-developed enquiry into the history and traditions of the island from circa 1770 to 1914. A small research unit was established in 1973, with funding from the Social Science Research Council. It consisted of a director (myself), a research fellow (Dr Margaret A. Mackay), and a research assistant (Mrs Jane MacGregor). While both Dr Mackay and I had studied Gaelic and Mrs MacGregor was a native-speaker, more extensive Gaelic interviewing was made possible with the assistance of Donald W. Mackenzie, who had been reared, and had worked, in the Hebrides. We had generous academic and technical help from our colleagues in the School. Four years of intensive work, followed by further, closely related research among emigrant families in Canada, yielded a large amount of data based both on traditional and written sources.

In the period up to 1977 (which includes the earlier work in Tiree from 1968, but only the earlier part of the overseas research) our oral material was collected from over a hundred and twenty informants in some five hundred interviews. Interviews varied in length, but averaged about three hours. Approximately three hundred hours of material were recorded on tape. Nearly all songs and oral texts were recorded in Gaelic, and much of the historical tradition was recorded in both English and Gaelic versions. Our informants were drawn from a wide social range, though with a pre-dominance of crofters and their wives, craftsmen and ex-seamen, and a sprinkling of shopkeepers, professional people and members of the business world. They lived in all parts of the island, in mainland Scotland and overseas. Some were young or middle-aged but the majority were in the range sixty to eighty and above. Most were interviewed at least twice and some informants, whose range and abundance of traditional lore would have earned them in former times the respected title of *seanchaidh*, were visited frequently in successive years and recorded a score or more times.

Our collection had a historical bias, but, within the context of a wide-based study of the island community, it was in fact impossible to distinguish what was historical from what was literary or folkloristic. All categories of traditional lore were of potential value and we recorded much that might be termed popular oral literature, embracing prose narrative, poetry and song. We might, had time allowed, have collected a fuller record of such items to supplement the earlier collections of the Revd Hector Cameron and others.

Other Hebridean islands might have matched our traditional sources but possibly none could have rivalled the written sources available for Tiree. They were, nevertheless, subject to the limitations common to all historical sources referring to the Highlands (and indeed frequently also to the Lowlands) in that parish registers of births and marriages are extant only from circa 1770 (and defective in the earlier decades); deaths were unregistered before 1855; official census lists did not exist prior to 1841; private correspondence and diaries were extremely sparse; travellers' accounts mainly dated from the nineteenth century. Some legal, ecclesiastical, parliamentary and government records were relatively detailed, though mainly for the period after circa 1850, when printed material also became more available. We had the advantage, however, that Tiree had been administered for nearly three hundred years by the earls and dukes of Argyll, whose estate records, preserved at Inveraray Castle, though uncatalogued, were unusually complete and detailed. My earlier historical work on these records had made me familiar with this invaluable source and the willing help of the present duke and his father enabled this project to be realised, despite the disruption caused by a destructive fire in the castle in 1975 and its subsequent rebuilding.

Gradually we assembled two contrasting bodies of evidence – on the one hand the written record of estate and government officials, inspectors, ministers, teachers, journalists and visitors and, on the other, the popular record of oral tradition which we recorded from the islanders themselves, sitting by their fireside or on a field bank. There was now an opportunity to compare and evaluate the written and the oral records.

The two bodies of evidence are separate and distinctive. Quite apart from their contrasting literary forms, they select different aspects of history to emphasise or ignore. Even when dealing with the same topics the treatment is quite different as will become apparent in the following pages. One cannot maintain that the process of oral transmission has been totally sealed off from the growing influence of the written word, but it played a relatively minor part until the late nineteenth century; literacy was restricted and little was available in print except religious works. We have evidence that songs composed in Tiree were occasionally written down by the composer or someone else; this practice goes back into much earlier times in the Highlands, but its part in the whole process of transmission of songs, stories and family lore appears to have been slight.[vii] In order to highlight what is characteristic of the oral tradition of Tiree and to indicate its degree of validity as a historical source, it is proposed in this article to cite a selection of the collected material, which relates to the island during the period *circa* 1770 to 1850.

In 1770 the island of Tiree, lying far out from the mainland of Argyll, lacking a good harbour and surrounded by turbulent seas, was remarkably isolated from the rest of Scotland. Its population, numbering between 1700 and 1800 people and scattered in small communities over the twenty-eight square miles of the island, was largely indigenous and untravelled and spoke only Gaelic. Agriculture was the basis of the economy and land was widely distributed among the small tenants, who in turn gave employment to the cottars, a group which provided the craftsmen, labourers and servants and was usually paid in grazing rights and the use of small plots of arable land. The island was relatively fertile and supported the population in greater comfort than was usual in the Highlands. Little was imported and the rents were paid from the barley crop and the proceeds of a flourishing trade in locally-distilled whisky. (*Instructions* xxvi ff.)

There were about thirty extensive farms on the island. Some were in the hands of tacksmen (upper tenants), three of them Macleans, the others Campbells who resided in Mull or elsewhere in Argyll. Most of the farms, however, were occupied by groups of co-tenants who practised a semi-communal system, in which the individually-worked and scattered strips of arable were periodically reallocated among the tenants. This runrig agriculture rested on cooperation and, at some cost in terms of efficiency and experiment, ensured rough justice.

Manufacture, apart from a feeble linen industry, scarcely existed, and there was no commercial fishery. Land and cattle were thus of vital importance to the islanders, and the object of constant striving and concern. The upper tenants had traditionally enjoyed extensive holdings of land by virtue of their kinship with the laird. Under the Campbell chiefs, the claims of blood were more grudgingly acknowledged, but were not ignored and tended to perpetuate the economic privileges of the tacksmen (Cregeen 1969).

Ordinary islanders regularly divided their holdings to support close relations, a custom which was already by 1770 producing serious fragmentation of land. More widely, they belonged to kinship groups which bound together tenants and cottars and were usually concentrated in particular localities. Thus many MacUolrigs (Kennedies) were clustered in a number of contiguous townships in the extreme west, a group of MacDonald kinsfolk at the east end, and a concentration of Campbells in and about Balenoe. The members in each group traced their descent from a common ancestor. Sometimes this ancestor was of high status as in the case of the *'Diùrach'* (Jura) Macleans, who claimed as their founder in Tiree a certain *Ailein Dubh* ('black Alan') who may date to the sixteenth century. In May 1974 John MacLean, crofter in Cornaigbeg, usually known as *Iain Alasdair*, gave me his genealogy, which included nine generations (excluding himself): thus *Iain* (himself)–*Alasdair–Iain–Dòmhnall–Iain Og–Iain–Iain Og–Ailein Diùrach–Tearlach–Ailein Dubh*. It is believed that *Ailein Dubh* was the first of the Diùrach MacLeans to settle in Tiree and that another member of the stock, *Aonghas Diùrach,* settled in Lewis. From comparison with documentary sources I have concluded that the traditional genealogy is correct. One of his forebears is found in a rental of 1663 as John McAllen Vc Carlich (evidently a great-grandson of Ailein Dubh). Thus consciousness of rank and class was contained within a framework of family and kin.

Clanship was dying out as a political force in the Highlands in the late eighteenth century, but the sentiment of clanship was still amazingly strong in Tiree. This was partly because of historical circumstances. The Campbells had acquired Tiree and other territories from the former chiefs and lairds, the Macleans of Duart, in the late seventeenth century. Maclean tacksmen and their allies and dependants had witnessed the alienation of much of their land to Campbell settlers and others favoured by the dukes of Argyll (Cregeen 1969, 96–99). Resentment against the intruders continued to fuel the loyalty of the islanders to the representatives of the Macleans even as late as the end of the eighteenth century. 'The small tenants of Tiry.' wrote an official of the new duke in 1771, 'are disaffected to the family of Argyll. In this disposition it's thought that long leases might render them too much independent of them and encourage the people to that sort of insolence and outrage to which they are naturally prone and much incited by their chieftains of the Maclean gentry.[8] These words, from the pen of a member of the Campbell settlers in Mull, reflect not only Maclean hostility to the

Campbells but the distrust which the Campbells entertained towards the Macleans and their supporters in the island.

The oral traditions of the island were inevitably much affected by events. The Maclean chiefs had formerly maintained bards, pipers and *seanchaidhs* (the *seanchaidh* was part story-teller, part historian) to celebrate clan deeds and provide entertainment in their halls. Such posts were hereditary in certain families, and served to transmit lore and skills from one generation to the next. Chiefly patronage ceased in the eighteenth century, except on a modest scale among the minor Campbell and Maclean gentry who resided in Tiree (Cregeen and Mackenzie 1978, 5–7). The last of the official bards, John Maclean, received patronage from the laird of the neighbouring island of Coll, as had his great-grandfather. Neil Lamont, but, for lack of sufficient material support, he emigrated to Canada in 1819.

As clan institutions for the transmission of lore and history withered, oral tradition of a more popular kind rose to prominence in Tiree as elsewhere in the Highlands. In the early 1790s the natives of the island were described as much attached to dancing, song and storytelling (*OSA* XX (1794), 1983, 276). This ceilidh tradition, with its nightly gatherings in house or barn for entertainment, persisted vigorously through the nineteenth century and into fairly recent times. The earlier, more aristocratic tradition still had an influence; after all the storytellers and 'village poets' were sometimes descended from the ancient families of official *seanchaidhs* and bards. But the focus of interest in bardic composition moved to the everyday events and familiar personalities of the contemporary scene, and the songs, with their fresh and topical flavour, convey the experiences and emotions of the ordinary islanders (Cregeen and Mackenzie 1978). The songs of the Maclean period appear to have fallen out of use and none survived to be written down or recorded in Tiree in the twentieth century.

It is now necessary, before discussing the oral evidence that bears on the late eighteenth and early nineteenth centuries, to explain briefly what emerges from a study of the written records of that period.

Tiree, in common with the Highlands in general, was profoundly affected by the industrialisation of the Scottish Lowlands. The growth of woollen manufacture brought extensive sheep-farming and depopulation to the interior of the Highlands, but Lowland industry affected maritime areas in a quite different way. There it stimulated the labour-intensive kelp-burning manufacture which used seaweed as its raw material. The rise of this industry discouraged emigration and thus tended to be associated with a rapid increase of population (Gray 1957, 124–137). The Napoleonic war period in Tiree was one of swift economic change, unusual prosperity and soaring population. The islanders benefited from the kelp boom, in contrast to many Hebrideans, largely because the Argyll estate left the kelp shores in the possession of the tenants under leases which gave them a generous share of the profits (*Instructions*, xxvii–xxxiii, 32ff., 46, 185–194, and unpublished 'Instructions').

Agriculture and settlement patterns underwent a most significant change during the war period. Under the paternalistic rule of the 5th duke of Argyll, one of the great improvers of his age, the landless cottars were settled on small holdings. This was made possible by his radical policy of depriving the non-resident Campbell gentry of their farms in Tiree and dividing them into crofts of six and ten acres. A commercial fishery was also established for the employment of the crofters. Most important of all, the duke finally gained the assent and cooperation of the islanders in a scheme he had long cherished: the traditional runrig system was abandoned and in its place compact individual farms, averaging about twenty-five acres (ten hectares), were created within the townships for the previous runrig tenants. Whilst retaining certain communal activities, the tenants were now free to develop their arable land as they wished. Aided by long leases, grants and technical and other assistance from the estate, the islanders began to adopt new crops and methods (*Instructions*, 73–79). This was a veritable revolution and it stands as one of the most impressive instances of beneficial improvement in Highland Scotland, where change was too often accompanied by clearance and hardship (*Instructions*, xxx–xxxv and 55ff.).

Conditions deteriorated in the post-1815 period. It was one of the penalties of becoming enmeshed in world markets that the local economies of the islands were rendered more vulnerable. Tiree suffered severely in the post-war decline in agricultural prices and especially from the collapse of the market for kelp. The hardship was intensified by the rapid growth of the population of the island, which doubled in the fifty years after 1790, rising from 2,416 in 1792 to 4,687 in 1841 (*Instructions*, xxxix and *NSA* 208). Younger islanders resorted to seasonal work in the Lowlands, but there was little permanent emigration until the late 1840s when blight destroyed the potato crop over a number of years and the threat of starvation brought a wholesale exodus (Tiree papers, Inveraray Castle).

We turn now to consider what oral record survives in the memory of the islanders about this period of growth and innovation. We found many traditions bearing on the late eighteenth and early nineteenth centuries, mainly among old people in their seventies and eighties. They took the form of songs, stories and anecdotes, place-name lore, sayings and genealogies. Like the written sources they varied in abundance, being sometimes amazingly full and detailed, sometimes sparse or non-existent. On the one hand they recreated the stir and bustle of vanished communities and breathed life into mere names; on the other hand they would sometimes ignore events of importance as if they had never occurred and took delight, it seemed, in mingling fact and fantasy. A brief acquaintance with the island and its traditions might have given the impression that historians had little to learn from this strange amalgam. Growing knowledge of the less obvious riches of our informants' minds was to prove more rewarding.

The leading figures of the times had left their impression on oral tradition, as one would have expected. In general the earlier dukes were august figures beyond the normal range of popular knowledge and recall, though 'Duke John' (*Iain diùc*) appeared several times in the tradition of one informant. But oral tradition has much to say about the duke's chamberlains, those grand officials who were entrusted with the administration of the island and whose word was law. In the traditional accounts they often appear as larger than life and are represented either as heroic personages or as sinister and awesome figures. Their persons have been magnified by the story-telling tradition of the *ceilidh*, and coloured by the imagery of the heroic tale, but they preserve an identity which we can recognise as the historical characters we know from the written records. Even in their exaggerated form they act, as it were, in character. The traditions which survive about Donald Campbell or '*Bàillidh Dòmhnull*' serve as an illustration.

Donald Campbell held sway as chamberlain from 1770 to 1800. He belonged to one of the Campbell families who had settled in Mull and were evidently descended from the Lochnell branch of the Campbells (*Instructions*, 3). Estate papers reveal him as a man of stubborn integrity, who consistently defended the interests of the islanders and irritated his superiors by pointing out the inadequacies of doctrinaire schemes of economic improvement (*Instructions*, 1–49). An old man called Donald Sinclair[9] sometimes spoke to me about the chamberlain, referring to him as *Bàillidh Dòmhnull* and praising his noble and benevolent character. It was striking that, although the oral traditions took the characteristic form of praise-song and heroic tale, their general tenor was in agreement with what one knew of him from written sources. According to the accounts which had been current in his township when he was young, the *Bàillidh* had two sons who fought in the Peninsular war and were killed in battle. He had heard old people sing eulogies of the sons and of their father, composed by a Tiree bard at the time, and he rendered some verses of one of the songs. Composed by Archibald MacPhail, who lived at Balephuil in his later life, the songs must have formed part of the local repertoire. These were evidently the songs with which Donald Sinclair was familiar, and the verses which he sang came from the lament '*Do Dhonnchadh agus do Alasdair Caimbeul, clann Bàillidh Thireadh, a chaidh a mharbhadh anns an Spàinn*' but include the following lines not found in the published version.[10] His was a genuine orally transmitted one:

> Nuair a theann sibh ri sèiseadh a thoirt a' bhaile gu geill d' ur command,
> 'N àm gluasad on bhatraidh, cha robh smuainteanan gealtach nur ceann;
> 'N àm dìreadh an àraidh thainig peileir o d nàmhaid na dheann
> 'S mun do bhuannaich thu 'n fhàrdraich, thuit thu gun chàil aig a bhonn.
>
> 'S ò an iongnadh do mhàthair a bhith euslainteach fàillinneach tinn!
> Chaneil duin' aic' an làthair de na chunnaic do dh'àraich a glùn;
> 'S e seo buille bu chràidhteach dhi, a' smaointinn mar bha thu gun chlí
> Call na fala san àraich 's tu cho fada bho d' chàirdean 's bho d' thìr.
>
> When you began the siege to bring the town under your command,
> As you advanced from the battery, there was no cowardly thought in your head;
> As you scaled the height, a bullet came at speed from your enemy
> And before you could gain the ground you fell lifeless at the foot.
>
> And oh, is it any wonder that your mother is sick in heart and soul,
> She is bereft of all those whom she raised at her knee;
> This was her sorest wound, thinking of you with all your strength gone,
> Your life-blood draining away on the battlefield, far away from friends and your homeland.

The two sons, according to the praise-songs, had all the courage, strength, beauty and ferocity that are usually attributed in traditional Gaelic poetry to heroic warriors. One of them set up a battery on a hill in Spain during the Peninsular war and is represented as carrying two massive cannons, one under each arm. The existence of the songs must have helped to perpetuate traditions of Donald Campbell and his sons, for they would be sung and discussed in the *ceilidh*. Donald Sinclair's account of the young men is influenced by them, but he also had other sources of information. When he was a child his family had known an old man whose father remembered them as boys playing shinty (Donald sometimes rendered the Gaelic term *camanachd* as 'hockey') on a grassy level land behind the shore.

> Macdonald was his name. Duncan Macdonald. He would tell you a story about Bàillidh Dòmhnull's children. When he was a boy he was brought up over somewhere at Hilipol there, and the Bàillidh's sons, you know between the pillar up at the Bàillidh's house and the church down at Balenoe, the level ground that is there, they used to be playing hockey there, and this Duncan Bàn, he used to tell my father when the factor's sons would be running you would fancy it was horses that was running, the ground was shaking under their feet. And the two of them were killed

in Spain. Aye, a pity, aye. (SA 1969/165B.)

There is no reason to doubt the authenticity of the story of the boys playing shinty on the Balenoe *machair*, but Donald's account is that of a story-teller and it echoes the imagery of the heroic tales which he had heard recited in his childhood.

The Napoleonic war formed the background of a good deal of anecdote and local tradition which bear the hallmark of authenticity. Some traditions crystallised around the battle of Waterloo. A fine informant, Hector Kennedy, gave the names of local men who had been press-ganged and had been at the battle.[11] He recounted that his own great-grandfather Archibald Campbell was present and survived the battle but died at the hands of a wounded French soldier afterwards. Hector showed us the croft at Barrapol which he had occupied and the two houses built by his sons when the croft was later divided between them. Another family still bears the nickname, which derived from their ancestor's action in evading conscription by cutting off the end of his thumb. The historical basis for these traditions cannot be put to the proof but it is clearly necessary to know what degree of veracity such local and family traditions have. Fortunately it has been possible to put traditions of similar age to the test, in particular certain traditions about a local migration.

A surveyed plan of the island made by James Turnbull in 1769 shows the settlement of Hough as a cluster of houses on the west side of the hill of Beinn Hough. At some time its location was changed and the present inhabitants of Hough live on the east side of the hill. In our search for information we learned from Hector Kennedy that a sandstorm had deluged the old settlement, the well had filled with sand, and the inhabitants had removed inland to Kilmoluag (SA 1979/75). The story of this event was amplified by others. Local tradition at Kilmoluag, we found, confirmed the Hough origin of a number of families. One old man in his nineties directed us to the site of the abandoned house of his forebear. Another informant. Alasdair Macdonald, a descendant of one of the migrants, ascribed the migration of his great-grandfather, Alan Macdonald, and of other inhabitants of Hough, to drifting sand.

The event was assigned by Hector Kennedy to the Spring before the battle of Waterloo and he connected it with the visit of the press-gang to Tiree 'for the first time'. Usually the chronology of an event in oral tradition has vaguer boundaries though the use of such phrases as 'when my grandfather was a boy' can limit an event to within a decade. It was important for us to explore historical sources to test the authenticity of this tradition. In favour of its credibility was the fact that he had learned it from a certain Willie MacPhail, a reputable tradition-bearer and bard at Kilmoluag, and that he himself had proved unusually reliable and well-informed on many occasions. It was also perfectly credible that a settlement should have been abandoned as a consequence of inundation by blown sand. Such occurrences are well authenticated in the Hebrides, and in Tiree it is known from Turnbull's 1769 Description that sand-drift had rendered as much as an eighth of the agricultural land useless in the late eighteenth century and that sand had overwhelmed a kirkyard at Kilkenneth near Hough some years before 1792 (*OSA*, XX (1794), 1983, 263–4). There was a major problem, however, in that relevant documents between 1810 and the early 1820s were not to be found. In no written source known to us was there any explicit reference to the events at Hough.

My colleague, Dr Margaret A. Mackay, went some way towards solving the problem when she examined the Tiree and Coll parish register. She found that there had indeed been a movement of population from Hough to Kilmoluag. In the years immediately following, children were recorded as born at Kilmoluag to parents who had not long previously had children recorded as born at Hough. An estate rental of 1823 showed tenants at Kilmoluag who had been earlier resident at Hough.

But did the events occur exactly as the traditional account represents? Since the migration was evidently in progress in, or shortly after, 1820, either the traditional association with the Spring before Waterloo was incorrect or else there was a series of minor migrations, starting off after a catastrophic storm in 1815 and continuing as the sand spread its havoc further over the settlement, until the whole population had moved. Such a development would accord with experience of the way in which coastal land is progressively damaged by blown sand. If this was the case, the tradition has presented a gradual movement as a single dramatic event in a manner characteristic of the story teller's art and well known to folklorists. Alternatively, we may suppose that the migration in fact took place around 1820 and was transposed in time, somewhere along the chain of oral transmission, either through a misunderstanding or for dramatic effect. There are other examples in traditional accounts of a great event, here the battle of Waterloo, exercising its gravitational attraction on minor events in its temporal field.

Whichever is the true explanation of this mysterious event, it was rescued from oblivion by oral tradition, and the substantial accuracy of the oral account is largely supported by such historical records as could be discovered. At the same time it is evident that, in matters of detail, tradition has taken certain liberties perhaps in the interests of dramatic effect, and requires the restraining hand of the sober historian. Dr Mackay sums up her conclusions after a detailed study of this case: 'Neither the oral tradition nor the written sources can tell the whole story of what happened at Hough, but used in combination each can illuminate the other and add a further dimension to the account.'[12]

If we consider the history of Tiree settlements more generally, the contrasting but complementary nature of the two bodies of data becomes more evident. The written sources, especially estate papers, often contain detailed evidence on the physical character of the townships, their agricultural system and economic value, social composition and demographic features. It is given in a coherent form and frequently statistically, combined with observations that show the historian that the writer is like himself in his thought-processes and values. This particular form of presentation is usually absent from the body of oral data. Its evidence is rarely given either in broad generalisations or with exact numerical precision. Its view is that of the insider and its language and images, familiar to the islanders, frequently have to be interpreted before they can be understood and utilised by the historian. Once understood, oral evidence was found to shed light on many aspects of social life, and complemented the evidence of officials and reporters in a fascinating way.

The topographic evidence was straightforward enough, though requiring some knowledge of Gaelic. It enabled us to fix the location of settlements which had almost vanished and identify their wells, folds, kilns, bothies and other structures. The ruins of dwellings, deserted over a century ago, occasionally preserved the names of their occupants. The remains of a church of eighteenth-century date, sometimes mentioned in the records but recently described as having left 'no identifiable remains' (RCAHMS *Argyll*, Vol. 3, 158n.) were yet shown to us, clear and unmistakable, by an informant on the open moor of Druimbuigh. The building was known to him and others as *an taigh-searmoin* ('the preaching house') and was connected with other lore, including the tradition that the first Independent minister in Tiree, Archibald Farquharson, had regularly preached there.

The destruction of a settlement by sand impressed itself on the folk-memory, but, strangely enough, there is no comparable tradition concerning the way in which the runrig settlements were transformed into townships of compact small farms and individual crofts. The impression derived from contemporary estate papers is of an island in a ferment of activity between 1803 and 1807 (*Instructions*, 93–97, and unpublished Instructions). Tenants occupied the new buildings which had been allotted to them in their townships and built houses and enclosures, dragging stones and timbers from the houses of the old settlements nearby, whilst landless cottars, eager to secure a holding, moved from their townships to the new crofting settlements at Scarinish, Heanish, Balemartin, Gott, Mannal and Balephuil. In the background of all the bustle was the enigmatic figure of the chamberlain, Malcolm MacLaurine, busy attending to the duke's orders or his own private and less respectable pursuits. The written sources point clearly to a relatively swift and radical change in a deep-rooted way of life. In the oral traditions of the island, knowledge survives of ancestors who moved to newly created holdings, but one would never suspect that a new policy had been introduced and with it a dramatic social change.

The contrast in what is conveyed by the two types of source can be demonstrated if we consider the township of Balephuil in the south-west of the island. The 5th duke withdrew this large farm from the chamberlain in order to accommodate cottars and returned fencible soldiers. In the estate records we find that in 1806 a number of soldiers moved into the crofts there and were soon followed by settlers from other townships (unpublished letters and Instructions at Inveraray Castle). These settlers are rarely named in the surviving records and their place of origin usually remains unknown. Some engaged in fishing and were assisted by the estate to acquire boats and lines. The new chamberlain, Malcolm MacLaurine, showed his resentment for the loss of the farm in the acts of petty vindictiveness against the settlers here and elsewhere, but the duke protected them and sternly reminded the official of the responsibilities of his position, as he had done in 1803 when he wrote: 'I sent you to Tyree to be my factor, to look after and promote my interest and the good of the people, not to be a great farmer seeking suddenly to enrich and aggrandise yourself.' (*Instructions*, 95).

These events and personalities are preserved in oral tradition but in a significantly different way. It knows nothing of MacLaurine's connection with these agrarian reforms, but several informants had accurate details of his personal life – that he was a doctor, that he lived with a sister at Hilipol and that he carried on amours with local women. Some verses of an unpublished bawdy song, composed by one of the Balephuil poets, narrate one of his affairs with a loose woman in the neighbourhood in vivid nautical imagery (SA 1968/263B). It was not until some years after the song was recorded that my colleague Dr Margaret Mackay discovered from the parish register that he had fathered two illegitimate children on two different women in the district.

Our informants also had tales of uncanny powers possessed by the chamberlain. He had succeeded in floating a boat marooned on the shore and had known where to find a stolen piece of timber which he had intended to use as a mast. The source of his knowledge was said to be a large black book which he kept in the house. Whilst he consulted it he wore an iron hoop on his head as protection against the powers he was invoking to his aid (SA 1969/165B and SA 1970/106A). These stories, told with perfect seriousness, evidently reflect what the islanders believed and felt about the chamberlain at that time.[13] They convey resentment and distrust, but, mingled with these, is a certain respect and awe for the man's power and esoteric knowledge. Whilst they incorporate *motifs* widely known in oral literature, they express a certain moral truth about MacLaurine and dramatise the self-seeking and sinister aspects of the man.

What has tradition preserved of the actual history of the creation of the crofting townships? It has retained nothing to suggest the sequence of events that created crofts in this and other townships or the upheaval in old-established practices they brought. What the oral traditions recorded at Balephuil do provide, however, are invaluable details of families and individuals who settled here and formed its character, and many sidelights on township life during a long period after the Napoleonic War when written sources are largely silent. This concentration on the experience of individuals, often kinsmen of our informants, to the exclusion of more general movements, is one of the distinctive characteristics of the oral record. It can be turned to advantage for historical reconstruction, as I hope to show in relation to the township of Balephuil, where I recorded a considerable body of information, mainly between 1968 and 1974.

These traditions concern a number of families among the early settlers in the township who eventually became linked by marriage. There are the Sinclairs, a family celebrated for traditions of all kinds, whose earlier associations were evidently with the north-west of the island; the Macdonalds who came from the east end of the island and were known as *'na Duibh'* (a name which referred to their dark colouring); the Macleans, who also hailed from the east end and possessed a gift for poetic composition so that other families still like to claim relationship with them; the Browns whose ancestor married into this stock and whose present-day representative is a notable *seanchaidh*; the Blacks, whose forebear came as a minor estate official and was given a croft at Balephuil. These are only five of the forty-three crofter families who originally settled at Balephuil, but their family traditions, which are interwoven with one another and with others in the township, will serve to illumine the early history of the community.

They tell us of a returned soldier named *Calum mac Iain 'ic Nill*, or Malcolm Macdonald, settling on a croft which is still pointed out above a shore where kelp was burnt in kilns. According to family lore he had served in the Peninsular War as a valet to a surgeon and on his return put his experience to good use by practising the art of bleeding on his fellow-islanders; hence his nickname 'Lancer'. A characteristic story describes how he quarrelled about the seaweed with a woman on the shore and how, calling her a witch he drew his lancer's knife and slashed her petticoat and marked her (SA 1969/165). Tradition says that he came from Caolas at the east end of Tiree and that he was one of the so-called 'black Macdonalds' who were known for their lawless behaviour. This traditional lore and his patronymic, naming him as *Calum mac Iain 'ic Nill 'ic Dhomhnuill 'ic Iain Duibh* (Malcolm son of John son of Neil son of Donald son of black John), enabled us to overcome the problem of defective estate and parish records and to attach him to a family of tenants who occupied land at the east end of the island a century before Malcolm moved to Balephuil (SA 1969/165 and SA 1971/90B). This is one among many instances in which oral tradition made identification possible and so provided the key to information contained in written sources which would otherwise have been inaccessible.

The Macdonalds became allied with the Macleans by the marriage of Malcolm's sister, Mary, to Donald Maclean.[14] A brother of the famous bard, John Maclean, Donald (otherwise known as 'the Cooper') could turn his hand to making a song as easily as he could fashion a barrel out of oaken staves. Donald and Mary settled at Balephuil on a poor croft which they later exchanged for a better one and established a thriving family, all of whom were talented and given to composing songs. His own songs were true 'village poetry', descriptions of local events and persons, and were passed on orally till recent times. From one of them we learn of his flitting from the old township, Caolas, at the east end of the island to the new croft at the west end, and the tasks which faced him in ploughing up the wet, rushy land with a plough repaired by the local blacksmith and a team of four horses made up with the help of number of fellow-crofters (SA 1971/92).[15]

A daughter of Malcolm MacDonald, Anne, married Alasdair Sinclair[16] (*Alasdair Og*), who occupied a nearby croft, and from them descended the remarkable tradition-bearer Donald Sinclair, who was usually known as *Dòmhnall Chaluim Bàin* – Donald son of fair Malcolm. Malcolm was a great storyteller, sought out by folklorists in the last century. I knew Donald as an old man and recorded a great variety of lore from him – charms, cures, sayings, place-names, genealogies, folk-tales, anecdotes, songs and reminiscences. He drew his vast store from many sources, from *ceilidhing* with old people, and from inheriting the accumulated traditions of Macleans, MacDonalds, Sinclairs, MacArthurs and other families connected with him. Although by the time that I knew him he was over eighty and his mind was occasionally confused, his traditional knowledge was remarkable in range, accuracy and depth. Among a group of outstanding tradition-bearers connected with Balephuil, he was recognised as the doyen.[17]

The written sources are often silent on the life of the crofting township in the years 1810 to 1840; births and marriages are recorded, and there are occasional lists of tenants and their rents, but little else, as the estate records for Tiree are incomplete in the second quarter of the nineteenth century. In the local songs and traditions however there is mention of fishing trips and boats bringing in smuggled tobacco and liquor; of illicit stills making whisky; of the herding of cattle and milking in the folds; of occupations carried on by local men and of young men and women travelling to the Lowland harvests; of marriages and deaths in the community; and tales of 'waking' the dead; of poets and storytellers in the township, and witchcraft and the second sight; of disasters and epidemics and emigrations. It would in fact be quite impossible to present an accurate and balanced social history of the island community without drawing upon oral traditions. Sometimes they are the only source of information about the normal events of daily life; at other times they supplement and illumine what written records provide.

Typical of such transmitted lore are the songs and stories about the herding of cattle on the commons, a subject which is little noticed in written sources. In oral sources it is often mentioned, sometimes with reference to fairly recent times, when the virtues and vices of the township herd are a recurring theme in the island's satiric songs, sometimes in the remoter past.[18] Children were much employed in herding, but the crofters of each township usually jointly engaged one or more professional herds. The remains of two drystone buildings on the slope of Beinn Hoighnis were shown to us in 1973 by a Balephuil crofter, John Brown, and identified by him as the former dwellings of herdsmen. The lower one, which was much dilapidated, was known as *taigh a' bhuachaille bhig* ('the little herd's house'), and the upper one as *taigh a' bhuachaille mhòir* ('the big herd's house').

The upper dwelling stood in a fold enclosed by a crumbling stone and turf dyke, where the grass still showed a more intense green than the surrounding hill. Above the fold was a strong dyke encircling the upper slopes and identified by our informant as *garadh nan each* ('the horses' enclosure'), a name which indicated where the tenants used to graze the sturdy ponies, so often referred to in eighteenth century estate papers and eventually banished early in the nineteenth century (*Instructions*, 55, 59, 67, 89). The substantial walls of the herdsman's dwelling contained a small chamber near the entrance which fitted the description of it as a dog's kennel, whilst two slab-lined pits against the outer wall were said to have been used to store potatoes, which were part of his pay. It would be difficult to date the structure exactly. According to our informant it had fallen out of use long before his father was born in 1882 but its well-built stone walls, its state of preservation and the mention of potatoes provided by the crofters suggest an early nineteenth century context.

The history of the crofting families of Balephuil was also greatly amplified by our oral sources, which could be used to enhance the potential of written sources by providing more certain identification and other key information. Written sources mention some of the crofters and cottars of Balephuil in the early nineteenth century, in brief entries in rentals, parish registers or the records of government departments. One may discover their occupations, age, marriage-partner and children's names, their rent and how it was paid and whether they were in arrears. With luck one may find out whether they made kelp or had a fishing boat. But their personal traits and habits are seldom revealed, and their family connections and origins are usually difficult or impossible to verify. Names such as John Maclean and Donald MacDonald are so common even within one township that sure identification in historical sources is often impracticable. This is not so in the oral record of the township. Our informants knew their grandparents and great-grandparents by their patronymic and could guide us unhesitatingly to their kin and often to their place of origin.

Duncan Macdonald is recorded in the official census of 1841 as a boatbuilder aged thirty-five, resident at Balephuil with his wife Janet and a daughter, Margaret. The records are otherwise unilluminating. In local tradition he is remembered as *Donnchadh Bàn mac Iain 'ic Sheumais* ('fair haired Duncan son of John son of James'), a skilled craftsman who travelled about widely, building sloops and smacks and whose family probably came to Balephuil from the neighbourhood of Hilipol. It was his father, Iain, who, in Donald Sinclair's account, witnessed the *bàillidh's* sons playing shinty on the *machair* (SA 1971/90A).

Neil Brown is listed in the same census as a crofter, aged fifty, living at Balephuil with his wife Margaret and five children. Earlier he had had two small crofts and a Rental of 1823 shows that he was more than able to pay the rent on these (£1 8s. 6d. and £2 8s. 6d.) from the proceeds of kelp (£4 15s. 9d.). From family tradition we know that he was *Niall Mòr mac Iain 'ic Dhughaill* ('big Neil son of John son of Dugald') and that he had worked as a young man at foundries in the Clyde area as well as at (probably seasonal) farm-work; that the wife he married was a daughter of Donald the 'Cooper' who from her devotion to Highland ways was known as *Mairead Ghàidhealach* ('Highland Margaret'), that two of the daughters went to be servants on Lowland farms and one of their sons, Charles, left to work as a carpenter at Greenock where he died of smallpox at the age of twenty. A nephew who died aged ninety in 1972 had been named Charles after him and with his son John, was my source for these traditions (SA 1974/83, SA 1976/120, and field-notes, 1972). From John Brown we know that his father and predecessors kept up the relationship with the Macleans at Caolas and attended their funerals at the east end – this for nearly a century and a half after Donald Maclean's removal to Balephuil. The origin of the Browns before their move to Balephuil is not retained, but the clues provided by the oral genealogy when combined with evidence in estate papers, strongly indicate the township of Balemeanach.

Here also in the census is John Black,[19] a widower and crofter of sixty years in 1841. The 1823 Rental shows him as occupying a croft for which he paid a rent of £8 17s. 0d. – but the 1851 census describes him as 'pauper'. Family tradition is much fuller and more accurate in some respects. The census of 1851 gives his birthplace as 'Tiree', whereas Donald Sinclair (his great-grandson) narrates that he was of a Lismore family (inherently more probable) and that he came to Tiree in the service of the chamberlain. MacLaurine, bringing with him a wife from Inveraray and eventually settled in a croft by the shore at Balephuil (though now in Hynish West) which he lost at the time of the potato failure. Donald had a great deal of information about John Black's descendants. One of his daughters, Isabella, also appears in the census of 1841, married to an agricultural worker, Archibald Maclean. Her husband, known as *'an cìobair'* (the shepherd) was to die in a fishing disaster. Isabella Black is of special interest and will appear again in the story of Balephuil.

Brief illustrations have been given of the combined use of written and oral sources in the areas of family history, personal biography and economic activities. In the historic reconstruction of social and cultural life the value of oral tradition is perhaps even more important, for written sources are rarely able to illumine the mental activities, spiritual values and customary practices of Highland communities. They belonged to a world beyond the reach and interest of the English-speaking traveller, official and improver. No-one familiar only with the written records would suspect the cultural vitality of this township of crofters and fishermen. Most Highland townships had a poet or two but Balephuil was *baile nam bàrd* ('the township of the bards') and had numerous poets of both sexes. The poetic tradition existed early, for Archibald MacPhail, who composed the eulogies on Donald Campbell and his two sons, lived here (Cameron 1932, 4). The tradition was reinforced by the arrival of other settlers given to poetic composition: Donald 'the Cooper' and his family, the Macdonalds at 'the *Sliabh*' (the upland area of Balephuil), the Blacks, the 'Manitoba' Macleans, and other talented families. From quite early in the nineteenth century there was a most remarkable burgeoning of song-composition in this township (Cregeen and Mackenzie 1978, 13ff). Some families like the Sinclairs were more given to storytelling and *seanchas* (historical tradition), and others to dancing and piping, but there was a general delight in songs in every section of the community, which we found still widespread and remarkable among the other people of Tiree. With this went a high regard for and a certain fear of the poets as men and women of special power. It was they who celebrated in their compositions the significant events in the life of the community – the deaths, disasters, marriages and rejoicings – and immortalised the virtues of the living and the departed; they also mocked and ridiculed those who incurred their dislike in witty, bawdy, often savage satires. Donald Sinclair, himself a bard, was well aware of their fearful power and told me 'A wise man would keep on the poet's side so that he would not expose them'.

Oral sources proved able to suggest the operation of new cultural influences and subtle changes in the township. Among the bardic families was that of Duncan MacDougall,[20] who came from Mull circa 1820 as a Gaelic teacher and remained in Tiree as a Baptist missionary. He had a croft at Balephuil, baptised converts in the loch on the north side of the township and composed hymns of unusual merit. He came of a family of poets, his sister Mary being remembered in Mull as an accomplished bard and known more widely as the composer of the hymn *Leanabh an Aigh* (translated as 'Child in a Manger'). He himself had a family of children given to poetic composition. Nevertheless it is evident from oral sources that evangelical religion began to affect the poetic and story-telling tradition of Balephuil. It weaned some of the bards away from their concern with secular poetry, as in the case of the fisherman Alexander MacDonald.

John Black's daughter, Isabella, wife of the shepherd, referred to earlier, expressed this new spiritual concern in a song which she made on seeing a thrush singing on a rock on the shore. Like most of the village songs it was never printed but I have heard it sung. After addressing the thrush and praising its song, she compares its fate with that of herself and other mortal men and women:

> Nach sona dhuit aig àm do bhàs,
> cha sàsaichear gu mòd thu.
> Tuitidh tu sìos air an làr
> 's gu bràth cha tig ort feòirich;
> Ach nuair a laigheas mise sìos
> 's a dhinnichear on fhòd mi,
> Mur bi mi beò an Iosa Crìosd
> gun dìtear aig a' mhòd mi.
>
> You are fortunate at the time of your death
> That you will not be dragged before the tribunal.
> You will fall down upon the ground
> But there will be no investigation of your life.
> But when I lie down
> And am pressed beneath the sward
> Unless I am alive in Jesus Christ
> I will stand condemned at the judgment-seat.
>
> (SA 1968/144A)[21]

It is evidence of this kind, drawn from oral tradition, that provides us with the clearest indications that social and cultural change, induced by contacts with the Lowlands, was taking place in Tiree in the early or middle decades of the century.

In the disastrous years between circa 1845 and 1850, the island, in common with much of the Highlands, was devastated by the failure of its potato crops and was drastically thinned by emigration. Balephuil lost many of its younger people including two sons of the Lancer and members of the Cooper's family and others who sailed to Canada. The sombre events can be followed in heartrending detail in documentary sources, which bring out the enormity of the crisis and the immense scale of relief measures organised by government, churches, lairds and private individuals. In oral tradition the calamities of these years have left only faint traces; there are excellent tradition-bearers who know nothing of this time of hunger, when over a third of the population had to leave the island. This strange ignorance is a reminder that sometimes the folk memory is faulty, or chooses to forget.[22] The explanation in this particular instance is a complex one which merits detailed treatment in a future essay but would be out of place here.

In July 1856 a great storm sprang up suddenly and scattered the little fishing fleet, which had set sail from Balephuil that morning. Twelve or more men and boys were drowned. The whole township was affected in one way or another. Except for notes left by one of the fishermen (Cameron 1932, 125–6), little is found in the written sources about the storm, but oral traditions still surviving at Balephuil and its neighbourhood about the '*Fuadach*' preserve the details of this event and the impact which it had on the district in a way which written sources could not rival. It is illuminating to consider them, for they illustrate the insights into basic patterns of thought and behaviour which oral sources afford. None of the five families mentioned earlier was directly involved except the Blacks; Isabel Black's husband, 'the shepherd', was drowned. The Sinclairs, though they were fishermen, sensed that the calm clear weather was deceptive and stayed at home. The scene was played out before the terrified onlookers:

> My mother remembered that day. She was a girl, a big girl at the time. And she saw two of the boats, they nearly made it but it was two old men and boys that was aboard and the boys was tired pulling at the oar. So they took the wind after them and made for Islay. But a good many were – There was two boys from Sliabh up there, two brothers, they were drowned. That's two, and there was Campbell, the steersman of this boat, three. And Maclean, the father of the people that was here, that's four. And two from Moss, that's six. There was about twelve or fourteen drowned.
>
> – SA 1968/243 B

One of the survivors, a fisherman called Alasdair Macdonald, composed a lament which, sung by Donald Sinclair, seems to carry the sorrow of the whole community in its cadences:

Oran an Fhuaidaich.

Refrain:
Tha mi fo chùram, fo mhòran cùraim

G' eil fear na stiùrach 'sa ghrunnd gun èirigh.

Seachad Colbhasa' dh'fhás i dorcha,
Bha uisge 's stoirm ann 's bha 'n fhairge beuchdaich

Tha fleasgaich 's maighdeannan taobh Beinn Hoighnis,
Cha chulaidh aoibhnis a bhi gan éisdeachd.

My heart is laden, so heavy laden.
The helmsman's grave's in the ocean floor-bed.

Passing Colonsay, the sky grown surly,
The rain came squalling, the sea was roaring.

The youths and maidens around Ben Hynish
No cause of joy was to hear them mourning.[23]

The echoes of the fatal day are still heard in houses in Tiree. An old woman living at Mannal told me that her grandmother described to her how she was just putting on the pot of potatoes for the family's midday meal when she heard the sound of the storm rising. Her husband Alasdair Macdonald was drowned and she left the croft with her young family to settle in a neighbouring village. The vacant croft and the adjacent one, where the crofter had also been lost in the storm, were given to a family called MacNeill from neighbouring Barrapol. The Browns at the Sliabh fared differently. *Niall Mòr*'s sons were not to succeed to the croft and the chances of the family acquiring land were remote. The *Fuadach* indirectly changed the situation. A family called Mackinnon held a small croft in the Sliabh of Balephuil. The crofter John Mackinnon had died earlier and his son was drowned in the storm, leaving a widow Margaret and three daughters in the croft. One of them, Ann, eventually married one of Neil Brown's sons, Archibald, who moved into the house and in due course inherited the land. Having no children, Archibald left the croft to his brother Malcolm, a fisherman, the father and grandfather of my informants.

For other families in Balephuil the *Fuadach* had a more sinister significance, as Donald Sinclair, a descendant of the Blacks as well as the Sinclairs relates. His great-aunt Isabella Black had married Archibald Maclean, 'the shepherd', and had several children by him. The unfortunate shepherd died of exposure in the boat. But Isabella was suspected of practising witchcraft, and the story got about that she and Mary Campbell, the wife of the steersman of one of the boats, who was also drowned, had wished to get rid of their husbands and had created the storm by using their black art. Donald Sinclair, my informant, was convinced that this really was the case.

In the following account, translated from the original Gaelic, Donald Sinclair speaks of his great-aunt Isabella (the composer of the song to the thrush) and refers also to her being one of two women discovered earlier making a *corp crèadha* or clay image to bewitch someone against whom they had a spite.

> A little pretty woman, but she had a really evil look about her all the same. They were saying that she was a witch, and so she was – a witch. And the disaster that befell Balephuil, when the men were drowned and the day turned bad, they were believing that it was this old woman and a sister of the one who was with her in the black narrows of Balephetrish, when they were making the clay body [image], that they were the two women who caused the Balephuil drowning disaster. Anyway they were blaming her. Neither of them had any great love for their husbands and they wanted to get rid of them . . . And people were casting it up against these two women that it was them who caused the wind, because a witch is able to do just about anything. She'll make wind or calm just as she pleases.
>
> – SA 1968/245 A[24]

Had some of MacLaurine's black art rubbed off on the descendants of his ground officer, John Black? This may, in a sense, be near the truth. In Tiree, and elsewhere in the Highlands, witchcraft is [said to be] a family characteristic, passed on to one's descendants, like bardic powers or the second sight. It was possessed by John Black's daughter, Isabella, and also by members of her sister Janet's family so that it eventually came into the immediate family of Donald Sinclair. We have come across other individuals and families in Tiree who have a reputation for witchcraft or for ill-luck, and frequently they are found, like the Blacks and MacLaurine, to be linked with the new régime as officials or settlers. They may in time have married in the island and appear to be assimilated into the population. But the stigma of witchcraft or ill-luck survives and prevents them from being wholly accepted within the community. Thus MacLaurine and the Blacks may have derived their reputation from the same source – association with the Macleans' clan enemy. This is speculation but perhaps the ill fame attaching to such individuals and families is the islanders' revenge for the Campbell conquest.

Oral traditions of widely different types have contributed to our study. Clearly not all proved to be of equal use and validity as an historical source. We recorded stories locally accepted as true accounts of historical events, which on scrutiny turned out to have been derived from Fenian heroic tales. In another type of tradition based on actual notables in the island's history, the representation of persons and events betrayed the strong influence of storytelling, literacy devices and motifs or the conventions of praise-poetry, but an important factual basis remained. The quasi-legendary character acquired by our historical personages was evidently the price they had to pay to ensure survival in the popular memory. In yet another *genre*, concerned with local history and the experiences of forebears, the content of reliable historical detail was usually high and the influence of folkloristic motifs slight.

One cannot deny that myth in some form or another is always likely to be present in oral tradition. It affects even family tradition, that most valuable of oral historical sources. Stories of origin are difficult to corroborate and tend to incorporate folkloristic motifs whilst bold, skilful and strong ancestors show a tendency to become even more colourful. But the knowledge and accuracy of a good *seanchaidh* are impressive, and his genealogical lore will sometimes match time-scales in some of the oldest surviving written records. A depth of genealogical core of five to seven generations was common in the lore of our informants; the most that we encountered extended to nine generations. In this latter case it was possible to find historical corroboration in unpublished papers of much of the genealogy, but, as I have demonstrated in the Appendix, genealogical lore may incorporate and transmit errors and misapprehensions.

Such errors, however, are found equally in written sources and can be discovered by critical investigation. They do not weaken the claim of oral testimony to be utilised in historical investigation. However, its peculiar characteristics must be understood and then exploited by appropriate methods. The most valuable oral tradition in Tiree was locally and family-centred, viewing events in a native focus and selecting and stressing what was of interest and importance to the islanders. The investigator must adapt to this. He must not expect a date but a reference to a family event or a phase in an ancestor's life. He must not enquire after John Maclean but for John son of Donald – and preferably in Gaelic. Neither the chronology nor the frame of reference of an oral testimony is arranged in a form familiar to historians nor does it turn about the same topics. Our best informants could not be expected to deliver information and opinions on matters that preoccupy the academic historian: the trend of population figures, changes in living standard, relations between social classes, the emergence of new economic and social structures. But, as the earlier case-studies have shown, oral testimony greatly extended the range of our knowledge and brought to light crucial aspects of social life and cultural activity ignored or not understood by the literate creators of the written evidence: oral tradition preserved a vivid knowledge of events such as the abandonment of a settlement and the migration of families, which had eluded the written record.

From traditional sources alone one would produce a strangely unstructured account of Tiree, but in our experience in dealing with oral as well as written sources, there is an unassailable case for the fullest study of oral traditions, even where written material is relatively abundant.

APPENDIX

Since much stress has been placed in this article on the value of family traditions, it is worth citing the genealogical lore of one of our main informants in some detail. Donald Sinclair could recite his genealogy thus: Donald son of Malcolm son of Alasdair son of Alasdair son of *Alasdair* son of Neil son of Brian [pronounced Brehan] (SA 1971/ 84A). Brian he claimed to have been a Barra man and on one occasion said that he came from Borve, eloped with the daughter of the MacNeill tacksman of Balnacreige and settled in Tiree, where he was given a holding (12/6/73). Donald was evidently uncertain about the earliest Alasdair (whom I have italicised) for sometimes he hesitated over the name and sometimes omitted it. The reason for this confusion may be that his great-great-grandfather's name was almost certainly not Alasdair, but Alan, a name with the same initial syllable. At any rate Donald's great-grandfather can be identified with fair assurance with an Alexander Sinclair, who is listed as aged six in the family of Alan Sinclair and Catherine Mackinnon in Kirkapol in Tiree in 1779 (Cregeen 1963, 53), whilst at the same date there is a Neil Sinclair a tenant in Ballamhulin who could be Alan's father (Cregeen 1963, 34). A 1776 List makes this even more likely since it gives Alan as aged thirty-six and Neil as seventy. There is, further, a Neill MacVrion who appears in other estate papers in the same generation and whom we can fairly safely accept as Donald's great-great-great grandfather.

Now I must draw attention to an interesting point. Neil in the genealogy is 'Son of Brian'; MacVrion (Gaelic *Mac Bhriain*) appears to mean 'son of Brian'. Donald assumes that Neil's father was called Brian and interpreted the genealogy in this sense. But actually Mac Vrion was used as a surname in eighteenth century Tiree and appears regularly in estate papers until it was replaced by the surname Sinclair in the 1779 List of Inhabitants. Brian was therefore the eponymous ancestor, and not the father, of Neil, and his ultimate origins were almost certainly in Ireland, like those of many Hebridean families, since the form, which it took in Tiree in the seventeenth century, was Mac O'Vrion.

What of the Barra origin of Donald's Sinclair forebears? There is likely to be some factual element in the tradition but enquiry in Barra from reliable informants provided no certain indication and the matter must be regarded as unproven. It has been our experience that the genealogies of our informants have often shown a high degree of reliability as far back as five, six or seven generations, but that it is seldom that ancestral lines deriving from an area outwith Tiree can be satisfactorily checked. This is mainly due to two factors. One is the deficiency of historical records (and particularly of parish records) in the West Highlands. The other is that non-native lines tend to be less well recorded in tradition; their genealogies rarely go back beyond the time of settlement. Their arrival in the island is sometimes presented in a semi-legendary form as in the story which I recorded in Mull of three brothers named Macfarlane, who settled respectively in Mull, Iona and Tiree and originated the families of that surname in these islands.

Donald Sinclair's family traditions bear out this generalisation. His mother Christine MacArthur's people were incomers. Donald knew that her father was a Gilchrist MacArthur from Mull but could trace the line no further. Her mother, Janet Black, was the daughter of an incomer, John Black, who appears to have been of a Lismore family. Donald had no pedigree of the Blacks beyond this John. He knew John Black's wife's history one generation further back, evidently because Black brought his mother-in-law, Janet MacCallum, to Tiree and her forceful personality left an enduring impression in the family traditions, as the following story shows, given here in an English translation from the original Gaelic.

> I am going to tell you about the time they were stealing cattle. It was going on far and near. And my mother's people were from Lorne on her father's and her grandmother's side. And at this particular time they were stealing cattle from the Duke of Argyll. And my great-great grandmother happened to be a dairy-maid to the Duke of Argyll. The boys wouldn't stay on the look-out to see what was happening, but this night she said – she was a hardy woman – 'I'll stay tonight,' she said, 'and keep watch on the cattle and see what happens.' And she put her tartan plaid on – the women were wearing tartan plaids instead of plain ones in those days – she put her tartan plaid on and made for the byre.
>
> She sat herself down at the cow's head. She wasn't long there before the thieves came, two of them, and they were feeling the cattle to see which were the fattest. And where did one of the thieves put his finger but in the mouth of the woman sitting at the cow's head. And when she got hold of his finger, with one snap she took off the end of it. The thieves fled, and in the morning when everything was in order the Duke said to her,'And how did you get on last night. Janet?' – she was called Janet too.
>
> 'Oh, I got on well,' she said. 'Here's a piece of the thief's finger and you can find the rest of it for yourself.'
>
> It was a farmer who lived not fearfully far away who was stealing the cattle, for he was found. He couldn't hide his finger and he was given

away by it. The Duke had the other bit of the finger. Well, I don't know if that man was punished but I'm sure he would be.

But when my great-grandfather married this MacCallum woman, the daughter of the one who did . . . the Duke was present, when he married [the daughter of] Janet MacCallum, the one who bit off the thief's finger. He came home to Tiree with one of the factors, and if my memory is right it was factor MacLaurine he came home with, and his house was over there on the *machair*, very near Island House, as we call it. And he is buried in Soroby, and the old woman who did this deed, she is buried in Soroby too.

– (SA 1968/247A)[25]

The tale catches the forceful personality of Janet MacCallum and its details accord well with conditions in eighteenth century Argyll, where, even as late as 1744, horses were driven off in a daring raid on the precincts of the ducal castle. Yet, even though the central theme is not to be found among classified folkloristic *motifs*, there is an aroma of the storytelling art in this tradition.

The two bodies of source-material are, in our experience, best treated as complementary and contrasting rather than as conflicting. The one body of material is largely that of the literate outsider (often an official, a minister or a teacher), presenting events in a way easily apprehended by the historian: the material can be readily arranged in a chronological framework and used for the analysis of social and economic structure and development. The other is the insider's story, told to friends and neighbours in the native language, presenting a world without clear historical contours, where events may sometimes float freely in time and be subject to the bidding of the storyteller's imagination or at the mercy of the supernatural. It is rich in lively personalities and in intimate values, customs, attitudes and knowledge which have tended to survive the most drastic changes in material circumstances. Without the written sources we would have lacked the form and structure of the island's history; without the oral traditions the very essence of its life would have escaped us.

ACKNOWLEDGEMENTS:

I gratefully acknowledge my debt to tradition-bearers in Tiree and elsewhere whom we have recorded; to the Argyll Estate Trustees and others who have allowed access to unpublished sources; to the Revd Donald W. Mackenzie and especially to my collaborator, Dr Margaret Mackay, for their important contribution to this research; and to Jane MacGregor, Peggy Morrison and Margaret Flanagan of the School of

Scottish Studies for their work of indexing, transcription and typing. Time has not allowed a full acknowledgment of my debt to various scholars and writers on folklore, anthropology and history, but I must not fail to mention the help and stimulus received from the work of Jan Vansina[26] and David Henige. The Social Science Research Council gave generous funding to the research.

REFERENCES

Cameron, H. (ed.) *Na Bàird Thirisdeach/The Tiree Bards*. Glasgow, 1932.

Cregeen. E. (ed.) *Inhabitants of the Argyll Estate in 1779*. Scottish Record Society. Edinburgh, 1963.

Cregeen, E. (ed.) *Argyll Estate Instructions: Mull, Morvern, Tiree, 1771–1805*. Edinburgh (Scottish History Society, Fourth Series, Vol. 1), 1964.

Cregeen, E. 'The Tacksmen and their Successors: A Study of Tenurial Reorganisation in Mull, Morvern and Tiree in the Early Eighteenth Century' in *Scottish Studies*, 13/2:93–144, 1969.

Cregeen, E. & MacKenzie, D.W. *Tiree Bards and their Bardachd*. Isle of Coll (Society of West Highland and Island Historical Research), 1978.

Gray, M. *The Highland Economy 1750–1850*. Edinburgh, 1957.

NSA New Statistical Account (Tiree), Vol. 7, 1845.

OSA Old (First) Statistical Account (Tiree), Vol. 10, 1794. Wakefield, 1983.

RCAHMS *Argyll, An Inventory of the Monuments. Vol. 3. Mull, Tiree, Coll & Northern Argyll*. The Royal Commission on the Ancient and Historical Monuments of Scotland, 1979.

SA Sound Archive, School of Scottish Studies, University of Edinburgh.

NOTES

1. This descriptive introduction is largely based on Cregeen 1964. xxviff. [Since this anthology consists of published articles only, it does not include the 1964 book. (Ed.]

2. Editor's note: In the 1960s, Cregeen was one of a number of international folklorists discussing issues surrounding the relevance of oral tradition to historical studies. In this article, Cregeen acknowledges especially the influence of Jan Vansina (citation added below). See also Robert H. Lowie, 'Oral Tradition and History', *Journal of American Follore*, Vol. 30 (1917), pp. 161–67; Herbert Halpert, 'Suggestions for the Collector', *Hoosier Folklore Bulletin*, Vol. 1.2 (1942) and 'Folklore Research in North America', *Journal of American Folklore*, Vol. 69 (1947), pp. 355–366; Richard M. Dorson, 'The Debate of the Trustworthiness of Oral Traditional History' in Fritz Harkort (ed.), *Volksüberriefung: Festschrift für Kurt Ranke*, Göttingen, 1968; and R. M. Dorson (ed.), *Folklore and Traditional History*, The Hague, 1973.

3. Editor's note: Scandinavian, American and Irish scholars in particular were leading the way in teaching their folklore students, both undergraduate and post-graduate, the techniques of the oral historian. Dr Herbert Halpert, founder of the Department of Folklore at Memorial University of Newfoundland in 1967, also recommended the work of Eric Cregeen as a Scottish 'model' to develop research into emigrant settlements in Eastern Canada, based on tape-recorded interviews of oral tradition. See M. Bennett, *The Last Stronghold: Scottish Gaelic Traditions of Newfoundland*, (St John's & Edinburgh, 1989), and *Oatmeal and the Catechism: The Story of Scottish Gaels in Quebec*, (Edinburgh & Montreal, 1998) Several seminal works relying upon oral history as evidence redress the balance called for by Cregeen; in particular, see W. Lynwood Montell, *The Saga of Coe Ridge: A Study in Oral History*, (Knoxville, 1970) and *From Memory to History*, (Nashville, 1981); George Ewart Evans, *Spoken History*, (London and Boston, 1987); Edward D. Ives, *The Tape-Recorded Interview: A Manuel for Field Workers in Folklore and Oral History*, (Knoxville, 1974); Neil V. Rosenberg (ed.), *Folklore and Oral History*, (St John's, Newfoundland, 1978). Furthermore, Cregeen's former colleague in Edinburgh, Professor Edward J. Cowan (appointed to the Chair in Scottish History at the University of Glasgow in 1993) encourages the study of oral tradition as an important resource for students and researchers. See also essays in *The People's Past: Scottish Folk, Scottish History*, edited by Cowan (Edinburgh, 1980).
4. See also 'Oral Tradition and Agrarian History in the West Highlands'; SA 1973/34. [Ed.]
5. There is a fuller transcription of this tape in Cregeen's 1974 paper, 'Oral Tradition and Agrarian History in the West Highlands'. [Ed.]
6. For example, Jan Vansina, 'Recording the Oral History of the Bakuba: I, Methods', *Journal of African History 1*, (1960), pp. 43–51. [Ed.]
7. The influence of written versions of Gaelic songs on transmission is discussed more fully by my colleague Dr John MacInnes in 'The Oral Tradition in Scottish Gaelic Poetry' in *Scottish Studies* Vol. 12, Part I (1968) 29–43.
8. The evidence strongly suggests that the anonymous writer of this report was Alexander Campbell, Chamberlain of Kintyre from 1767, possibly a member of the Braglen branch of the Campbells who had settled in Mull. He was the brother-in-law of Donald Campbell (*'Bàillidh Domhnull'*) who was Chamberlain of Tiree from 1770.
9. My colleague Dr John MacInnes, who first suggested I should visit Donald Sinclair, also recorded a great deal from him in the 1960s.
10. The Revd Hector Cameron published two songs about Donald Campbell and his sons in *Na Bàird Thirisdeach* in 1932 (6–8 and 13–15).
11. *Tocher* 32 (1979), 69–106 contains a biographical feature on Hector Kennedy by Dr Margaret A. Mackay, together with a selection of his recorded material.
12. A detailed account of this illuminating case study was presented in September 1982 by my colleague Dr Margaret A. Mackay, and appears in the printed volume of papers given at the *IVe Colloque International d'Histoire Orale* held in Aix-en-Provence under the auspices of the University of Provence and the *Centre National de la Recherche Scientifique*, Paris, 1982.
13. Stories about the Black Art are common in both Gaelic and Scots tradition.

14. Marriage of Donald MacLean and Mary MacDonald, Caolas, 4 December 1798 (Parish Register). Both Mary and Malcolm MacDonald were children of John MacDonald and Mary McConnel (MacDonald).
15. Donald Sinclair sang this and other songs by 'The Cooper'. He said that he acquired them from his father and it is noticeable that they differ markedly from versions collected by Hector Cameron and published in *Na Bàird Thirisdeach*. Our research revealed a great deal of detail about 'The Cooper' and his family in and beyond the island.
16. Their marriage is recorded in the Parish Register on 1 August 1830.
17. A biographical feature on Donald Sinclair with a selection of his traditions and reminiscences appears in *Tocher* 18 (1975). He recalled his father Malcolm's connection with the collector and local minister the Rev. John Gregorson Campbell, working for him in the manse garden and providing him with traditions (SA 1972/78A).
18. Oral traditions about herds and others jointly employed by the tenants of townships in Uist and Benbecula to look after their animals are illustrated and discussed by the writer in 'Oral Tradition and Agrarian History in the West Highlands', *Oral History* Vol. 2. No. 1 (1974).
19. The surname Black hardly ever occurs in Tiree before the nineteenth century, whereas it is a characteristic Lismore surname.
20. For further information, see J. McNeill. *The Baptist Church in Colonsay* (Edinburgh, 1914), which tells of MacDougall's conversion while working at kelp there: *Laoidhean Spioradail a chum cuideachadh le cràbhadh nan Gael* (Glasgow, 1841) for his hymns as well as G. Yuille, *History of the Baptists in Scotland* and the *New Statistical Account* of Tiree. *Tocher* 24 (1976) includes traditions about the MacDougalls in Mull and Cregeen and Mackenzie 1978, 16 gives details of the family's poets.
21. Translation by the Revd Donald W. Mackenzie.
22. Editor's note: 'Choosing to forget' is more likely in this case, as human experience teaches that if the mind 'chooses' to recall every ill of life, the result is usually bitterness. There is a striking similarity among the collective memory of emigrants from the Isle of Lewis to Quebec whose descendants have no oral tradition, and therefore no apparent 'memory' of the potato famine that precipitated their eviction. (M. Bennett, *Oatmeal and the Catechism,* 1998)
23. The verses sung by Donald Sinclair are printed together with a translation and musical transcription in *Tocher* 18 (1975), 60–61.
24. The original Gaelic (a fuller version) is printed together with an English translation in *Tocher* 18 (1975), 56–58.
25. See *Tocher* 18 (1975), 48–49 for the Gaelic original and notes.
26. Jan Vansina, *Oral Tradition: A Study in Historical Methodology*, translated by H.M. Wright, 1961 & 1965. [Ed.]

13

TRADITION AND CHANGE IN THE WEST HIGHLANDS OF SCOTLAND: A CASE STUDY

The Satellite State (1979), edited by Ståle Dyrvik, Knut Mykland, Jan Oldervoll Universitetsforlarget, Bergen, Oslo, Tromsø pp. 99–121

In this paper I wish to discuss the West Highland area of Scotland, and by focusing attention on one limited part of it, to try to understand what kind of social, political, economic and cultural development was in progress in one major sector of Scotland between the 17th and the 19th centuries. It may throw some light on the problem of Scotland's relationship with her bigger neighbour, England. It should certainly suggest some of the complexities lurking below the surface in studying relationships between states and within states.

The Scottish nation developed in the early Middle Ages out of a number of distinct peoples and cultures, and for long was a nation-state with inadequately developed central institutions and central power. Partly owing to the misfortunes of the royal house, the component parts of the kingdom tended to assert themselves as independent entities. And nowhere was central authority less respected or enforceable than in the Highland area, this extensive region of mountains, moorland, glens, islands and sea-lochs lying to the north and west of the settled Lowlands.

It was a region that formed no single political entity to challenge government. Indeed, its powerful clans were frequently in conflict. But it had cultural unity and common social institutions, and a combination of Highland clans could, and often did, pose a threat to the central authority. There was in fact a tradition of political unity in the West Highlands, dating back to the 11th to 13th centuries, when the western sea-board and the Hebrides had maintained an independent existence as a Celto-Norse kingdom owing allegiance, not to the Scottish king, but to the king of Norway. Although it was incorporated in Scotland in 1266, this kingdom was in a sense re-created under the chief of the Clan Donald, the Lord of the Isles. From 1380 to 1493 the Lord of the Isles ruled much of the North and West Highlands, and controlled most of the western chiefs and their clans, whilst a branch of the Macdonalds also held power in Antrim. This era represented a peak in Gaelic civilisation; religion, and the arts were cultivated; poets and harpers travelled from Ireland to the court of Macdonald and lesser chiefs; dissension within this extensive lordship was usually under control.

In 1493 this powerful lordship was destroyed by King James IV of Scotland, and there followed a century of recurrent warfare as the chiefs who had been Macdonald's vassals struggled for land and dominance. It was a situation that the government encouraged. In particular it used the clan Campbell to destroy the Macdonalds and take over their lands, a task it went far to carrying out. The beginning of the 17th century finds the Crown determined to complete the work of reducing to law and order a region that was described as 'the Hielands, where nane officer of the law may goe for fear of their lives'. To achieve this and exploit the natural wealth that the western seas were thought to hold, the king was prepared to transport or even extirpate the whole population of the islands.

In this the Crown probably had the backing of most Lowlanders. Whatever earlier relations had been between the Highlands and Lowlands – and they shared the same Gaelic speech until the 13th century or later – they were seen by the 14th century to belong to distinct and incompatible systems. In Lowland terms, unfair but understandable, you had on the one hand the thrifty, industrious, order-loving Lowlanders, speaking Scots, skilled in trade and civilised; on the other, the barbarous Highlanders, speaking Gaelic, caring only for war, cattle-lifting, songs and indolence. The Lowlanders exaggerated. The Gaels were not as uncivilised as they were represented, and the Lowlanders themselves were not so advanced in many skills as their neighbours in the South and on the Continent. In the 16th and 17th centuries the Lowlands showed themselves in many ways as subordinate to English commerce and foreign cultural influence as the Highlands were, indeed more so.

There the comparison ends. The Lowlands proved capable of assimilating English and other influences and of using that influence to promote a powerful surge of intellectual, cultural and industrial reformation in the late 18th and early 19th centuries. Though Highlanders as individuals participated in this development, its centres were in the Lowlands, and the Highland region as a whole, for a variety of reasons, fell into social, economic and cultural decay. It resembled, by the early 19th century, a semi-colonial territory – where a largely alien élite controlled the fates of a native population.

To bring this study into sharper focus, I will discuss in more detail those parts of the former Macdonald territories in Mull and adjacent coasts and islands which had fallen into the hands of the clan Maclean.

In the time of Sir Lachlan Maclean of Duart, chief from 1630 to 1648, his clan consisted of several thousand people. Some were on his lands, others on the lands of prominent Maclean land-owners, like the Macleans of Ardgour, of Lochbuie and of Torloisk, but most accepted his chieftaincy and followed him in war, as did a number of independent clans like the MacQuarries, MacNeills and Buchanans. In this way, a force of a thousand or fifteen hundred warriors could be rallied to the chief. Sir Lachlan Maclean brought 1100 men to support Montrose, and of these, 750 were Macleans, the rest MacQuarries and MacNeills. They were commanded by officers drawn from the principal men of the clan, each of whom had his own following. (*Account of the Clan Maclean*, London, 1838)

It made an impressive array when the clan was mustered. In 1675 the sheriff of Argyll and his posse brought a royal order that Castle Duart be surrendered. The defenders fired on the posse, and 'at the same time, the better to strengthen, encourage and fortiffie those within the house of Dowart in their rebellious opposition, McLaine of Brolois and his complices, to the number of seven score armed men, armed with fyrelockes, swords and targets, in a posture ready to fight, with their plaids thrown from them, standing and drawn up hard by the house of Dowart,' threatened, 'upon the last attaq and putting our lawes in execution, they would meet resistance to blood.' Next year, fiery crosses sent around the country (a traditional method of raising the clan) brought together three to four hundred men armed 'with swords, hagbuts, pistols, dirks and other weapons invasive and munitions bellicale'.[1]

It was a society cast in the heroic mould of the ancestral Irish society from which it stemmed. The principal men, who were close kinsmen of the chief, enjoyed large portions of the chief's land at low rents and were freed from the need to earn a living. Keeping a proper distance from the plough and the dunghill, they could devote themselves to the pleasures of war, cattle-raiding and the chase. The warrior virtues of courage, loyalty and open-handed liberality were admired, and must be possessed by a chief worth his salt. A Mull poet, *Eachainn Bacach*, in a eulogy on the dead Sir Lachlan [translated here by Derek Thomson], says:

> Well I've seen the day
> when you joined in the hunt,
> the rough slope did not stop you;
> no yew-bow was fashioned
> that could daunt you or stress you:
> you could draw to the limit
> while the timber stayed supple
> and send the tail-feathers at speed.

> Good was your dispensing
> in the big house at evening:
> pot-still whisky being poured
> into goblets of silver
> while the harp was being tuned to sing.[2]

It was an unequal society, in which wealth and status went according to one's degree of kinship with the chief, who represented the founder of the clan. Thus the gentry or 'tacksmen' (known in the Highlands as *daoine uaisle*) had extensive farms and numerous cattle. The ordinary clansmen, further removed from the chief in kinship, had to be content with a holding as a sub-tenant or as one of a partnership of a farm, and owed labour service and rent to the upper tenant or direct to the chief, whilst there were landless men who laboured for the principal tenants. In the 17th century Maclean still perambulated his lands to consume his rents in kind, and when he visited his fortress in the island of Tiree with his retinue, he stayed all winter, whilst the small tenants supplied their needs in food, peats for the fire, corn for the horses and lambs for the falconers' hawks.

There is plenty of evidence of clan feuds, but signs of social conflict within the clan are rare. Not only the nearer privileged kinsmen but the ordinary commoner took pride in his blood-ties with the chief and preserved his genealogy carefully, for it was his pass-port to honour and land. The chief for his part counted his wealth in the number of his clan. What made the clan formidable as a fighting force was its close-knit, exclusive nature, and the blind devotion of the fighting men to their chief. That the Gaelic term *caraid* means both 'friend' and 'kinsman' suggests the narrow limits of approved social contacts. Marriages of the common folk were almost invariably between people in the same or adjacent townships. The gentry, like the Macleans of Brolas and Treshnish, usually married into other branches of the clan Maclean. The chief and his family married, for political reasons, outside the clan – in the 17th century with the house of Argyll, the Seaforths, the MacLeods of Dunvegan, but were fostered with families of the clan.

In the early 17th century Highland chiefs usually lived in the clan territory, spoke the language of the district (but also understood Lowland Scots) and might indeed themselves compose poetry or perform well on the harp – as did some of the Macleans of Coll. Parish schools were less common than they were in the Lowlands, but there existed a system of patronage whereby families of professional poets, bards, harpers, physicians and genealogists were maintained by the chiefs to exercise their skills, provide entertainment and conserve knowledge. We know of such families in Mull, like the MacNeills, who were harpers, and the Beatons, who were physicians.

The songs and stories, historical accounts and genealogies of this learned class spread through the whole community as a common stock of tradition and helped to integrate the clan in subordination and loyal service to the chief. Though not necessarily members of the clan proper (they were often of Irish origin), they enjoyed high status and prestige and were regarded as gentlemen, not commoners.

Living conditions in the West Highlands are not well documented before the 18th century, but they were clearly simple and sometimes inadequate to support life. The houses of commoners were probably constructed in the windy and tree-less island of Tiree much like the thick-walled 'black-houses' familiar in our day, but in Mull and adjacent parts they were made of walls of sods or wattle-and-daub built about a timber framework that rested on the ground and supported a thatched roof. The hearth, set on a mud floor in the centre of the house, burned peat and lacked a chimney. The houses of the upper tenants were somewhat better and had more elaborate furnishings.

The commoners' diet was based on oats and barley, grown in a primitive fashion, with fish and dairy products but rarely any meat. They had frequent recourse to shellfish, especially in times of scarcity, such as that series of years at the end of the 17th century. Traditions existed late in the 18th century that all the population of the extensive district of Brolas in Mull perished except a few families. Productivity may have been declining in the Hebrides in the late 17th century as a result of strong winds operating in sandy areas. (Possibly something similar was also going on in the island of Laesø in the Kattegat, where one of the parish churches had to be abandoned early in the 18th century after being deluged by sand). Imports of meal were a regular feature of the West Highland economy, but there were favoured areas, like Tiree, which actually exported it.

The gentry, or tacksmen, paid their chief a rent in cattle or by bills of exchange resulting from cattle-sales. From their own subtenants they received a variety of payments in labour and kind that enabled them to live in comfort. The chiefs could afford luxuries, and accounts exist for imported French wines, tobacco, spices, fruit, tapestries etc. But it was customary for them to entertain their kinsmen and retinue, and one does not find criticism expressed about chiefly extravagance. Nevertheless a man like Sir Lachlan Maclean, who sometimes visited the royal court, and acquired sophisticated tastes, was probably living at a higher rate than his rents in cattle and the rest could sustain. He built large extensions to his castle at Duart and incurred considerable debts.

For the Maclean territory, as for the Highlands as a whole, the Union of Crowns in 1603, and the abolition of the Scottish Parliament in 1707, meant that their destiny was interwoven with events which were taking place on a wider scene than Scotland and of which they had no real control. During the Civil War of the 1640s and early '50s the most powerful clan, the Campbells, under their chief, the Marquis of Argyll, linked its fortunes with the opponents of the Stuart Monarchy. The Macleans, Macdonalds, Stewarts and other western clans, who had suffered from the expansion of the Campbells, supported the Crown, probably more faithfully than it deserved but partly in the hope of recovering their lands. Although the restoration of the Stuarts in 1660 postponed the day of reckoning for the clans, the Revolution of 1688, which expelled the Stuart James II and VII, put the family of Argyll into a position of immense power in the Highlands.

The accession of the Hanoverian dynasty to the throne in 1714 brought many of the western clans into a state of more or less permanent opposition to the government, whilst it confirmed and enlarged the influence of their arch-enemy, Argyll. This government, now based in London, could command much greater military and financial resources than the Scottish Crown had ever had, and ruthlessly crushed the Jacobite risings of 1715 and 1745. Between the risings, 'rebellious' chiefs were deprived of their estates, a network of military roads was created in the Highlands, and a system of surveillance by loyal military companies, the Black Watch, was established. The defeat of the rising of 1745 was followed by further forfeitures and by the proscription of arms and Highland dress. In the period of roughly half a century from 1688 the virtual independence of the Highland chiefs, who had formed the core of the Jacobite cause, was brought to an end.

For the Maclean chief, the defeat of the Risings only confirmed a fate that had been decided earlier. Sir Lachlan's personal debts, increased by war-time expenses for the Crown, were bought up by the Marquis of Argyll, and eventually, circa 1690, after much legal wrangling and armed conflict, brought the Duart lands into the Argyll family's possession. Sir John Maclean, passing his last years at the Jacobite court, could bring only 300 men into the 1715 Rising, and it was left to other branches of the clan to support that of 1745.

The Forty-five was a watershed in the history of the Highlands because, after this, change gathered a momentum of a different order. But it is worth remarking that many of the features of this change were recognisable long before in the late 17th century, in the spread of Lowland education, manners and dress among Highland lairds. Early in the 18th century the Mull bard, John Maclean, chided his chief for his extravagance in the new habit of taking tea:

> What has brought you these new debts
> is your liking for the Lowlands,
> the little pot beside the hearth,
> with honey-tasting brew in it,

spending what your father used
to keep an armed household.³

His contemporary, Roderick Morrison, *an Clarsair Dall*, was more bitter, more like the later poets, in his strictures on MacLeod for giving up traditional ways and burdening his tenants in Skye to pay for his extravagances.

Prolonged residence outside the Highlands in the 17th century was unusual however, except for aristocrats like the Earl of Seaforth or the Earl of Argyll. Some chiefs and chieftains had already caught the taste for improvement in the early 18th century, and went in for gardens, new houses and agricultural experiment. And a number, like Archibald Campbell of Knockbuy in mid-Argyll and Alexander Macdonald of Boisdale in Uist were dealing extensively in cattle droves in that period. A Maclean merchant from Glasgow (of the Griminish branch of the Coll Macleans) undertook to improve a farm in Tiree for the Duke of Argyll, as well as making trials at the undeveloped commercial fisheries. There is indeed much to suggest that new influences were penetrating the Highlands very effectively – almost too effectively if one recalls the two chiefs in Skye (Sir Norman MacLeod and Sir Alexander MacDonald) who were detected in 1739 in complicity in a scheme to carry off poor families to be sold as indentured servants in the American plantations.

The process of change speeds up after 1746. Within half a century, or in some cases much less, many chiefs had transformed themselves into wholly non-resident landlords and had moved out of the confined circle of their clan into the sophisticated world. It was a road taken much earlier by the aristocracy of the Highlands, who had been drawn into court life and politics in the 17th century and were accustomed to its demands and extravagance. The chiefs who, in the aftermath of the '45, when their private armies were banned, attempted to live on equal terms with rich English landlords and Lowland gentry did so on the basis of a very unequal income. The humiliation and defeat at Culloden made them ready imitators (and victims) of all that the new society offered and that theirs could not: a place in the Hanoverian establishment, with its vigorous and expanding commerce; its conquering armies and navies; its lavish wealth and conspicuous display; its superb achievements in the arts; its elegant manners, dress and taste seen in the Assembly Rooms at Inverness, Perth and Edinburgh, but ultimately approved by the Hanoverian court. Admission to this society gave access to army appointments, posts in the East India Service, jobs in the customs and excise and many more, in the gift of some powerful controller of patronage like the Duke of Argyll (or, later, Henry Dundas).

The transformation of the chiefs happened with great rapidity, as Dr Johnson observed and deplored in 1773. We have seen that its beginnings were much earlier than 1746, but, after the destruction of the chiefs' military role, they showed themselves more ready to change and to find compensations in a place in the new establishment. The Lowland society which now attracted was not the same as the Lowlands of 1700, with its cramped stage and petty bourgeois manners, but a Lowland society itself in the process of transformation and considerably more attractive to Highland gentry. Without the dimension given by the existence of Court, ministers, army, high society, and immense wealth and opportunities, one may well doubt if the Highlanders would have been impressed by what they saw at Edinburgh, Perth and Inverness. The greatest transformation was to come later, in the time of the old chiefs' sons, but the career of Norman, 22nd chief of MacLeod of Skye, is fairly characteristic of the first generation.

Born in 1706, he was brought up in Perthshire (in part at least) and his estates were managed by a 'tutor' or guardian. He was Gaelic-speaking and for some years lived on his estates. But in 1741 he entered Parliament for Inverness, and in London learned the life-style that complicated his finances and destroyed much of the goodwill of his clansmen. A single visit to London cost him £700, at a time when his rental was less than £2,000. He built a costly house near Edinburgh and continued to live there until the expense forced him to sell and move to St. Andrews. He educated his son at Haddington and gave each of his daughters a 'season' at Edinburgh. In his purchases of clothes, jewellery etc. he dealt mostly with London firms. He drank and gambled heavily and died £40,000 in debt.

His grandson and heir, the 23rd chief, made at first immense efforts to restore the estate's finances, and spent his career largely in the Indian army as a means to this end. But he acquired equally lavish tastes and is said to have gone through prize money amounting to £100,000. Parliament and elections were disastrous to a modest income such as his. In the 1790's more than half the estate, including Harris, Bernera and Waternish, had to be sold to pay the creditors.

For the tenants these trends often proved distressing. Rents increased even beyond the rising cattle prices of the latter half of the century. By 1800 few of the chief's kinsmen, or tacksmen, survived, having emigrated to North Carolina or Canada, and several thousand other tenants also left, often under their tacksmen. The clan biographer comments that the clan's troubles can be traced to the 22nd chief's election to Parliament in 1741 and his residence in London. (Grant, 1959: 485)

This is no isolated example: witness the tacksmen and tenants emigrating from North Uist in the early 1770s when Sir Alexander (later Lord) Macdonald greatly increased rents and brought in sheep. In his *Oran do na Fògaraich* the bard John MacCodrum could not stay silent: 'Look around you and see the nobility without pity for poor folk, without kindness for friends.' (Translated by William Matheson; 1938: 314–316)

These were the trends that caused the bards to send up their smoke signals of alarm, as they observed the Highland way of life in jeopardy. But one cannot say that in the 1770s or 1780s positive reformation might not take place that would bring new life to the Highlands from its black cattle and fish and even from new industries. Hope and enterprise were in the air, and there were men of vision and humanity among the land-lords. Might it not turn out, as it was doing in the Border hill countries, that the old society would evolve and adapt? Here the old order of clans (Scotts, Elliots, Armstrongs) and of lairds, tacksmen and sub-tenants, became the foundation of a modernised, commercially successful society. Even though English interests discouraged the young cloth manufacturing industry, it became well established in the later decades of the century in the Border towns of Hawick, Selkirk and Galashiels. (Robson 1977)

If we look at Mull and the adjacent lands, the prospect circa 1780 is not without its promise or at least its redeeming features. The remaining Macleans were perhaps too conservative to adapt production on their estates to serve Lowland demand, but the lairds showed no wish to escape their responsibilities and clan sentiment was still very much alive. On the estate of Brolas, the chief, Sir Alan Maclean, maintained his kinsmen much as they had always been, each one occupying an extensive farm, which also supported a numerous community of tenants or sub-tenants and servants. The military life still kept its central place for the gentry of the clan, though now in the service of the Hanoverian crown. By offering army commands to the chief and chieftains – as to Sir Alan in 1757 through the patronage of the Duke of Argyll – the Government also gained the service of the clansmen, and nicely harmonised clan sentiment, Highland tradition and State policy. Highlanders were thus finding a role in the new order, and through the lead provided by the chiefs, clanship was proving reconcilable with law and order.

The best promise of reform and revival in the West Highlands lay, *mirabile dictu,* on the vast estates of the dukes of Argyll, so much of them taken by violence or stealth from the clans. One would not expect much after the initial basic reform of the 2nd duke, who abolished clan tenures on his lands in Mull and adjacent districts in 1737 and introduced a modern system of leases, as a preliminary to what was virtually a rack-renting policy. (Cregeen 1969) But his successors, notably the 3rd duke (succeeded 1743, died 1761) and the 5th duke (succeeded 1770, died 1806), seriously attempted to translate practical schemes of agricultural and industrial innovation into effect in their wide-spread lands. Agricultural improvements such as enclosures, new crops and tree planting were written as conditions into leases. Larger-scale tasks – drainage, road-making and coastal and harbour works – were carried out with the unpaid labour of tenants. Flax growing was promoted in the remote island of Tiree, along with a spinning school, and tenants were ordered to make their wives and daughters spin – or lose their farms.

In an ambitious and elaborately planned phase, in the last decades of the century, the 5th duke grappled with the most difficult problem: that of the small, highly traditional tenants working in their farm partnerships, suspicious of Lowland ways, and too poor to innovate. He envisaged creating modest tenant-farms as the basis for Hebridean agriculture and as the complement to more extensive grazing farms adapted for cattle and sheep. Newly established villages would absorb the landless population. These he would train as craftsmen and fishermen and help to provide with boats, gear and marketing facilities. Emigration would be unnecessary; indeed with industries expanding, there might be a labour shortage. (Cregeen (ed.) 1964) In the event, these and similar High-land schemes had to be modified and even abandoned in the face of trends that asserted themselves strongly in the last decade or so of the 18th century. Among the most serious was the demographic situation, with an island population that doubled in the second half of the century and threatened to produce pauperism. Cattle and barley prices were high in the war years, but sheep and kelp (the burnt ash of seaweed) were the most lucrative. On many island and coastal estates this led to a pattern of settlement, which left the hilly interior to the sheep and created townships of small-holdings or 'crofts' on the coasts for the bulk of the population. They were employed at fishing, small trades and kelp-burning. On some estates, though not on the ducal lands, this redeployment of resources was associated with forcible removals.

Nevertheless, the duke's island estates suffered equally with others in the aftermath of the war years, when kelp and agricultural prices declined fast and landlords saw their rents disappear. Every level of Highland society was affected – lairds, upper tenants and small tenants. When in the 1820s, large parts of the Argyll lands in Mùll and Morvern were sold off to pay the creditors of the pleasure-loving 6th duke, the purchasers in many cases made short work of evicting the people and turning their estates over to sheep. Between 1813 and 1838 every property in Morvern changed hands. (Gaskell 1968) Other estates had been coming on to the market. The estate of the ancient MacQuarries of Ulva was in the hands of creditors in 1776, and that of Maclaine of Lochbuy in 1804. In 1798 the bankrupt son of Allan Maclean of Drimnin finally severed the family's 400 year old connection with Morvern. Such sales were followed by clearances and the extinction of the tacksmen.

The situation in the 1820s and 30s contrasts in many ways with what we saw in the 17th century. Instead of a graded and pyramidal social structure, representing chief, kinsmen, and commoners, we find a disunited society which has lost its native leaders. The new masters were the factors, often representing a non-resident land-owner and usually disliked. In Tiree and Mull the new leaders were the ministers of evangelical religious movements, notably Independent and Baptist. In place of the tacksmen there were Lowland sheep-farmers with no share in Highland culture or speech and little contact with the crofters and cottars who composed the bulk of the population. The deep division between Gael and Lowlander had been brought into the heart of the Highlands, and though the Gaels acquired a smattering of Scots through attendance at school or seasonal work in the Lowlands, they retained a deep distrust of the Lowlander and his ways, the more so now that he had the upper hand. This polarised social landscape was a novel phenomenon in the Highlands, but we have seen it in other guises in overseas colonies. There was a rich class of English-speaking farmers and proprietors, many of them new men, controlling the bulk of the land, producing meat and wool for the southern markets and industries. It included a number of Highlanders like John Sinclair of Lochaline and the notorious Patrick Sellar of Ardtornish, but there was no question where their sympathies lay. The rest were Gaelic-speaking crofters and cottars, occupying what was often marginal land and supporting themselves in various degrees of poverty by small-scale subsistence agriculture, minor trades, fishing and seasonal work. A few of the original lairds and tacksmen survived, but they were under a growing pressure, and most disappeared in the middle decades of the century.

The physical hardihood of the crofters was remarkable. They survived environmental conditions of the most extreme kind of reducing their wants to a minimum. They were skilful in using rocks, driftwood and grasses for their houses, and in utilising herbs for salves and cures and dyes. Crofters could produce much of their clothing and most of their food from their holdings, and would barter their dairy products for fish from the cottars. They hired extra help at harvest by paying the cottars in land for potatoes and perhaps a little grazing. They could pay their rent to the factor with a beast and relied on a pig for their own meat supplies. The crofter's economy in the 19th century was, in contrast with that of the big farmers, almost as much a subsistence economy as that of the small tenants in the 17th century. Were crofter and sheepman, in their opposing ways, examples of the survival of the fittest – the sheepman by his superb adaptation to the market forces, the crofter by his very lack of needs and his ability to accommodate to the climate and environment? Both were poles apart from the native chiefs, who had first unleashed a revolution and, failing to control it, became its victims.

The crofter-cottar class were the ultimate heirs of the Gaelic tradition and brought into the 19th century values and attitudes that may have seemed hopelessly out of tune with the times, but had in fact a powerful effect on morale. The communal habits of the earlier multiple tenancy townships persisted in many of the practices of the crofting townships; the making of peat, shearing of sheep, grazing of cattle and horses, thatching of buildings still depended on the co-operation of families. Clanship had lost much of its force, but one can see, in an island such as Tiree, how the whole community was in fact linked together by kinship groups of remarkable extent and cohesion and by informal associations of neighbours.

The disappearance of the resident chiefs meant that the hereditary harpers, bards, historians and other men of the arts lost their patrons. The last of the professional bards, the bard of Maclean of Coll, emigrated to Canada in 1819. But the crofters and cottars carried on a very vital tradition in Gaelic song, poetry and storytelling, so that much of Highland culture persisted, not as mere survivals but as an integral part of everyday life. The bards of the 19th century composed songs for every occasion – a wedding, a death, a shipwreck, an amusing incident – and sang them in the cottage-gatherings or 'ceilidhs'. The talent for composition was widespread but was found especially among the descendants of the former hereditary bards. Now the praise-songs to the chiefs were superseded by praise-songs and laments for their member of parliament or their local postman. As they were caught up in religious movements, the bards' compositions became tinged with serious concern. To commemorate her receiving the Old Age Pension, then a novelty, an old woman composed a short song, epigrammatic in its conciseness:

> Mine is this crown of silver
> By the king guaranteed me.
> What's it worth when my kinsfolk
> To the kirkyard will bear me?
> He who for me suffered anguish,
> If His truth I despise not,
> A true Crown shall give me
> And my birthright in Zion.[4]

We have discussed the development of a West Highland area from the 17th to early 19th century and have seen an ancient and highly integrated society fall into a dependent condition. This dependence has social, cultural, economic and also political aspects. It is possible, though not certain, that even without the Union a similar development might have taken place, but the dimension given by the Union is important and it clearly speeded up the whole process and increased its impact on Highland society.

One may distinguish three principal stages in this transformation:

1. In the first stage, mainly occurring in the last half of the 18th century, the native chiefs are attracted by the centres of power and social importance – 'sucked into the vortex of the nation and allured to its capitals' as the 23rd chief of MacLeod expressed it. They may attempt, in the 'age of improvement', to adapt the amenities and values, even the technology, of this new culture to Highland life but are usually unsuccessful. They cease to maintain the professional families, who have transmitted the native cultural traditions. They tend to become non-resident landlords, eventually losing touch with the Highland environment, and often become insolvent. The sale of their estates delivers the land and the destiny of its inhabitants over to a new and tougher breed of land-owners. Dr. Johnson may have been right in declaring: 'The Highland chiefs should not be allowed to go further south than Aberdeen . . . in general they will be tamed into insignificance.'

2. In the second stage, extending over much of the first half of the nineteenth century and into the second half, the native population of the Highlands existed in a semi-colonial situation on the fringes of a more developed Lowland economic system. In some areas, though by no means most, they are removed from the land and forced to emigrate. Where this does not happen, as on the Argyll estates, the crofters and cottars maintain the native culture vigorously and attempt to adapt to changing conditions – for example by supplementing the living gained from their crofts and ancillary trades by seasonal migration to Lowland farms and east-coast fishing. But rapidly growing numbers result in falling standards of living. A series of failures in the potato crop in the 1840's, and the subsequent threat of starvation, leads to massive emigration. It also virtually ruins a number of chiefs, including the MacLeods of Dunvegan, whose finances cannot stand up to loss or rents and heavy demands for charitable relief.

3. The third stage falls outside our period and is still in progress. It takes its rise very largely from the introduction in 1872 of a system of compulsory education designed primarily to inculcate values, skills and aspirations appropriate to a modern industrial society. It is at variance with the Highland outlook, habits and beliefs. Reinforced by the effects of contacts with emigrants and closer links with the Lowland area, the new educational system effectively educates the young to reject tradition and to leave their region. The Highland area has recently been going through social and cultural decline more rapid and widespread than anything previously experienced.

BIBLIOGRAPHY

Cregeen, E.R. (ed.) *Instructions of the 5th Duke of Argyll,* Scottish History Society, (Edinburgh, 1964).

Cregeen, E.R. 'The Tacksmen and their Successors', in *Scottish Studies,* Vol. 13, no. 2 (Edinburgh, 1969).

Gaskell, P. *Morvern Transformed,* Cambridge University Press, (Cambridge, 1968).

Grant, I.F. *The Macleods,* (London, 1959).

Matheson, W. *The Songs of John MacCodrum* (Scottish Gaelic Texts Society, (Edinburgh, 1938).

Robson, M.J.H. Doctoral thesis on 'The History and Traditions of Sheep-Farming in the Scottish Border Hills', (Edinburgh, 1977).

NOTES

1. Quoted from the Maclean papers printed in J.R.N. MacPhail (ed.), *Highland Papers* vol. I (Scottish History Society, 1914).
2. D. Thomson, in his *Introduction to Gaelic Poetry,* pp. 129–132.
3. D. Thomson, *Introduction to Gaelic Poetry,* p. 147.
4. H. Cameron *The Tiree Bards* (Stirling, 1932), page 288. Translation here by Revd D.W. Mackenzie, Auchterarder. [The original text is re-instated in 'Tiree Bards and Their Bardachd: The Poets in a Hebridean Community'. [Ed.]]

14
BIBLIOGRAPHY OF ERIC CREGEEN'S PUBLISHED WORKS

1954 'Skeealyn Edard Karagher', Cre'neash (Manx fishing taboos), Coraa Ghailckagh, Isle of Man

1955–63 Notes on approximately fifty sites and finds in annual issues of *Discovery and Excavation Scotland*

1957 'Extra-Mural Classes in the West Highlands', *Scottish Adult Education*, Vol. 20, 6–10

1959 'Recollections of an Argyllshire Drover' *Scottish Studies*, Vol. 3/2, 143–161

1960 'In Partnership: Adult Education in the County of Argyll', *Scottish Adult Education*, Vol. 30, 16–21

1963 *Inhabitants of the Argyll Estate 1779*, (ed.) Scottish Record Society, Edinburgh

1964 *Argyll Estate Instructions: Mull, Morven, Tiree, 1771–1805*, (ed.), Scottish History Society, Edinburgh

1965 'Flailing in Argyll' *Journal of the Society for Folk Life Studies*, (ed. J. Geriant Jenkins), Vol. 3, 90

1967 'The Ducal House of Argyll', *Chambers' Encyclopaedia*,

1968 'The Changing Role of the House of Argyll in the Scottish Highlands' *History and Social Anthropology*, ASA Monograph 7, ed. I. Lewis, London, 153–192

1969 'The Tacksmen and their successors: a study of tenurial reorganisation in Mull, Morven and Tiree in the early 18th century' in *Scottish Studies* Vol. 13/2, 92–144

1974 'Oral Sources for The Social History of the Scottish Highlands and Islands' *Oral History* Vol. 2, No.2, 23–36

1974 'Oral Tradition and Agrarian History in the West Highlands.' *Oral History*, Volume 2, No.1, 15–33

1975 'Donald Sinclair', *Tocher* 18, 41–65

1976 'Donald Morrison' (with D.W. MacKenzie), *Tocher* 24, 289–319

1978 'Oral History in Scotland', a report of the conference of March 1978, *Oral History* Vol. 6, No.2,, 19 22

1978 *Tiree Bards and their Bardachd,* with. D.W. MacKenzie, Society of West Highland and Island Historical Research, (Original Gaelic texts incorporated in the current edition)

1979 'Hector Kennedy' (with M.A. Mackay), *Tocher* 32, 69–106

1979 'The Changing Role of the House of Argyll in the Scottish Highlands' condensed version in *Scotland in the Age of Improvement,* N.T. Philipson & R. Mitchinson, eds, Edinburgh, 5–23 (Reprint 1996)

1979 'Tradition and Change in the West Highlands of Scotland' in *The Satellite State in the 17th and 18th centuries,* eds, S. Dyrvik, K. Mykland, & J. Oldervoll Universitetsforlarget. Bergen, Oslo, Tromsø, 98–121

1981 'Oral History', *Phonographic Bulletin* 29 (March 1981) pp. 9–14

1981 'The Highlands since 1745', *A Companion to Scottish Culture* (David Daiches, ed.) 164 and *A New Companion to Scottish Culture,* (David Daiches, ed. 1993), 140–42

1983/1998 'Oral Tradition and History in a Hebridean Island' *Scottish Studies,* No. 32: 1993–98, (1998), pp. 12–37

1985 Preface in Nancy C Dorian, *The Tyranny of Tide: An Oral History of East Sutherland Fisherfolk,* Ann Arbor, pp. ix–xiii

2011 *Kintyre Instructions: The 5th Duke of Argyll's Instructions to his Kintyre Chamberlain, 1785–1805,* with Angus Martin. The Grimsay Press, Glasgow.

www.ingramcontent.com/pod-product-compliance
Lightning Source LLC
Chambersburg PA
CBHW060832190426
43197CB00039B/2570